SIX

THE REAL JAMES BONDS
1909–1939

MICHAEL SMITH

SIX

THE REAL JAMES BONDS

1909–1939

Biteback Publishing

First published in 2010
This paperback edition published in 2011 by
Biteback Publishing
Westminster Tower
3 Albert Embankment
London
SE1 7SP

ISBN 978-1-84954-097-1

10 9 8 7 6 5 4 3 2 1

A CIP catalogue record for this book is available from the British Library.

Set in Bembo by SoapBox
Printed and bound by CPI Group (UK) Ltd, Croydon, CR0 4YY

'Between the wars, the profession and practice of espionage did not much change. Invisible inks and false beards were still standard issue.'

ROBERT CECIL,
Personal Assistant to Sir Stewart Menzies,
Chief of the Secret Service 1939-1951

In memory of
Nigel Antony Richard Backhouse, MVO
(1956–2008)

CONTENTS

ACKNOWLEDGEMENTS

I am grateful to some indefatigable researchers into the secret archives for their assistance in this project, most notably David List, but also Phil Tomaselli, Nick Hiley, Yuri Totrov, Rolf Dahlø, Craig McKay, Andrew Cook, Yigal Sheffy, Ann Trevor, Nina Staehle and Oliver Lörscher. I am also grateful to Richard Cafferata, Roger Fairholme, Shirley Durrant, Hannah Charnock, and Edward and Susan Harding-Newman, Henrik Sinding-Larsen, Yolande Whittall, Elizabeth Moulson, Molly Megson, Ian Sumner, James Stephens, Jonathan Wadman, Hollie Teague, John Schwartz, Sylvia Vetta, Robert Kirby, Charlotte Knee, and last, but certainly by no means least, my wife Hayley and my children Ben, Kirsty, Louise, Leila and Levin.

JOHN Merrett slouched along the Nevsky Prospekt, a big scruffy bear of a man hugging the stucco walls, his attempt to merge into the background assisted only by the dingy surroundings and the lack of street lights. The agents of the Cheka, the Extraordinary Commission, were everywhere and there was said to be a substantial price on his head, although the likelihood of anyone who went to the Cheka getting any money seemed remote.

Once the Nevsky had been one of the most fashionable streets in the world; now its cafés and shops were shuttered against the misery imposed by the Soviets. Here and there a huddle of men gathered around a hawker selling half-rotten vegetables, or hacked at the carcass of a horse driven into the ground by an owner with too little food for himself, let alone a nag.

Merrett had once been one of the smartest businessmen in St Petersburg, clean shaven with a frock coat, top hat, twirling cane and a sparkle in his eye. Not now. To all outward appearances, he looked like a tramp, a man hidden even from himself. It was a false picture. Merrett was very far from the withdrawn, shabby image he presented to the outside world. He was simply doing a job. Jim Gillespie had left him with firm orders to look after the British spy networks. He was determined to stick to what he saw as his patriotic duty. He'd never been a spy, never trained for it, but someone had to do it. Why not him?

At first, Merrett disguised himself with a thick red beard. Then one of the agents in the British network got rattled and gave him up. Merrett only escaped the Cheka agents by jumping out of a window and shinning down a drainpipe, but they managed to grab his wife Lydia. As if he didn't have enough on his plate, now he worried constantly for her safety and what they might persuade her to say of him.

With the Cheka knowing he had a beard, he'd shaved it off, but the stubble was growing back. He badly needed a shave, though probably now it didn't matter one way or another. They knew him with or without a beard. If they couldn't find him, they could do nothing to harm him or the networks. So he kept on moving, never sleeping in the same place twice, adopting the pseudonym Ivan Ivanovich, Russia's equivalent of John Bull.

It was grinding work, collecting the intelligence, paying the agents and, most difficult of all, in the midst of the 'Red Terror', keeping them calm. Hundreds, thousands, of Russians had been taken from their homes and some would not be going home ever again. Small wonder the agents were jittery. 'Babysitting' was how Gillespie put it, and at times that's what it felt like. The MI1c man had promised him before he went that someone would come soon to take over, a professional who wouldn't have to worry constantly if he were doing the right thing, or what the Bolsheviks were doing to his wife.

Merrett hoped the new man would come soon. The 200,000 roubles Gillespie gave him had long since run out. He and the agents were surviving on his savings and money loaned by the members of the city's British community he was getting to freedom. He'd just left another six of them waiting for 'an old woman in a white apron', who would collect them at dawn and pass them on to one of the couriers. Those were the boys running the real risks. They were paid to smuggle intelligence over the Finnish border, where Gillespie had set up shop waiting for them. They still did that – no-one was going to argue that Merrett wasn't fulfilling his part of the bargain – but he'd had them running a different kind of package down the lines as well, more than 200 Britons all terrified of being scooped up by the Terror and left to rot in Butyrka prison.

As Merrett passed Meltzer's furniture store, its windows boarded up to protect what little was left, a hawker stepped out from the shadows in front of him and he recognised one of the agents.

'Ivan Ivanovich,' the man whispered, looking anxiously around, 'you have to come with me. The new fellow's arrived. He's looking for you. Says his name's Paul Dukes.'

ONE

'Capital sport'

THE British 'secret service' that would eventually become known as MI6 was set up in 1909 following several years of growing concern, verging on panic, at the idea of German spies marauding across Britain preparing for war. There is no doubt that Germany was sending spies to Britain, including an increasing number of army officers who claimed to be on holiday 'learning English', but were in fact collecting information that might be useful in the event of an invasion. Nevertheless, they were doing so in relatively small numbers and, for the most part at least, the information they collected was openly available to anyone who cared to look for it. They did not constitute anything like a major threat and the spy scare that swept Britain in the early 1900s was in fact out of all proportion to the reality. It was stoked, even orchestrated, by the author William le Queux, who produced a series of best-selling books – with titles like *Spies of the Kaiser: Plotting the Downfall of England* and *The Invasion of 1910* – that deliberately set out to blur the lines between fact and fiction. Le Queux protested vigorously to anyone who would listen, and many influential people did, that the authorities were negligently ignoring the German threat. Lord Northcliffe, proprietor of the *Daily Mail*, serialised *The Invasion of 1910* in his newspaper, carefully rerouting the hypothetical marauding Hun troops through towns and villages where the *Mail*'s circulation was at its highest. 'Among the thousands of Germans working in London, the hundred or so spies, all trusted soldiers, had passed unnoticed,' wrote le Queux. 'But, working in unison, each little group of two or three had been allotted its task and had previously thoroughly reconnoitred the position and studied the most rapid or effective means.'[1]

As the public excitement grew, so too did the number of alleged German spies. Lord Roberts, taking up the theme in Parliament, said:

> It is calculated, my Lords, that there are 80,000 Germans in the United Kingdom, almost all of them trained soldiers. They work in many of the hotels at some of the chief railway stations, and if a German force once got into this country it would have the advantage of help and reinforcement such as no other army on foreign soil has ever before enjoyed.

The *Daily Mail* instructed its readers that they should 'refuse to be served by a German waiter', adding as an afterthought: 'If your waiter says he is Swiss, ask to see his passport.'[2]

Even senior military officers not generally known for taking their lead from the press were convinced by le Queux's claims, not least because Colonel James Edmonds, the Royal Engineer who was in charge of 'secret service' at the War Office, was a friend of the author. Edmonds asked the police what could be done about 'the systematic visits to this country by Germans'. He complained of Germans 'of soldierly appearance' who had rented a house close to Army ranges on Romney Marsh and spent most of their time out on the marshes sketching. Two or three would stay for a month or so before being replaced by others. But the police pointed out that what the Germans were doing was actually not against the law and were unconvinced by Edmonds's claim that German tourists were 'assiduous in collecting other information concerning the topography of the country, roads, dockyards, military magazines, which might be considered of value from the military point of view'.[3]

Despite his concentration on the threat from German espionage, Edmonds was also aware of what was in fact the far greater threat to Britain – its failure to create an effective espionage system of its own to collect intelligence on Germany. Unlike their German colleagues, most British army officers saw espionage as immoral, an occupation to be avoided by any true gentleman. Charles à Court Repington served as military attaché in Brussels and The Hague in the early 1900s. Both cities were ideal posts from which to monitor the German military build-up, but he dismissed any such thought. 'I would never do any Secret Service work,' he wrote. 'My view is that the military attaché is the guest of the country to which he is accredited, and must only see and learn that which is permissible for a guest to investigate. Certainly, he must keep his eyes and ears open and miss nothing. But Secret Service is not his business and he should always refuse a hand in it.' Not even Sir William Everett, the British military attaché in Berlin, was happy about being asked to collect intelligence on his German hosts. 'You will not have forgotten when we talked this matter over some months ago, that I mentioned how distasteful this sort of work was to me and how much more distasteful it would be to me when it no longer formed a necessary part of my duties,' he said, when asked to act as a spy. 'I so dread the thought of being compelled to continue in communication and contact with the class of man who must be employed in this sort of work, while the measures to which we are obliged to resort are repulsive to me.'[4]

By 1905, the War Office had begun drawing up plans for a 'Secret Service in the Event of a War in Europe'; any ambiguity suggested by that title was swiftly removed a few months later with the drafting of the more explicit 'Secret Service Arrangements in the Event of War with Germany'. Both sets of plans worked on 'a general system of Observers, Carriers, Collectors and Forwarders' set up in peacetime. The second set proposed a precise system of networks run by 'Collectors', who would be British officers based in neighbouring countries – Denmark, Sweden, Switzerland, Belgium and the Netherlands. They would use 'Carriers' to receive information from and pass messages to anything from five to a dozen 'Observers' who were to be based in various German towns and were candidly described as 'spies, pure and simple'. The 'Carriers' were to be people who might travel in and out of the country without arousing suspicion, such as 'commercial travellers, gypsies and women'. The 'Collectors' would then use the nearest British embassy or consulate as the 'Forwarder' to pass their intelligence back to London.[5]

At the end of 1908, with no real improvement in the situation, Edmonds produced a long paper on 'secret service' in which he compared the British system unfavourably to those of other European countries, including Germany, Russia and France, and then proceeded to prove his point with a banal, even naïve, section on 'procuring intelligence'. Fortunately, it seems unlikely that the senior officials to whom it was addressed would have got that far, since most had little if any enthusiasm for finding out how 'this dirty business of espionage' was carried out. They would, however, have read the covering letter from Major-General Spencer Ewart, the director of Military Operations, who summed up the situation succinctly: 'We have so far I think failed to realise the value of Secret Service and have neglected to study the question sufficiently. It is impossible to extemporise a system of espionage after hostilities have broken out and any arrangement to be of value must be elaborated in time of peace.'[6]

It would be wrong to deduce from this that Edmonds did not have any agents at all. Five years earlier, the War Office had recruited an undercover intelligence officer, William Melville, a former head of the police Special Branch and a man who had achieved a certain degree of public notoriety. His exploits against Irish republican bombers and anarchists were widely celebrated by the popular press, which often recorded unlikely detail apparently designed to make him appear more heroic and attractive to their readers. Despite this publicity, Melville managed to adapt with ease to a life that was completely incognito. He was known to his bosses as 'M' and operated out of offices at 25 Victoria Street under the cover of William Morgan, general agent. While his main role was to watch out for 'suspicious Germans that might come to my notice, the same as to Frenchmen and foreigners generally', he was also tasked to seek out and recruit 'suitable men to go abroad to obtain information'. Melville not only recruited and controlled a small number of 'Secret Service agents' in Russia, Belgium, Germany and Africa, but also acted as what would now be regarded as a London-based 'fireman', carrying out a number of secret missions of his own around the world. He was regarded by his bosses as 'very resourceful', with 'a great capacity for picking up suitable persons to act as agents'.[7]

By the beginning of 1909, the War Office had four different agents in Germany (two of whom were shared with the Admiralty); one in Belgium; one in German South West Africa; and three sub-agents operating in Russia, controlled from Berlin by yet another German-based agent, an Austrian named Byzewski. There was also a deputy fireman, Herbert Dale Long, who had a good deal of experience operating in Africa, but with war looming had been recalled to London to carry out missions in Europe, spending the early part of 1909 in a fruitless search for the German spies alleged to be preparing invasion routes through East Anglia. In April, Colonel Schultz, one of the agents in Germany, died and Melville returned to Germany to recruit a replacement. The new agent, described as a retired officer in the armed forces of 'a friendly power', was so well regarded that he was placed on a salary of £600 a year. This extraordinarily high payment resulted from 'K' being not one person but in fact three, all of the same name, Christmas, the most important of them being Captain Walter Christmas, a well-connected former officer in the Royal Danish Navy, who was also a personal friend of Crown Prince, later King, Constantine of Greece. Christmas was designated K or WK, perhaps because it was simply assumed that being Danish, his name began with a K, or possibly it was deemed unwise to use the designation WC for an agent. Christmas's family were based in Esbjerg, with at least one of them travelling in and out of Germany to collect the intelligence as well as reporting it to London once safely back home.[8]

Galvanised by a combination of spy fever and the lack of a proper intelligence collection system, both Edmonds and Ewart lobbied hard for some form of action. The problem they faced was that the Liberal government then in power was unconvinced that Germany posed any great threat. So Edmonds and those within the military who agreed on the threat took to referring to the Germans as 'TRs'. This stood for 'tariff reformers', a reference to protectionist policies shared both by the Germans and by the right wing of the British opposition Conservative Party, and appears to have been an attempt to emphasise the German threat in a way the Liberal politicians would understand. As a result, Germany itself was constantly referred to by British intelligence officers as 'Tiaria'.[9]

The persistent lobbying worked and, in March 1909, Herbert Asquith, the British Prime Minister, instructed the Committee of Imperial Defence 'to consider the dangers from German espionage to British naval ports'. A sub-committee was set up, chaired by the Secretary of State for War, Richard Haldane, and including both Ewart and the director of naval intelligence, Rear-Admiral Alexander Bethell, as well as the Home Secretary, the postmaster-general, the first lord of the Admiralty, the commissioner of police and the permanent under-secretaries at the Treasury and Foreign Office, who between them administered the secret service vote. The terms of reference concentrated on the threat internally from foreign espionage, adding only as an afterthought that the sub-committee should also consider 'whether any alteration is desirable in the system already in force in the Admiralty and the War Office for obtaining information from abroad'. At first, many of the sub-committee members were sceptical of the alleged German threat. Edmonds, who also attended the meeting, describing himself as 'employed under the Director of Military Operations on Secret Service', said a secret service's motto should be 'trust no one' and quoted Kipling's adage: 'trust a snake before a harlot and a harlot before a Pathan'. Haldane's adviser Viscount Esher, who was clearly not an avid reader of either Kipling or the *Daily Mail*, described Edmonds as 'a silly witness from the War Office' and asked him sarcastically if he was not worried about 'the large number of German waiters in this country'. Esher noted in his diary that 'spycatchers get espionage on the brain'.

Nevertheless, despite the high level of scaremongering, the sub-committee recognised that some German spies were indeed active in Britain and, even if not at the level that William le Queux and others suggested, the threat was real. Just as importantly it accepted that 'our organisation for acquiring information of what is taking place in foreign ports and dockyards is defective, and that this is particularly the case with regard to Germany'. It also recognised that the Admiralty and War Office were 'in a difficult position when dealing with foreign spies who may have information to sell, since their dealings have to be direct and not through intermediaries' and it would be a good idea to have an organisation that could handle such delicate matters and ensure government officials did not have to dirty their hands by dealing with spies. The solution was to be the creation of a secret service bureau;

> To deal both with espionage in this country and with our own foreign agents abroad, and to serve as a screen between the Admiralty and War Office and foreign spies who may have information that they wish to sell to the government . . . By means of this bureau, our naval and military attachés and government officials would not only be freed from the necessity of dealing with spies, but direct evidence could not be obtained that we were having any dealings with them.

So secret was the creation of the bureau to be that the sub-committee's recommendations were not to be printed or circulated among its members. Just one copy was to be made and handed to Ewart, who was to be in charge of organising the bureau 'without delay' with assistance from Bethell and the commissioner of police, Sir Edward Henry.[10]

The sub-committee ruled that the bureau should be run by two officers, one each from the Army and the Royal Navy. The Army chose Captain Vernon Kell, whose fluency in French, German, Russian and Cantonese and experience in the Far East both with the military and as a correspondent for the *Daily Telegraph* appeared to mark him out as the ideal chief of a foreign intelligence service. Bethell's choice was at first sight far less promising. Commander Mansfield Smith Cumming was fifty years old, an obscure naval officer who had been forcibly retired from the active list owing to chronic sea sickness and had spent the past decade experimenting with the best methods of providing boom defence for Southampton harbour. Bethell claimed that Cumming 'possesses special qualifications for the appointment', although what these were seemed initially unclear.[11]

Bethell wrote to Cumming two weeks after the Haldane committee reported, suggesting that after more than ten years he must be pretty bored with boom defences. 'You may therefore perhaps like a new billet.

If so I have something good I can offer you and if you would like to come and see me on Thursday about noon I will tell you what it is.' Two days later, Cumming presented himself at the Admiralty, where Bethell told him that the appointment he had to offer was 'chief' of the new secret service. Cumming would be in charge of 'all' of the Admiralty's and War Office's agents alongside 'a junior colleague'. He accepted the post as 'a wonderful opportunity of doing more work for the Service before I am finally shelved'.[12]

The new headquarters of the Secret Service Bureau was set up in a second set of offices in Victoria Street under cover of a private detective agency run by a former CID officer, Chief Inspector Edward Drew, who as well as working as an assistant would receive £500 for the cost of the accommodation and the use of his name. In accordance with plans agreed by Haldane's committee, Herbert Dale Long was to be asked to go to Brussels, then seen as the espionage capital of Europe, to act as controller of the European agents. The committee had also instructed the navy to recruit another agent in Germany to report on German shipbuilding. As a result, Bethell sent Max Schultz, a 34-year-old shipbroker who had a Prussian father, to northern Germany. Before taking on the secret service mission, Schultz was based in Southampton and as a result quite possibly already known to Cumming. Despite Kell's apparent qualifications for foreign intelligence-gathering, he was to take charge of the domestic security section of the bureau, which would later become MI5, and would be known as K, from the first letter of his surname; Cumming was to control the foreign intelligence service. In reality this simply reflected the main interests and priorities of their respective services. Cumming and Kell met with Edmonds and his successor, Colonel George Macdonogh, another Royal Engineer, on 4 October 1909. They were then briefed on what work had already taken place, what agents existed and what their main qualifications were. The two agents Christmas and Byzewski both came up in the discussion and evidence of the attitude towards such agents was evident from the way Edmonds referred to them as 'scallywags'. The bureau opened for business officially six days later with Kell and Cumming each earning

£500 per annum, somewhat less than the £663 per annum paid to William Melville, although the latter sum seems to have included the rent for his offices.[13]

The new head of Britain's intelligence operations abroad, now to be known only as C, from the first letter of his name, was seen by most of those who met him as an extraordinarily charismatic man. Despite appearing to have been sidelined by his long role in developing boom defences, Cumming was seen as something of a pioneer, always open to new ideas, which might be what Bethell saw as his 'special qualifications'. He had a passion for yachts, cars and the very new pursuit of flying and, as a result, was not only an influential member of the Royal Automobile Club but in 1905 became a founder member of the Royal Motor Yacht Club and, a year later, the Royal Aero Club. But perhaps Cumming's best qualification was that he had already been sent abroad by the Foreign Office on a spying mission to study 'the development of motor propulsion in fishing fleets in Sweden and Holland'. This was allegedly in order to ascertain 'the reliability of internal combustion engines running paraffin', and shortly after taking over his new role, Cumming noted in his diary that he 'would like to get in touch with certain Danes and Swedes – with some of whom I made acquaintance when sent abroad recently by the FO [Foreign Office] in connection with Marine Motors.' He was it seems the ideal candidate for what was by any standards a pioneering and highly exciting role.

'This extraordinary man was short of stature, thick-set with grey hair half covering a well-rounded head,' one of his intelligence officers later wrote. 'His mouth was stern and an eagle eye, full of vivacity, glanced – or glared as the case may be – piercingly through a gold-rimmed monocle.' Another of Cumming's recruits described entering his office for the first time:

> Seated at a large desk with his back to the window, and apparently absorbed in reading a document, was the most remarkable man I have ever met in my life. The thing that struck me most about him was the shape of his large, intelligent head, which I saw in profile against the

light. Without paying the slightest attention to me as I stood by the door, he went on reading, occasionally making a note on the papers before him. Then with startling suddenness he put his papers aside and banging the desk hard with his hand said: 'Sit down, my boy, I think you will do.' I knew then that something really eventful had come into my life. This was my first introduction to C – the name by which this man was known to all who came in official contact with him. He had, of course, other names and one quite well known in London society, but to us, or rather to those who served under him, he was always known and referred to by this single letter of the alphabet.

Such was Cumming's influence that 'C' was to become the title given to all subsequent heads of British intelligence, evolving from the initial of his name into an abbreviation for 'chief' of the secret service. But initially he struggled to impose his undoubtedly powerful presence on those in charge of the new Secret Service Bureau. Macdonogh refused to deal with him directly, insisting that Kell be in charge of relations with the War Office. He also refused to allow Cumming to take any of the agent records away from the War Office and insisted that one of either Kell or Cumming should be in the Victoria Street offices at any time in case he wanted to get hold of them. Cumming protested to Bethell that it would be impossible to set up agent networks if he were never to leave the office. By now Cumming was seriously concerned that he was being sidelined and that Macdonogh would ensure that Kell, who had been sold to him by Bethell as his junior colleague, was in charge of all of the bureau's operations. In his diary he complained:

Cannot do any work in the office. Been here five weeks, not yet signed my name. Absolutely cut off from everyone while there, as cannot give my address or [be] telephoned under my own name. Have been consistently left out of it since I started. The system has been organised by the Military, who have just had control of our destinies long enough to take away all the work I could do, hand over by far the most difficult part of the work (for which their own man is obviously better suited) and take away all the facilities for doing it. I am firmly convinced that K will oust me altogether before long. He will have quantities of work to show, while I shall have nothing. It will transpire that I am not a linguist, and he will then be given the whole job with a subordinate, while I am retired – more or less discredited.[14]

Fortunately, the problems, and Cumming's concerns, appear to be the natural consequence of people with little if any experience in intelligence matters trying to set up a system virtually from scratch. Within days, the idea of a joint bureau had been abandoned, with Macdonogh accepting that the foreign and domestic espionage operations should be completely separate. Cumming was to be in sole charge of foreign operations and was tasked 'to correspond with all paid agents desirous of selling secrets' and to 'organise an efficient system by which German progress in armaments and naval construction can be watched'. The plan for Long to go to Brussels was put on hold, with Kell adamant that he and Melville must work solely for him and could not be spared. Cumming was told to 'hunt up a retired officer in Brussels as agent'. Macdonogh had initially suggested the War Office should continue to run its old agents abroad, in particular Byzewski, but Cumming, backed by Bethell, insisted that as head of the foreign intelligence service he must be in charge of all agents overseas and eventually won the argument, also obtaining permission to move into offices of his own at a flat in Ashley Mansions. The flat – for which he received an additional grant of £100 a year – had the advantage of being close to the bureau's Victoria Street headquarters while at the same time establishing the independence of his foreign espionage section.

On 26 November 1909, Cumming met the first of the agents he had inherited. The meeting with Byzewski did not begin particularly well, in part justifying Macdonogh's reluctance to hand him over. Edmonds, who had run him until now, introduced him to Cumming and left. Byzewski, who was an Austrian national, was understandably cautious. He had run what was by all accounts an efficient intelligence service into tsarist Russia for the British with three agents, all of whom he controlled from Berlin. Now suddenly he was being asked to switch his organisation to collecting intelligence on German shipbuilding – something that ran counter to his natural loyalties – and to add to his concerns, he was to be working to a completely new man he had never met before, who was telling him how to do his job. He agreed to recruit one man in Wilhelmshaven and another to travel between the main ports but baulked when he was asked to find out details of four large Austrian battleships allegedly being built in the Adriatic port of Pola. 'He jibbed at this immediately and said he was an Austrian and could do nothing that could hurt his native country,' Cumming noted, adding: 'He will be of little use should Austria join Germany in a war against us.' But after discovering that Byzewski was fluent in French, a language in which Cumming was more comfortable than German, the atmosphere improved somewhat. 'He is definitely an intelligent and bold man and I think he will probably prove my best aide,' Cumming noted later in his diary. 'But the difficulty about his patriotic feeling for Austria will have to be considered.'[15]

A few days later, Cumming met Captain Walter Christmas, the best of the three WKs. They met at the lodgings of Captain C. H. 'Roy' Regnart, a Royal Marine officer and assistant director of naval intelligence loaned to Cumming by Bethell as an assistant. Christmas reported seeing some new German weaponry. Unlike Byzewski, he was very keen to spy on the Germans, at one point saying: 'I have always looked upon myself as at least half English.' Cumming concluded in his diary that Christmas 'seemed straightforward, but I am not quite certain he ever saw those guns!'

Christmas was in fact very straightforward indeed. He was willing to spy for what were already the standard inducements of sex and cash and would go on to provide Cumming with a regular supply of the Danish navy's ship-watching reports of German vessels passing through the Skagerrak and the Kattegat, the channels joining the North Sea to the Baltic. On top of his £200 salary, the 48-year-old insisted that the go-between who collected his intelligence should always be a 'pretty' young woman who was to meet him in a hotel in Skagen, the town at the northernmost tip of Denmark. The women concerned were almost certainly prostitutes procured and paid for the purpose by the real collector of the intelligence. When a few years later, the Germans got too close to Christmas and Cumming had to have him exfiltrated to London, he was lodged in the notorious Shepherd Market area of Mayfair, where there were plenty of pretty young women, all pursuing the same business as the go-betweens who used to collect his intelligence from the Skagen hotel. The close links between what are alleged to be the world's two oldest professions were to be repeated persistently throughout the Service's history. Sex and money often represented far better inducements to spy than patriotic or moral beliefs.[16]

By the beginning of 1910, Cumming had drafted a strategy to collect intelligence from Germany that appears to have been based on the previous War Office schemes and their plans to use collectors based in neighbouring countries. So-called 'third-country operations' were to become the standard response for Britain's secret service when faced with a difficult target like Germany. Cumming also set up a cover organisation – Rasen, Falcon and Co., Shippers and Exporters – and a number of telegraphic addresses for contact with agents, including Sunbonnet London for routine communications and Autumn London for use in emergencies, with arrangements made with the Post Office to ensure that he would receive such messages at his flat at any time, night or day. He also set up a number of deals with businessmen travelling to Germany to collect intelligence, relying on their patriotism and the occasional offer of expenses. This would become standard practice for a perennially cash-strapped British intelligence service – Cumming's initial budget was a mere £2,700 and he was forever fighting off Treasury attempts at cuts. 'Much useful information was obtained by enthusiastic Englishmen while travelling in Germany and Austria,' one of the naval officers who worked with Cumming later wrote. 'This was not ideal since reports from such sources often contained more chaff than wheat.' However, given the lack of funding, it was a necessary way of supplementing the work of the professional intelligence agents.

Intelligence work, however hazardous it may be, and however valuable the results, was never sufficiently recognised by our home authorities as deserving of reward. The work of our intelligence correspondents was severely handicapped by the exiguous funds available. It may be that this pointed neglect is due to an inherent prejudice against the whole business of espionage.[17]

There is evidence in the accounts of severe financial cutbacks early in 1910, with two of B's sub-agents, including the recently installed man in Wilhelmshaven, laid off, the two other members of Christmas's family collectively known as WK let go, and another agent in Germany, designated D, who had failed to impress Cumming, also dropped. Others were either to be put on retainers with extra money for good reports, or paid simply on results alone. Byzewski and Walter Christmas, the remaining member of the WK family, were now the two main agents on the accounts and the only ones paid a full-time salary regardless of results, with Byzewski based in Berlin and Christmas described as a 'traveller' doing 'general work', although clearly his base in Denmark made him an ideal agent to collect intelligence in the main German ports at Kiel, Bremen and Hamburg. There were four other agents in Germany. Three of them were the remaining Byzewski sub-agent, a man called Hans Reichart, who was based in Hanover; Max Schultz, who travelled to Germany on a regular basis, using his cover as a shipbroker to collect intelligence in the shipbuilding yards; and A, a German woman based in Berlin, who was supposedly only to warn of any imminent preparations for war but whose usefulness could not therefore be tested. The last of the four was a Belgian called Arsène Marie Verrue, who also went under the pseudonym of Frédéric Rué, and 'travelled in Germany'. He was inherited from James Edmonds, who had recruited him on the recommendation of the Courage brewery, which Verrue represented in Germany. Known, slightly oddly, as U, rather than V or R, he was also working for a freelance espionage agency based in Brussels. It is not clear if either Edmonds or Cumming was aware of this or indeed that Verrue was a convicted criminal, who had served a number of prison sentences for various offences ranging from fraud to assault, although this might not have been regarded as a disqualification given that Cumming regarded most of his agents as 'rascals'. What Edmonds and Cumming would certainly not have been aware of at the time, although it was later to prove disastrous, was that the Brussels espionage agency's preferred customer was the far more generous German intelligence service.

The accounts also show two other agents on the Service's books. The first was a man called JR, who was based in Brussels and appears to have been recruited temporarily until Cumming could find someone to run his continental base. Given his low retainer of £50, it was no surprise that he was also working for French intelligence, telling Cumming disarmingly that they would happily provide him with a reference. The other agent was a TG, who had apparently agreed to 'join a regiment in Kiel and send us periodical reports for fifty pounds', which seems at first sight extremely low for the highly dangerous role of infiltrating the German army to spy for the British. But the accounts note this down as 'a retainer', suggesting that he would be paid extra for any reports, and after protests from TG, it was doubled to £100 a year.[18]

Cumming described the various agents in a report on the first six months of his work for the committee overseeing the work of the Secret Service Bureau. They split into two main types:

1. Those who are not required to collect definite information or send in periodical reports, but who are expected to keep a good look out for any unusual or significant movements or changes – either Naval or Military – and report them. From these agents 'no news is good news' and in the absence of any evidence to the contrary, it is to be believed that they are doing their duty and are earning the pay they receive. It has been pointed out that this negative news is of great value and that although we may wait for years for any report, it may be invaluable when it comes. On the other hand this class of agent should be very carefully chosen and should be of proved character, as very much will depend upon them, and the temptation will be strong when the critical moment arrives, to avoid risk by doing nothing.

2. The other kind – those who in addition to giving warning of extra-ordinary activity on the part of those they are deputed to watch, are expected to collect information of all kinds and forward it to me at stated intervals – I cannot as yet speak with any authority, as sufficient time has not elapsed since their appointment to enable me to form an opinion.

He then added a third group, which given the straitened circumstances of the British secret service for most of its existence was to become an important supplement to its agent networks:

A valuable source and one which it is hoped will be greatly extended, is that of the voluntary help given by those whose business or profession gives them special facilities for finding out what is going on abroad. I have received intelligence in this way from several whom it is not necessary to specify by name, and have sent in reports of their information from time to time. I am afraid that it will always be difficult to get voluntary help from people living abroad – even those of British birth. The risk they run is so great, and the consequence of detection so serious, that it is only in rare cases that they are likely to be of any use. I have, however, found one man – a Scotchman who occupies a position which will give him exceptional opportunities of knowing if anything in the nature of war is impending, who has promised that in such a case he will come over himself, or if that is impossible, will send a messenger in whom he has absolute confidence, to give warning. I feel bound to say that I place more reliance upon this man – who is of sturdy and independent character – than upon any of the others who have undertaken this important duty.

Cumming wrote the word 'Rollo' alongside this report, in the green ink that has become the trademark of every 'C' since (its use was originally a naval tradition), possibly suggesting it is the name of the mysterious 'Scotchman'. The most obvious candidate is George Rollo, a former 'volunteer' reservist of Scottish descent who worked for his family's Liverpool-based marine engineering company – and so would have had the perfect opportunity to conduct business in Germany's Baltic ports. But one businessman of Scottish descent who undoubtedly provided valuable information to Cumming during the pre-war years was Frederick Fairholme, a director of the Sheffield steel firm Davy Brothers who certainly could have been described as having 'exceptional opportunities' of gathering intelligence on the Imperial German Navy. Fairholme's father was Scottish and his mother was a Bavarian baroness, and he had spent his childhood partly at the family home in Austria. As a result, he spoke fluent German and dealt with the massive German steelmaker Krupp on his company's behalf. He met Cumming in January 1910 and was immediately able to supply important new intelligence on the German navy's latest guns and the newly developed shell they would fire, leading to the earliest report still in existence to have been circulated by the newly formed British secret service:

The following information has been received from a reliable source. It is reported that Krupp are making a very large howitzer, 29.3cm, firing a projectile weighing 300 kilos, with a muzzle velocity of 450 metres per second, which pierces a nickel steel 'deck armour' plate of 10cm at an angle of 55 degrees. The projectile penetrated the plate at a velocity of 253 metres per second and was unbroken. The projectile was filled with tri-nitro-toluol [TNT]. It is stated that the new 30.5 gun is to throw a projectile weighing over 500 kilos, with a muzzle velocity of 2800ft, and which will penetrate a 12in Krupp plate at 1600 feet per second . . . It is claimed that Krupp is using Nickel-Tungsten steel for all small guns. A great deal of the segregation [a stage in the steel-making process] trouble is got over by its use, and a longer life is claimed for the gun on account of the less erosion.

A few days before the report was issued, Walter Christmas produced what appears to be the first of a series of monthly summaries of his travels around Germany's naval shipyards and docks. It covered the month of December 1909 and gave details of work underway at the Imperial Yard in Wilhelmshaven, the Imperial Yard at Danzig and the Germania Yard at Gaarden, near Kiel. He reported a new shipyard under construction on Heligoland, and the speeds achieved in trials by the new dreadnought warship *Nassau*, and by the armoured cruisers *Blücher*, *Gneisenau* and *Scharnhorst*. He also described the 'remarkable speed' of 34.62 knots achieved by a new torpedo boat fitted with turbines, and the continued construction of U-boats, with two new submarines doubling the German navy's submarine fleet and a further two due to be built during 1910. This was probably the first of many monthly reports from an agent who was among Cumming's most successful in the run-up to the First World War. Christmas was also the first of what was to become a long line of British secret service employees who used their experiences to write spy novels. He began sooner than most, publishing *Svend Spejder* ('Svend the Scout') – in which the hero hunts down German spies in Denmark – in 1911, relatively early in his career for the British secret service.[19]

Christmas was not the only agent beginning to produce the goods. January 1910 was highly productive for Cumming, who also received and disseminated a comprehensive report from the Austrian Adriatic dockyards at Trieste, Pola and Fiume. The report was written by an agent who was not only clearly well informed about the latest naval equipment and weaponry, but was also looking out for potential agents, apparently under orders to do so from Cumming. Once again 'Scotchmen' were seen as the most likely recruits. Cumming sent the report verbatim, with a brief introduction of his own. 'The agent reports that none of the English residents were of any use to him, as they were either afraid of injuring their business interests, or were openly Austrian in sympathy,' Cumming said. There were, however, 'some Scotchmen who are of good type' and had helped him get into the best places to collect intelligence. These included the main Austrian navy base at Pola, where he found a 30.5cm naval gun on a parked lorry. 'I crawled under its tarpaulin and measured its muzzle.' The agent particularly recommended the manager of the Adria Steamship Company, a man called Rolland who was due to visit England in the near future and would be staying at the Charing Cross Hotel.

He is a very old and very canny Scotchman and I am not certain that he did not get some inkling of my object, by the broad hints he gave me as to his visits to England and his willingness to give information. He is absolutely straight and I fancy is anxious to tell anything he knows.[20]

The new head of Britain's secret service was not above going on missions of his own across the continent, journeying to Brussels and Paris, where he set up an intelligence-sharing agreement with the French Deuxième Bureau under Major Jean Wallner. This link was seen as so important that Cumming sent an officer to the British embassy to liaise with his counterparts in French intelligence. He frequently affected elaborate disguises, even for meetings with agents in London, and was always armed with a swordstick, a walking stick that pulled apart to reveal a rapier. Compton Mackenzie, who would serve as a secret service officer during the First World War, described how Cumming gave him the swordstick he had taken with him on spying expeditions before the war. 'That's when this business was really amusing,' Cumming said. 'After the war is over, we'll do some amusing secret service work together. It's capital sport.'[21]

TWO

Preparing for war

THERE was in fact another source of intelligence besides Cumming's various agents. It came from army and navy officers looking for adventure. They were apparently inspired by the spirit of Erskine Childers's 1903 novel, *The Riddle of the Sands*, in which Charles Carruthers and his friend Arthur Davies uncover German preparations for an invasion of Britain while sailing and 'duck-shooting' in northern Germany.[1] Large numbers of British officers volunteered to go to Germany on intelligence-gathering missions, few of them seeing themselves as 'spies', a word still seen as having underhand connotations not worthy of a man holding the King's commission. These men, often naïve and excessively enthusiastic amateurs over whom Cumming had too little control, were to provide him with his greatest problems in the early years. The situation was not helped by the fact that he had his own over-enthusiastic amateur to cope with in the shape of his part-time assistant Roy Regnart, who was primarily responsible for the earliest of a number of German arrests of British spies. The Brandon–Trench affair, as it was to become known, was the first of a series of scandals which led to British spies being paraded before the German courts.

Clearly keen to make his mark, Regnart decided to send a fellow Royal Marine, the thirty-year-old Captain Bernard Trench, on a tour of areas of northern Germany to map out the defences along the North Sea coast, which was where British planners had suggested any forced landings should take place. Trench had made a previous trip to Germany to report on the naval dockyard at Kiel with a friend, a Royal Navy lieutenant, Vivian Brandon, and asked if Brandon, a hydrographic expert, could come with him. Regnart happily agreed. Trench was allocated the codename Counterscarp while Brandon was to be known as Bonfire in what Regnart must have seen as clever jokes – rather than easily identifiable and therefore highly insecure. The two were to be contacted via the Thomas Cook office in Hamburg, an early use of a company that would repeatedly be of assistance to British intelligence. A third person was codenamed Orange. This appears to have been a Lieutenant Peel – the pun was clearly intended and yet again highly insecure. Peel was moored in a yacht flying the Norwegian flag at Delfzijl in the Netherlands, a short ferry ride across the Ems estuary from Emden in Germany, and was acting as a 'letter box' for the intelligence gathered by Trench and Brandon. The idea of sending the reports through the German postal system was sprung not just on Trench and Brandon, but also on Cumming, at the very last minute. 'This is quite contrary to my wishes in the matter,' Cumming wrote. 'I feel very strongly that it is utterly wrong and mistaken policy, and has no single advantage to support it, but on speaking to Roy about the matter he says that Bonfire was to write to him only on a particular matter, that of a man who had been recommended to him by a ship's captain. I did not see why this should be separate from the rest, but let it pass.' Regnart was in fact lying to get himself out of a difficult situation, which is almost certainly why he was so unpopular in the Admiralty.[2]

Brandon left for Germany on 6 August 1910 to rendezvous with Trench, who was in Denmark, studying Danish, and appears to have carried out reconnaissance of Kiel and the Kiel Canal before meeting Brandon in the town of Brunsbüttel, on the mouth of the Elbe, at the start of their 'walking tour'. Brandon had a list of questions on the German defences, some of which Trench was able to answer immediately as a result of the reconnaissance work he had already carried out. Trench then went to Sylt in the North Frisian Islands, which was seen as a likely British landing site, while Brandon went to Cuxhaven and Heligoland. One or both of them also visited Bremerhaven and Bremen, before they made their way to the East Frisian Islands. Here Trench visited

Nordeney, apparently alone, but they visited Wangerooge together, mapping an area of shallows while swimming. They were throughout maintaining contact with Peel at Delfzijl, and asked him to send them a detailed map of Wangerooge. Ten days into the trip, Regnart asked George Macdonogh for permission to send Trench and Brandon to Danzig to watch the entire Imperial Navy, a total of eighty-eight major warships, mounting full-scale manoeuvres which were to end with the Kaiser reviewing the fleet. This would have the critical impact of forcing Trench and Brandon to rush the remainder of their 'tour'. The sudden change of plan, and the way it was presented, left Macdonogh singularly unimpressed with Regnart, and he asked Cumming for a report on the man. Anxious not to criticise someone he would have to work with, and rely on, in the future, Cumming begged Macdonogh not to force him to write the report 'as it would be a very awkward thing to do and might lose us the services of a good man. To this he agreed, but he said that I must promise not to take Roy into any more of my schemes.'[3]

A few days later, Trench and Brandon arrived together on the East Friesian island of Borkum, one of the most important points in the German North Sea defences and the main target of their mission. They were now in something of a hurry to finish gathering the required intelligence before they left for Danzig. Trench managed to infiltrate a searchlight battery that was being tested for the first time and, after coming out, suggested to Brandon that he go in and have a look. Brandon had a camera and flashlight with him. Having managed to get in, he took a photograph, not the cleverest of things to do in the middle of a searchlight battery that was at its most alert. The flash was spotted by a sentry and the area was scanned by one of the searchlights, which immediately picked out Brandon. He was arrested and escorted to Emden on a boat. Trench, who was still free and apparently not seen as a suspect, travelled on the same boat and was allowed unhindered access to his colleague. He then went to their hotel in Emden and ineptly hid the various maps, notes, sketches and photographs from their mission in rather obvious places around the room. Having made a poor fist of trying to conceal the evidence, he attempted to escape across to the Netherlands but was arrested.

A search of their hotel uncovered the hidden intelligence with embarrassing ease and the two were held pending a full trial before the imperial court in Leipzig that had been specially set up to deal with espionage cases. The British press might have been obsessed with spy fever but it was as nothing compared to the near hysteria of the German newspapers. A German spy caught 'spying' at Portsmouth at around the same time was only collecting information he could 'have learned more cheaply and with less trouble by buying picture postcards', one German newspaper reported. Brandon and Trench on the other hand were 'specially trained men who undertook the work, men who did not need to take their results home in black and white, but for the most part could carry them in their heads. Thus these gentlemen have become very dangerous.' The *Berliner Neueste Nachrichten* outraged the correspondent of *The Times* by demanding that the prisoners 'be made incapable of reporting what they may have seen by means of appropriate mental treatment so that they may not retain too clear a memory of what they have seen'.

By comparison, the trial was a relatively polite and restrained affair. The general mood in Britain was that the Germans were intent on incarcerating two innocent officers and gentlemen. But all the evidence, much of it admitted, showed that Trench and Brandon were in fact guilty as charged. They did attempt to disguise their intentions, but the evidence hidden by Trench at their hotel made it clear that they had been in the process of assembling an intelligence guide to the German North Sea defences. They admitted pacing out the lengths of quays and landing docks, but insisted that they had only estimated the depths of the water, a claim rendered improbable by the fact that Brandon, a trained hydrographic surveyor, was equipped with a naval depth-sounding lead line. Nevertheless, Trench and Brandon were treated throughout not as criminals but as officers doing their job.

The atmosphere in the court room was remarkably relaxed. At one point, their barrister held up a copy of *The Riddle of the Sands* and asked them in turn if they were familiar with it. Trench simply said that he knew of it. But Brandon replied: 'Yes, I have read it,' before adding, to raucous laughter from the court, that he had liked it so much that he had in fact read it three times. The prosecution focused on the list of questions given to Brandon by one 'Reggie', which it said was designed to improve and correct a 'naval Baedeker' of Germany's North Sea coast produced by the Royal Navy's Intelligence Division, the Baedeker being a reference to a famous German publisher of tourist guides. But it was the evidence from the hotel that was the most conclusive. It included a series of sketches, photographs and notes taken at all the various points on their tour. These were read out in court, with the distances and dimensions replaced by the letter X. At Sylt, Trench had noted: 'Breakwaters, coal-sheds, coal stores here. There are no cranes. Railway lines by bridge – bridge (X) yards long, (X) yards wide. Cement wall all round promenade. Wells in all villages. Indifferent roads. White reefs not visible at flood tide.' On Wangerooge, Brandon had made a similar note: 'Landing piers (X) high, (X) long, (X) broad. Milk and eggs come from the mainland. Only five buildings on the west side. Seen no building which can contain mines. The beacon furthest out is occupied and has telegraphs.'

While this left no doubt that they were collecting intelligence, some of the most damaging evidence was the correspondence from Regnart 'obtained from Delfzijl by the German authorities'. One letter from Reggie to Trench referred to a sum of money for a second mission and openly implied it was being carried out on behalf of British intelligence, while another, written after Brandon's arrest, began – in a direct reference to the arrest – with the words: 'I am rather worried about what I have read in the *Daily Mail*...' Both Trench and Brandon resisted the prosecution's attempts to get them to name the mysterious 'Reggie' as a senior member of British intelligence or to admit that their communications with him through Peel on board the Norwegian yacht moored at Delfzijl were part of 'a pre-concerted plan to spy and report to the Intelligence Department of the British Admiralty'. Regnart, whose view of his role was such that he signed one of the letters with the initials CA, standing for 'C's assistant', would undoubtedly have been flattered by the persistent references to him as someone 'influential within the headquarters of the British intelligence department'. But the whole affair damned him with both the Admiralty and the War Office, while Cumming was appalled at the lack of sensible tradecraft, and Regnart's willingness to ignore his rulings on how secret service operations should be run. The communications methods had been a mess – compromising the Sunbonnet telegraphic address in the process – and seemed designed to bypass Cumming, allowing Regnart to take the credit. While the blame, as a result, fell entirely on Regnart and the naval intelligence division, Cumming later reflected that it was 'merely a fortunate accident' that none had attached to him and his section of the Secret Service Bureau. Trench and Brandon were sentenced to four years each, to be served in the relative comfort of military fortresses – rather than common prisons – because, in the words of the German attorney-general, they 'were not German traitors betraying the Fatherland' they were simply doing their job as 'servants of their government'.[4]

No doubt, the Brandon–Trench case was in part responsible for an influential memo, in October 1910, in which Macdonogh urged that more money be put into Cumming's secret service so that it could recruit the agents it would need when, as by now seemed inevitable, Britain went to war against Germany:

As matters stand at present it is probable that our secret service system compares unfavourably with that of other first-class powers, and that consequently we should find ourselves at a great disadvantage in case of war. It is still in its infancy, and though great progress has been made since the bureau was started a year ago, much remains to be done before it can be considered in any way efficient, in fact in the event of war with Germany we cannot now point to a single agent that would be likely to be of use to us.[5]

Despite Macdonogh's pessimism, Cumming did not have to rely on amateurish British officers who thought they could replicate the heroes of *The Riddle of the Sands*. He replaced the compromised Sunbonnet telegraphic with the more opaque Verbloske, London and resumed his fledgling operations in Germany, which included the reports from British businessmen like Frederick Fairholme and Max Schultz, the German-speaking Southampton shipbroker sent to Germany in 1909 on the orders of Richard Haldane's committee. 'I was there ostensibly ship buying, a business in which I was an expert and therefore well qualified to cover up my real business – discovering the secrets of the German navy,' Schultz later recalled. The Admiralty had asked Cumming to obtain the plans for the Imperial Navy's latest big warships, the *Thüringen*, a battleship, and the *Moltke*, a battle cruiser. Schultz had been making frequent trips to the country on business and was enjoying some success. He had also uncovered yet more amateur tradecraft from a Regnart-controlled agent.

Schultz was asked to meet up with a Danish agent run by Regnart, a man called Neilsen, who had singularly failed to produce anything worthwhile. Schultz was immediately suspicious.

This man had a camera and had been doing work and been paid for it, but had never given proper value for what he received. I called upon him and he came to my hotel, and from the moment he first called upon me, he never left me. I came to see what he had done with a certain camera, but I got my suspicions of the man because one night we were in a cafe and he was trying to fill me up pretty well, and in the middle of the large room he pulled out a plan and offered to sell it to me. I jumped up and said if he did not talk common sense I must do him some violence. I put the wind up the fellow; he looked around, and as he was folding his plans up I got my suspicion then that the man was not quite right. I left him – he did not know I was coming back to England. When I came home I went up to the office and asked if he was quite right, and would not see him again. I told them what I knew about this Neilsen and that the camera was not worth bothering about and if they took my advice they would get rid of the fellow.

It was good advice, but it was too late. Schultz had set up a network of agents across the country, not just in the ports but also in the main industrial area of the Ruhr. In August 1910, he recruited a businessman called Ernst von Maack, who agreed to 'correspond' with English friends of Schultz 'interested in naval matters'. Von Maack handed over a description of how German merchant navy ships were to be used by the Imperial Navy in the event of war and then in December went to London with Schultz to meet Cumming. He agreed to try to find out details of a diesel U-boat engine the British knew to be under development at the MAN factory in Augsburg, Bavaria. He was also asked if he knew anyone else who might be able to help.[6]

The man he recommended was a marine engineer called Karl Hipsich, originally an Austrian, but now a naturalised German, who had worked in the Weser naval shipyard at Bremen for more than ten years. In January 1911, Hipsich was duly invited to the UK, where he was feted by Cumming, who went out of his way to impress him, recording in his diary that 'an elaborate scheme has been arranged in order to attract a certain Mr Hiccough, whose acquaintance had been made by Max S when abroad'. Hipsich was, like Cumming, 'super interested' in aeroplanes and had in fact designed one. This provided the hook. Schultz was told to tell him that a friend of his in London knew Claude Grahame-White, the British aviator whose exploits had won him worldwide fame. Grahame-White had only a few weeks earlier told *The Times* that he planned to set up a factory to build high-speed aircraft before going on to make the then incredible prediction that 'next summer, practically for the first time in a complete and finished way, people will be able to enjoy the sensations of air travel'. This burgeoning aircraft industry would need revolutionary designs like Hipsich's. Schultz's friend would introduce the German to his friend Grahame-White and if the great man liked the design, Hipsich would be in line to make lots of money.

The German engineer was in a fairly prominent position within the Weser shipyard but he appears to have been desperate for money, possibly to feed the spending habits of his 27-year-old landlady, Ida Eckermann, who accompanied him to London. She was living with another shipyard engineer called Bernhard Wulff, who had also been recruited by Schultz, and her presence in London with Hipsich raises questions over her relationship with the two men living under her roof. Cumming, masquerading as 'Maurice Carter', introduced Hipsich to Grahame-White, who was indeed a close personal friend; not only was he a fellow member of the Aero Club, his family were close neighbours of the Cummings at their Hampshire home.

Sadly, the German's aircraft design was deemed impracticable by Grahame-White. But given Cumming's use of a false name, he must have been fully briefed on what was going on and, as recompense for turning down the aircraft design, he offered to drive them all down to Hendon the next day to watch him fly his aircraft. Cumming noted in his diary that this suggestion revived Hipsich to such an extent that 'he threw his arms around Max's neck and kissed him loudly on both cheeks'. So happy was Hipsich that Cumming only narrowly managed to escape the same fate. The following day, as promised, Grahame-White took them all to Hendon, where they saw the Farman biplane in which he had attempted to fly from London to Manchester, just failing to win the *Daily Mail*'s £10,000 prize for the first to accomplish the feat, but capturing the public imagination by flying part of the journey in total darkness in an attempt to win. The prize exhibit, however, was the specially modified 104-horsepower Blériot XI monoplane in which he had won the prestigious Gordon Bennett Trophy in America four months earlier. Grahame-White offered to take Hipsich up in the flimsy-looking Farman and, when he declined, Cumming enthusiastically took his place. The upshot was that Hipsich provided Cumming with a large number of documents and plans collected from shipyards across northern Germany, evoking 'surprise and unconcealed pleasure' that he was able to provide material of such quality. He agreed to work for the British for the miserly sum of £2 a week. Cumming gave him a £20 advance and clearly had high hopes of further good results. But he also seems to have decided that Hipsich was too big for Schultz to handle, writing presciently in his diary that the difficulty would be getting the documents Hipsich promised out of Germany and weaning him away from Eckermann, Wulff, von Maack and Schultz, all of whom were too obviously and closely associated with each other. 'I can control Max S, to a certain extent, but no-one can control the woman or her partner Wulff,' Cumming wrote. 'At first her demands will stimulate H, but as she becomes more greedy, he will find himself hard put to keep pace with them and will either quarrel with her or get caught trying to do too much.'[7]

It is not clear whether Hipsich tried to do too much too soon, or whether the complex relationships within Eckermann's house simply unravelled following her trip to London with Hipsich and his emergence as the more important, and profitable, of the agents living under her roof. Schultz believed, rightly or wrongly, that Neilsen was a German spy who had given Schultz, and therefore the entire network, away, and this seems entirely plausible. But Hipsich behaved extremely stupidly, pulling out plans in a cafe to which he, Schultz and a woman, almost certainly Eckermann, had been tailed by German police. Schultz managed to create a diversion which allowed him to slip the plans into his pocket. They then left the cafe, followed by the police, and headed for Hamburg's main station, where Eckermann was to catch the train to Bremen. Schultz slipped the plans into an envelope. Creating another diversion, an artificial argument between them, to distract the police, he put the envelope containing the plans inside a second envelope and during the confusion posted it. The outer envelope was addressed to PO Box 500 in London, an early use of a post office box address, which was apparently shared by both the foreign and domestic departments of the Secret Service Bureau, but would subsequently become associated solely with MI5.[8]

On 19 March 1911, Schultz, Hipsich and Wulff were arrested in Hamburg. When Schultz was arrested, someone suggested to him that it was unlucky. 'Oh no,' the naïve Schultz replied. 'It was lucky, because if I had not been arrested I would have done a great deal more, and I would not have got out of Germany in less than twenty years.' Schultz, Hipsich, Wulff, von Maack and Eckermann were all put on trial at Leipzig that December.

The hearing was held in camera, an indication of the level of secrets that had been passed to the British. The only details of what was said in court came with a statement announcing the sentencing, which said:

Schultz used the journeys which he made to Germany as a ship dealer in order to get into touch with all sorts of people with a view to learning military secrets. In particular, he addressed himself to Hipsich and Wulff, acted as intermediary in their communications with the English Intelligence Service, supplied them with the code addresses and code words for their correspondence, and himself assisted in despatching their communications.

He was to be jailed for seven and a half years, a sentence which apparently took into account his willingness to provide much of the evidence used in court, not just against himself but against his agents. Hipsich had handed over 'a large collection of drawings and other important material' to the British intelligence service, the judge said, sentencing him to twelve years imprisonment. 'He has surrendered secrets of which he obtained knowledge in his official capacity, and he has in a grave degree imperilled the German Empire.' Eckermann and von Maack were jailed for three years, while Wulff received just two years, allegedly because it had not been proven that he passed information to Schultz. However, the contradiction between that claim and the charges laid against Schultz that he helped Wulff pass secrets to London, the much shorter sentence Wulff received, and the complicated situation inside Eckermann's house inevitably give rise to suspicions that a jealous Wulff may have assisted the police in their detection of the network.

Once in prison, Schultz was repeatedly questioned with regard to details of the British espionage system. Since the Germans knew that Cumming had used the identity Captain Curry and Roy Regnart had used Captain Robertson, he confirmed both names in the hope that this would emerge in the German press and warn Cumming that those covernames were blown. The Germans also showed him a book of spy biographies with photographs, which included both Neilsen and another of Cumming's spies, a man calling himself Enrique Lorenzo Bernstein. The latter had been born in Australia of a Polish father and American mother and his real name was Henry Lawrence Bernstein. He was a former soldier turned arms dealer, who had been operating in South

America, a real rogue who would cross the Service's path on a number of occasions in the future. Bernstein was believed by Vernon Kell, quite wrongly as it turned out, to be working for the Germans, although it was certainly true that he was prepared to work for anyone who would pay him.

Sadly for Schultz, and his hope that his testimony would warn Cumming of areas where his service or his agents were blown, the Germans were not so stupid as to allow the press to publicise what they already knew. Schultz's apparent willingness to provide evidence against his own agents and others he knew, which led to a number of other Germans being jailed, left his bosses in London believing he must be mad. But Alexander Bethell and Cumming remained surprisingly loyal to him, giving his wife Sarah, dubbed 'Mrs Max', an allowance of a perhaps symbolic £13 a month, a substantial proportion of her husband's secret service salary, throughout his time in jail.[9]

There was of course the consolation of the valuable intelligence provided by Hipsich during his brief time as an agent but that was clearly not all that Cumming received during the pre-war period. There were also the monthly reports from Walter Christmas and the intelligence produced by Frederick Fairholme, who appears to have followed up on his interesting material on a new German naval delayed-burst shell with more detailed intelligence, presumably having been asked to do so by Cumming. 'A full and illustrated description of the new shell was furnished to our Admiralty in the early part of 1911, together with an account of its performance against many varieties of armoured targets,' one of Cumming's officers later wrote. 'The shell was made of Krupp crucible nickel chrome steel, a metal unsurpassed for toughness and hardness. It tapered at the nose to a very fine point, which was protected by a cup of softer metal. Long and costly experiments were necessary before the right material for this cap was discovered. The bursting charge was inserted into the shell through the base, and represented about three per cent of the total weight. As the object was to secure a most destructive burst with the smallest fragmentation, it was desirable to employ a highly explosive aromatic compound. But as such compounds are very sensitive, and liable to explode on impact against armour, it was necessary to "phlegmatise" the charge in order to bring it intact through thick plating, though without impairing the violence of its disruption.'[10]

The report set an unhappy precedent in that the crucial capabilities of the shell failed to ring the right alarm bells in the Admiralty, or if they did, they were ignored. The delayed-burst shell caused major damage to the British Grand Fleet during the Battle of Jutland, destroying three Royal Navy battle cruisers, while the less advanced British shells often had little impact on the German warships. This was to be a regular occurrence for Britain's secret service, the production of a good report that was then ignored by policy makers. Cumming also obtained information on tests of the new diesel engine for the German U-boats; whether from von Maack or another source is unclear. 'The completion of this engine, subsequently installed in *U19*, constituted a landmark in the development of submarine navigation,' one of Cumming's former officers said. 'A few months after the initial tests at Kiel the British Admiralty had at their disposal all the requisite facts pertaining to the new engine, and, in addition, a report on the sea trials of the *U19*.' Given that the engine was not introduced more widely into the U-boat fleet until 1914, obtaining this information in 1911 was, like the details of the delayed-charge naval shell, a considerable coup and Cumming appears to have deserved the increase in pay to £600 a year he was granted in May.[11]

Cumming finally managed to get the reliable spy in Germany he craved with the appointment in late 1911 of Hector Bywater, a journalist based in Dresden who wrote on naval matters for a number of US and British newspapers and journals. The first attempt at recruitment appears to have taken place in early 1910 but taking on Bywater would have meant getting rid of Byzewski, a move persistently vetoed by George Macdonogh. It was to be more than a year before Cumming, with heavy backing from Bethell, managed to get his way on the basis that since being asked to concentrate on Germany rather than Russia, the Austrian had 'not provided any information of value'.

Bywater gave one of the better descriptions of the inside of Cumming's office:

The apartment, airy, is furnished as an office. Its most conspicuous feature is a huge steel safe, painted green. The walls are adorned with large maps and charts and one picture, the latter depicting the execution of French villagers by a Prussian firing squad in the war of 1870. There are three tables, at the largest of which sits a man, grey-haired, clean-shaven, wearing a monocle. His figure inclines to stoutness, but the weather-tanned face, with its keen grey eyes, stamps him as an out-of-door man. He is, in fact, a post-captain on the retired list of the Royal Navy. Let us designate him as C. At a smaller table is seated a very different figure. Tall, spare, and dark, with aquiline features, his soldierly bearing betrays him for what he is – an officer of the regular army. This is F, perhaps the most capable intelligence officer of his generation. He is a linguist of the first order, his mind is a storehouse of naval and military knowledge, and his memory rivals that of Datas. Against his inclination, F was seconded to the intelligence service from a Highland regiment some years before the time of which we are writing. It was put to him as a matter of duty, and he knew no other mistress. The third occupant of the room is C's secretary, an incorrigibly cheerful soul who works fourteen hours a day for the pittance which a grateful country bestows on its devoted Civil Servants in the humbler grades.[12]

'F' was Captain Kenneth Forbes-Robertson of the Seaforth Highlanders, who after gaining a reputation for intelligence-gathering during operations in Somaliland and on the North-West Frontier had been seconded first to the War Office and then to Cumming, while C's 'secretary' was in fact his first full-time member of staff, Tom Laycock, a former Royal Artillery chief clerk who volunteered his services to Cumming and, in November 1912, left the Army to join the secret service for a salary of just £200 per annum. Laycock would subsequently be commissioned as a full-time intelligence officer and, although he was not very successful in that role, Cumming would later pay him a fulsome tribute for his 'valuable service', adding that 'for a considerable time he was my only assistant and I could not have carried on without him'.[13]

Bywater appears in the accounts as a 'fixed agent abroad' with the designation H.H.O., or sometimes H2O, a typically Cummingesque play on his name – he could not have been B since this would have caused confusion with Byzewski, the man he replaced. He travelled around Germany mapping out defences and using his role as a naval journalist as an excuse for talking his way into the dockyards. Bywater later published the notes he made of visits to survey the defences at Borkum, which he probably carried out in early 1912 since he described the trip as his first important mission.

On island, three hours, with crowd of trippers, but large part of it Sperrgebiet [prohibited zone], sentries with fixed bayonets and plenty of barbed wire. Persistent reports have been current that Emden is being developed as a naval base, but am unable to find any sign of this. Barracks are being enlarged, however. Borkum defended by twenty guns of various calibres, from 24cm downward, and including several 15cm high-velocity pieces on field carriages. I find in Emden a general impression that, in the event of war, Borkum will be one of the first objectives of the British Fleet. Since the Brandon–Trench affair it has been dangerous for any foreigner to visit the island as an individual. But the Ausflüge [excursions] from Emden provide one with an opportunity to cross to Borkum as one of the crowd, and in comparative safety, so long as German-made clothes are worn. Next to Nordeney, by Norddeutscher Lloyd Seebäderdienst steamer from Bremen. Make a careful survey of the island, and find no traces of the fortifications which had been reported as being in progress. This report came from R in Hamburg. This is not the first fairy tale he has told, and henceforth his reports will be suspect.

The unreliable R in Hamburg was probably Hans Reichart, the one sub-agent of Byzewski to survive the 1910 cuts, and like his former chief agent unable or unwilling to produce the same level of reporting against Germany as he had against Russia. The arrests of British spies continued intermittently, four cases at least on the basis of information provided to the authorities by Max Schultz. In July 1912, a Siemens and Halske technician called Ewald, who installed communications equipment on board German ships, was arrested for trying to obtain the Imperial German Navy's signal book on behalf of the British Admiralty. He was subsequently jailed for seven years after the Leipzig court heard that he had visited England and been put on a monthly retainer supplying the British with 'seven reports and plans regarding matters that ought to be kept secret'.[14]

At the end of 1912, Cumming took on two new agents, a father and son codenamed Sage and Sagette, to set up a ship-watching service in Norway and Denmark. Sage was Walter Archer, a former assistant secretary at the government's Board of Agriculture and Fisheries who had been forced to retire earlier that year through poor health. His son Edward was a former naval lieutenant, a specialist navigator, and they were 'intimately acquainted with both countries'. Walter Archer, a key figure in early research into the sex life of the salmon and in efforts to protect it from commercial netting, had set up a second home in Norway, having secured the fishing rights to the Suldalslågen, a major salmon river. Father and son planned to sail around the coasts of Norway and Denmark in a private yacht, recruiting lighthouse keepers, ships' pilots and coastguards to report German naval movements. They were to be paid a total of £660 a year between them with estimated travelling expenses of around £900 a year and payments to the ship watchers put at around £250. This was based on the extraordinarily optimistic payment of just two kroner – two shillings – for every report sent. The project was backed but clearly under-funded – even on the basis of these highly optimistic estimates – at £1,200 a year. By the time they finished setting up the network in May 1914, Sage and Sagette had predictably run well over budget and refused to hand over their agents until Cumming promised to pay what they were owed, which was considerably in excess of £2,000 for the whole enterprise. The coast-watching network was extended still further by having Captain Walter Christmas rejoin the Danish Navy to provide unofficial access to its reports on the movement of German warships and submarines into the North Sea, and while Cumming grumbled over the bills run up by Sage and Sagette, they were in fact a relatively low price to pay for what would be an extremely successful coast-watching service, its reputation surviving into the Second World War when it was held up by naval intelligence as a shining example of what was required.[15]

The problems dealing with agents like Karl Hipsich had convinced Cumming that he needed his own 'branch centre' on the continent to 'organise the sub-agents abroad, and more especially a system by which any information collected by them could be securely and expeditiously forwarded both in peace and war'. Alan Johnstone's recommendation of Copenhagen, with its easy access to the northern ports, was attractive to the Admiralty and was initially, it has to be said surprisingly, backed by the military. But by May 1911, Macdonogh was expressing a preference for Brussels, with its ensured access to Germany's western borders. Bethell had no problem agreeing to this proposal since the branch centre was to control four new agents to be recruited in the main German ports, replacing the likes of Reichart and ensuring good naval coverage, and 'Brussels is full of foreign agents and persons anxious to dispose of information'. What he did not say, of course, was that experience ought already to have shown that the majority of these foreign agents were not entirely reliable.

The man chosen by Macdonogh to set up the Brussels branch centre was a 38-year-old Etonian lawyer and Army reservist, Captain Bertrand Stewart, who, angered by rising tension between Germany and Britain in the summer of 1911, went to the War Office offering his services to gather intelligence on the German North Sea defences. Macdonogh decided, against Cumming's advice, to 'give him a run'. He was taken on to head up the branch centre in Brussels at £600 a year. Unfortunately, his first task was to link up with Arsène Marie Verrue, who had by now been sacked by Courage for dishonesty. This had led to him being taken off Cumming's list of full-time agents and used only on an irregular basis. But Verrue had recently produced some 'valuable intelligence', allegedly from a woman he knew in Hamburg, and Stewart was tasked to pay him for this information and to persuade the two of them to obtain more. It seems likely the woman never existed – Verrue declined to take Stewart to see her, claiming it was too dangerous. The information was almost certainly completely false or, if not, accurate but inconsequential 'chicken-feed' designed to create trust without giving anything important away, since Verrue and the Brussels-based agency that employed him were working for the Germans, both as intelligence gatherers and as counter-espionage agents. They were not only paid by the British to help Stewart but were also paid by the Germans to mount the sting that trapped him. Stewart played completely into their hands: he gave Verrue £15 for the intelligence he had already provided, and he went on a spying mission of his own to the newly reinforced German defences on Heligoland, taking a codebook given to him by Verrue, which he foolishly had on him when he was arrested in a public lavatory. Verrue was completely open in subsequent interviews with the German press that Stewart was only given up because Berlin were prepared to pay more money than London.

The trial evoked an outcry in England, where Stewart was seen as completely innocent, a belief he bizarrely seemed to share, reacting to his 3½-year sentence in the same fortress as Bernard Trench with an anguished cry from the dock: 'I am innocent and desire that everyone in England shall know about it.' Whether Stewart was simply deluding himself or playing a part in the hope of drumming up support for a successful appeal is unclear, but certainly his friends in England had no doubts, with one writing to *The Times* to protest that Stewart – an Old Etonian and a member of a string of London clubs, the Athenaeum, the Carlton, Arthur's and White's – was 'absolutely incapable of a mean or dishonourable act and would never stoop to play the miserable *rôle* of a spy'. Stewart was of course guilty as charged and once again, as with Trench and Vivian Brandon, Cumming had found himself dragged into a spy scandal arising from an ineptly run operation over which he had little or no control. Worse was to come: in March 1914, on the very eve of the war, Stewart took the War Office to court, naming Cumming as head of British espionage operations abroad no fewer than nine times, while at the same time claiming improbably that he, Stewart, had done nothing wrong and if only the British government had intervened to point this out he would not have had to suffer the indignity of being locked up in a German castle for six months. The case never came to court. Stewart was bought off with an inquiry and the promise of a cash payment he never saw. He was killed in action in France in September 1914 and the money went to his widow.[16]

Stewart's arrest still left Cumming without a Brussels branch centre. The initial solution was to send Herbert Dale Long, who was transferred from Vernon Kell's books to Cumming's in late 1911. He was only the first of a succession of officers sent to the Belgian capital. They included Cecil Aylmer Cameron, an artillery officer who had been imprisoned by a Scottish court for fraud and whose case had become a *cause célèbre*. Cameron's wife had insured a pearl necklace which she had never in fact owned for £6,500 and then claimed it had been stolen. The case saw prominent witnesses lined up to testify to having seen the pearls but the evidence was firmly against both Cameron and his wife. Nevertheless, the military establishment in England smelled a Scottish stitch-up of a fine officer who it was assumed – against all the evidence – had at worst acted chivalrously to protect his wife. A high-profile campaign was started to see him pardoned and on his release he was taken on Cumming's books as AC, almost certainly at the insistence of Macdonogh, who was one of Cameron's defenders, and sent to Brussels, where his ideas included sending British Army officers on cycling tours along the German border in two-man intelligence-gathering teams.[17]

Cumming still wanted to send Roy Regnart to Brussels to take charge of co-ordinating the intelligence collected on the continent. Captain Thomas Jackson, who had taken over from Bethell as director of naval intelligence, was opposed to this plan on the grounds that Regnart had proved himself neither 'clever or tactful', nor indeed 'loyal to C'. But surprisingly, given Macdonogh's previous attitude, the Army supported the move, describing the Royal Marine officer as 'an artist in secret service'. Regnart, who was a member of the family which ran the international furniture retailers Maple & Co., doesn't seem to have been an artist in much at all. He set up the new base under cover of an agency selling the firm's goods but it soon became clear both to C and to Maples that he was not the man for the job. Two other officers were sent to Brussels. The first was Baron George Marie de Goldschmidt – referred to by Cumming as GG. This appears to be typically Cummingesque humour, given that Goldschmidt was a cavalry officer. Goldschmidt represented the War Office's interests. The other was a Royal Marine representing the Royal Navy's interests, Captain James Cuffe, who was Macdonogh's nephew and took over Regnart's role as the lead agent.[18]

Cumming had one other man in Belgium. This was the writer Demetrius Boulger, who was based at Dinant and was a genuine expert on the country. Boulger, listed in Cumming's diaries as DB, had lived in Belgium for some time, collecting information on behalf of the War Office, and had influential friends within the Belgian establishment including members of the royal family. Under orders from Cumming, he began recruiting agents across Belgium and, according to his obituary in *The Times*, 'closely studied the military possibilities on the French and Belgian frontiers'.[19]

The preparations for war with Germany – on which Cumming was spending 'considerable sums of his own money' – were picking up pace at just the right time, rewarded in April 1913 by an increase in pay to £700 a year, with Macdonogh pointing out that 'C's work is particularly anxious and trying'. At some point during the pre-war years, Cumming also recruited Richard B. Tinsley, a retired naval reservist who was running the Rotterdam offices of the Uranium Steamship Company. Tinsley's useful position and background may well have come to C's attention in the spring of 1911, when the Dutch briefly expelled him for allowing would-be Russian émigrés rejected by America to land illegally in Holland. It remains unclear when precisely he was recruited. Given the speed with which the Foreign Office had him put back in place it may even have been before this incident, but he was certainly in place and ready to play a key role when war broke out.[20]

Meanwhile, Cumming's agents continued to collect good intelligence on the Imperial German Navy's preparations for war. Hector Bywater described how he managed to get on board the battle cruiser *Von der Tann*, which was anchored off Hamburg. 'I determined to visit her, though the risk was considerable,' he said, resisting any false modesty. 'By a stroke of luck, I found that a local shipping man, to whom I had a letter from a mutual friend in Berlin, knew several officers of the ship, and had visited them on board. He was going again, and by very tactful manoeuvring I got him to invite me to accompany him. We went across in a launch, but on arriving at the ship's ladder I remarked to my companion that, being a foreigner, I might not be welcome on board. He then spoke to the officer of the watch, who was one of his friends, explained who I was (or, more strictly speaking, who he thought I was), and I was promptly invited to come up. We spent two hours in the ship, and saw nearly everything except the inside of the gun-turrets and the engine-room. I memorised all the important details, and subsequently wrote an elaborate report on the ship. This was the first German battle cruiser to be personally inspected by a British Secret Service man.'[21]

Even as war approached, money remained tight, as reflected in the arguments with Sage and Sagette which took place in May 1914, just three months before the war. In spite of this handicap, the British intelligence system was 'on the whole, wonderfully efficient', one former intelligence officer claimed. Thanks in no small part to Sage and Sagette's efforts, and the well-positioned Captain Christmas, Cumming was particularly good at detecting movements of German ships into and out of the Baltic. Evidence of any intelligence on German military capabilities or plans is in fact sparse, but there is certainly evidence of substantial intelligence on German naval capabilities, even if its significance was often ignored by the Admiralty. 'Every "surprise" which the Germans sprang upon us at sea was foretold and elucidated in full detail,' the former officer wrote. 'Practically complete diagrams of every German capital ship down to the *König* class, showing the extent and thickness of their armour, the layout of their underwater compartments and bulkheads, and every other protective feature, were obtained by our intelligence service. It was thus known, long beforehand, that the German ships were built to withstand the severest punishment, and it is a thousand pities that this knowledge was not taken into account by the Admiralty officers who were responsible for the design of our armour-piercing projectiles.'[22]

THE German artilleryman saw Sister Marie-Mélanie fussing over the rose bush in the convent gardens and limped over to talk to her. It was early 1918. The soldier's spell of convalescence at the convent, in the southern Belgian town of Chimay, had been his first chance for months to speak to a woman. Some of the military nurses in the German field hospital based in the convent were good to talk to, and a few weren't bad looking, but they kept their distance. Oddly, Sister Marie-Mélanie was more approachable. She seemed to understand that, after months on the front, he needed simply to hear a gentle voice far removed from the brutality of the trenches. Although she didn't seem to mind too much if he did occasionally talk about his work and the big new gun he and his bosses were so proud of.

If only the German gunner had known the truth, he would have realised why Sister Marie-Mélanie was so interested in the big gun and held his tongue. Fortunately for the British secret service, he had no idea that the kindly French nun was a member of La Dame Blanche, the network of more than a thousand British agents across Belgium controlled by the MI1c officer Henry Landau. Named after the legendary ghost whose appearance would supposedly signal the downfall of the Hohenzollerns, the German royal family, it was based around a train-watching network, but it gathered intelligence from wherever it could. The Sisters of the Doctrine Chrétienne had been forced out of their convent in France by the war and relocated to Chimay. When the German military took over the convent as a field hospital, two of the nuns had volunteered their services to Anatole Gobeaux, commander of the 'Chimay Company' of La Dame Blanche, offering to collect intelligence from the German soldiers being treated there, which was why Sister Marie-Mélanie was such a good listener, especially when the thoughts of the German soldiers returned to the work they carried out on the front.

The good sister had a particular reason to speak to the German gunner. During their last conversation, he had bragged to her that the Germans had a big gun, the 'Kaiser-Wilhelm-Geschütz', that would change the shape of the war, turning it in Germany's favour. She needed him to give her more details, but she could not appear too keen, for fear of rousing his suspicion. Fortunately, the simple German soldier saw no harm in talking to a nun about it; after all she was not part of this war. She was not really interested in it all, her thoughts were surely only of God. Without any prompting, he told her the gun he had been talking about could fire shells more than 120 kilometres, enough to reach the city of Paris.

'It hardly seems possible that it can shoot that far,' she said. It certainly could, he replied. He had seen it himself in the Laon sector. He was about to give her the name of the village, but at the last moment stopped himself, just in case.

His reticence came too late. The sector was all Sister Marie-Mélanie needed. A few weeks earlier, a French refugee, seeking food and shelter at the convent, had told her that the people of his village, Crépy-en-Laon, had been forced from their homes so the Germans could place artillery there. How did he know it was artillery they wanted to put there, she asked. 'Well, they've laid down concrete gun platforms and ammunition pits in Dandry's Farm,' the refugee said. 'At least, that's what everyone thinks they are.'

Sister Marie-Mélanie passed the details of the big gun and its location back to Gobeaux, who sent one of his agents to Crépy to confirm she was right. Sure enough, the agent saw the biggest gun he had ever seen, with a barrel 30 metres long. The intelligence was sent back with the couriers to Landau, who had himself recently received a report from a spy inside Germany of trials of a big high-trajectory gun. Landau later said it was with appropriate 'exultation' that he reported back to his bosses on the existence of the new gun.

THREE

Turf wars with the military

WHEN the Serb nationalist Gavrilo Princip shot dead Archduke Franz Ferdinand, heir to the Austro-Hungarian empire, in the Bosnian city of Sarajevo on 28 June 1914, it was far from clear that it would lead to war between Britain and Germany. But a retaliatory attack on Serbia by Austro-Hungarian troops triggered a series of alliances and ultimately confrontation between the Entente powers – France, Britain and Russia – and the so-called Central Powers of Germany and Austria-Hungary. The first indication of full-scale German preparations for war came just over three weeks after the assassination, when Mansfield Smith Cumming received a report that Germany was mobilising. He recorded the one-word entry *'Mobilmachung'* in his diary for 23 July 1914. This warning is most likely to have come from Hector Bywater's agents in the northern ports, where the Imperial Navy's ships were to be among the first to be mobilised. The warning does not seem to have been taken seriously in some sectors of Whitehall, possibly because under German law mobilisation could only be ordered by public decree and no such decree had been announced. Eight days later, on the morning of 31 July 1914, Pierre-Paul Cambon, the French ambassador to the Court of St James, told Sir Arthur Nicolson, the head of the British Foreign Office, that the report was true. The Germans were definitely mobilising, albeit secretly, in the hope that this would force France to act and provide a 'provocation' to justify the German attack. Sometime later that day, one of C's agents in Germany – possibly Bywater himself – arrived in London with confirmation of troop trains passing through Cologne on their way towards Belgium and France.[1]

Cumming was now based in Flat 54 at 2 Whitehall Court, just behind the War Office, while continuing to maintain the offices in Ashley Mansions. His operations at this stage were described in one official report as 'still amateurish in execution' although it added that the secret service 'quickly assumed a more responsible position owing to the increasing demands made on it from all quarters'. Cumming had deployed a number of officers in France and the Low Countries. Demetrius Boulger was in the Belgian town of Dinant, on the main path of the anticipated German attack. Herbert Dale Long, Cecil Aylmer Cameron, George Marie de Goldschmidt and James Cuffe were in Brussels, with the Rothschilds merchant bank providing the funding. Major John Charteris, a high flyer in the still very small British military intelligence world, had been sent to Paris to take over liaison with the Deuxième Bureau. Cuffe was setting up the only secret agent reporting networks the British had at the start of the war, but as the Germans swept across Belgium, forcing C's men in Dinant and Brussels to pull back, control of the networks reverted to Richard Tinsley in Rotterdam.[2]

Tinsley would be widely demonised by other intelligence officers, both in the Admiralty and at the Army's general headquarters, but he was the ideal man for Cumming to have in charge of his longed-for branch centre on the continent, helping it to become the most important intelligence collection point on the Western Front. Tinsley was certainly no intelligence expert, leaving this largely to his subordinates. He was in fact a 38-year-old merchant seaman from Bootle, who had served in a number of junior officer posts on commercial ships for Cunard before taking a minor management role in the Liverpool docks and eventually securing the rather more prestigious post of Rotterdam manager for the Uranium Steamship Company. Tinsley was a bit of a crook – one intelligence officer described him as 'a very rough looking character, rather like the cartoon pictures of convicts' – and was just the sort of 'rascal' that fascinated Cumming, but he was a trained naval gunnery officer, having been commissioned into the Royal Naval Reserve (RNR) in 1903, with a recommendation from his superiors as a 'zealous, painstaking and able officer'. How reliable this recommendation was is unclear, since he also had the persuasive skills of a natural con-man, having talked his company out of very serious trouble when one of its liners caught fire in mid-Atlantic with the loss of 133 of those on board. Cumming needed someone who could take on a difficult job defending his corner against all comers. He picked the right man.[3]

Another intelligence officer who worked with Tinsley described him as 'a short, though broad-shouldered man, somewhat over-dressed, ruddy of complexion, with small piercing eyes, who looked like the combination of sea captain and prize fighter'. Brought up on the Liverpool dockside and having served as a first or second mate on a variety of merchant vessels, Tinsley was without doubt an adept street brawler. Whether it was dealing with the Dutch or Belgian authorities, or as it mostly was, the British military, 'his outstanding quality was as a fighter', the officer said. His role was not to be the hands-on intelligence collector; other officers who worked for him did that. 'T hardly spoke a word of Dutch, and knew no French or German; he had no military knowledge, and not the least conception of how an organisation could be mounted in occupied territory,' one of them said. 'He was, however, a shrewd executive and helped to keep the various branches of the Service under him in close co-operation. His chief function, the handling of the Dutch authorities, he carried out admirably. He undoubtedly rendered splendid service.'[4]

Quite how he got the Dutch authorities on his side is unclear. In all probability it was by a mixture of sharing a good deal of intelligence and liberal amounts of alcohol, not necessarily in that order, and with no small assistance from the Germans, who constantly threatened the Netherlands' neutrality. Certainly from wanting Tinsley expelled, it was not long before the Dutch police regarded him as one of their closest allies. By the end of August 1914, operating from Uranium's offices on the Boompjes, right on the Rotterdam waterfront, Tinsley was already running locally recruited agents into Germany to report on troop movements. Dimitri de Peterson, the son of the Russian consul-general in The Hague, was the main agent handler, using a kiosk in Amsterdam's Westermarkt as a 'letter box' to receive the agents' reports. While two of the agents inside Germany were arrested by the Dutch police, others were not and by the time the Germans squared off against the French, Belgian and British forces across Flanders and north-east France, Tinsley was operating the only agents behind enemy lines that were available to British commanders.[5]

Unsurprisingly, perhaps, Tinsley was not the only dubious character that Cumming had on his books in the early months of the war. When 'Enrique Lorenzo Bernstein' turned up at the Admiralty in early August offering 'his services, which had been accepted in the past', to spy for the secret service, the new director of naval intelligence, Rear-Admiral Henry Oliver, called the police. They searched Bernstein's Hammersmith home and found plans for an 'inflammable aeroplane projectile' and codes and ciphers. He was charged under the Official Secrets Act. Oliver's scepticism was perhaps understandable given that, for the previous eighteen months, Bernstein had been touring Britain's music halls as a conjurer, using the stage name Lu Chang, and appearing at the Belfast Palladium, the Shoreditch Empire, the Imperial, Canning Town, and the Canterbury Theatre. His list of theatrical credits, and his entirely justified insistence that he had in the past spied for the British secret service, failed to prevent the magistrate from ordering him to be deported. But at the last minute, Cumming stepped in to have him released into his custody, visiting him in Brixton prison to have 'a long talk with him'. A few days later, he collected him from Brixton and personally drove him home to Hammersmith. Cumming told Oliver that Bernstein was in fact 'a very noted international spy'. He resumed working for the British, this time for the naval intelligence division, dropping his surname and calling himself Henry Lawrence, although it is difficult to see how he could have produced any reliable intelligence.[6]

Cumming's domination of secret service activities on the continent was about to change, with the inexperienced new secret service very nearly wrongfooted by the military, led by another of C's crooks. At the beginning of October, Cumming travelled to France to see his 24-year-old son Alastair, an officer in the Seaforth Highlanders, who at the start of the war had joined the newly created Intelligence Corps. The story, as told repeatedly within the secret service, was that Cumming and his son were driving a Rolls-Royce in the woods to the east of the town of Meaux when it suffered a puncture. 'The car going at full speed had crashed into a tree and overturned, pinning C by the leg and flinging his son out on his head,' one former officer later recalled. 'The boy was fatally injured, and his father, hearing him moan something about the cold, tried to extricate himself from the wreck of the car to put a coat over him; but struggle as he might, he could not free his smashed leg. Thereupon he had taken out his penknife and hacked away at his smashed leg until he had cut it off, after which he crawled over to the son and spread a coat over him, being found later lying unconscious by the dead body.' The story is of the type that invariably leads to scepticism and the full truth is unclear but the existing documentation backs up the major part. The crash happened, Alastair died and Cumming certainly did have his right leg amputated below the knee. Just as importantly perhaps, the story survived without correction. It is unlikely that Cumming managed to hack his way through his tibia with a penknife but if his foot was partially severed and trapped under the car, it would be perfectly feasible for him to have cut through the tendon and cartilage to free his leg.[7]

While Cumming was in hospital, the intelligence section at the general headquarters (GHQ) of the British Expeditionary Force, based in the Château Beaurepaire at Montreuil, attempted to take over his operations. The section came under George Macdonogh, who had been sent to France as Brigadier-General Intelligence. His protégé Cecil Aylmer Cameron, whom he had foisted on Cumming in the first place, took charge of setting up new networks under Major Walter Kirke, who was a member of the newly created Intelligence Corps and another staunch believer in Cameron's innocence. Far from being innocent, Cameron was in fact a proven liar and a convicted fraudster, scarcely the best qualifications for an intelligence officer, yet Kirke and Macdonogh were convinced he was a good officer who had been badly treated and their sponsorship not only ensured that he was put in charge of all military agent-running in France and Belgium, it also gave him an arrogant belief that he could do, and demand, anything he wanted.

James Cuffe and George Marie de Goldschmidt were absorbed into the new GHQ system, and ordered to hand over details of some, but critically not all, of their agents to Cameron. Demetrius Boulger had been brought back to London and paid off when Dinant fell, early in the campaign, leaving Long the only remaining officer Cumming had in Belgium. Long had two problems: not only had he made the unfortunate mistake of being on holiday in Italy when war was declared, but he was also a civilian and in Kirke's book was therefore not to be trusted. Having carried out a wholesale takeover of C's agents in Brussels, and with Cumming laid up in hospital, Kirke and Cameron now tried to take over his networks but were blocked by Tom Laycock, who had fortunately been commissioned at the start of the war and was now a captain in charge of liaison with the War Office as head of a newly created military operations section called MO6c. It is not clear whether he was briefed beforehand by Cumming from his sick-bed, but he bravely stood up to the takeover bid, insisting – much to Kirke's irritation – that Tinsley's Rotterdam bureau was quite capable of running all of C's operations in Holland and Belgium.[8]

Cameron initially had difficulties persuading any Belgians to work for him, mistaking their natural suspicion of his clumsy approaches for a misplaced love of the Boche. But he began to make headway after Kirke took on an agent offered by the French, a Parisian called Ferdinand Afchain, to act as a go-between – in espionage parlance, a cut-out. Afchain dealt with the potential agents on Cameron's behalf and was far more successful than his boss had been in persuading Belgians and French to go back behind enemy lines and set up some useful train-watching services, observing the railway lines bringing in fresh German troops. It was Afchain who recruited the man who was to be Cameron's most important agent at the start of the war. Dieudonné Lambrecht, a 32-year-old Belgian, was the part owner of a factory producing precision machinery. A devout Roman Catholic, Lambrecht lived with his wife Jeanne and their young daughter Riette in Liège. His Catholic faith was important since two of his first recruits were Jesuit priests, Father Arthur Dupont and Father Jean des Onays, who in turn brought his brother-in-law Oscar Donnay on board. The four set about recruiting railway workers to monitor the movement of German troop trains along the main railway line that ran from Aachen through Liège and Namur towards the German front.[9]

The beauty of the train-watching services was that the Germans sent their troops to war in 'constituted units' with each regiment taking up a full train, sometimes more than one, to carry all its equipment. Details of what was on the train – much of which could be determined by the different types of wagon used – allowed British intelligence officers to work out whether it was an infantry, artillery, cavalry or engineer regiment. If the train watchers were able to spot insignia on the weapons, vehicles or uniforms, they would even be able to determine the precise unit.

Cumming returned to work on 11 November, remarkably swiftly given the loss of his right leg below the knee and the trauma that must have accompanied the accident. Three days earlier, during the first Battle of Ypres, Kenneth Forbes-Robertson, who on the outbreak of war had insisted on rejoining his regiment, was killed leading a company of the Seaforths to counter a German advance in Ploegsteert Wood. Cumming had lost first his son and now his former deputy in the first few months of the war. But there was little time to consider such matters. He soon found himself embroiled in discussions that would set the scene for more than two years of turf wars between his secret service and its equivalent at GHQ. A conference at the provisional Belgian capital of Furnes, involving representatives of the British, French and Belgians, agreed to set up a joint bureau at Folkestone, where most of the refugees from the war were arriving in Britain. Known as the Bureau Central Interallié (BCI), it was to share intelligence and recruit new agents who could be sent back behind the lines to collect information. Cumming also agreed to put his own liaison officer into the BCI, but the main British representative, and the officer in overall charge, was to be Cameron. He was not the right man for the job and swiftly became the central figure in a series of squabbles over control of secret service operations in Belgium and Holland. These began in earnest at the Furnes conference with the GHQ representatives attacking the standard of military intelligence produced by Tinsley and pushing Cameron as the man to take things forward. Kirke clearly believed Cameron could do no wrong, while, whatever lessons Cameron's previous misfortunes had taught him, humility was not among them. Both Macdonogh and Kirke had supported him, wrongly believing him innocent but apparently leaving him with a belief that he was untouchable. He appears to have believed, like Regnart before him, that he could sideline Cumming, but made a serious mistake in basing himself in Britain rather than on the continent. Kirke recorded in his diary the somewhat naïve view that Cameron would be able to 'organise a large system' in occupied Belgium and France from the BCI's offices at 8 The Parade, Folkestone. It was always obvious that organising a number of train-watching networks from the other side of the Channel would be a difficult task. Cameron seemed determined to make it even more difficult, for everybody.[10]

The criticism of Tinsley's reporting on military matters was swiftly solved by filtering his agent reports through the British military attaché in The Hague, Lieutenant-Colonel Lawrie Oppenheim. His role was to analyse the information, turn it into military intelligence reports and send them on to London, with the War Office then passing them on to Macdonogh in France. Oppenheim would then task Tinsley, telling him what further information was required to fill in the gaps. The agents were still to be run centrally from Tinsley's office on the Boompjes, not least because some were producing highly valuable naval reporting, an area which Tinsley understood far better than Oppenheim, and the Admiralty was not prepared to lose this rare source of intelligence. The decision to put Oppenheim in charge of the military reporting was inspired, turning an inadequate military reporting system into a consistently reliable one. He was a skilful interpreter of intelligence who not only improved the reports on the Western Front that were produced by C's fledgling secret service but was also to become a loyal supporter of Tinsley's 'intelligence branch centre'.[11]

Oppenheim was in his early forties, a senior and experienced army officer who, according to one of Tinsley's men, was the exact opposite of T: fairly tall, and somewhat frail, scholarly in appearance, highly strung, and retiring in disposition. His sole function was to analyse information and telegraph reports, and having nothing to do with the procuring of information or with the secret service organisation, he did not quite realise the difficulties that we had to contend with. He was, however, a brilliant staff officer, as I found out afterwards from his masterly analyses of the reports I sent him. He got every scrap of information there was to glean from them, and in the examination of train-watching reports, he was an expert in gauging the exact volume of each troop movement.[12]

By the end of November 1914, C was spending £4,310 a month running a number of officers in Belgium, the Netherlands, Denmark, Norway, Germany, Switzerland and Russia, with the bulk of that money, a very respectable £1,250, going to Tinsley for operations in Belgium, the Netherlands and Germany. The rapid expansion meant that by December, C was asking for another £2,190 a month. By now there were four officers working at the Whitehall Court headquarters: Cumming, Laycock and two new recruits: Captain Patrick Kenny, a 31-year-old Intelligence Corps officer who was the son of a Dublin judge, and Major Archibald Campbell, who was there only temporarily, having been recalled from a mission in Petrograd at the request of Captain Reginald 'Blinker' Hall, the new head of naval intelligence, whose nickname derived from a chronic facial tic suffered since childhood. Campbell had been upsetting virtually everyone he met in Petrograd and was now endeavouring to do the same back in London. There were also four clerks, two typists, one messenger and two 'outside men' to deflect unwelcome visitors. The office was expanding all the time with Francis Newnum, a mining engineer, and Stanley Garton, an Olympic gold medal rower, recruited in December. Garton's hands were so muscular from his rowing that he could sprinkle tobacco on them and fill his pipe upside down, one colleague said. 'It was fascinating to watch the tobacco wriggling its way up into the bowl, like a snake.'

Some of Cumming's officers abroad had also begun to prefix reports with the letters CX, a practice that continues to this day, with the

Service's product routinely known as 'CX reports'. The bigram had been traditionally used within the Foreign Office for 'Confidential Exchange' and dated back to the mid-nineteenth century at least. The extension of its usage followed a discussion between Cumming and the man who was his main liaison with the Foreign Office, Ronald Campbell, private secretary to the permanent under-secretary, Sir Arthur Nicolson. Campbell would turn into a high-flying member of the diplomatic service who went on to become ambassador to France, but he was then a very young and relatively junior official. 'It used to annoy us younger ones when C called that young FO official "sir",' one of Cumming's officers later recalled. 'We ought to have understood his reasons.' It was a key feature of Cumming's approach to protecting his still fragile empire that he cultivated his relationships with his three main customers – the Foreign Office, the War Office and the Admiralty – with great skill, sometimes playing them off against each other, but always seeking to keep them on side. Campbell was certainly young but he had Nicolson's ear and was to be a key supporter of Cumming throughout the war. The need to discuss the use of 'CX' with Campbell suggests that Cumming might have been simply borrowing a Foreign Office reference. But the anecdotal history within the Service has always been that it derived from Cumming telling an agent in Brussels: 'If you have urgent material you want to get to us quickly you should put "CX CX CX CX" on the report' – denoting that it was for C and urgent. The reference to Brussels is itself interesting given that, by this stage, Cuffe, Long, and Cameron had all long since withdrawn.[13]

Despite the obvious drawbacks in Cameron running his agent networks from Folkestone, he now had three different train-watching services in play of which the Lambrecht service, with around thirty agents, was by far the most important, ensuring that for eighteen months, from November 1914 until the spring of 1916, Cameron was able to provide commanders with good detail of which German units were fighting where on the front. This included the news that several German divisions were being moved from the Serbian front to Flanders in May 1915, providing reinforcements for the second Battle of Ypres, which had seen the first use of gas on the Western Front. Later that year, the Lambrecht service picked up the heavy movement of German troops from the east to counter a planned French offensive expected in Champagne that autumn, leading the French to bring the offensive forward. But it was a constant battle to keep the networks secret from the Germans, who acted ruthlessly against any suspected agents, even – it was alleged – jailing an eight-year-old caught holding a secret message. Macdonogh's staff at GHQ also had additional intelligence reporting from a small train-watching service set up by Major Ernest Wallinger in April 1915. A former artillery officer who had lost a leg during the Battle of Aisne in September 1914, he provided reporting that was universally regarded as being highly reliable. He was initially based at Folkestone but perhaps unsurprisingly did not get on with Cameron. This and the need to be better placed to capitalise on refugees coming into Tilbury led to Wallinger setting up his own offices at Lincoln House just behind Harrods in Knightsbridge.[14]

By the middle of 1915, Tinsley's agents in the Netherlands had managed to set up a relatively large train-watching service, a network of forty observation posts and 200 agents covering Belgium and north-east France and reporting via a British agent across the Dutch border in Maastricht. The Service Frankignoul, as it was known, used a novel form of courier system, albeit one that was dangerous in that it had no fallback procedures of any kind. All the messages were hidden in a 'dead letter box', a secret compartment on one of the two trams that ferried passengers from Lanaken in Belgium across the Dutch border to Maastricht and back. The trams and their passengers were repeatedly searched by the German secret police but since the system did not require any of the British agents to travel across the border on the tram, it was an ideal means of passing the reports back to the British agent, who then took them to Tinsley in Rotterdam from where they were handed to Lawrie Oppenheim and reported back both to London and to the army's headquarters at the Château Beaurepaire in Montreuil.[15]

Viewed from Whitehall, the system worked, and yet Cameron and Kirke continually lobbied to take over Cumming's networks in Belgium

and Holland, the former's efforts made more urgent by the way in which
the Germans were picking off his own agents. Both men were deeply
unhappy at the way in which Oppenheim had given authority to the
reports coming out of Tinsley's networks and were clearly stirring trouble
with Macdonogh, who gained the mistaken impression – almost certainly
originating from Cameron – that Oppenheim was running his own
separate series of networks. Back in Whitehall both Brigadier-General
George Cockerill, the War Office director of Special Intelligence,
and Ronald Campbell, on behalf of the Foreign Office, threw their
support behind Cumming, which, given the breadth of intelligence
both men were seeing, suggests Oppenheim's was superior to that now
coming from the networks run by Cameron. Nevertheless there were
still genuine problems with the system caused by the slow War Office
distribution of the intelligence. Macdonogh was not seeing the material
in time for it to have an immediate impact on operations, a problem
easily solved by having Cumming send urgent material, particularly
anything relating to the movement of Germans troops, directly to GHQ.
This satisfied Macdonogh but was, perhaps predictably, not enough for
Cameron or Kirke, who, within days, were again trying to take control
of Cumming's reporting from the Netherlands.[16]

This was now substantial with a major expansion of the entire
service underway. By the summer of 1915, Cumming had forty-seven
staff and his organisation was growing all the time, with bureaux in the
Netherlands, Greece, Malta, Gibraltar, Russia, Switzerland and Egypt
as well as operations in Denmark, Norway, Germany and Italy. By
August, there were thirty-three staff in London alone, although twelve
of these were typists and the number of actual intelligence officers was
far smaller, including Cumming, Tom Laycock, Lieutenant-Commander
Talbot Ponsonby, a pre-war officer who had recently returned, and
Maurice Cockerell, another of a number of mining engineers taken on
by Cumming. Their recruitment raises the question as to whether he
was unduly influenced by John Buchan's mining engineer turned spy
Richard Hannay, the hero of *The 39 Steps*, who made his first appearance
in print that summer. Francis Newnum's brother Eric also joined, as did

George Jolley, who had previously worked for the *Tatler* and appears to have originally been Laycock's replacement as clerk. Jolley was now Cumming's private secretary with a commission in the RNVR as a sub-lieutenant. The expansion, which would continue throughout the remainder of 1915 – suggesting a dramatic boost in budgets – led to the takeover of more space in Whitehall Court and the rental of an additional two flats in Ashley Mansions.[17]

The second half of 1915 was largely taken up by the continuing turf battles over control of the various train-watching operations inside Belgium, largely caused by Cameron's influence on both Kirke and Macdonogh. At a conference in London in late July, Cumming, backed by the Foreign Office, suggested that the only logical way of having the train-watching networks controlled by one organisation was for Tinsley to take them all over. Kirke protested that since the information was being collected on behalf of the Army in the field, the networks should come under Cameron. Meanwhile, Macdonogh attempted to take over Cumming's network by the back door, insisting that Oppenheim work to him, a move opposed not just by Cumming and by the head of War Office intelligence, Lieutenant-Colonel Charles French, but by Oppenheim himself. There was a brief respite during a conference of all the Allied powers' intelligence operations at the Hôtel de Crillon in Paris, when Kirke backed down from his demands that Cameron take over Cumming's networks, recording in his diary that he had 'soothed C down' and asking Macdonogh to write to him saying how useful Oppenheim's reports were. He also tacitly admitted that Cameron's refusal to take anything less than total control of the networks was the fundamental cause of the problems. 'If Cameron does a little bit of giving and taking I think that the scheme should run,' he wrote. But this brief moment of perspicacity was immediately followed by the usual naïvety. If the scheme did not work then he and Cameron 'must take over the whole thing root and branch', cutting out Cumming completely, he wrote, still apparently oblivious to the support Cumming had at the War Office, the Admiralty and the Foreign Office. Having been told repeatedly by Kirke and Cameron that the information produced by

Cumming was no use, Macdonogh presumably felt some difficulty in fulfilling Kirke's promise of a letter praising it. He waited until mid-October and then wrote to the director of military operations recording his 'appreciation of the services of Major Oppenheim and C's agents during the past few weeks especially the rapidity with which they had transmitted their information'.[18]

Alongside the unremitting battle for control of the British networks, there were a number of smaller-scale rows with the Belgians, led by Commandant Mage, the head of the Belgian secret service, who according to Kirke was 'excitable, nervy and difficult to deal with'. Although there was undoubtedly an element of the pot calling the kettle black in this claim, it was for once an opinion shared by C's men in Rotterdam. The Belgians had apparently given them 'the most trouble' of all the Allied services, repeatedly claiming that Tinsley had poached their agents and trying to have Belgian members of the British secret service networks called up for military service. The British had less trouble with the French, in part because of a good relationship between Oppenheim and his French counterpart in the Hague, General Paul Boucabeille, that left the British effectively in control of the French networks. Nevertheless, there were complaints from London that the French officers based at the Folkestone bureau had released details of methods used by Blinker Hall's naval codebreaking section, known as Room 40, and the names of some of C's agents, with Cumming harbouring suspicions, denied by Kirke, that Cameron was responsible.[19]

The way in which Kirke dismissed the naming of agents raises serious doubts over his ability and his understanding of an intelligence officer's basic responsibilities to the sources who provide the intelligence. By any standards, the naming of agents was a major security breach. It is not clear whether it had any effect on the way in which the German counter-espionage agents tore through the British intelligence networks from the late summer of 1915 and throughout the first half of 1916 since by the time the agents were named, the German successes had already begun. But it can scarcely have helped.

The damage to the British networks began in August 1915. As part of his secret service work on behalf of the War Office, Cumming had set up an escape organisation to help British and other Allied servicemen stranded behind enemy lines to get back to safety. This appears to have included the escape lines organised on the ground by a number of Belgians and Edith Cavell, the British matron of a Brussels hospital. It seems likely that, despite British denials, Cavell was also collecting intelligence from the German soldiers treated in her wards and passing it on to Cumming. Certainly, Cumming still had an agent of some sort in Brussels and Cavell reportedly had a meeting shortly before the Belgian capital fell with two British men who only just got out before the Germans arrived. Cavell was arrested by the Germans in August 1915 as a result of her work with escapers, although she was initially charged with espionage. She was sentenced to death on 11 October and, despite repeated pleas for clemency, she was executed at two o'clock the next morning. While the British propaganda machine made hay over her 'barbaric' execution, the links to Cumming suggest a more nuanced story. James Langley, who was in charge of escape operations during the Second World War, recalled that the belief that Cavell was working for Cumming and was only discovered because of the assistance she gave to Allied servicemen 'seemed to dictate the whole attitude' within British intelligence to his work. This was backed up by Langley's deputy Airey Neave, who recalled Stewart Menzies, the head of the British secret service during World War Two, regularly repeating 'his favourite War Office theme', that Cavell had 'mixed help to British escapers in the First World War with sending out military information'.[20]

The rows between London and the intelligence officers at GHQ continued at a conference held in London in November 1915. There was no longer any doubt as to who would win the arguments. Cumming's status within Whitehall, where the final decisions were made, had risen to the extent that his original 'foreign department' of the Secret Service Bureau had now officially become the Secret Intelligence Service (SIS), with his own title chief of the secret service – rendered either as CSS or as C. Both titles have survived to the present day. From having been simply the first letter of Cumming's name, used as a simple disguise, C had become the title of the chief of the secret service, to be passed on to all his successors. Indeed, such was the importance of the title, and the reluctance of many officials to admit that Britain actually had a secret service, that from these early days until well into the 1950s, the Service was often only referred to as 'C's people', 'C's organisation', or in the case of the military, 'C's show'.

Cumming's impressive new title did not appear to cut much ice with Kirke, who again insisted Cameron should control everything relating to military operations. This claim was immediately overruled by George Cockerill, who was clearly not one of Cameron's supporters. Tinsley was not just providing information on German troop movements, he was also collecting intelligence on German trade and running a counter-espionage service, neither of which could be done by Cameron from the safety of Folkestone. 'Any secret service in a neutral country should be controlled by someone with whom they are in close touch,' Cockerill said, adding that it would have been better if Tinsley – whose qualifications were 'very exceptional' – had been put in charge of the whole enterprise from the start. That was no longer possible but he was not about to collapse the whole system by putting Cameron in charge of Tinsley, with the risk, if not the certainty, that the latter would resign. Tinsley emerged from the arguments with his position enhanced as 'head agent' for all secret service organisations in the Netherlands. But by far the most important outcome was that Cumming was now to oversee all secret service operations on the Western Front. All contact with Tinsley was to be conducted through Cumming, who would pass on requests from Kirke or Cameron only 'as long as they did not contradict his own orders'. On the ground, Cameron was still in charge of his own operations and of reporting their intelligence to GHQ but he could only run networks to the west of a line running from the town of Lier in the north, passing to the east of Brussels and Charleroi down to the French border in the south, while Cumming's men were restricted to operating to the east of that line. Ernest Wallinger was to stay where he was and not expand his networks at all, an odd decision given that the one thing everyone agreed on was the reliability of his reporting. The Belgians were in charge of operations in Brussels itself but crucially, although the Belgian capital lay

5 miles to the west of his area, Cumming was to be allowed to continue to run operations inside the city, or at least those not caught up in the Cavell round-ups. Cumming was to be the final arbiter over who was operating where, settling any disputes through Oppenheim. Cameron felt he was being sidelined and predictably he railed against it, insisting that there should be an investigation into Tinsley's alleged attempts to poach his agents, although the evidence suggests that the poaching was very much a two-way street.

Kirke complained that the Foreign Office were 'trying to get incessant power for C over our organisations', even though it was in fact the War Office that had forced through the changes. As ever, Kirke seemed to have attended a completely different conference to everyone else, altering the draft of the conference agreement so that Cameron was to be in charge. His amended draft did not survive contact with either Cumming or the War Office. Having met Tinsley in London, Kirke recorded his considered opinion of C's main man on the continent. It was clouded by a large degree of snobbery, not to mention Kirke's habitual naïvety. Tinsley, he noted,

> strikes me as being a smart fellow but not a man for whom any really high class agents would work. With him it is a matter of business and I doubt his imparting patriotic enthusiasm to agents. He therefore misses the best people and I should never consider him capable of running our show without an officer in charge and always at his elbow.[21]

Cameron and Kirke saw Tinsley as the cause of all their woes and the main villain of the piece. But in fact by now he was rapidly becoming just the front man for a much larger organisation. There were twenty-seven staff in his offices on the Boompjes, split into four separate divisions, one collecting military intelligence, which did not just concentrate on the train-watching services in Belgium reported through Oppenheim. It was also reporting on intelligence from agents inside Germany itself – which took up a quarter of Tinsley's £5,000 annual budget – and from a press-monitoring unit which scanned the newspapers coming out of

Germany and occupied Belgium looking for anything relating to the navy or military, as well as information on the internal situation within Germany, and garnering a remarkable amount of intelligence. There was also a highly successful naval intelligence section, a section monitoring illegal trade with Germany, and a counter-espionage section, working against German spies operating in the Netherlands and travelling through on their way to the UK. After the war, MI5 acknowledged the 'brilliant work of "T"' in relation to the activities of the Imperial German Navy intelligence officer Alexander Blok, a Dutch former banker based in Hamburg who was running intelligence operations into the UK out of Antwerp and Copenhagen. Sir Everard Ratcliffe, who served in MI5 during the First World War, looking out for German spies trying to enter Britain, was full of praise for the contribution made by Tinsley and his counter-espionage section. The German spies uncovered as a result of Tinsley's operations included a number travelling on US passports, including several sympathetic US journalists. 'Many were the interesting cases,' Ratcliffe recalled. 'But what remains most vividly in my mind was the brilliance of our agent in Holland, who rarely failed to advise when an important spy was en route to England, and almost invariably was able to apprise for what purpose and where he intended to go.'[22]

Cameron and Kirke's refusal to accept the rulings made at the Folkestone conference ensured the rows over the Belgian networks would continue for another year, but they would no longer be anything other than an irritant, not least because at the beginning of January 1916 George Macdonogh came back from France to take over as director of military intelligence at the War Office, where he swiftly became aware of the real situation and the full extent of Tinsley's operations. This extended way beyond the train-watching services, important as they were, and involved a number of exceptionally talented intelligence officers and agents.[23]

FOUR

La Dame Blanche

GEORGE Macdonogh's return to London coincided with a complete reorganisation of military intelligence which separated the intelligence sections from the operations division. The title of the 'Special Intelligence Service' liaison section with the War Office was changed from MO6c to MI1c and it was under this latter designation that the Service was to be widely known within military circles right up until the Second World War. Mansfield Smith Cumming was also given a senior army officer, who effectively became his deputy. Lieutenant-Colonel Freddie Browning was almost certainly attached to the Service to represent the military viewpoint, but he was to prove a staunch ally for Cumming. Browning was a great sportsman, having played rackets for Oxford and cricket for the MCC, and was a director of the Savoy Hotel. He swiftly became Cumming's 'chief mainstay', one former officer later recalled:

> A brilliant games player, living as hard as he played, making friends everywhere and never losing them, as ready to play his part in the crisis of the war as he had been to bat on a sticky wicket or to fight an uphill battle in the racket court. The game he was now playing was catch-as-catch-can with enemy agents. I can say without fear of contradiction that as a general staff officer and an organiser of Intelligence he played a part of really first-class importance. His was the inspiring force behind the most secret branch of our military intelligence.

Another colleague confirmed that Browning only made life easier for Cumming:

> His amazing humanity, knowledge of men and women and 'people that mattered', put the 'C' organisation right in the picture all round. Browning's hospitality was unbounded and, being distressed at the way the female element of the staff had buns for lunch, he got a canteen built on top of Whitehall Court, extracted a chef from the army, an old Savoyard, and used the buying agencies of the Savoy to secure cheap food in a time of food stringency. As for Browning's relations with 'C', they were inimitable. He brought happy evenings to the Old Man by having gay parties with all the stage beauties that he had at call and, in more serious ways, he was the perfect link; seldom doing anything himself, but linking up with those who knew what was what in any particular line. The marvellous thing about 'C' and Fred Browning was that no field of enterprise was outside their scope.[1]

Macdonogh also made a number of alterations to the reporting system for military intelligence from occupied Belgium, putting Ernest Wallinger's networks under Cumming's overall control, with Lawrie Oppenheim producing the reports and ordering Cecil Aylmer Cameron's Folkestone bureau to ensure that all their reports went not just to their main customers, the military commanders in France, but also to Oppenheim so they could be incorporated into the more extensive reports he sent to the War Office. Cameron's networks were still producing some of the best intelligence on German troop movements, with Dieudonné Lambrecht providing a detailed warning of the German plans to attack French positions at the strategically and morally important town of Verdun after a German officer billeted with his sister was flattered into revealing the plans. But it was the last useful information Lambrecht was to produce.[2]

The German construction of a large electric fence along the border with the Netherlands had prevented the couriers from getting through with their information. Reports from Lambrecht's service were delivered to a 'letter box' in Liège, a cigar shop owned by one of his relatives. But in early 1916, as the Germans cracked down on the Allied agents, Ferdinand Afchain had difficulty getting anyone to go through the wire to collect the reports stacking up in the cigar shop. Under pressure from Cameron, he first grew desperate and then careless, with the result that, in February 1916, the German secret service obtained a letter he had written to Lambrecht, who was arrested, tried and, on 18 April 1916, found guilty of espionage. In a letter to his wife, written the night before he was to be executed by firing squad, Lambrecht's thoughts lay only with consoling his family:

> He who dies is quickly rid of his pain, but for you others, how much suffering. Let my resignation be a comfort to you. Think of my life as being given up for my country – it will make my death seem less painful to you. Jeanne, in heaven we will meet again. For our darling little daughter, for my parents and for you, receive on this letter the last affectionate kisses of he, who was your, Donné.[3]

Richard Tinsley dominated operations in northern Europe but Cumming also had a number of geographical sections based in Whitehall Court, covering Scandinavia, Switzerland and Spain, which were all attempting to get agents into Germany. Perhaps his most interesting section was one designated 'Nemesis', which was attempting to organise sabotage inside Germany itself, blowing up weapons factories, sabotaging armaments and derailing trains, with some evidence of success. An MI1c training manual for agents going into Germany included the postscript:

> It is well for agents who show themselves to be resolute, to be instructed in the use of explosives on railways (choice of point, installation of charge). They should be advised to use these only during large movements executed by the enemy by rail, at a time when an important engagement is certain to take place.[4]

There were also some reports coming in via prisoners of war in Germany. Conrad O'Brien-ffrench, a captain in the Royal Irish Regiment, was sent to France at the start of the First World War, only to be captured almost immediately. Incarcerated at Burg bei Magdeburg, along with a large number of Russians, he took the opportunity to learn the language. He also corresponded with a friend, Cathleen Mann, daughter of the artist Harrington Mann and later a leading artist in her own right.

> She was a very pretty girl and, above all, she had the talent of a quick wit. She wrote to me regularly during my four-year absence as a prisoner-of-war. I conceived the idea of establishing a secret mode of communication with her by which I could reveal things I did not wish the censor to know.

O'Brien-ffrench used the crude code of talking about a Mrs Washit, of Inink Road, Bath, to indicate that he was hiding messages in the letters, using secret ink, made from a solution of potassium iodide that he obtained from the camp medics to treat his wounds. O'Brien-ffrench knew that Mann worked in the War Office; what he did not know, and could not be told, was that she worked in MI1c.

> Many Royal Flying Corps pilots shot down over the enemy lines had undelivered reports which they had memorised and such valuable facts as troop movements or gun emplacements, etc., were worth relaying on to the girl for transmission to the appropriate department. I felt that in this manner I was doing even more good than being in the trenches.[5]

Cumming had a small but surprisingly professional PoW operation which sent genuine sealed food packages and recreational equipment, including a gramophone, to British prisoners based in Germany with hidden compasses, maps and directions on how to pass secret communications back to London. It was run by Major John Snepp of the Royal Marine Light Infantry and Lieutenant Harry Brickwood RNVR of the Brickwood brewing family and a fellow member with Cumming of the Royal Motor Yacht Club. The Germans sent a series of protests in late 1917 and the first half of 1918, passed via the Dutch government, that the British were breaking the rules with regard to sending parcels to PoWs. One protest concerned a box of biscuits sent to an officer in a German PoW camp in the Harz Mountains. When the box was opened and the biscuits removed, it was found to have a double bottom. 'The box made the impression as though it was in its original packing and had not been opened,' the German protest said. 'Between the two bottoms, seven excellent maps of the Harz and Dutch frontier districts were hidden.' At another camp, an unopened 2-pound box of Quaker Oats was also found to have a false bottom, under which were hidden two maps of the German–Dutch frontier, one compass with luminous dial, a ruler to measure distances on the map and directions for escape. Compasses, escape plans, maps and directions for 'the production of secret writings' were found in a tin of meat, while a gramophone sent to one British officer was packed in a double-sided crate with a variety of escape equipment hidden between the two sides. The Foreign Office was concerned over the affair, worrying that while MI1c had not used the Red Cross symbol on its parcel, it might be deemed to be a breach of the Geneva Convention governing treatment of prisoners.

'I know very well how these things were sent,' one official said. 'They are some of the things habitually sent out by MI1c, 2 Whitehall Court, a department presided over by Major Snepp. One of Major Snepp's associates, Lieutenant Brickwood, is often here and has on several occasions taken away supplies of coupons for officers' parcels. These of course do not bear the Red Cross and we are very particular that our Red Cross labels should not be used for such purposes. We can, however, hardly refuse the coupons. I never liked this business much and of course so long as the Red Cross label is not abused, we have no locus standi to object from. I do, however, think that the time has come to consider whether more harm than good is being done by the operations of this MI1c department.'[6]

The difficulty of getting reports out of Germany without being detected led MI1c to make extensive efforts to find a reliable, and easily available, invisible ink, one of Cumming's officers recalled:

Secret inks were our stock in trade and all were anxious to obtain some which came from a natural source of supply. I shall never forget C's delight when the Chief Censor [Frank] Worthington came one day with the announcement that one of his staff had found out that semen would not respond to iodine vapour and told the old man that he had had to remove the discoverer from the office immediately as his colleagues were making life intolerable by accusations of masturbation. The Old Man at once asked Colney Hatch [lunatic asylum] to send female equivalent for testing and the slogan went round the office – every man his own stylo. We thought we had solved the problem. Then our man in Copenhagen, Major [Richard] Holme, evidently stocked it in a bottle, for his letters stank to high heaven and we had to tell him that a fresh operation was necessary for each letter.

Walter Kirke was distinctly unimpressed by the discovery. 'Heard from C that the best invisible ink is semen,' he wrote in his diary. 'Does not react to iodine vapour, charring or anything so far tried. Asked C what it does react to.' When the disarray in Cameron's train-watching networks forced Kirke to send one of his officers, Captain Thomas Traill, to London, to act as liaison with the secret service, he was told his first priority was to 'get invisible ink research put on proper basis'.[7]

The loss of Cameron's Lambrecht network left the military heavily dependent on the Frankignoul network run by Tinsley's Dutch agents. But in May 1915 the Frankignoul network was ripped apart. Its sole method of passing on its reports, via the tram to Maastricht, was discovered by the Germans, who tracked the entire network, assisted by the fact that Frankignoul had allowed all his agents in Belgium to know the identities of their fellow agents. 'His [Frankignoul's] method of communication was ideal because it was so direct and simple as to forestall detection for a considerable time,' one MI1c officer said. 'But it had worked so smoothly for months that he had lulled himself into the belief that it would go on working forever.'[8]

Cameron and Kirke now began a new tack in their turf war with Cumming, sending Captain Lachlan McEwen, Cameron's deputy, to

Flushing to interview refugees in the hope of finding replacements for their lost train watchers without any consultation with Cumming or Tinsley. The unfortunate McEwen made such a hash of it that he soon had to go into hiding with the Dutch police on his tail, causing problems for Tinsley, whose name was published in the Dutch press. Kirke was irritated to discover that Cumming blamed him for both Tinsley's exposure and, with far less justification, the critical loss of the Frankignoul network. Kirke evidently put this down to the fact that Cumming, as a naval officer, had never been through the army staff college, then based at Sandhurst. He noted in his diary that 'if a staff college man were in C's place, say French, we should never have had the slightest trouble as he like ourselves would be working for the common good and not for self-aggrandisement'. Cumming was in fact simply trying to ensure the safety of his own operations, and if anyone was working for self-aggrandisement it was Kirke's deputy, Cameron; but the last thing Kirke wanted was to be blamed, unfairly it has to be said, for the loss of the Frankignoul network, which left commanders lamenting that 'in the absence of agents' information we have no idea whatsoever which divisions have gone or where they have gone'.[9]

Army–navy rivalries certainly played a part in the turf wars. Despite the introduction of Lawrie Oppenheim into the reporting chain, and its widely acknowledged success, Cameron and Kirke continually questioned Tinsley's ability, as a naval officer, to run a military network, and the loss of the Frankignoul network gave them the excuse to insist that Cumming's military networks should be run by an army officer, with the intention of putting in their own man and effectively taking control. Cumming's response was to recruit an army officer to work under Tinsley and in July 1916, he found the perfect man. Henry Landau was a young South African who had obtained a commission in the Royal Artillery. Sent on leave to London, he became friendly with the sister of another officer in his regiment. By coincidence, she was one of Cumming's secretaries. On finding out that he spoke French, Dutch and German, she pronounced him 'just the man my chief is looking for' and when an illness separated him fortuitously from his regiment, he was recruited to go to The Hague to head up Tinsley's military operations. Given that Landau had been brought up speaking Afrikaans, the Dutch language test proved no obstacle at all and he soon found himself ordered to report to Freddie Browning at Whitehall Court.

> He informed me that I had been transferred to the Intelligence Corps, and that as I had been attached for special duty to the Secret Service, he would take me up to the chief immediately. Up several flights of stairs I went, until I reached the very top of the building. Here, in a room which resembled the stateroom of a ship, I was confronted with a kindly man who immediately put me at my ease. It was the chief, Captain C. He swung round in a swivel chair to look at me – a grey-haired man of about sixty, in naval uniform, short in stature, with a certain stiffness of movement which I later discovered to be due to an artificial leg. After a few preliminary remarks, he suddenly came to the point: 'I know all about your past history. You are just the man we want. You are to join T in Rotterdam, leaving tonight via Harwich and the Hook. Our train-watching service has broken down completely in Belgium and north-eastern France – we are getting absolutely nothing through. It is up to you to reorganise the service. I can't tell you how it is to be done – that is your job. You have carte blanche. You are in complete charge of the military section; responsibility for its success or failure is on your shoulders.'[10]

Landau was in Rotterdam quite literally within twenty-four hours of meeting Cumming, having been provided with a ticket and expenses by Paymaster Commander Percival Stanley Sykes, the Royal Naval officer who was Cumming's main administrative officer and who was to remain in that post until after the Second World War. He was known to everyone as 'Percy', even though the name he preferred to use was Stanley. Landau set about picking up the threads of the operations as well as mounting two separate investigations, one into what had gone wrong with the Frankignoul network and the other into the loss of military reports when the Germans captured the *Brussels*, a British steamship operating between

Rotterdam and Harwich. Captain Charles Fryatt, the ship's master, had earned popular acclaim in both the UK and the Netherlands for ramming a German U-boat, the *U33*. This infuriated the Germans, who set out to capture the *Brussels* on 23 June 1916. Despite being a civilian, Fryatt was court-martialled and executed by firing squad.

Landau was able to reassure London that the capture of the *Brussels* had not – as previously thought – caused any major problems, while the investigation into Frankignoul gave him a good understanding of some of the things he needed to avoid in setting up his own networks. He started slowly, recruiting a Belgian head agent called Victor Moreau, whose father was a senior official with Belgian Railways and who therefore had good access to railworkers who lived close to the railway lines. Landau and Moreau, who worked under the codename Oram, set up half a dozen *tuyaux* (literally 'funnels'), points along the border with the Netherlands through which messages could be passed. Reports from the train watchers were deposited with 'letter boxes' in Liege, Antwerp and Brussels and then collected by couriers who took them to the *tuyaux*, where Oram's men would collect them and take them back to Landau in Rotterdam.[11]

Concerned to avoid repeating the inherent insecurities of the large Frankignoul network, Landau concentrated on a dozen small, but completely unconnected, networks. He also recruited a number of *promeneurs* (literally 'ramblers'), who were simply tasked to travel around acting anonymously but collecting details of German troop movements and locations. Local civilians could walk relatively easily around the districts used by the Germans as rest areas taking note of the different uniforms and insignia from which precise regiments could be deduced. One of Landau's earliest train-watching services was led by a patriotic Belgian lawyer, Henri van Bergen, who did well for four months. But he broke a key rule in that he failed to merge into the background. Van Bergen was smartly dressed, in stark comparison to the railworkers who passed him the information. He was not the sort of man who would have frequented the workers' bar at which he was to leave his reports, and this almost certainly led to his capture.[12]

By the autumn of 1916, Cumming had more than a thousand people working for him across the world, albeit that the vast bulk of these were agents rather than officers, a title based originally on his use of military or naval officers that continues to this day within the now civilianised British Secret Intelligence Service – an officer being a long-term staff employee of the Service, while an agent is the person providing intelligence or assistance on the ground. There were several hundred officers and agents around the Near and Middle East controlled by Major Rhys Samson in Alexandria, most of them agents but including some notable 'officers', not least the author Compton Mackenzie, who was in Greece, and Gertrude Bell, the famous Arabist and archaeologist, based in what is now Iraq. Samson's operation was larger even than Tinsley's, which had ten officers plus around twenty clerical staff in Rotterdam and some 240 agents operating in Belgium, France and Germany. There were even small contingents in South America, South Africa and New York. Cumming and Vernon Kell had also sent military or passport control officers to Alexandria, Athens, Christiania (now Oslo), Lisbon, Madrid, New York, Paris, Petrograd, Rome, Rotterdam and Stockholm, to track the movements of international travellers, looking for German spies. The military control officers operated in countries involved in the war, while the passport control officers were based in neutral countries where military control did not apply. The control officers were responsible to Cumming for any intelligence they produced but to Kell and MI5 for any British visas they issued. Cumming also recruited the distinguished inventor and physicist Thomas Merton as scientific adviser, the Service's first 'Q'. Lieutenant Thomas Ralph Merton RNVR, who shared Cumming's love of experimentation, would subsequently become a noted scientist whose pioneering work on spectroscopy would lead to his appointment as Professor of Spectroscopy at Oxford and a fellowship of the Royal Society. Ironically, his interest in science was said to have been awakened by a German governess, a Fräulein Richter. Merton's first success was in tracing invisible ink absorbed into the underwear of German agents. The agent would simply immerse the material in water to create the ink. Despite his experiments with underwear, Merton, who was independently wealthy and agreed to work without pay, brought a somewhat more scientific approach to Cumming's search for secret inks, creating a better, if less immediately available, option than semen. This expansion also saw the actor and playwright Harley Granville-Barker taking charge of the Service's written records, although he was originally recruited with the intention of sending him on a 'special mission' in the Netherlands or Switzerland and subsequently appears to have combined a speaking tour in the US with surveillance of German-funded Indian anarchists.[13]

The Germans continued to seize civilian ships, albeit without any apparent intelligence success until 10 November 1916 when the Dutch mail boat *Koningen Regentes* was intercepted by two German U-boats and taken to Zeebrugge. This was 'most disastrous' for MI1c, with the Germans apparently intercepting an original agent report. It was almost certainly a train-watching report sent to London for adjudication as a result of the disputes with Walter Kirke and Cecil Aylmer Cameron. Certainly, six weeks after the mail boat was captured, the Germans executed eleven Belgians as British spies. The arguments had come to a head in early December over a proposal from John Charteris, who had replaced George Macdonogh as the brigadier-general in charge of intelligence in France, proving himself far less able. Spurred on by Cameron and Kirke, Charteris was insisting that they should be allowed to put two of their own men into the Netherlands, a move that risked upsetting Tinsley's relationship with the Dutch. The proposals were viewed 'with alarm' by Cumming and outright opposition by Tinsley and Lawrie Oppenheim, not least because one of the officers proposed was Cameron's deputy, Lachlan McEwen, who had created such havoc during his previous visit to the Netherlands. Tinsley was expert at keeping the Dutch on side but wary of anything that might upset the apple cart. His relationship with the Dutch police and intelligence services was delicately balanced, Landau said:

> As they could at any time discriminate against us if they chose to do so, we decided to give them no cause for unfriendliness and so issued strict instructions to all our agents not to do any spying against them. We

ingratiated ourselves with various officials by supplying them with all information coming into our hands concerning Germany, which in any way affected their country. This brought them into favour with their own authorities; and as they were eager to obtain these reports it was perfectly natural for us to demand and obtain from them, in exchange, all information they knew about the Germans which concerned us.

This intelligence exchange with the Dutch was by no means one sided. The Dutch authorities provided Tinsley with a copy of every telegram sent out by the German legation and consulates in the Netherlands, enhancing his reputation in London for being able to obtain valuable intelligence even without the information provided by his agents inside Germany.[14]

Tinsley and Oppenheim, backed by the minister Alan Johnstone, insisted that introducing new British officers into the Netherlands would only create friction and risk upsetting the Dutch, who were already under pressure from Germany to act against the British intelligence operations. Tinsley said 'he could not take responsibility for the effective working of the present system or indeed for its maintenance and future safety since he considered that the carrying out of the proposal and its consequent risks did not warrant the grave consequences that might ensue'. The situation was not helped by Cameron, who appears to have been going behind the backs of Charteris and Kirke to inform Tinsley and Oppenheim that he was sending two of his men to the Netherlands whether they liked it or not. In a letter to London, Oppenheim lamented 'the unfortunate result of Major Cameron being in any way connected with the proposal'. Cameron had tactlessly claimed there were 'direct orders for the legation's compliance with the proposal' and was issuing 'a constant stream of instructions' to the legation, creating a situation that was 'frankly impossible'.[15]

In the midst of all this, *The Times* reported the deaths of the unfortunate eleven Belgian agents and death sentences on nine others; the Foreign Office complained that it had never been consulted about the idea of sending two of Cameron's men to the Netherlands, and would not have backed the scheme if it had been consulted; and it emerged that Cameron had set up sixteen train-watching posts in Cumming's area. Evidently no longer so impressed by his protégé, Macdonogh realised the rows had to end. The only effective solution was to replace Kirke with someone more capable of controlling Cameron. The man he chose was Major Reginald Drake, who had previously worked for Kell. 'I can strongly recommend him,' Macdonogh told Charteris. 'He has a regular flair for the work, knows all there is to know about counter-espionage, gets on well with C, is up to all the tricks of the German spies and has a good knowledge of the permit system. He is also a very good chap in himself. I am sure there is no-one who could take on Kirke's job so easily or with so good a chance of carrying it on successfully.'[16]

The Charteris proposals were discussed in detail at a conference at the War Office on 19 January 1917, with Colonel French representing the views of Charteris, Kirke and Cameron. But despite Kirke's belief that a 'staff college man' would inevitably support his and Cameron's position, French did not and the conference did not go the way Kirke, Charteris and Cameron had hoped. Colonel Edgar Cox, who was in charge of the War Office section analysing information on the German military, 'declared emphatically that it would be a great mistake to endanger T's organisations and the reports sent by Major Oppenheim'. The conference was unanimous that to obtain the best results there should be just one organisation exercising central control and that it must come under Tinsley. It concluded that 'as soon as was convenient all agents should be subordinated to T and all reports sent through Major Oppenheim'. The conclusions were endorsed by Macdonogh, which ought to have ended all arguments. But the best that can be said of the response from Charteris is that it was naïve. In a letter to Macdonogh, Charteris made the mistake of invoking the name of Field Marshal Sir Douglas Haig, the British commander, who would be 'most averse to giving up direct control of sources of information which affect our operations here'. He then rubbished recent MI1c reporting. 'You will remember we have got nothing at all of any value from the Military Attaché Hague from June to December last year,' Charteris said. 'Since then the stuff has not been really of much good that we are getting from him. I think there is therefore no necessity to consider further the proposal of handing the whole thing over to Tinsley.'

It is impossible to see how Charteris thought writing to Macdonogh in such terms would further his cause. He seemed completely oblivious to the fact that Macdonogh had personally backed the proposals he was so blithely dismissing. Macdonogh's response was to call Charteris to London to discuss the proposals at a second conference. At the same time, he had Cox draw up a report comparing MI1c reporting for the last four months of 1916 with that produced by Cameron. Cox concluded:

> In addition to a certain amount of information received only through C, Major Cameron's train-watching reports would not have been complete without corroboration of C. As regards the form in which the reports were presented, C's organisation was undoubtedly superior, having the advantage of the expert knowledge of the military attaché at The Hague to edit and control. The value of the GHQ [Cameron] reports would be enhanced if they could be treated similarly by an expert.

Charteris came to London and argued his case, but with the evidence against him, and the other delegates pressing 'the remarkable qualities of T', he not only failed to push through his proposals, but Cameron ended up with even less control than was previously the case. The final 'compromise' was that Tinsley should control a 'clearing house' for intelligence from all the various services, including the Cameron, Wallinger, Belgian and French services. He would then pass this intelligence direct to Oppenheim, who would be in charge of all reporting. Cameron was allowed to send a junior officer, Captain Francis Verdon, to work as Oppenheim's deputy, but Verdon, who had no great expertise at handling agents, was not to have any contact with them. Tinsley and Oppenheim would be the only ones who saw all agent reports, thereby ensuring that they would never again be sent to London, risking agents' lives. All Cameron's agitation had achieved was to ensure that Tinsley, the man he saw as his great rival, controlled all the intelligence coming out of the train-watching networks based in Belgium and occupied France, a move which Cumming declared to be 'a good and practicable step in the right direction'.[17]

It was left to Drake to sort out the practicalities of the new system, which largely forced an end to the unhealthy competition between the various services, but he recalled that 'it was impossible in some cases to forget the bitternesses of the past and personal feelings which these had left behind, especially among the subordinate personnel'. This was a reference to Cameron, who to the last insisted action should be taken against Tinsley for his alleged theft of agents. While there was in Drake's words 'little doubt that denunciations, buying up of other services' agents, duplication of reports, and collaboration between agents of the various allied systems were not uncommon', ironically the largest and most important appropriation by Tinsley of Cameron's agents was yet to come.[18]

The remnants of Dieudonné Lambrecht's organisation had reorganised under the leadership of Walthère Dewé, one of Lambrecht's cousins, setting up their own counter-espionage service to try to keep one step ahead of the German secret police. They had a large network of train watchers collecting intelligence, which they christened the Michelin service, but no-one to whom they could send their reports. They contacted the French and then the Belgian intelligence services but on both occasions pulled out when their counter-espionage experts reported that the courier systems were compromised. They eventually, in August 1916, got in touch with Liévin, one of Cameron's agents, but contact swiftly broke down and did not resume until February 1917. By now, the Michelin service was running out of cash but when it sent Cameron a request for more money and for all its members to be enrolled in the British army, a consideration they believed would show their contribution was recognised, there was no response. Cameron's agent had been betrayed by one of his couriers and several members of the Michelin service were subsequently arrested, including Father Jean des Onays. The network again found itself without any way of passing its valuable train-watching reports to the Allies.

Fortunately, shortly before the arrests, the leaders of the Michelin service had sent one of their men to try to contact the British in the Netherlands and appeal for funding and military recognition. Gustave Lemaire, a Belgian engineer, went to the British consulate-general in Rotterdam and from there was sent to Tinsley's offices on the Boompjes, where he was met by Henry Landau, who said:

As soon as Lemaire mentioned the name of the Michelin service, I was all attention. A week previously, through one of my Maastricht agents, I had received a number of train-watching reports from posts at Liège and Jemelle. The nature of the reports showed that they emanated from a well-organised service in Belgium, but all that I had to guide me was the signature 'MM' and the information that they had deposited at a 'letter box' in Liège which was serving for one of our organisations in the interior. A few minutes' conversation with Lemaire soon convinced me that I was right in my estimation of the Michelin service. I knew who Liévin was and could have sent Lemaire along to him, but I also knew how Liévin was struggling to keep communication open with the interior. On the other hand, the British secret service had half-a-dozen frontier passages, which they could place at the disposal of the Michelin service. To me, my duty was clear. Without hesitating, I offered to attach the Michelin service to our organisation. My enthusiasm had a marked effect on Lemaire. Already, I was visualising the super-service of my dreams, and I was getting ready to dismiss him with instructions to meet me again in the afternoon, when he suddenly shot at me: 'There are two conditions. Suitable arrangements must be made to cover their financial expenditure. They also insist on being enrolled as soldiers.' I looked at him in blank amazement, even though I could understand the desire he expressed. The demand seemed quite impossible. How could the War Office make British soldiers out of Belgian subjects? How even could the Belgian authorities do it? Above all, how could either of them make women soldiers? For there were many women enrolled in the Michelin service.

Landau realised this was a make-or-break moment and played for time, saying he would contact his chief in England but it would take a day or two to get a reply. Knowing there was no way the demands could be met, he then said the deal was agreed, without even bothering to contact London. The money was easy. The recruitment would have to wait until the end of the war. Cameron was predictably furious that his network had been 'stolen' from him and Liévin attempted in vain to take back control of the Michelin service. 'After the war, I happened to see some of Liévin's notes,' Landau said. 'Opposite the Michelin service was written "Stolen from me by the War Office Service".' The note of personal possession which Liévin sounded typified one of the baneful effects of the competition among the allied secret services in the Netherlands. Each in its endeavour to get ahead of the other, unintentionally, lost sight of the main objective – the defeat of the Germans.[19]

In fact, given that Liévin's role was already known to the Germans, the severing of the Michelin service's link with Cameron probably saved it from being rolled up by the Germans. One of the first things its leaders did was to reorganise on a military basis and change its name. The hope was that the disappearance of the Michelin service would give the Germans the impression they had been successful in breaking it up. It changed its name first to B149 and then to La Dame Blanche, after the legendary ghost of a white lady whose appearance was supposed to signal the downfall of the Hohenzollerns, the German royal family. Having been assured by Landau that they were now a fully fledged military organisation, they created three separate battalions of agents, based on the cities of Liège, Namur and Charleroi. Each battalion was divided into three companies and each company into four platoons, with the fourth platoon collecting the reports and dropping them off at a local 'letter box', usually an agent's house or shop. The letter boxes were run by separate sections within each battalion, which collected all the reports and took them to three central letter boxes in Liège, one for each battalion. The extensive network of letter boxes, with every part of the organisation separate from each other and not known to the next link in the chain, provided it with far more security. Each battalion had a secretariat where the reports picked up at its central letter box were scrutinised before being typed up and sent to Dewé or the network's other leader Herman Chauvin. Once passed by the leadership, the reports were sent on to a final letter box close to the frontier where they were collected by one of Oram's men, who was smuggled through the electric fence by specialist *passeurs* who ran the *tuyaux*, the individual crossing places along the wire.

Landau said:

> Border characters of every type were used at these frontier passages. There were the smugglers Tilman and his son, who on their smuggling trips across the Meuse to Maesyck never forgot that extra package, the White Lady reports. Then there was that large band of frontier guides who frequented the scrub and bush of the Campine, the area to the north of Liège, bordering on the Dutch frontier. Strong, fleet of foot, fearless, quick with the knife and the use of the guns, they were the terror of the German sentries and Secret Police detailed to watch them. Smugglers and poachers in peacetime, they knew every inch of the frontier and the passing of refugees, soldiers' letters and finally spy reports came natural to them.

Concealing the reports was less of a problem than getting through the wire. They were hidden in a variety of ways, in hollow keys, false bottoms of tins, the handles of baskets, on silk paper that was then sewn into the courier's clothes, in a hollow tooth, and in the case of one woman, in boxes of Belgian chocolates. She carried a number of boxes of chocolates only one of which had a false bottom and flirted with the German guards, often giving them chocolates in order to throw them off the scent. One particularly effective method of getting the messages through the wire was to use the German guards themselves, with the Belgian laundrywomen wrapping the guards' clean clothes in brown paper on which the reports were written in secret ink. Once across the wire, the discarded wrapping was collected by British agents.

The militarisation of La Dame Blanche enabled its leaders to impose far more security on the network, with every individual agent using false worknames to disguise their identity and messages encoded, initially using the Pater Noster, the Latin version of the Lord's Prayer, with each letter spelt out using two numbers separated by a comma. The first number indicated the position of the word from which the letter was taken within the prayer and the second number the position of the letter in that word; thus the Q from '*Pater Noster qui es in caelis*' at the start of the prayer would have been indicated by 3,1. This was a very simple but effective cipher that was difficult to break without knowing the passage on which it was based. The instruction in what was required became much more organised with Tinsley's agents giving instruction in specific aspects of train-watching, which formed the bulk of the work carried out by agents in Belgium and occupied France.[20]

'It is absolutely essential from our point of view that every agent is able to identify the most important troop formations of the German army and can recognise each type of unit,' one MI1c training document said. Every train watcher needed to know the breakdown of a German army division by heart, it said. 'The division is the most important formation as far as we are concerned because the division is the smallest tactical formation that includes every type of unit. Movements of smaller units never take place without the rest of the division to which they belong.' A normal-sized division would need fifty-one trains to move it and with troop trains travelling no faster than 20 kilometres per hour, and the average gap between each train being as much as ninety minutes, it could easily take three days and nights for all the division's trains to pass by.

Reports on the movement of 'constituted units' had to include the place through which the trains were passing, the direction in which they were going, the date and time that the trains passed by and the precise number of trains and their make-up. Different units could be recognised from the type and number of trucks used: an infantry battalion would have twenty-five covered wagons containing the men, eight covered wagons for the horses, a single standard railway carriage for the officers and ten open-topped wagons for vehicles. The covered wagons would always go at the beginning or end of the train, the open-topped wagons would always be in the middle.

Each division would have between nine and twelve infantry battalions. The other main units in the divisions were the artillery and cavalry regiments, with each artillery battery having a train of its own made up of six covered wagons for the men, twenty-five for the horses, four open-topped wagons for the guns and a single standard carriage for the officers. Each cavalry squadron would also take up a train in its own right with four covered wagons for the men, between twenty-five and thirty for the horses, four open-topped wagons for the vehicles and one standard carriage carrying officers. Recognition of specific units was difficult but not impossible: the helmets, shoulder straps and patches and the vehicles and artillery guns all had distinctive markings identifying the troops' regiment or division.[21]

The agent networks inside Belgium and occupied France were by no means Landau's only source of intelligence on the German army. He obtained useful intelligence from German army deserters who sought asylum in the Netherlands and were paid for the information they provided. One deserter who turned up at the offices on the Boompjes produced what Landau described rather extravagantly as 'the biggest Secret Service scoop of the war', a complete German field post directory, stolen a day previously from Düsseldorf, which gave the British the exact location of every German army unit and could be kept up to date not just by the train-watching units but by the addresses on letters from and to German soldiers which were intercepted by the Dutch authorities. Since these used only field post numbers, they had previously been useless but, with the directory to decipher them, they helped the British to keep up-to-date locations for all the German army units on the Western Front.[22]

One German deserter even went back into Germany to collect intelligence for the British. Heinrich Fleischer had vowed to desert after going home to Berlin on leave and discovering his family white and emaciated, with nothing to eat but turnips and watery potatoes. He saw his responsibility to look after his wife and children as more pressing than his duty to fight for the Kaiser and fled to the Netherlands to earn some money that would keep them alive. Fleischer collected a wealth of intelligence on this first trip back into Germany, including the strength and tactics of the stormtroopers who were to lead the so-called *Kaiserschlacht*, Germany's last main offensive in March 1918, as well as details of the economic difficulties inside Germany, where many people were close to starvation. Landau then tried to get Fleischer to set up a train-watching service inside Germany itself – a highly dangerous proposition. Eventually, Fleischer agreed and was given a large sum of money to set up the network. Landau never heard from him again and was never sure if he was caught and shot or simply decided to take the money and go back to his family. Openly admitting that he had set Fleischer 'an impossible task', Landau clearly hoped that it was the latter:

> I have a suspicion that having found out that the papers we gave him were perfect forgeries that could pass muster with the Germans, and having saved a fairly large sum of money, he returned to his family in Berlin. They were obviously his greatest and only consideration in life, and as he had refused to sacrifice them for the Kaiser, we could not expect him to sacrifice them for us.[23]

Having sorted out the problems between MI1c and military intelligence in France, George Macdonogh set about reorganising the secret service. He was unhappy with the way in which sections had been created in an ad hoc fashion to deal with specific areas, largely, although not entirely, geographic regions. In August 1917, Macdonogh brought in Lieutenant-Colonel Claude Dansey, an assistant director of MI5 who had been in America advising on the creation of a US intelligence service, to take charge of War Office liaison with MI1c.

Dansey's ostensible role was to look at the MI1c military reporting and make recommendations as to changes, although in effect his recommendations meant a complete reorganisation of the MI1c structure, removing the geographical sections completely and replacing them with sections dealing with specific areas focusing on the individual departments for which MI1c produced its intelligence. Macdonogh's main aim appears to have been to reinforce his own control over Cumming's military reporting, and a key element of the reorganisation was to place liaison officers representing the main customers for each type of intelligence inside the relevant sections. This led to the creation in late 1917 of what was to be the basis of a key section of the MI1c headquarters structure right up to the Second World War with five specific 'Requirements' sections, later known as 'Circulating' or 'Liaison' sections, dealing with air, naval, military, political and economic intelligence respectively, as well as more administrative sections dealing with pay and personnel, cover, communications and secret devices. The sections were numbered using Roman numerals from Section I to Section V. Section I was economic intelligence, reflecting the importance of the economic blockade in the attempt to bring Germany to its knees, with Browning in charge. The Air Section, which already existed, was made Section II. There was a new naval section, Section III, with Admirality appointing Captain Boyle Somerville, who had until now spent the war on convoy duty, to head up the section and be its representative inside MI1c. The military section, Section IV, also dealt with counter-espionage abroad – and therefore liaised directly with MI5 – as well as escape lines for prisoners-of-war held in Germany and Turkey. As the head of the War Office liaison section MI1c, from which the secret service's name came, and the army's representative inside the actual service, Dansey assumed control of Section IV; while the section dealing with political intelligence for the Foreign Office was Section V, run by Colonel Rhys Samson, formerly the controller of Cumming's operations in the Near and Middle-East. Perhaps predictably, Cumming was unhappy with the results of the reorganisation, telling one senior diplomat that some of his 'best men' had been taken away from him. The requirements sections led to a closer relationship with the various government departments that was undoubtedly needed. But there was a distinct feel that the removal of the geographical element, and the expertise in particular areas that went with it, was a case of throwing out the baby with the bath water and it would take a further post-war reorganisation to get it right.[24]

Cecil Aylmer Cameron's last train-watching service, the Biscops or Sacré Coeur, so called because of the large number of nuns and priests involved, was broken up in September 1917 and from that point on he was largely sidelined, with his subordinate Captain George Bruce taking charge of the more innovative military intelligence operations from offices in the Rue St Roch in Paris. Cameron's relationship with Bruce had been little better than those he enjoyed with MI1c, and Reginald Drake noted that 'the situation, partly again owing to the personalities of persons engaged, had become unworkable'. A few months later, Cameron was moved to other work 'because of the strain'. Drake was generous in attributing his abrasive attitude to good intentions. Cameron had pioneered the train-watching system, with some good results, but 'competition and bitterness were the natural outcome of the system then in force, and of the vital necessity, coupled with keenness, to obtain information for the armies in the field'. La Dame Blanche continued producing vital intelligence, correctly predicting the timing and main point of attack of the *Kaiserschlacht*. The value of the service to the Allied cause was laid out in a message from Cumming to its leaders in which he said:

> The work of your organisation accounts for 70 per cent of the intelligence obtained by all the allied armies not merely through the Netherlands but through other neutral states as well. It is on you alone that the allies depend to obtain intelligence on enemy movements in areas near the front. The intelligence obtained by you is worth thousands of lives to the allied armies.[25]

FIVE

Air operations – Cumming's Jesuit priest

CUMMING'S fascination with aviation led him to create an air section to collect intelligence that would be useful to the Royal Flying Corps (RFC) and its navy equivalent, the Royal Naval Air Service (RNAS), long before George Macdonogh's organisational changes created army and navy sections. It was run by one of his best and most enthusiastic agent handlers, Pierre-Marie Cavrois O'Caffrey, a French Jesuit priest of Irish stock who had been working as a missionary in Ceylon when war broke out. His family on his father's side were descendants of an Irishman called O'Caffrey who had settled in France – 'Cavrois' being the French rendition of the Irish name. Pierre-Marie Cavrois added the Irish version to his name in an apparent attempt to anglicise himself and arrived unannounced, together with a French general, at an RNAS airfield at Dunkirk on the outbreak of war. O'Caffrey, who had been born and brought up in the town, immediately set the tone for his subsequent exploits by volunteering to travel through the German lines, by tram and in civilian clothes, to Lille to report on German activity there. Having succeeded in getting himself into Lille, he recruited a lawyer as an agent and told him that when he wanted to report any information he was to wait in a certain place wearing a white waistcoat, checking the identity of his British contact using the password 'Eastchurch' (the location of the naval pilots' UK base). The RNAS commander at Dunkirk, Charles Rumney Samson, found O'Caffrey's intelligence-gathering ability so useful that he had him commissioned into the Royal Naval Volunteer Reserve.

O'Caffrey's initial intention appears to have been to become a Roman Catholic naval chaplain – a move that evidently had the backing of the Archbishop of Westminster, Francis Cardinal Bourne, the leader of the Roman Catholic church in Britain – but his native ability as a French speaker made him too valuable to Samson, who presciently sent him out to gather intelligence on possible targets and threats to the Dunkirk base. Aside from the Lille lawyer, O'Caffrey's first agent network operating inside German-occupied territory was a group of young French boys, Samson later revealed. 'We provided each with a bicycle and paid them one franc a day,' he said. 'They were most useful, as they could get into places that were occupied by the Germans without fear of capture.'[1]

Samson soon realised that O'Caffrey's capabilities extended far beyond the role of unit intelligence officer. He sent him to the headquarters intelligence staff with an offer to find out about Zeppelin sheds in Brussels, but Walter Kirke evidently misunderstood O'Caffrey's intentions, dismissing him as an irrelevant nuisance. The fact that he was a Frenchman, a missionary and a naval officer appears to have determined Kirke's disparaging attitude, although the order of precedence of these curious impediments is not entirely clear. Whatever it might have been, nothing concerned Kirke quite so much as the fact that O'Caffrey was a Jesuit and would therefore not have 'our ideas of what is correct'. There was no need for intelligence on the Zeppelin airship sheds in Brussels, Kirke noted, since the Royal Flying Corps already had the 'job in hand'. He sent O'Caffrey off to the Admiralty with a flea in his ear.[2]

O'Caffrey may have been rejected by Kirke, but he was grabbed with both hands by Captain Murray Sueter, director of the Royal Navy's Air Department, who did not share Kirke's confidence in the British army's attempts to locate the German Zeppelins. In the years before the war, warnings of the likelihood of bombing raids on the British capital by the Zeppelins had been rife and the RNAS, with more aircraft than the RFC, was ordered to provide homeland air defence, albeit with no clear idea of how to go about bringing down an airship. This led Winston Churchill, then First Lord of the Admiralty, to tell the cabinet that he did not believe any adequate measures to counter the Zeppelin threat were in place and as a result 'loss and injury, followed by much public outcry, will probably be incurred in the near future'. Uncertain whether the British aircraft could bring down a Zeppelin, Sueter saw O'Caffrey's attempts to track down the Zeppelin sheds as the answer. If the airships could be destroyed at their bases before they even left for Britain, the threat of 'loss and injury, followed by much public outcry' would be kept to a minimum and Churchill and the cabinet would be happy.[3]

O'Caffrey recruited agents and collected intelligence behind the German lines with remarkable ease, not merely because of his fluency in French but as a direct result of a personable and sympathetic character that persuaded his agents they could trust him. Within days, he already had a reliable agent in place in Brussels who was producing valuable intelligence on the construction of Zeppelin sheds at Berchem-Sainte-Agathe and Etterbeek, two of the main airship bases in the Brussels area. Both reports were accurate and the sheds were subsequently the subject of repeated bombing raids. In a report on 17 November 1914, O'Caffrey said his agent in Brussels would wire him as soon as the Zeppelins were moved to the bases. He also revealed that he had already fallen prey to attempts to poach his agents by a rival intelligence officer who 'has made use of a Belgian lady who has first offered her services to me'. Whether this was Richard Tinsley or Cecil Aylmer Cameron – both of whom were perfectly capable of poaching other officers' agents – is not clear, but O'Caffrey managed to retain his important agent in Brussels and, four weeks after his original report, a naval pilot dropped twelve bombs on the Etterbeek base, causing extensive damage.[4]

Just as important as O'Caffrey's reporting was his assessment of how much more intelligence might be obtained. 'It struck me as I travelled to and from Holland by the Flushing boat last week that information obtained from Belgian refugees who having just left Belgium landed daily at Folkestone could be turned to very good use by our intelligence service,' he said in a letter to his boss. O'Caffrey's suggestion came as intelligence officers were preparing for the November 1914 conference at which it was decided to set up the Bureau Central Interallié at Folkestone and was almost certainly the genesis of the idea. His report was largely based on intelligence already gained from refugees arriving at the port with details of a number of important targets, including the precise locations of the guns protecting Ostend and a large 'petrol works' north of Brussels, which provided most of the German fuel – 'a few bombs might do a great deal of damage there', O'Caffrey suggested, although his approach was generally far from gung-ho. An early report on potential targets in Bruges highlighted the German military governor's residence, where senior German officials passing through Bruges stayed, but added the rider: 'It must be pointed out that this building is of great architectural value and rather difficult to hit without touching at the same time the adjoining buildings of the Town Hall where about 100 Belgian clerks are employed daily.' The report, 'compiled from various sources and confirmed by a very reliable informant who lived in Bruges from 12 February to 23 April', also gave the precise location of the Germans' main wireless communications hub for the city, a major German petrol dump 'easily recognisable as it is almost surrounded by the hot houses of the Sanders Nursery', the electric power station for the city, and the locations of the main air defence guns.[5]

As a result of his success, O'Caffrey was moved in January 1915 to Cameron's new Folkestone offices to provide air intelligence, boarding all ferries coming from the Netherlands to collect intelligence and recruit agents among the Belgian refugees. 'He soon had a splendid service going,' said Samson. 'I think there is little doubt that our intelligence at this time was quite the most reliable.' This was largely because the Admiralty was willing to pay good money for intelligence and so O'Caffrey's agents were 'a good class of men'. His reporting was not restricted to potential targets; he also provided the first 'bomb damage assessments' of how well the British attacks had been carried out, thereby prompting renewed visits to destroy targets not hit in the initial raids. Sueter swiftly realised that, while O'Caffrey's reports had 'proved unusually correct and of considerable value in drawing up plans for our air raids', his agent networks needed to be co-ordinated with those run by the professionals. He handed O'Caffrey over to Blinker Hall's naval intelligence division. Hall worked extremely closely with Cumming

throughout the war, putting forward a number of people for the secret
service who were then actually run and paid for by Cumming, a model
adopted by both the Admiralty and the War Office and based on the
original 1909 concept of a foreign secret service organisation that would
'act as a screen between foreign spies and government officials'. Hall
passed O'Caffrey on to Cumming and from this point onwards, what
Cumming described as 'O'Caffrey's ménage' was effectively part of the
British secret service.

After a series of meetings with Cumming, the Frenchman opted,
with Cardinal Bourne's permission, to remain a spy rather than become a
naval chaplain. He and Cumming devised what O'Caffrey described as 'a
scheme for getting fuller information on German aeronautics on a much
larger scale than I had anticipated'. This included the intelligence that led
to the spectacular destruction by RNAS pilots of two Zeppelins in June
of 1915. The raids were in retaliation for a Zeppelin attack on London
a week earlier, in which seven people died and thirty-five were injured.
Three days after the British response, O'Caffrey was reporting from a
number of informants that the *LZ38*, one of the Zeppelins that had been
used to bomb England, had been destroyed in its shed at Evere, north of
Brussels. Two of his agents spent the night in woods near the Evere base.

> In the early hours of the morning they heard the explosion of a bomb
> followed by several smaller explosions. A few minutes later, a much
> louder explosion was heard, which according to other people caused
> a considerable shock to be felt a good distance from the aerodrome.
> Informants saw flames issuing from the shed. About 25 foot of the
> Brussels end of the shed had been destroyed. The interior was full of
> wreckage and the fire hoses were pouring torrents of water on both
> ends of the shed.

Two days later, O'Caffrey was able to confirm that the *LZ38*
was 'completely destroyed'. The bombing led to a crowd of Belgians
standing in their night attire around the outside of the base. 'When the
airship exploded and caught fire the crowd cheered and clapped hands,'

O'Caffrey said. His informants confirmed that the second Zeppelin to be destroyed, the *LZ37*, blown up near Ghent by bombs dropped onto it from above by Flight Sub-Lieutenant Rex Warneford of the RNAS, had been on its way to bomb London. The *LZ37* exploded in mid-air killing all fifteen of its crew, the debris landing next to a convent in the village of Gontrode, one of O'Caffrey's sources reported:

On Monday morning, 7 June, at 1.45 a.m., guns were heard firing at Allied aeroplanes. At 2.15 a.m., a Zeppelin [*LZ37*] was sighted flying over Mont-Saint-Amand. It was attacked by an aeroplane and seemed to have been hit in the fore part. Flames burst out of the airship and were soon seen to envelop it. Two terrific explosions were heard and the airship, broken in two, crashed down to the ground; one part falling in the street between the church and the St Elizabeth Convent, the other in the garden of the same convent. There was a pile of burning wreckage heaped up in the streets, on the roofs, hanging from the trees, etc. Corpses, many of them horribly burnt and charred, were seen amidst the debris, others on the roofs and even in the trees. It was said that a corpse fell right through the roof of the 'Café St Amand' and was found horribly mutilated in the kitchen of that establishment. In the evening, about twenty corpses had been identified. It is believed that there were altogether twenty-seven killed. One of the convent nuns as well as a ten-year-old child were also killed. A fire broke out in the convent stables; but luckily the cattle were saved. A number of men were dispatched from Ghent to deal with the situation. During the day, little boys were selling pieces of the wrecked Zeppelin to the inhabitants.

Meanwhile, O'Caffrey reported that an attack on the *LZ39*, which was moored at Berchem-Saint-Agathe, had missed its target, the bombs landing in a nearby field. O'Caffrey again quoted his agent verbatim:[6]

The sound of a loud explosion woke me up. I went out of the house and heard a second and a third explosion. It was 2.10 a.m. I heard the guns firing, walking towards the place where the sound of the explosion came from, I heard from some farmers who were taking vegetables to the Brussels market that Allied airmen had just tried to drop bombs on the Berchem shed and that the bombs had fallen in a field where some horses were grazing. At 2.55 a.m., other explosions were heard in an opposite direction. I gathered that the aeroplanes were then attacking Evere or Etterbeek. I saw in the distance huge flames and volumes of black smoke, the guns firing all the time. All the sentries along the railway line had deserted their posts and were hiding in the ditches. After hearing the good news from Evere, I went to see the results of the bombs dropped on Berchem. The three bombs fell in a field situated between the Ghent railway line and the fence that runs around the aerodrome. The first bomb fell at about a distance of 300 metres east of the shed, the second 30 metres east of the first and third about 60 metres east of the second, the latter being about 20 metres off the railway line. Five horses were killed and seven seriously wounded. They belonged to a man who had been commissioned to buy horses for the Germans. There was a rumour that the sentries on duty along the fence had also been killed; but this was not confirmed. There was a real panic among the men quartered in the huts and sheds, all taking to flight in all directions without taking the trouble to dress. The only guns which fired at the aeroplanes were those at the Hooghof Farm. The machine-gun on top of the old mill did not fire, nor the guns at the Villa des Couscous. There was a mist and the aeroplanes could hardly be seen.

Although, in this particular case, it was ultimately a report on a failed air raid, it was in fact extremely useful intelligence that could not only be used for assessing where the raid had gone wrong but also, given that the airfield was likely to be revisited to make another attempt to destroy the *LZ39*, where the air defences were located and how they were likely to react.

Warneford, the RNAS pilot who shot down the *LZ37*, had been in action for just over one month. The blast turned his Morane-Saulnier

Type L monoplane upside down and stopped its engine, forcing him to land behind enemy lines. Fortunately for him, given the carnage he caused and the likely reaction from the German forces, he managed to restart the engine and return to base. Four days later, he was awarded the Victoria Cross and, ten days after the attack, received the Knight's Cross of the Légion d'Honneur from the French. But he was killed later that day when an aircraft he was collecting fell apart in mid-air.

By now, O'Caffrey had recruited a large network of agents across Belgium and, a few weeks after the destruction of the Zeppelins, he moved to London to take charge of a new air section set up by Cumming at 11 Park Mansions. O'Caffrey's offices overlooked Vauxhall Park on South Lambeth Road and were a stone's throw from the Service's current headquarters at Vauxhall Cross. In order to facilitate payment to O'Caffrey's agents, his operations were funded from Richard Tinsley's budget. His reports concentrated on building up an extensive picture not only of all the German airfields in occupied Belgium but also of any potential bombing targets. Cumming's files were soon bulging with detailed reports on German military installations in Belgium. Every major town was assessed by O'Caffrey's agents for potential targets. All German airfields and any major military target were sketched out with precision, not just in words but in detailed, professionally drawn plans of the airbases themselves, and the results of every Allied bombardment were laid out in extensive reports, with the reports, where appropriate, referring directly to the relevant location as marked on the airfield plans. Some airfields were also photographed by O'Caffrey's agents on the ground. This was the early beginning of the now standard air intelligence system of providing target intelligence as a precursor to air raids and bomb damage assessment afterwards – a process evidently pioneered by O'Caffrey. He did not just deal with military airfields, he also collected intelligence on any other areas of interest, reporting extensively on the damage caused by the Royal Navy's bombardment of Zeebrugge in August 1915 and providing detailed sketches of new submarine shelters built to protect the German U-boats, as well as a full breakdown of what the roofs of the shelters were made of, allowing those planning raids on the submarine shelters to work out what would be required to destroy them.

O'Caffrey's reports included intelligence that had much wider significance than targeting and bomb damage assessment for British air forces. A report on 26 September 1915 gave the location of a Belgian factory west of Lommel which had been turned over to the production of 'asphyxiating gases'. The Belgian engineer in charge of the factory had resigned along with a number of other key workers and had managed to persuade most of the Belgian workers to go on strike. The factory was being kept going round the clock by workers brought in from Germany. It was protected by around thirty German Landsturm (Home Guard) soldiers with old rifles and had no machine guns or air defences. Two weeks later, he reported on another gas factory, this time at Etterbeek, which had two buildings and five gasholders, one gasholder being 50 feet in diameter, three being 36 feet in diameter and the remaining one being 10 feet in diameter. The factory was kept going day and night by two shifts of workers, each made up of 120 German soldiers and thirty civilians. A large number of empty lorries arrived at the plant each morning, leaving each night loaded with gas cylinders.

Nor did O'Caffrey stop at reporting from Belgium. By the end of 1915, his networks were so good that they extended into Germany itself, just one of a number of different operations Cumming was running inside Germany. As at 29 November 1915, O'Caffrey's own budget was just under £2,000, no less than 40 per cent of Tinsley's total annual budget of £5,000, with £1,200 spent on O'Caffrey's networks in Germany alone. He was also using intercepts of German bombers to plot the routes they were taking in their raids on Allied positions.[7]

O'Caffrey's reports from occupied Belgium and France are a model of neat, tidy, succinct reporting. How much reporting from inside Germany O'Caffrey was producing, and how accurate it was, remains unclear, but he and Tinsley were not the only ones running agents into Germany. Walter Kirke noted in September 1915 that Cumming was getting 'good German reports' from Cologne, Aix, Berlin, Dresden and Dirshau (now Tczew in Poland). It is not clear if these reports were coming via the Netherlands, Denmark or indeed Switzerland, since MI1c was now running operations into Germany from all three countries. One officer reported mounting two missions into Germany from Denmark:

> Entering Germany from the Schleswig frontier was not very difficult unless one attempted to pass through the custom house, with all its surrounding formalities and searches. In the angles of the frontier near Ribe, and on the mainland, of course the whole line was trenched and guarded, and any attempted passing or even approach was both difficult and dangerous. But by skipping round either end, at sea on the east, and between the islands on the west, no insurmountable difficulty presented itself.

The real problem, the former officer said, was that the Service was perpetually short of cash.

> The British Intelligence Department probably suffered least of any in this respect. Its actual managing chief never wasted a shilling where he could personally see a way of saving it. To my knowledge he never over-paid anyone, whilst he was not at all averse to using the persuasive argument of patriotism, in order to get a mass of useful work done for nothing at all. Throughout the period that I was connected with the BSS [British Secret Service], there were constant difficulties about money. In the early days most of the agents travelling abroad seemed to labour under the same difficulty: a shortage of funds and overdue accounts wanting payment. It may not have been any fault of, but merely an eccentricity of, our good old managing chief; be that as it may, impecuniosity never bothered me. Some of the others got very angry about it, whilst their irritation increased as their banking accounts became more heavily overdrawn.
>
> So far as actual pay went, a BSS man drew the equivalent to his ordinary army or naval pay, with nothing over for rations or extras. He, however, returned a list of his travelling expenses and hotel bills which were agreed to be refunded each month. If he were a married

man, he had to pay his wife's and his family's expenses out of his own
pocket, should it be necessary for any of them to accompany him,
which often absorbed the whole of his pay and a good bit above it.
If he entertained anyone with a view to drawing out some point of
useful intelligence, it would be passed in general expenses, provided
the outlay was exceedingly moderate. The Chief preached economy
at all times and he religiously practised it. Those who sit in chairs
in Whitehall take their regular fat salaries and periodical distinctive
honours as a matter of course and are ever in the official limelight,
whilst the reckless, devil-may-care workers over the horizon, the men
who carry their life in their hands and who go right into the lion's
den to collect facts and data which often mean success or defeat in
battles raged elsewhere, or who manipulate and pull the strings on the
spot, seem to be ignored and forgotten. The secrecy of the Service is
so absolute that no mention of the way their work is accomplished
may be made. The cloak of mystery is drawn so completely over the
whole department that no matter what sacrifice a member may make
for his country's sake, no matter what bravery he may have exhibited in
almost every instance alone and unsupported, probably in an enemy's
domain as one man facing a host of his country's enemies, his deeds are
unrecorded, unhonoured and unsung.[8]

O'Caffrey was replaced as head of the air section in early 1917
and sent to Greece to work for Compton Mackenzie, but the section
continued producing reports on German air movements and bomb
damage assessment following British raids. On 19 October 1917, eleven
German Zeppelins attacked the UK, flying at such great heights they
could not be seen from the ground, but as they dropped down over the
North Sea to come into land in Germany, they were picked off by RFC
Sopwith Camels and French Nieuport 11s. A. L. Hudson, the passport
control officer in Copenhagen, reported that one of the airships had
crashed into the sea about 4 miles off the Danish coast, while another,
the *L55*, which had bombed Birmingham and set a new world altitude
record of 24,606 feet in her attempts to avoid the British and French

fighter aircraft, had crashed in central Germany. A few weeks later, Hudson reported that the Danes had done a deal with the Germans, whereby the Zeppelins were to be allowed to land in Denmark. A series of signals had been worked out which would warn the Danish anti-aircraft defences 'and prevent the Germans being fired on'.

Then in late January, Hudson reported that a number of airships and hangers had been destroyed in a series of explosions at the Ahlhorn airbase, near Oldenburg in Lower Saxony. More than eighty German airmen had been killed. The agent report was confirmed by signals intelligence intercepts and by a Frenchman who had recently escaped from Germany and who said that he had heard a 'formidable explosion' in the Oldenburg area in early January. Later reports confirmed that the explosion on 5 January 1918 had destroyed all the airships and hangers at Ahlhorn as well as killing some 300 German servicemen. The bomb damage assessment reports put out by Section II included sketches of the damage culled from German newspapers. The section also continued to watch the progress of German military aircraft in post-war Germany.[9]

SIX

Hunting the Hun from Switzerland
– 'Deny everything!'

THE precise status of Cumming's operations in Switzerland at the start of the war is unclear. An internal service history suggests he had no-one based there until May 1915, but he certainly had operations there as early as November 1914. These may have used agents shared with John Wallinger of Indian Political Intelligence, who had been sent to Europe in 1910 to monitor the activity of Indian seditionists, based largely in Britain and Switzerland. Wallinger worked originally with Scotland Yard, but was subsequently attached to the general staff in France and began using his networks to collect military intelligence. Switzerland offered good potential for sending spies into Germany, but was a lower priority than either the Netherlands or Denmark, both of which were closer to the North Sea and Baltic ports.[1]

As a result, Walter Kirke decided – apparently with some justification – that Cumming's operations in Switzerland were insufficient and, early in 1915, began making moves to set up his own networks. 'C's Swiss system not as extensive as it might be and we decided that there should be no objection to our trying to start an independent one,' he recorded in his diary in early 1915. Kirke ignored a Foreign Office decision to ban him from using the British consuls, amid concerns that this would lead to confusion and damaging rivalries, and recruited George Pollitt from Brunner Mond, a chemical company, which would later form one of the main components of ICI. Pollitt had joined the Royal Engineers on the outbreak of war before being commissioned into the

Intelligence Corps. Kirke's initial plan was to send him to Switzerland as a civilian under cover of the British representative on a commission on hand dyes. Ultimately, Pollitt's only real contribution was to recruit a colleague from Brunner Mond to work in Switzerland permanently. Edward Béla Josepff Harran, a specialist chemist whose family were Hungarian immigrants, was so enthused by the offer of taking charge of the military networks in Switzerland that he immediately moved his family to Zurich. Harran was commissioned into the Intelligence Corps and tasked to run a network of German socialists, based in Mannheim, Nuremberg, Stuttgart, Bremen and Frankfurt, who were producing intelligence reports from inside Germany. They sent their intelligence on to a prominent German socialist in exile in Switzerland, believing it would help him plan a socialist coup, and were blissfully unaware that their exiled hero was a British agent. The operation appeared promising, but was highly insecure, and only briefly produced any worthwhile information.[2]

Kirke's justification for his expansion into Switzerland forced Cumming to beef up his own operations. There was some talk of sending the actor and playwright Harley Granville-Barker to Switzerland on a 'special mission', before he took over the secret service records, but it was not until May 1915 that Cumming set up his own permanent presence based around two men. He deliberately sought out former Swiss nationals who had taken British citizenship to take charge of MI1c operations in Switzerland, a policy that met with mixed success. Major Hanns Vischer, recruited by Cumming from the Colonial Office in April 1915 and sent to Berne as an assistant military attaché, was the first of several former Swiss nationals who were to work for him in the country of their birth. Vischer, who was born in Basel in 1876, had been naturalised in 1903 so that he could take up a post as British agent in northern Nigeria, and had subsequently achieved a level of notoriety by travelling across the Sahara from Libya to Nigeria. The way in which the Colonial Office insisted to *The Times* that this journey had 'not the slightest political significance' only served, rightly or wrongly, to reinforce the impression that it was an intelligence mission.[3]

The second recruit was Major Lewis Campbell, another mining engineer, who was commissioned into the Intelligence Corps and, in May 1915, sent to man a bureau in the French town of Annemasse, across the border from Geneva. Campbell's role was to use Annemasse as a base from which to cross into Switzerland to recruit and deal with agents, collecting intelligence from refugees from Germany and watching out for German agents trying to infiltrate France. But he was out of his depth, unable to tell whether the intelligence provided by his agents was credible or not, and admitting to Cumming that he had no idea of the order of battle of the German army. His reports made no military sense and were eventually sent via Vischer to be edited and turned into something the military could understand.[4]

The Germans, who had a much larger espionage operation based in Switzerland, were not slow in reacting to the increase in British spies and, on 6 September 1915, Cumming recorded in his diary that Wallinger had lost 'seven or eight of his bridge-watchers, jugged in Switzerland'. Vischer was withdrawn – presumably seen as vulnerable as a result of his previous reputation and Swiss origins – and moved to MI5.[5]

Wallinger began rebuilding his networks, sending the author W.Somerset Maugham to Geneva under the pretext of writing a play. Maugham did not spend long working as a spy, but it was long enough to inspire the *Ashenden* short stories, an authentically downbeat depiction of the life of a typical intelligence officer.

> He saw his spies at stated intervals and paid them their wages. When he could get hold of a new one, he engaged him, gave him his instructions and sent him off to Germany. He kept his eyes and ears open and he wrote long reports, which he was convinced no-one read, till having inadvertently slipped a jest into one of them he received a sharp reproof for his levity. The work he was doing was evidently necessary, but it could not be called anything but monotonous.

Maugham also immortalised one of the real couriers who smuggled intelligence across the border into France, describing how, every market day, his allegedly fictional spymaster would go down to the market place and meet 'the old butter woman', who would travel from France to sell her butter, eggs and vegetables, carrying messages from Wallinger, and go home with Ashenden's reports stuck down the top of her dress. The woman was in fact a real person who took Maugham's reports across the border.

> This old lady looked so bland and innocent, with her corpulence, her fat red face, and her swirling good-natured mouth, it would have been a very astute detective who could imagine that, if he took the trouble to put his hand deep down between those voluminous breasts of hers, he would find a piece of paper that would land in the dock an honest old woman and an English writer approaching middle age.[6]

By the end of 1915, Kirke was offering to pull out of Switzerland entirely and hand everything over to Cumming, albeit so long as there was a substantial boost to operations there. Wallinger had, in the meantime, managed to recruit agents in Frankfurt, Coblenz, Trier and Mainz, proving it was possible to get agents inside Germany, but Campbell had not been so successful and, given his poor grasp of the German army's order of battle, clearly needed to be replaced. In April 1916, he was given two months to improve and, when he failed to do so, was replaced by Redmond Barton Cafferata, owner of a Nottinghamshire gypsum company, who had been organising volunteer recruitment for the forces before deciding to offer his own services. Cafferata was sent to Switzerland as part of a complete revamp of Cumming's operations there in the second half of 1916 and the first half of 1917. This saw Cumming take control of Harran in Berne, who was put in overall charge of MI1c operations in Switzerland. Harran was assisted in Berne by MacInroy Este Vibert, a French-speaking sergeant in the Royal Fusiliers, and mainly dealt with intelligence on Austria and on potential enemy agents collected through the passport control system. Cumming also sent Major Cuthbert Binns to Switzerland. Binns was a fluent German and Turkish speaker who had lived in Constantinople before the war and had been talent-spotted while working for the army as a Turkish interpreter at Gallipoli. He worked initially under civilian cover, but later as military attaché, partly against Austria, but more particularly against Turkey, since a large number of Turkish opposition figures were free to visit neutral Switzerland. There were two other main bureaux set up inside Switzerland, one at Lausanne, focusing largely, but not entirely, on counter-espionage – watching for German agents trying to enter France – and one in Zurich, which focused on putting agents into Germany and Austria and on watching the large German intelligence operation based in the city. There were also bureaux at Montreux and Basel, both set up in mid-1917.[7]

In the meantime, Kirke had caused more trouble by trying to take over Wallinger's network. He began by telling Wallinger that he must no longer speak to Cumming and then sent Captain Francis Verdon from Paris to replace him, a move that was naïve at best, given that Wallinger was subordinate to the India Office, not the military, and was made worse by the fact that Kirke did not even tell Wallinger what he was doing. Kirke's attempted takeover was blocked by a furious George Macdonogh, who told John Charteris that Kirke was breaching 'our original agreement' that MI1c should be in charge of operations in Switzerland. 'His one idea seems to be to run a separate show of his own,' Macdonogh said. Kirke's manoeuvrings were counter-productive. Cumming ended up in complete control of operations in Switzerland. Wallinger stayed in place, with his networks concentrating on the increasing problem of Indian subversives financed by Berlin.[8]

Cafferata was trained on agent-running by Richard Tinsley in Rotterdam, commissioned as a lieutenant in the RNVR and sent to set up a new base at Pontarlier, in the French Alps, the closest French town to Lausanne. This base was known as 'the Nunnery', although whether it was based in the town's real convent is not clear. Cafferata took the codename Zulu, the letter Z being particularly popular among Cumming's recruits. He not only looked for potential spies among the refugees crossing the border, but also liaised with the French Commissariat Spécial de Police to prevent German spies getting through.

He was assisted by Captain Frederick 'Fanny' van den Heuvel, a papal count, which might explain the reference to 'the Nunnery'.

Harran had trouble with the British consuls, who complained to the Foreign Office about his attempts to involve them in his espionage operations, but Cafferata managed to secure a compromise. After arriving in Pontarlier in June 1916, he set about reorganising the agents operating from Switzerland and, in November 1916, proposed the use of specially appointed vice-consuls to act as 'letter boxes' for reports from agents inside Switzerland and to provide a link between himself in Pontarlier and Harran in Berne, keeping the consuls themselves untarnished by any involvement. 'Although it is undoubtedly a sound principle that HM consular officers should not jeopardise their position and standing, by mixing themselves up with espionage on behalf of Great Britain,' Cafferata wrote, 'it is an undoubted fact that a Consul is in an exceptionally favourable position to obtain information of a commercial and a military character which might prove of great service to the country in this period of national stress.'

Cafferata's system was agreed in a limited form, initially using just two vice-consuls, and was put in place in January 1917. Bertie Maw, codenamed Petrol, was appointed vice-consul in Lausanne and M. Chaplin, codenamed Cyprus, was given the same position in Zurich. The vice-consul's role was restricted to giving occasional advice and providing the 'letter box' for the intelligence reports, which were passed on initially via the Foreign Office, but later direct to Cumming and to GHQ in France. The Zurich bureau included another former Swiss citizen who had been naturalised as a British citizen and sent out from London – Robert Sahli, a 38-year-old chiropodist whose Old Bond Street practice presumably brought him to C's attention. Sahli took the codename Mabel, touchingly, though somewhat insecurely, the name of the English wife he left at home in Leytonstone, east London, with their two sons. Although Harran was in overall charge in Switzerland, the bulk of the espionage operations against Germany and the counter-espionage operations were in fact controlled by Cafferata, who relied on Sahli as his chief agent runner in Zurich.

One of Cafferata or van den Heuvel was always moving between the various bureaux inside Switzerland, under cover of working for the British Ministry of Munitions, while the other stayed at Pontarlier training agents. Instructions for agents going into Germany, probably devised by Tinsley's agent runners in Rotterdam, included training in how to build up a protective cover for their spying operations.

Especially at the beginning of an agent's visit to G, he should devote a considerable amount of time every day to the building up of his business connections. Especially in the case of a neutral, certain suspicion is attached to every arrival in a German town, and it is essential that for some time at least an agent should occupy himself entirely with his cover business, by calls, correspondence, note books etc. This would apply to a man who is going to G under the cover as representative or traveller of a neutral house. The agent who takes up a fixed post in a German firm, which will tie him to definite office hours, can obviously be of little or no use to us, whilst so employed, but this may be a means for him to get into G and after some time he could find an excuse to leave his employment and launch out for himself. Students in art, music, medicine etc. find good cover for train watching, as also do professionals such as doctors, dentists, architects, and those whose profession or business enable them to dispose of their time as they will and to establish themselves as they wish in localities of their own choice.

There were very few agents operating in Lausanne, which was largely a counter-espionage operation, but it did have two good Swiss agents: Pourchot, codenamed Mary, and Jim de Teux, codenamed Walfisch, who worked closely together and not only managed to get a number of German agents in Switzerland arrested and expelled, but were also successful in recruiting sub-agents to go into Germany to collect military intelligence. Pourchot's work was described as 'most valuable' while de Teux had two well-placed sub-agents in Germany who were 'men of considerable knowledge and position'.[9]

The bulk of the agents sent into Germany were, however, run via Zurich. They varied considerably in terms of productivity. One of the better agents was the Vickers representative in Switzerland, a man called Wagner who was based at Winterthur and was recruiting employees of the Swiss engine company Sulzer to collect intelligence during their business trips to Germany. Sulzer's headquarters was in Winterthur and the company had a large German subsidiary at Ludwigshafen, producing diesel engines. Wagner 'has supplied military intelligence of some value', Cafferata said. Another agent, called Elminger and codenamed Munch, recruited among his friends, 'who go to Bavaria on short visits selling foodstuffs'. He was providing military intelligence and 'promises well'. An agent called Weber was based full-time in Leipzig under the false name of A. Thommen and was 'operating in code fairly well', although his 'ink' letters had never got through. But access to Germany was no guarantee of success. One agent had been to Munich, Ulm, Friedrichshafen and Karlsruhe but was 'not much good', while another who had been to Munich and Metz had produced 'very weak' reports. Others had never even made it across the border.[10]

'It is no use hiding the fact that it is getting harder and harder to find men to go over to G, owing to the severe precautions taken by the Huns, and conditions such as civil conscription etc. in G,' Cafferata wrote in April 1917. 'Even the best of our men will consider himself lucky if he finds on average one agent every three months to go into G and, unfortunately, out of every four or five agents sent over, usually only about one will be found to be of any real use.'

As a result, Cafferata's vice-consul system relied on men like Sahli who were there to carry out the real secret service work, liaising with the agents and acting as 'cut-outs' to protect the vice-consuls from the Swiss police. These men had to be British citizens, Cafferata said:

We refer to the agents who were intended to act as the VCs' [vice-consuls'] right-hand men, and without whom the VC is almost useless. It is only such men who can do our most important work, viz recruit agents for Germany, and who are able to do the hundred and one things for us which a man in an official position cannot do. It is almost impossible to get the men of the necessary qualifications out here – they must be essentially 'our men', just as much as the VCs themselves, as their position of close co-operation with the consular officers must place their integrity and reliability above suspicion. These men can only be recruited in England. It is easy enough to get what may be called second class agents in Switzerland, but these men are usually not reliable enough to put in direct touch with the Consuls and can only be used as sub-agents through the intermediary of our own men.[11]

Cumming set up a bureau at Geneva in the spring of 1917 under Commander Hugh Whittall, who had been based in Greece until January 1917 when he 'strained his heart' and was sent to Switzerland. According to the author Compton Mackenzie, who worked with Whittall in Greece, he was 'as handsome as the most admired film star, strong and athletic too, with a masterful personality and great physical and moral courage'. Whittall operated from the consulate and began issuing political reports on the attempts by the American George Davis Herron, a Congregationalist minister and Christian socialist based in Geneva, to put out peace feelers to Germany on behalf of US President Woodrow Wilson. Whittall was not the only MI1c officer in Geneva; he was assisted by William George Middleton Edwards, who operated under cover of a correspondent for *The Times*, although there is no record of him ever writing anything for the newspaper. Both men knew Cuthbert Binns well as a result of previous service in Constantinople, where the Whittalls and the Middleton Edwardses were prominent traders and merchants.[12]

Around the same time, Cumming also moved Captain William Heard, an Intelligence Corps officer and Bulgarian specialist initially based in Salonika, to work alongside Binns in Berne. Heard's role was to conduct negotiations with Bulgarian politicians in Switzerland as part of an attempt to persuade the government in Sofia to withdraw from the war. The peace overtures followed Heard's recruitment in Salonika of a Bulgarian politician whose identity is protected in official files by the codename M4. Cumming's Salonika bureau had been holding covert talks with the Bulgarians since at least November 1915. Agent M4 declined to provide intelligence, but offered to act as a go-between in secret peace talks between his fellow Bulgarian politicians and the British. George Macdonogh suggested Greek and Serbian territory might be offered to Bulgaria in return for an agreement to pull out of the war, with the British and French reimbursing Greece and Serbia financially for the loss. 'The results would be far-reaching as German communication with Turkey would be cut and the Mesopotamian campaign strangled,' Macdonogh said. 'Greece and Serbia should be indemnified in money, which they need more than territory. This indemnity should be generous. England and France are spending each day some ten to twelve million pounds sterling so the shortening of the war by a week would supply ample funds for satisfying the Greeks and the Serbs. The detachment of Bulgaria would produce an immense saving to the Allies and might well involve the difference between victory and defeat.'[13]

The laws against espionage were rigorously enforced by the Swiss police and as a result, agents were given detailed instructions on how to avoid being caught. There were two main rules, the first of which was to avoid women and alcohol. 'The greatest possible prudence is required from an agent in the Service,' one MI1c training manual said. 'Never confide in women. Before being sure of anyone, act as if he were a German agent. Never give a photo to anyone, especially a female. Cultivate the impression that you are an ass, and have no brains; it is the greatest possible compliment to hear that you have the reputation of being an imbecile. Never get drunk; when you drink, you do not know what you say. If you are obliged to drink heavily on occasions, take two large spoonfuls of olive oil beforehand; you will not get drunk but can pretend to be so. If dealing with a suspect, make him drink as much as possible; he will probably tell you something interesting.' But the main edict was a very clear ruling that you should never admit to espionage in any shape or form:

As a general rule always deny everything when in the hands of the police. They cannot do anything if you persist. If you are taken red-handed, never say anything about any of your chiefs, nor of anyone in the Service. You can invent a few names if necessary, to throw them off the scent. Never have anything written on you if you can help it, make your reports as concise as possible, roll them up into a small ball, place them in your handkerchief and if arrested pretend to blow your nose and swallow the 'pill'. Never have anything in your rooms, if arrested there will be a perquisition made at once there. Never ask anyone for information unless the said person is alone with you.

If arrested simply deny all knowledge of the affair. If you are formally denounced by someone, deny what they say. If confronted, continue to deny. You must continue to deny everything. If two people are confronted with you, deny all the same. It is all in your advantage to continue to deny, nothing can be done if you do. If you are confronted with other agents, who have been arrested and have confessed, and it is known that you were often in their company, do not deny that you know them, admit it, but state that you made their acquaintance in such and such a manner, but that you were ignorant of what they did and, under no circumstances, admit that you work with them. In general, therefore, confess nothing. Never write in your own hand. Never have anything on your person, or at home, which could give you away. Have good cover and give a certain amount of time to your supposed occupation. Never leave incriminating documents in the hands of anybody. Never denounce anybody; you will only aggravate your own case. Never admit having received money; this would tell heavily against you. NEVER ADMIT ANYTHING. NEVER MAKE A CONFESSION.[14]

The dangers of being caught mounting espionage operations affected the Germans even more than the British. The German secret service had well over 100 men in Switzerland at any one time and the MI1c Lausanne bureau in particular went out of its way to assist the Swiss or the French in capturing them. A December 1918 summary of operations in Switzerland describes how a beautiful, well-educated Belgian woman, who had 'good cause to hate the Boche', was recruited and persuaded to penetrate the German secret service organisation in Switzerland. Agreeing that 'nothing be shirked in order to obtain a successful issue', she seduced a German intelligence officer. She agreed to act as an agent for him and then – having been given the addresses of the German agents who were to be her contacts in France, as well as undergarments impregnated with secret ink, persuaded him to accompany her into France, whereupon he was arrested and the other German agents rounded up. Meanwhile, her instructions from two other German intelligence officers, including details of Swiss frontier police who were helping the Germans, fell into the hands of a friendly Swiss secret police officer. One of the Swiss frontier officers who had been assisting the Germans blew his brains out rather than be arrested and the German espionage network was destroyed at a cost of around £60.[15]

Redmond Cafferata told Claude Dansey in September 1917 that as many as thirty German agents operating in Switzerland had been expelled as a result of the activities of his 'agents provocateurs' inside the German intelligence service. He was not alone within the Service at feeling frustrated by Cumming's notorious scepticism of counter-espionage operations. Cafferata told Dansey that he had infiltrated a number of his own men, and women, into the German networks on the basis that the best form of defence lay in 'having our own men in the enemy's camp' from where they could neutralise the German espionage operations from within. 'I have it on the authority of one of our present Agents Provocateurs that the Huns are very much concerned with the recent arrest of so many of their agents in Lausanne and France, which shows that they at least know the value of the work that we have been recently carrying out,' Cafferata said. 'After all, can we afford to scoff at the destruction of their organisations and the arresting of masses of their agents as recently done in Lausanne, where some fifteen or sixteen have been arrested, including their German chief von Zynda, alias Trichler, of Berlin? It seems to me a scandal that if such work can be done, and I have proved that it can, that it should be neglected.'[16]

In common with the entire operations of MI1c, the Swiss-based espionage and counter-espionage system was the subject of an extensive review in the late summer of 1917. Colonel Rhys Samson, the head of Cumming's operations in the Middle East and Mediterranean, who controlled the Swiss operations that targeted Turkey and the Balkans, was sent to carry out an inspection. The result was a recommendation that Edward Harran be replaced – Samson even went so far while in Switzerland as to suggest to Cafferata that he should take over. But the whole affair became caught up in Dansey's more general review of MI1c as a whole and it was decided in London that Hanns Vischer should be sent back to take over in Berne. This led to a furious reaction from Harran, who resigned on the spot and was moved to MI5.

Cafferata was deeply unhappy with his own position in Switzerland. During the review of the Swiss operations, Samson had given him the impression that he would recommend him as the new MI1c bureau chief in Berne, and Vischer's appointment had left him feeling 'shabbily treated'. He was sent to Greece to sort out the counter-espionage section there. An internal service history of operations in Switzerland suggests that Vischer was unpopular, although Cafferata and Robert Sahli both speak affectionately of him, referring to him as 'padre', and Cafferata went out of his way to make clear to Dansey that he had no problem working under Vischer at all.

Shortly after Cafferata left Switzerland, one of his Zurich agents was recruited as a German spy. Franz Bruno Grob was a 21-year-old soldier who was born in Zurich. He had worked for a number of stockbrokers in London and had become naturalised in order to sign up. He was picked out for MI1c in a trawl of the armed forces for any former Swiss nationals who had become British citizens. Recruited by Cumming, Grob was sent out to Zurich in January 1917, to assist Chaplin. He failed to impress Cafferata, who soon wanted to send him home, but found it was impossible since he had been called up for service in the Swiss army. Once Grob's army training was over, Cafferata gave him the task of recruiting agents and watching two leading German intelligence officers, Adolph Löwengard and Leon Strauss, in the Zurich and St Gall areas. Unfortunately, Löwengard was himself a stockbroker in London before the war and knew Grob personally. He engineered a meeting with Grob in Lausanne in January 1918. 'Löwengard suggested to me that I should go to the British consulate and act as an agent provocateur on behalf of Germany,' Grob later admitted. 'On 14 January, Löwengard and I went to see Strauss, who asked me whether I would be willing to work for them in England. When I said yes, they gave me the addresses of their friends in London.'

Grob was given a number of tasks, some of which were simply errands for Löwengard, but most involved contacting various stockbrokers in London with cryptic messages about Löwengard and Strauss, the people they were in contact with, and their readiness to 'deal in stocks'. All this might have been perfectly innocent had not Grob admitted having spent eight days in the Elite Hotel in Zurich with Strauss before his departure being talked through the details of his mission. 'Löwengard advised me to learn these addresses by heart and to have none of them on me in writing, which I did.' He told Chaplin he was leaving and going back to London and crossed the Swiss border into France, only to be arrested by the French police at Pontarlier.

Having extracted a full confession and found evidence that Grob had been living beyond his means in Switzerland, the French shared their investigations with the British. They then incarcerated Grob for more than a year before sending the British Foreign Office a dossier of his alleged links to the German intelligence service and offering to return him for trial in the UK. The case was handed to MI5, who interviewed Grob and ruled that it was 'not considered either possible or desirable to prosecute him in this country'. Had he not been stuck in a French jail for more than a year, this would open up the possibility that he had been operating as a British agent provocateur attempting to expose Löwengard and Strauss as spies. It seems more likely that – since he had failed as miserably in his mission for the Germans as he had for the British – the affair was deemed to be not worth the potential embarrassment of a court case that would expose the methods of the British secret service to the public eye.[17]

The departure of Walter Kirke and Cecil Aylmer Cameron dramatically improved relations with the British army in France and the MI1c officers in Switzerland provided back-up to a successful army operation run through Switzerland in which Mme Lise Rischard, the wife of the medical adviser to the Luxembourg Railway Company, helped the British to set up a network of train watchers in Luxembourg providing vital intelligence on German military movements during the crucial last months of the war. The operation was set up and overseen from Paris by Major George Bruce and Cumming's former man in Annemasse, Major Lewis Campbell, with 'Fanny' van den Heuvel tasked to exfiltrate Rischard from Switzerland if things went wrong. An official account, written by Reginald Drake, described the creation of the Luxembourg train-watching network as 'one of the most successful pieces of intelligence work, from an SS [secret service] point of view, within my knowledge'.[18]

One of the most interesting aspects of the work in Switzerland was the extent to which Hugh Whittall was in contact with the Independent German Social Democratic Party (USDP), formed after the pacifist faction of the German Social Democratic Party was expelled from the party over its opposition to the war. At least one leading Independent German Social Democrat, quite possibly more, was working for Whittall. Karl Ludwig Krause was recruited some time in 1918 and designated agent G69, the G standing for Geneva. Krause was producing intelligence on the revolutionary socialist movement from inside Germany, and was, Whittall said, 'ready to go to any length for the good of the cause'. One former member of the party, recruited by the Service in the 1930s, alleged that the chairman, Hugo Haase, and two of his close allies, Georg Ledebour and Wilhelm Dittmann, were also working for the Service and receiving funding from London for their party. Johann de Graaf said Frank Foley, the Service's Berlin bureau chief in the 1930s, told him all three were employed by the British and that through them money was channelled from MI1c to fund a 1917 mutiny within the German armed forces. 'The three leaders were in our employ, and the USDP, whom we financed, was all part of it,' Foley allegedly told de Graaf. 'In the beginning, everything started out well, but somewhere there was a leak and the whole plot failed. It would have succeeded too, since the navy was all set to go, but the army did not move as planned.'[19]

By the beginning of March 1918, George Herron's peace efforts were gathering pace, with Count Max von Montgelas, the head of the German Foreign Ministry's political department, visiting him in Geneva to discuss what terms the Germans were prepared to accept, information the British were anxious to obtain. 'Since sending you my report, Whittall and [Middleton] Edwards have been to me, begging for any information I can give them on Germany,' Herron said in a letter to the US President. 'They surmised the Count was here through information of their service, I suppose. How much, if anything, shall I tell them?' The two sides agreed that Herron should pass his reports on to the British Foreign Office Political Intelligence Department, via Whittall, who sent them on in CXP reports, the P standing for 'political', but, in May 1918, details of a German peace proposal given to Herron by Professor Ludwig Quidde, a German emissary, leaked to the *Daily Mail*. The Americans suspected, probably correctly, that MI1c was the source of the leak, but Herron accepted Whittall's assurance he had nothing to do with it, telling Wilson he believed the head of British intelligence in Switzerland to be 'morally speaking, a sportsman and a gentleman'.[20]

Colonel R. J. MacHugh, who like Vernon Kell was a former *Daily Telegraph* war correspondent, was sent to Geneva as vice-consul in October 1918, to take over from Whittall as MI1c bureau chief. MacHugh, an Irish Catholic, had combined his journalism with a reserve commission in the Territorial Army and commanded an artillery unit in France during the early part of the war but, after suffering severe wounds in German shelling, he was unable to return to the front and was sent to work for Cumming in Switzerland. Not content with acting as a 'letter box' for the locally recruited agents, MacHugh, a fluent Spanish speaker, 'penetrated into the heart of Germany disguised as a Spaniard, a daring achievement which gained us valuable information and brought him warm official acknowledgements'.[21]

MacHugh was not the only Briton to use Switzerland as a base to go into Germany as a spy. Wallace Ellison, who had been lecturing in economics at Frankfurt University at the outbreak of war, was one of a number of British civilians interned in a prison camp but, after several failed escape attempts, he succeeded, in October 1917, in getting out via the Netherlands, and was then sent by Cumming to Switzerland, from where he carried out a number of spying missions across the border to collect intelligence on conditions inside Germany. He later wrote:

> After my escape and an intensive short period of training at the War Office, I was sent out, under cover of my choice, to the German–Swiss frontier and worked there as a secret agent until the Armistice was signed. I was the first Englishman, when Germany was in the throes of revolution and counter-revolution, to travel through Germany from Berne to Copenhagen and back and report through my chiefs to Mr Lloyd George at Versailles. When I got back to Berne after that first trial trip through Germany, I found waiting for me a cable from the then editor of the Sunday Pictorial reading 'Offer you thirty guineas or more for article of 1600 words on present conditions in Germany'. I shall never discover how he learned that I had been there. I could have put those thirty guineas – or more – to quite useful purpose and the writing of such an article would have been as easy as falling off a wall, but I could not respond.

Given that MacHugh was Irish, Ellison's claim to be the first Englishman to travel through Germany at war's end may well be true.[22]

SEVEN

Navies and Nemesis

ONE of Richard Tinsley's most valuable agents – possibly even the most valuable agent Cumming had throughout the First World War – was a former German navy officer who was collecting naval intelligence in Germany's northern ports. Karl Krüger was, in intelligence parlance, a 'walk-in', having approached the British legation in The Hague in November 1914 offering to spy for the British. He admitted openly that he was intent on wreaking revenge on the Imperial German Navy after being court-martialled for having hit another officer, a relative of the Kaiser. There is some evidence that, after making the original offer, Krüger had second thoughts, with the Service's archives suggesting he may have had to have his arm heavily twisted by Tinsley before he agreed to go through with the deal. The war and the anticipated increase in agents had brought a new designation system based on the location of the agent. Krüger was designated TR16, as in the sixteenth agent run by Tinsley from Rotterdam, which is evidence of the relatively low numbers of agents that Tinsley had at the start of the war, and since he had more than anyone else, the low numbers Cumming had. Krüger was given in Tinsley's reports simply as R16 until the middle of 1916, when his designation was changed to H16, most likely standing for Holland, or possibly The Hague, agent number 16.

Perhaps the best indicator of Krüger's importance from the start, and the reason Tinsley worked so hard to ensure he carried through on his promise to work for the British, was his pre-war designation – GTA1, German Travelling Agent 1, the only man the British secret

service had in Germany at the time.[1] According to Henry Landau,
within the Rotterdam offices Krüger was known in hallowed terms as
'the Dane', although he was in fact very much a German, and lived in
Bad Godesberg on the west bank of the Rhine.

> Slight of build, fair, with blue eyes, he looked the reserved well-bred
> Scandinavian of cultured and professional interests. He certainly did
> not look the arch-spy he was. When I came to know him better,
> however, I realised why he was so successful. He was a marine engineer
> of exceptional quality. He was a man without nerve, always cool and
> collected. Nothing escaped his austerely competent eye and he was
> possessed of an astounding memory for the minutest detail of marine
> construction. He covered every shipbuilding yard and every Zeppelin
> shed in Germany. The key to his success was that he made the Germans
> believe that he was working for them against us. He was allowed to
> travel freely to Kiel, Wilhelmshaven, Hamburg, Bremen, Emden,
> Lübeck, Flensburg and other shipbuilding centres. His popularity with
> German clients and their trust in his apparently candid nature were
> unbounded. When in due time he applied for a pass to proceed through
> Germany to Holland it was readily granted.

Once every few weeks, on a regular basis, Krüger went to Rotterdam,
initially to meet Tinsley, or from late 1915, Captain Charles Power, the
head of Tinsley's naval section, in one of a number of safe houses the
British had dotted around the city, writing out his reports from memory
alone. Landau said:

> He never carried any incriminating materials whatsoever – notes, lists,
> letters, even special papers or inks. On his arrival in the house, the
> Dane immediately got down to writing his report, which he did in
> German, and this occupied sometimes three to four hours. With his
> extraordinary memory, he was able to sit down and write out page
> after page of reports, giving an exact description of the ships which
> were under construction or repair, and supplying us with the invaluable

naval information on which the Admiralty relied absolutely. As soon as his reports were completed, they were rushed to our office on the Boompjes for translating, coding and cabling to London. From him we got full engineering details of the submarines which the Germans were turning out as fast as they could in order to put over their unrestricted submarine warfare campaign.

Surviving reports from Krüger begin in April 1915, with two on submarine construction which contain some errors but largely agree with the facts as they are now known, including what would have been very interesting, and was certainly accurate, evidence that some U-boats were being built with only one skin, making them much more vulnerable to being rammed. Subsequent reports dealt with all types of vessels, although submarine construction remained a key interest. He covered the main northern ports at Emden, Wilhelmshaven, Bremerhaven, Hamburg and Kiel, as well as some of the smaller ports like Cuxhaven and Rostock. He also made frequent trips to the eastern ports at Danzig and Stettin. Some of his intelligence derived from long-term sources in the individual cities, while other information came from officials or sailors he befriended on his visits. It is clear from some of his reports that he had been tasked to answer specific questions, for example a briefing in January 1916 on the ships moored in the various northern ports that were capable of carrying troops and – amid continuing concerns over a possible German attack on Britain – a special trip to Emden and Wilhelmshaven to investigate unfounded reports that troops were gathering there in preparation for an invasion. Tinsley and Power initially rated him as only 50 per cent reliable, but much of what he wrote accords with the known facts and the assessments of reliability increased as more and more of his reports, which were checked against the Room 40 results, proved to be correct.[2]

By the beginning of 1916, Tinsley had a number of other naval sources reporting from Germany, with agent designations rising to R34. Krüger's reporting continued to dominate, however, and on 9 February 1916 a series of revelations included the fact that the battle cruiser *Seydlitz* had lost 128 men in an explosion during the Battle of Dogger Bank just over two weeks earlier. We now know the final death toll was in fact 160. One of his most impressive reports, although not by any means the most significant, came in April 1916 when, while routinely recording the German naval operations in each of the ports, including Stettin and Danzig, he described trials on a new German weapon, the *Fernlenkboot*, or FLB, a wire-guided remote control boat which was designed to be packed full of explosives and rammed against the Royal Navy ships that were cruising off the Belgian coast, bombarding Zeebrugge and Ostend. Krüger described these boats and how they looked when operating at speed in great detail, even correctly giving the name of the company, Siemens-Schuckertwerke, that was producing them, before continuing with a detailed report of what was taking place at other German shipyards. Bernard Trench, who was now working in naval intelligence, wrote at the end in pencil: 'This man should be encouraged, his reports have all been very much above the average.' The significance of the report would become more apparent eighteen months later, in October 1917, when one of them hit the Royal Navy ship HMS *Erebus*, albeit merely damaging her rather than sinking her.[3]

The Battle of Jutland, which took place from 31 May to 1 June 1916, led to an urgent request to all MI1c's agents operating in Germany for information on the German losses. The long-awaited clash of the Royal Navy's Grand Fleet with the German High Seas Fleet was initially portrayed by many as a defeat for the British, with the Kaiser claiming that his navy had 'torn down the nimbus of invincibility of British sea power'. There had been unrealistic expectations in Britain of another Trafalgar, a war-winning blow of the kind that seemed impossible in the stalemate on the Western Front, and there was palpable shock that the British losses in men and ships were much greater than those of their German opponents – more than 6,000 dead, compared to the 2,500 Germans killed, and fourteen Royal Navy ships sunk, while the Germans claimed initially they had lost only seven, although the real figure was in fact eleven. The heavier British losses were in large part a result of the Admiralty's failure to take note of Cumming's pre-war reports on the superior German naval shells and it badly needed to show that Britannia still ruled the waves. Cumming's request for intelligence from inside Germany read: 'Reliable information urgently required regarding German losses in North Sea action yesterday.' The first response came seventeen days later from a Danish-based agent, D15. His report, based on a single visit to Wilhelmshaven, was broadly accurate on the German losses in terms of men – it claimed 2,473 dead and 490 wounded, while the final revised German figures are now known to have been 2,551 dead and 507 wounded. It also rightly named the *Seydlitz, Derfflinger, Markgraf* and *König* as being among the worst damaged of those German ships that survived. But there was little else in D15's fairly extensive report that could be described as accurate. Five of the other seven ships it named as being damaged in the battle had not been hit, with two of them not even taking part.[4]

When D15's report arrived in Whitehall, Krüger was still touring the German ports assiduously gathering information. He arrived in Rotterdam at the end of June and, over the next two days, sat in one of Tinsley's safe houses and compiled two reports on the damage to the High Seas Fleet. The first, sent on 27 June and received in the Admiralty the following day, began by citing Cumming's request for intelligence. 'In accordance with instructions received from you on 2 June, I went at once to Bremen, travelling from there to Danzig, Kiel, Rostock, Geestemünde, Emden, and to Sande near Wilhelmshaven, in order to ascertain the exact German losses in the North Sea action of 31 May,' Krüger said. What followed was an extraordinarily detailed report obtained, as ever, from conversations with naval officers and dockyard officials who believed him to be a loyal German citizen, one of their own. He occasionally got the precise location in which a ship was hit wrong, but he was accurate on the extent of the damage to all the various ships under repair. He also located all of them to the correct shipyards, as well as accurately identifying the location of the torpedo nets on some of the German ships as an indirect cause of the loss of the battle cruiser *Lützow*, one of the two largest and most powerful German warships, the other being its sister ship, the *Derfflinger*.

'I went to Sande, near Wilhelmshaven, as this latter place is closed to all traffic,' Krüger continued. 'Here I met men of the *Lützow* and learned that part of her torpedo nets had got entangled in the propellers, which was the cause of reducing speed, and eventually of her loss.' The *Lützow* filled with so much water that she had to be sunk by a German torpedo boat. The *Derfflinger* also suffered with the same problem and had to limp back to port trying not to let her loosened torpedo nets foul her propellers; as a result of these problems all anti-torpedo nets were subsequently removed from the German warships. The top of this first report is marked '100%' followed by Blinker Hall's initials, W.R.H. But it was Krüger's second report from the MI1c safe house, dispatched the following day, which must have been the most welcome in Admiralty, providing it with the intelligence it needed to make its case. It began badly, reporting accurately that the *Hindenburg*, one of the ships the British claimed to have sunk, had not even taken part in the battle. 'Contrary to the rumours that have been about, that the *Hindenburg* was lost in the action off Jutland, I can definitely report that this ship is not commissioned yet, but is being finished as quickly as possible,' Krüger said. But he continued with much better news. 'Having spoken to some naval officers about the action in the North Sea, they said that the German Fleet had only been saved from annihilation by the failing light and the mist. The impression in the Fleet is that this experiment will not be repeated.' This confirmed the arguments being made by the Admiralty that in relative and perhaps more importantly psychological terms, the German losses had been more damaging. The British Grand Fleet remained much larger than the High Seas Fleet, which would never again attempt to take on its British counterpart, leaving the Royal Navy free to enforce a key part of the economic blockade that helped to ensure Germany's eventual defeat.[5]

Naval movements were also reported by the North Hinder Lightship, based in the southern part of the North Sea, between the Thames estuary and Holland. The lightship reported the movement of all shipping without any identification of its nationality, but a small section within MI1c, Section XVI, which appears to have been experimenting with wireless communications with agents, arranged that the lightship's wireless operator would insert certain indicators into his messages when the ships were German.[6]

Krüger also reported on the increasing difficulties the German naval industry was having with labour problems as conditions deteriorated inside Germany. 'I spoke to an Engineer of the Weser Wharf, who told me that they were short of skilled labour, and that it was no pleasure to work the way they were working now,' he reported in April 1917. 'One day they have to stop work on a certain ship, and push ahead with another, whilst the position may be reversed again in a week, all according to orders from Headquarters.' A few weeks later, he was reporting on socialist-inspired unrest that had led to a number of strikes. Krüger also provided detailed plans of the mines and anti-submarine nets around Kiel harbour. The information was obtained during a number of long walks with a German officer, whom Krüger befriended, through the restricted area from which the routes of German ships entering the harbour could be observed.[7]

There were occasional lapses – a report from April 1917 said the Germans had 357 submarines, when in fact they had around 150 at this stage of the war. This might even be a simple typographical error by the translator, replacing a 1 with a 3, since Krüger correctly estimated the number put out of action as being fifty-three. Nevertheless, there is criticism of the 357 figure on the report and this may have been what led Krüger to flirt briefly with the French in the wake of this report before returning to the British four months later. Whatever the case, most of his reports were in fact accurate and are littered with praise from naval officers normally cynical of the value of intelligence, including the words 'our most reliable agent' scrawled in pencil across the top of one report from Kiel, Stettin and Hamburg, in November 1917.[8]

Krüger also reported from the Krupp factories at Essen and Kiel on a German supergun, developed from a naval gun, to allow the Germans to shell Paris. The Kaiser Wilhelm gun had a 92-foot barrel and a range of 80 miles, and was the first weapon capable of projecting a shell into the stratosphere. 'In Essen, my friend could give me no news of the new guns,' he reported in March 1918. 'He told me that only the oldest and most trustworthy workmen were working at them. They had all been sworn to secrecy and would tell nothing. I have repeatedly heard during the last weeks in Kiel from conversations between officers and from my friends that the new guns were exclusively manufactured for the navy. Firing practice has begun in the Strander Bucht and in the Flensburger Föhrde [north of Kiel].' Three days earlier the gun had hit a church in Paris, killing eighty-eight people, but its ability to cause damage was in fact limited and only 250 people died throughout the war as a result of its shelling.[9]

At the same time, Krüger reported further on the situation inside Germany.

> Just as before, for a lot of money, everything can be bought secretly, such as butter, fat, meat, flour etc. Illegal trade is in full operation. On 9 April, I was in the Eifel, in a few villages of the Katen area. In one day, I bought the following goods: 7 kilos of butter, six hams, about 300 eggs, and sausages of the best quality. A farmer even offered me 120 kilos of slaughtered pig, to be delivered to my house. My friends have the same experiences. Persons having sufficient means can now live as in peacetime. The farmers are very strictly watched, but they always find a way of hiding some of their products. Large quantities of potatoes are still in the hands of the farmers and people go to them to buy them. The police have received orders not to stop these poor people, as no disturbances must take place.'[10]

Krüger also provided valuable feedback on the effects the British air raids were having on the German population. 'I was in Cologne during the air raid the day before Whitsunday,' he wrote in May 1918. 'The effect of the raid was frightful. The number of those killed (forty-five) given in the papers is generally contested in Cologne, for the authorities have not included in that number the casualties caused by anti-aircraft gunfire and falling houses.' The real number of dead was more than 100, Krüger said. Following a subsequent British raid on the city, in August 1918, 'the destruction was great and the streets were closed for several days'. Meanwhile, Krüger said, labour unrest was spreading. 'In Westfalia, the miners are on strike. About forty pits are idle. In Oberhausen, on 2 August, I saw considerable damage to houses, done by the miners. The newspapers are silent.'[11]

By October, Krüger was reporting widespread mutiny among the German troops.

Already on my return from Rotterdam at the end of September, things were pretty unsettled in the Rhine district. At the victualling stations in Rheydt, Düsseldorf, Mehlem etc. the troop transports refused to proceed to the front. This was in particular Bavarian and other south German troops, who commenced to mutiny already in Bingerbrück. Several companies of infantry with machine guns from the neighbouring garrisons were posted at the victualling stations in order to arrive on the troops by force, but without success. The troops were then sent back as prisoners. Such occurrences take place every day as I heard. Before everything else the principal reason is the bad and insufficient feeding of the troops and, since the new offensive, the hopelessness of the German fighting. Large bodies of soldiers indulge in plundering in their own country. Three-quarters of all the thefts are perpetrated by soldiers. The railway trains all carry military patrols to arrest the deserters who stream along continuously.

With the end of the war in sight, opposition to the regime was becoming more open, Krüger said. 'In consequence of the democratisation, the spirits of the people are good and they speak very openly and demand the dismissal of the militarists.' He continued reporting even after the armistice, noting that German troops were returning from the front in disorder, with government officials blaming the new workers' and soldiers' councils set up as part of a left-wing backlash that looked to replicate the Russian revolution. 'I read his reports from time to time and marvelled at them,' said Henry Landau. 'He was paid huge sums, far in excess of any of our other agents. In my opinion, he was undoubtedly by far the most valuable agent the allies ever had working in Germany.'[12]

Krüger was certainly Richard Tinsley's most effective agent collecting naval intelligence but he was not the only one. Shortly before the outbreak of war, Cumming had arranged with the London representative of the shipbrokers William H. Müller & Co., ironically a Dutch company founded by a German, to have agents placed at six points along the Dutch coast to report on German warship movements. Tinsley also had a number of Belgian agents reporting on ship movements, although by early 1918 these were deemed by the Admiralty to be either grossly inaccurate or of little or no value. One naval assessor, apparently unaware of the difficulty of getting the reports out of Belgium, complained that those which might have been accurate were not received in time to be of use:

> In many cases the movements referred to had taken place a fortnight before the report was received in this section, and occasionally considerably more. The attached list should be enough to damn any agent, even if he sometimes sent in reports that were of use, and T Rotterdam can scarcely be accused of doing that. It is suggested that the services of T Rotterdam might well be dispensed with.

Needless to say, the intelligence Tinsley provided across the board put him in an unassailable position that was unlikely to be jeopardised by the erratic nature of the naval reporting coming out of Belgium, although it was not the only criticism Tinsley received as a result of his attempts to obtain intelligence on the High Seas Fleet. The most controversial source of intelligence collection was alleged to be a blackmail operation in which Tinsley kept a 'black book' containing the names of those shipping companies operating out of Rotterdam that were breaching the British embargo, using it to twist their arms into providing intelligence and allowing Tinsley to infiltrate his agents into Germany as their representatives. Certainly, there is evidence of Tinsley removing companies from the 'black book' in return for intelligence on German agents coming to the UK. Allegations that Tinsley demanded financial payments from those listed in his book in return for allowing their continued passage through the blockade, under pretence of taking their cargoes to Denmark, Norway or Sweden, were never proven, but were certainly credible and he is said to have ended the war £200,000 richer.[13]

Claims of British officials turning a blind eye to shipping companies finding ways around the blockade also bedevilled Cumming's naval intelligence operations in Denmark, albeit in a markedly different way. The Danish operations came under the overall control of Frank Noel Stagg. He joined the Royal Navy at the turn of the century, qualifying across the board, in seamanship, navigation, pilotage, gunnery, surveying and torpedoes, with excellent reports. He was sent to Copenhagen University in 1910 to learn Danish, and on his return the following year gained language qualifications in Dutch, Norwegian and Swedish. When war broke out, he was on board a minesweeper in the Humber but as a result of his language qualifications was swiftly called in by the Naval Intelligence Division and in October 1914 attached to Cumming. Stagg's obvious skills in Scandinavian languages led to his being sent to Copenhagen to run Walter Christmas and a number of other agents together with Major Richard Carlyle Holme, a Royal Garrison Artillery major who spoke Norwegian and Danish. Early in 1915, Stagg made a tour of the Netherlands, Denmark and Sweden during which he persuaded key personnel in the postal authorities in each country to send 'important business mail' that was destined for Germany 'by mistake' to England, where it was rapidly 'dealt with' before being sent on to Germany. Stagg was also tasked to monitor trade between Scandinavia and Germany as part of the efforts to reinforce the Royal Navy's blockade, which was designed to prevent anything useful to the war effort, including imported foodstuffs, getting through to the German ports. He travelled widely between Denmark, Norway and Sweden, leaving most of the day-to-day work in Copenhagen to Holme.

At some point, Holme's wife Louise, a Norwegian and therefore more able to blend into the local community, was asked to undertake a special mission to the Jutland coast where items from a sunken ship were reportedly washed up on the shore. The use of the wives of local service representatives abroad to mount surreptitious missions was to become a regular occurrence which continued into the Cold War. Louise Holme is said to have recovered some documents which were dispatched to

London and resulted in Cumming buying her a diamond ring, although family tradition has it that the ring was given to her on the orders of the then First Lord of the Admiralty, Winston Churchill. Given the latter's deep interest in intelligence, this seems entirely possible.

By the middle of 1915, there were just half a dozen agents in Denmark attempting to gather intelligence from inside Germany, and Cumming's budget in Denmark was £860, of which £120 was provided by the French in exchange for the intelligence Stagg and Holme produced. They used the herdsmen who regularly drove cattle across the border into Germany as couriers for the representatives of Danish companies based in Germany who were collecting intelligence for Cumming. One of the most inventive of the schemes run from Denmark was the 'Nemesis' sabotage ring, encouraging left-wing activists who aimed to overthrow the Kaiser and set up a socialist republic to carry out bombing attacks on railway lines and weapons factories. The Foreign Office was furious to hear of plans to stockpile explosives for Nemesis in Denmark, with Ronald Campbell laying down the law that no explosives were to be stored in neutral countries, while the German legation – having learned of Stagg's schemes – was trying to get the Danish authorities to expel him. None of this will have put him in the good books of the British minister in Copenhagen, Sir Henry Lowther. Stagg was pulled out of Denmark and brought back to London in September 1915 to take overall control not just of Scandinavia – and Nemesis – but also liaison with the naval intelligence department, the Baltic and Russia. The last, Stagg recalled, was 'quite a big proposition as the German bags on the Siberian mail train were being extracted and opened and yielded much useful stuff which was dealt with in the Board of Education.'[14]

Despite this extra responsibility, Stagg's main focus of operations during the second half of 1915 was reporting on the effectiveness of the blockade, amid anger in Westminster over the way material was bypassing it via Scandinavia. Christmas had rejoined the Royal Danish Navy on the outbreak of war and was feeding the British reports from the official Danish ship-watching posts, which included details of every ship whether part of the High Seas Fleet or a merchant ship breaching the blockade. Following the row with the German minister, Stagg travelled on an American passport, spending a lot of time in Copenhagen and Christiania, as the Norwegian capital was then called, monitoring the situation. He was assisted in no small part by the Danish navy's own data supplied by Christmas. This suggested Britain's legation in Copenhagen, and the commercial attaché, Richard Turner, in particular, were turning a blind eye to widespread breaches of the blockade by Danish and Swedish shipping companies. Turner had served before the war as a consular official in Leipzig. Stagg discovered, in late 1915, that Turner had forced Robert Erskine, a vice-consul in Denmark, to issue an illegal certificate of non-enemy origin for ermine furs exported from Leipzig to America via Denmark and the UK. The furs had been seized by customs on arrival in Britain and the American company's UK manager, William Goodsir, arrested and prosecuted for 'trading with the enemy'. Stagg wrote a letter to a friend in the Foreign Office, enclosing a newspaper report of the case, and pleading with him to get someone to ask Erskine why he had signed a certificate of non-enemy origin when the furs clearly came from Germany:

I cannot insist too strongly on the absolute vital necessity of dealing with this. I tell you honestly and earnestly that, if you will only take this matter up, you will be doing a most enormous service, not only to our poor old country, but to your much maligned friend Erskine. Turner is a perfect danger to our country and the sooner he is cleared out of it the better. In Bergen, one consul and two vice-consuls were full of his iniquities and the fact that he was nullifying all efforts at restriction of enemy supplies in Norway by whitewashing Danish firms which were known to be as black as black could be. I hear the same story here in Christiania and I tell you plainly everyone is spitting blood about him. Stuff is pouring through Denmark under the noses of Lowther and Turner. Now please don't waste a minute, Turner is, I am convinced, a national danger. I am going to work quietly in Copenhagen to find out what Turner has been doing. There appears to be an awful mess down there.

Stagg warned his friend not to divulge the source of the information but, unable to get anyone to deal with the issue, the friend showed the letter to Sir Eyre Crowe, the powerful head of the Foreign Office Contraband Department. The immediate Foreign Office response was to close ranks, with Crowe accusing Stagg of 'gross charges against the honour and integrity of our whole delegation at Copenhagen'. Turner angrily denied doing anything wrong, claiming that as a result of his time in Leipzig he had known that 'the exporter was an American and there was no German capital in the concern'. Meanwhile, Stagg testified before a cabinet committee that material was pouring through the blockade in both directions via Copenhagen. Although Turner's name was never mentioned in this testimony, he took it as a personal attack. The Foreign Office demanded an explanation from the Admiralty but feeling itself bound by the confidential way in which it had obtained the original letter from Stagg, failed to mention it. As a result, both Stagg and the Admiralty were left under the impression that the complaints were over his testimony to the committee and he was asked to write a letter explaining that he had not accused Turner of anything. The result was unlikely to mollify either the Foreign Office or Turner himself.

'I understand that charges affecting the personal integrity of Mr Turner are said to have been made by me before a Sub-Committee of the War Trade Advisory Committee,' Stagg wrote. 'I wish to emphatically deny that I then made or now make any such charges against Mr Turner's personal honour. The statement I did make was that there was a lamentable lack of British control over imports into and exports from Denmark and the only manner in which Mr Turner could be affected by this charge is as a part of the system that fails to exercise the control which is necessary in the interests of the British Empire. I was only induced to make this statement, owing to the fact that in my opinion this absence of control is prejudicial to the satisfactory conduct of the war and has probably already cost the forces of Allies many thousands of lives.'

Oddly, given that they had never disclosed the existence of the original letter, the Foreign Office took issue with this because it did not address the specific allegations on the furs exported from Leipzig, although they could not of course say this to the Admiralty or to Stagg. Crowe set up an inquiry under a senior barrister, but given that Stagg could not be allowed to know they had the original letter, the barrister confessed he could get nothing relevant out of him. The Foreign Office took this to mean that there was no evidence against Turner, who must therefore be absolved of any blame, while Stagg was, by contrast, damned for 'his wild attacks about the efficiency and integrity of the Copenhagen legation'. Given the previous trouble Stagg's operations had caused him, Lowther was no doubt very happy to stick the knife in. His laconic response was that 'if Lieutenant-Commander Stagg's present performance is a fair sample of secret agent work, that only strengthens the conviction I have long ago held that Admiralty receive many statements on the subject of contraband trade which cannot be substantiated as well as some which have no foundation in fact.' Lord Cecil, a junior foreign minister, demanded that Stagg's 'employment in Scandinavia should cease'. The Admiralty agreed only that he should not return to Denmark, issuing their orders on Christmas Day, Stagg's birthday. Privately, they backed their man and merely accepted the fait accompli, since Cumming had already removed all his people from Denmark, at the insistence of the Foreign Office. To make matters worse, Christmas was betrayed by one of the prostitute couriers, and was forced to resign from the Danish navy, citing ill health, and in November 1915, both he and Richard Holme were brought back to London. Cumming records in his diary that Christmas stayed initially at the St Ermin's hotel, which was to have a long history of use by the British secret service, and that on 26 November 1915 Christmas and Holme dined with Cumming and Stagg at the Royal Automobile Club, of which Cumming was a prominent member. The identity of the three ladies who joined them is not divulged.[15]

No-one seems to have been the slightest bit concerned during all this that Goodsir had been sent to prison for a transaction which, according to the Foreign Office, was completely legal. Nor is there any evidence that Crowe, Lowther or Turner were in any way embarrassed when, a few months later, the Treasury sent the Foreign Office an affidavit sworn by Stagg, which the British government intended to use to justify the confiscation of a number of Swedish and Danish freighters. Making full use of the Danish navy intelligence supplied by Christmas, it extensively detailed the way in which Swedish and Danish shipping lines were making a fortune breaching the blockade via Malmö, Trelleborg, Gothenburg, Karlskrona, Stockholm and, in particular, Copenhagen.

'The direct sailings from Copenhagen to German ports during the first six months of 1915 averaged two per diem,' Stagg said. 'In addition to the German vessels *Lübeck* and *Walter Leonhardt* and those of the Hugo Stinnes Line, and the very large German lighter *Reichsanzeiger*, the following vessels have been observed among others regularly engaged in this traffic, namely: (Swedish) *Najadén*, *Nassau*, *Halland*, *Svanen* and (Danish) *Bogo* belonging to the United Shipping Company. This company's SS *Ydrun* also ran a weekly service during the greater part of 1914/15, doing a round trip from Copenhagen to Gothenburg, Gothenburg to Stettin, and Stettin back to Copenhagen, and until recently their lighters plied regularly between Copenhagen and other Scandinavian ports and Germany.'[16]

Stagg and Holme travelled frequently to Norway and Sweden to oversee operations there. Stagg travelled under a fake American passport, spending most of his time in the Norwegian capital, Christiania, from where he took charge of operations and agents throughout Scandinavia. These included nine agents in Sweden run originally by Cumming's man in Stockholm, William Savage, a British businessman who was living there when war broke out and was originally recruited by the legation to monitor the local press, before being taken over by Cumming. But by mid-1916, the intelligence produced was such that Cumming appointed Captain Rolf Berner, an army officer whose family were Swedish, as his Stockholm bureau chief under cover of passport control officer. Clifford Sharp, editor of the *New Statesman*, who had close pre-war links with German socialists that continued during the war, was called up in 1916, and also sent to Stockholm as an MI1c officer under a 'natural' journalistic cover, writing as a special correspondent for *The Times*, with a brief to use his contacts within the German and Swedish socialist parties to gather intelligence and encourage anti-war feeling inside Germany.

Stagg's liaison with the Norwegians, particularly the police and the navy, was extremely productive. He not only had the ship-watching network set up by Walter and Edward Archer, he had access to reports from the Norwegian navy's own coastal observation stations, ensuring that no German ship passed along the Norwegian coast without Cumming being able to report its movements to the Admiralty. Peter Tennant, who worked with Stagg in the Special Operations Executive in Scandinavia during the Second World War, recalled that he had been 'deeply involved in subversive activity' across Scandinavia during the First World War. 'One of his more amusing exploits was to have tins of Norwegian sardines filled with croton oil' – a very small amount of which is a very effective laxative – shipped to the Germans 'with dire results for their troops at a critical moment of the war'.[17]

One of Stagg's greatest coups – although he modestly attributed it to 'the Chief' – came with the arrest in January 1917 of Baron Otto Karl von Rosen, a German officer who was attempting to disrupt British horse- and reindeer-drawn sleighs taking supplies to Russia. The baron was stopped by Norwegian police at Karasjok, close to the border with Sweden, after a tip-off from Stagg to his close personal friend Redvald Larsen, a senior Norwegian detective. 'That good friend of Britain told me he would always help in any way he could without letting down his superiors if we passed word on to him,' Stagg said. 'Savage in Stockholm then heard of the journey of Baron von Rosen and two German agents "on a scientific visit to the Lapps" via Narvik. Redvald Larsen was informed and, before they crossed the Norwegian frontier, had them searched. The rest is history.'

The baron's luggage included a number of bombs, poisons and nineteen sugar lumps that were to be fed to the horses and reindeer and contained tiny glass phials of anthrax. Among the material found by the Norwegian police were tins of 'Swedish beef', which in fact contained high explosive; bottles of curare poison labelled as mouthwash; and cans of table salt which also contained explosive. When one official suggested von Rosen cook himself some of the 'Swedish beef', he was forced to come clean about the real contents of the tins. The Germans' luggage also included so-called 'pencil bombs', pencils in which the lead was replaced by a thin glass tube which, when sharpened, released acid onto other chemicals causing an explosion.[18]

The forced decision to pull out of Denmark left the naval attaché Captain Charles Dix running Cumming's large number of agents – the D designators indicating agents controlled from Copenhagen ran to at least D104 – resulting in a number of poor results of which D15's Jutland report was by no means the worst. In the spring of 1916, there was a brief discussion of whether John Wallinger could run the agents in Denmark, but Cumming remained concerned it might lead to trouble with Sir Henry Lowther and the plan was dropped. Instead, Cumming appointed the Royal Naval Reserve officer Lieutenant-Commander Charles Hudson as Copenhagen bureau chief, again with the cover of passport control officer, with Lieutenant-Commander Hastings Taylor, RNVR, briefly taking up the same role in Christiania before being replaced by Major Kenneth Lawrance, Royal Marines.

The Foreign Office vendetta against Stagg over his investigations into the breaches of the blockade continued, with Lord Hardinge, the permanent under-secretary at the Foreign Office, insisting at the end of 1916 that he be reprimanded 'severely'. Cumming noted in his diary that he did not think this 'quite satisfactory as if explanation is correct, minister is wrong'. Eventually, in July 1917, his position untenable, Stagg left MI1c and went back to the Navy, taking command of HMS *Grayfly*, a river gunboat operating against the Turks in Mesopotamia.[19]

'COME on, Tucker. You can do it, old man.'

Charles Tucker, deputy chief of the British secret service in Greece, struggled up the mountain, dragging yards behind as Whittall and the six Greek agents strode on. Hugh Whittall, in his mid-forties but still with the looks of a Hollywood film star and an athleticism to match, stopped the party and waited.

They'd force-marched nearly 20 miles over the mountains of Andros in the hunt for the renegade policemen, traversing the island at its longest point, from the port of Andros in the south-east to Gavrio in the north-west. It wasn't surprising that Tucker was struggling to keep up. His kindest friends would not describe him as anything less than portly. He was noticeably thinner now than when they started. Both Tucker and Whittall had grown up in the Middle East, part of the big British expatriate community in Turkey. Exiled by the war, they were part of AEGIS, the Aegean Intelligence Service, set up in the Greek islands by the novelist Compton Mackenzie as part of the region's extensive British secret service network.

The mission that brought them to Andros was to track down royalist police chiefs from the neighbouring island of Tenos. The fugitives had absconded with 30,000 drachmas of public money and were hiding out in the Monastery of the Fountain of Life, in the mountains just above the fishing village of Gavrio. The high white walls and towers of the fourteenth-century monastery were only a few hundred yards away. The route march was almost over, but Tucker needed to catch his breath. As they sat waiting for him, taking in the sweet scent of warm pine, the agents wanted to know what Whittall was planning to do once they got there.

'What do you think we'll do?' Whittall grinned. 'We'll knock on the door, of course. We're travellers seeking refuge for the night. It's late at night and this is a monastery. They can't turn us away. Come on, Tucker. It's not far now, quarter of a mile at most.'

Once they reached the monastery, Whittall strode up to the wooden door and grabbed the rope of the large bell, pulling down on it repeatedly. At first, there was no response, but eventually they heard the sound of sandals shuffling across flagstones and a monk opened a little grill to ask who dared disturb them at this hour.

'We're weary travellers seeking refuge for the night,' Whittall said.

Disbelieving and anxious to get a better view of the strangers, the monk drew the bolts and opened the door slightly, struggling to get his lantern to shine on *their faces. Whittall threw his weight against the door, sending the monk tumbling backwards over the flagstones and into a flower bed. Whittall and Tucker and their six agents barged past him, pistols drawn, into the refectory, where the police officers were sat with the abbot tucking into a large pie.*

'What have you done with the money?' Whittall asked the police chief, who opened his arms out, insisting he knew nothing of any missing money.

'You've grown very fat since you started eating that pie,' Whittall replied, whipping out a hunting knife and slashing the police chief's shirt to unleash a hoard of gold and silver coins that tumbled out on the floor. The MI1c men arrested the police chiefs and took them back to Tenos before returning to Mackenzie's base on Syra, where they sat counting up the loot, feeling for all the world like pirates rummaging through a treasure chest.

'The variety of the coins was fantastic,' Mackenzie said. 'The history of the Aegean for the last 200 years could be read in their images and superscriptions. There were even golden louis d'ors and Venetian ducats of the early eighteenth century.'

EIGHT

Englishmen in New York

FOR the first year of the war, Cumming had no officers based in America. Intelligence operations there were controlled by Blinker Hall through the British naval attaché, Captain R. Guy Gaunt. But in August 1915, the British authorities in Falmouth detained James Archibald, a US journalist who was acting as a courier for the German military attaché, Captain Franz von Papen. The documents confirmed evidence from the interception of secret telegrams that Germany was involved in espionage, sabotage and sedition in the United States from offices on the twenty-fifth floor of 60 Wall St, Manhattan. They also implicated Constantin Dumba, the Austrian ambassador to the US, in efforts to sabotage arms and munitions supplies to the British. This evidence was supplemented by information obtained from Captain Franz von Rintelen, a German agent brought in to set up the sabotage operations. Von Rintelen had been arrested by the British two weeks earlier while on transit through Falmouth for the Netherlands. As a result of the revelations of his 'illegal and questionable acts', von Papen was expelled – suffering the ignominy of having his own papers seized as his ship stopped off in Falmouth. He left his assistant Wolf von Igel in charge of German espionage and sabotage operations in the US. Cumming set about creating a team to counter them.[1]

Cumming recruited Guy Standing, a 42-year-old actor, to man a new American desk at his Whitehall Court headquarters. Standing, who had just been signed up by a leading US film studio when war broke out, knew America well. An accomplished yachtsman, he broke off from his film contract and returned to the UK in August 1914 to join the Royal Navy's motor boat reserve, but after being wounded in action, he was sent off to work for Cumming. A few days before recruiting Standing, Cumming had taken on a 32-year-old subaltern in the Duke of Cornwall's Light Infantry, whose eyesight had been damaged by a German gas attack during the first Battle of Ypres. Sir William Wiseman, whose family baronetcy dated back to 1628, had been a reporter on the *Daily Express* before going into banking, working for the Hendens Trust in North America and Mexico, and eventually becoming the company's chairman. Cumming took him on initially for 'general work', but a few weeks later Wiseman was sent to New York to set up a bureau in the British consulate at 44 Whitehall Street, Manhattan, with a brief to concentrate on counter-espionage, counter-sabotage, and watching Irish republicans and Indian seditionists. The cover was as the US transport department of the British Ministry of Munitions.[2]

One of the first agents Wiseman recruited was Manuel del Campo, a Mexican diplomat he had known since his time in Mexico before the war. Del Campo's assistance was important because Germany was trying to stir trouble with Mexico to divert US attention away from the war in Europe. Wiseman paid del Campo \$350 a month, around \$5,000 at today's prices. He recommended another of his British friends to be deputy bureau chief. Major Norman Thwaites, also a former journalist, had worked for Joseph Pulitzer at the US newspaper *The World*. Well known in New York high society, Thwaites joined the Royal Irish Dragoon Guards on the outbreak of war, but was shot through the jaw and the throat at Messines and invalided home, where he was recruited by Wiseman. His extensive connections in the US were to prove invaluable. Thwaites arrived in New York in January 1916 and began setting up the counter-espionage and counter-sabotage service, watching German attempts to disrupt Britain's war effort, while Wiseman concentrated on 'political matters'. They had also been told by Cumming to be on the lookout for expatriate Belgians who might be prepared to return home as British spies. Their arrival put Gaunt's nose considerably out of joint. The Australian-born naval attaché continued to see himself as the head of British intelligence in the US, trying everything he could to prevent his replacement, without success, and continuing long after the war to claim that he had been Wiseman's boss. When Cumming appointed Lieutenant Henry Fitzroy RN as military control officer (MCO) in New York in July 1916, to provide visas to anyone coming to Britain via the US, an attempt to weed out German spies, Gaunt tried to insist Fitzroy came under his control, again without success. Fitzroy was one of a dozen MCOs sent to various capitals with a brief to report intelligence to Cumming, but responsible to Vernon Kell and MI5 for the visas he issued. He received lists of outbound travellers, both to Europe and South America, from all the local shipping companies, but his 'unfortunate manner' made him highly unpopular and he was eventually recalled, leaving the military control function to Wiseman and Thwaites.[3]

Wiseman and Thwaites took a relaxed view of Gaunt's position, gradually edging him aside rather than confronting him head on. Their position was enhanced almost immediately by a remarkable success by Thwaites. Von Rintelen spent his time in America trying to stop the US exporting arms and munitions to the British. A key part of his mission had been to provoke a rebellion in Mexico on the basis that the US military would intervene and would then need all the arms and munitions it could get, so preventing supplies being sent to Britain. While he failed to achieve this aim, he was more successful with a secondary effort, the sabotage of transatlantic arms supplies. Provided by his bosses in Germany with unlimited amounts of money, he set up a bomb factory producing incendiary devices, including pencil bombs, and recruited Irish dockworkers to hide the bombs in the holds of ships bound for Britain. Von Rintelen said later:

Our dockers only put the detonators in the holds which contained no munitions, for we had no intention of blowing up the ship from neutral territory. When the ship caught fire on the open sea the captain naturally had the munition hold flooded to eliminate the most serious danger. None of the ships reached its port of destination, and most of them sank after the crew had been taken off by other vessels. In every case the explosives were flooded and rendered useless.[4]

A few months after Thwaites arrived in New York, the consulate received a 'mysterious' telephone call from the port of Hoboken, across the Hudson River from Manhattan, where many of the dockworkers were of German or Irish descent. Thwaites recalled:

A voice indicating some agitation stated that if a British official would come to the Kaiserhof Hotel in Hoboken at once and ask for a Mr Witte, he would receive valuable information of German activities against the British. The voice suggested that an official who spoke German should be sent, and that, furthermore, he should bring $2,000. As the only British official who spoke German, Gaunt asked me to go to Hoboken. 'You had better take a gun with you,' he said.

The informant was eventually persuaded to come across the Hudson to the relative safety of Manhattan, bringing with him an incendiary device produced by a chemical factory run by Dr Walter Scheele, an expatriate German chemist who had taken US citizenship. The incendiary devices had been responsible for the destruction or partial destruction of thirty-six ships during the first fifteen months of the war, Thwaites said. 'My young friend Witte, reluctant at first, warmed up as the story proceeded. He named Germans, German-Americans and nondescripts. He described laboratories and he named ships. In short, he delivered the goods.'

Thwaites had an extremely good relationship with Captain Thomas J. Tunney, the head of the New York bomb squad. Tunney was of Irish Protestant extraction, with a brother in the Royal Irish Constabulary, and therefore sympathetic to the British cause. The police swiftly rounded up eight of the main suspects in the 'ship bombs plot'. Scheele escaped briefly to Cuba, but was later brought back to face jail. They also raided von Igel's Wall Street offices, seizing large numbers of papers detailing the various German plans and plots, including those involving German-funded IRA attacks, and a plan to use Indian dissidents to provoke insurrection in India.[5]

In order to counter the plans for revolution in India, the British had already sent their most accomplished Indian secret service expert to

America to work alongside Wiseman and Thwaites. Sir Robert Nathan was a former chief commissioner of Dacca who had retired in 1914 due to ill health and returned to the UK, but was now working for both MI5 and the India Office. Nathan had already been involved in breaking up German-backed Indian networks in Europe, in particular Switzerland. He and John Wallinger had infiltrated and broken up an anarchist plot to kill a number of Allied leaders, including the British War Secretary, Lord Kitchener, the Foreign Secretary, Lord Grey, King Victor Emmanuel III of Italy and French President Raymond Poincaré. But the US, and particularly the west coast, was now one of the main centres of Indian sedition. Nathan arrived in March 1916 and swiftly began investigating the Indian revolutionary networks. Given he was well known to the Indian seditionists as a 'master plot breaker', he operated under the pseudonym of Napier, or simply N.[6]

Thwaites's contacts in the journalistic world allowed him to generate a considerable amount of useful propaganda for the British, but he insisted that one of the most effective stories concerned the German ambassador in Washington, Count Johann von Bernstorff, and the wife of a wealthy US businessman, a former singer called Celeste White. 'There was much gossip at this time about Count von Bernstorff and a lovely lady,' Thwaites said. 'It was alleged that Mrs Black, as we will call her, was aiding and abetting the enemy. Among my various assignments was the instruction to investigate this pretty lady.'

Thwaites met with little success until, at a dinner party given by a prominent New York socialite, one of his fellow guests produced photographs of von Bernstorff taken at the Whites' summer lodge in the Adirondack mountains, where Mrs White was said to entertain 'Bohemian friends' and behave like a latter-day Cleopatra.

> The gallant Ambassador figured largely and intimately. Apparently the members of the house-party were bent on a return to nature. Among the pictures were several of the ambassador posing upon the springboard, an arm about a lovely companion. Yet another showed the German plenipotentiary in more generous mood, with both arms

encompassing the waists of bathing nymphs in ravishing, if strictly rationed, costume. As I leaned over the table, engrossed, as we all were, I felt slipped beneath my hand what was obviously one of the snapshots. A little later copies of an illustrated paper arrived in New York, with a whole page illustration prominently displayed showing: 'A representative of one of the Central Powers who, in spite of the anxieties of office, finds time for relaxations' – or words to that effect. As a piece of anti-enemy propaganda, I have no hesitation in saying that this incident was more effective than pages of editorial matter the British were alleged to inspire.[7]

The German agents persistently attempted to wrongfoot their British counterparts, with Thwaites recalling how Paul König, one of the more aggressive of the German spymasters, tried to bribe his batman into providing him with a list of Cumming's men in America. The batman reported the approach immediately and took part in a sting operation which led to König's arrest and the seizure of documents detailing the agent network he was running from the Broadway offices of the Hamburg-American shipping line.

'But before that event, we had some fun,' Thwaites recalled. König's batman did indeed provide a list of British secret service officers in the US.

We sought to please. Lists were made out of the rascally British officers; a formidable list, of those belonging to Britain's 'vast' organisation. It consisted of that little band of British subjects who behind their hands whispered that they hated to be away from the firing line, but that they had been appointed to the British secret service. We accommodated them and also added the name of a German official in the consul-general's office, a poisonous fellow altogether too curious about our affairs. This caused great consternation in the enemy camp.[8]

Not all the confrontations between the British and the German agents attempting to disrupt US supplies to the UK were so humorous. Once

America entered the war, the activities of some of the German agents became ever more deadly, and even involved sending bacteriological bombs across to America to be placed in cargoes of grain. Many of the British agents recruited by Thwaites to track down the ship bombers were American private detectives, overseen by John Gillan, an Irish-born member of the Metropolitan Police Special Branch loaned to Cumming. They also kept a close watch on German ships trying to break through the Royal Navy blockade carrying supplies purchased in the US. One former officer revealed:

> Persons in the employ of the British intelligence service were stationed at every port on the Atlantic coast of the United States. In consequence no movement of any enemy ship could take place without almost instant notification to British headquarters. Many of the people who kept watch and ward at these ports were humble individuals who performed a very dangerous duty from purely patriotic motives. The writer has in mind one person who was responsible for observing enemy shipping at a port not a hundred miles from New York. Although a working man, his dispatches and memoranda sent to headquarters were standard examples of terse English, reflecting the keenest powers of observation. For two and a half years, he performed his duties admirably, though in constant danger from the machinations of the central European agents, who swarmed in the eastern states. Then one morning, his body was found floating in the dock, riddled with bullets. There can be no question that this man died for his country just as heroically as any of our uniformed soldiers who fell at the front.[9]

By October 1916, there were eight members of staff in the MI1c bureau at 44 Whitehall Street. They included Gillan; Captain William Boshell, who had been born in Colombia and occasionally went into Latin America on espionage missions; Lieutenant Tom Furness, who had the by now standard MI1c cover of an officer in the RNVR; and Frank Blyth Kirby, a former British consul in Russia, who was cultivating influential members of the city's Russian community. There were also occasional visitors from London conducting their own intelligence operations, albeit informing Wiseman of what they were doing, a practice that seems to have been common throughout the Service's history. The actor and playwright Harley Granville-Barker took time off from minding the Service's records in early 1917 to stage a play off Broadway and make a speaking tour of America. He wrote to Wiseman in November 1916 giving him the dates of his thirty-venue lecture tour. 'C thinks it may be useful to you to have as soon as possible this preliminary list of my travels,' Granville-Barker wrote. His brief was to use the tour to gauge the strength of feeling across the country in support of Britain or Germany and of the US joining the war on Britain's side.[10]

Undoubtedly, Wiseman's best contact was a US official he met in December 1916. The British ambassador, Sir Cecil Spring-Rice, who was close to a number of prominent Republicans, had a poor relationship with Democrat President Woodrow Wilson and used Guy Gaunt as a liaison with Colonel Edward Mandell House, the president's closest aide. In December 1916, with Gaunt away on leave, Spring-Rice sent Wiseman to House's Manhattan apartment to discuss a confidential issue with House. The two men hit it off immediately, with House noting in his diary that Wiseman was 'the most important caller I have had in some time' and describing Wiseman as 'a kindred spirit'. The two men had a series of meetings during which they developed a relationship of trust, leading Wiseman to reveal to House 'in the gravest confidence' that he had his own direct line to Whitehall. House noted in his diary: 'I am happy beyond measure with this last conference with him, for I judge he reflects the views of his government.' From then on, he determined that Wiseman should be used as the main US conduit to the British government, sidelining Spring-Rice. It has been suggested that this also sidelined Cumming, but there is no evidence to back this up. Wiseman immediately wrote to Cumming alerting him to the fact that he was taking 'a more active interest in politics' than he would ordinarily have considered his duty 'because the ambassador and his staff have practically all their friends in the Republican Party', as a result of which Wilson regarded British officials as 'Republican partisans'. Wiseman also passed on to the Foreign Office 'through my chief in London certain information and suggestions which Colonel House thought they ought to have'.

The majority of Wiseman's messages back to London went through the CX channels, with serial numbers beginning CXP, the P denoting politics. It was, like the conversations with Bulgarian and Turkish officials in Switzerland, an early example of what would become known within the Service as 'parallel diplomacy'. The close relationship between MI1c and the US administration was further enhanced by the friendship between Thwaites and Frank Polk, the head of the State Department intelligence service, whose assistant, Gordon Auchinloss, another important contact for both Wiseman and Thwaites, was House's son-in-law. Wiseman briefed Polk on the true nature of his US role in mid-February 1917, setting up an informal intelligence exchange and passing on details of German submarine positions to assist the US merchant ships.[11]

The bellicose attitude of Spring-Rice did not chime with the general mood of Wilson's administration, which, while it recognised the reality of German aggression, and the likelihood that it would eventually be forced to act, had come to power on an anti-war ticket and had striven to find a peaceful solution. Wilson could not be seen to be pushed into war by the British, nor would he have wanted to be, something Wiseman appears to have understood far better than Spring-Rice and managed to make clear to London. When Germany announced at the beginning of February that it was going to use its submarines to sink any vessels helping the Allies, Wilson waited. When a German submarine sank a US cargo ship off the Scilly Islands three days later, the US broke off diplomatic relations with Germany but accepted that because the crew were taken off and made safe before the ship was torpedoed there had been no overt act of war. Nevertheless, the administration began preparing for war.

The US entry into the war was now inevitable. What it needed to go to war was some overt act by the Germans, which the US public would feel threatened US integrity. This was provided by the British in the form of a timely telegram, deciphered by Blinker Hall's Room 40 codebreakers, in which the German Foreign Secretary, Arthur Zimmermann, told the German ambassador to Mexico that if war broke out with the US, he was to offer the Mexicans an alliance and promise them the return of land lost to America in Texas, New Mexico and Arizona. The British passed this to Wilson via the US ambassador in London and the anger it caused contributed to the US decision to declare war, adding to the picture Wiseman had painted, through House, of German spies exploiting America's neutrality. Asking Congress to declare war, Wilson accused Germany of having 'filled our unsuspecting communities and even our offices of government with spies'. On 6 April 1917, Congress duly declared war on Germany. Three weeks later, House told the British Foreign Secretary, Arthur Balfour, that Spring-Rice no longer had access to the President and that all really important messages would be sent through Wiseman.[12]

Robert Nathan's investigations into US-based Indian seditionists had come to a head a few weeks before the US entered the war, on 6 March 1917, when Captain Tunney arrested Chandra Kanta Chakravarti, who was in charge of the US-based operations of 'the Berlin Committee', a German-backed Indian revolutionary group. The federal authorities had been reluctant to act against the Indian seditionists, but Nathan and Wiseman bypassed this inconvenient problem by giving Tunney details of a German bomber they were tracking in return for the arrest of Chakravarti and his German contact, Ernest Sekunna. The extent of the British involvement is demonstrated by the presence of Thwaites and Nathan during the interrogation of Chakravarti and Sekunna. The two British spies sat hidden behind a screen, with Nathan prompting Tunney with occasional notes.

Chakravarti, described as a 'thin-faced, falsetto-voiced' Bengali, was 'glib but evasive', Thwaites recalled.

On the other side of the screen we listened. Now and then, Nathan would write a note on a scrap of paper which would be passed in to Tunney. These hints would indicate the line of inquiry to take.

They showed that we had already a considerable knowledge of what Chakravarti had been doing. They mentioned fellow conspirators, made reference to orders transmitted from Berlin, alluded to sums of money paid over. More than once a fragment of some letter was quoted, and occasionally a few words of Hindustani shook the little man and suggested to his mind that one of his colleagues had double-crossed him. At midnight, however, we had obtained little useful information from the cautious and clever fellow.

The progress of the investigation changed rapidly when Tunney interrogated Sekunna, Thwaites said.

He was informed that his friend had revealed his part in the plot, and that as a matter of form it would be of interest to have Mr Sekunna's corroboration. It was suggested to him that he was more guilty than anybody else. Explosively, the German denied it and put us wise. In half an hour, more information had been extracted from Sekunna than in six hours had been divulged by the obdurate oriental. It was a story of the shipment of arms to India that never reached their destination, of appointments not kept, of rendezvous ill timed, of money squandered with no result, of clumsy mismanagement and ill-luck that was almost laughable when one considers the reputation we gave the Germans for their organising capacity.

When this was put to Chakravarti, he admitted virtually everything, Tunney said.

He sat there and unfolded an amazing story. He touched gingerly upon his own part in it at first, then evidently sensed the fact that there were others in the plot guilty of perhaps no less reprehensible but more violent crimes, and the little doctor's capture and confession not only gave clues to the authorities which enabled them to follow up the outstanding German–Hindu plots in America, but developed prosecutions of the first magnitude and the keenest general interest.

Thwaites recalled the Indian revolutionary as being 'lamb-like' at the second interrogation, having 'come to the conclusion that the game was up'. They finished at four in the morning and Nathan, 'in high spirits', took Thwaites off to get a meal at Jack's, a popular Manhattan all-night eatery.[13]

The confessions led to the arrest of Heramba Lal Gupta, an Indian student, whose safe provided what Tunney said were further details of the network of Indian agents across America.

It may be wondered how he [Chakravarti] was able to perfect an organisation. The answer to that we found in Gupta's safety deposit box – a list of two hundred or more members of an Indian society in the United States, a large proportion of whom were students in American colleges, sent here for education on scholarships, in the hope that they would return to their native country and uplift it. Some of them were influential agents, and they were scattered conveniently about the country. Add to this force the co-operation of almost innumerable German agents and pay it with a share of the $32,000,000 which Chakravarti said had been set aside in Berlin for anarchistic, race-riot and Hindu propaganda in the Western world, and you have a real factor for trouble.[14]

The arrests led to others, including that of Ram Chandra, the leader of the German-backed seditionists on the west coast. Assisted by information supplied by Nathan, a major trial took place in San Francisco, beginning in November 1917. It lasted nearly six months, culminating in one of the other defendants shooting Chandra dead in the courtroom. The German consul-general in San Francisco and several of his staff were jailed, together with a number of German agents and fourteen Indians, including Chakravarti, whose minimal sentence of thirty days reflected the extensive evidence he provided.[15]

Wiseman and Nathan were also interested in Russian activities, and particularly those of the Russian revolutionaries living in New York. During the early months of 1917, these included Lev Bronstein, better known as Leon Trotsky, who was collecting money to fund a revolution in Russia. Much of this was being provided by the Germans in order to relieve pressure on the Eastern Front. Tipped off by Casimir Pilenas, a Lithuanian who was MI1c's main agent inside New York's Russian community, Wiseman warned Cumming in early 1917 that 'an important movement has been started here among socialists backed by all-Jewish funds, behind which are possibly Germans'. The main leader of the group was Trotsky, who addressed a mass meeting at New York's Beethoven Hall on 20 March 1917 and outlined the movement's aims including a revolution in Russia and 'promoting socialistic revolutions in other countries, including the United States'. According to Tunney, who had his own agents at the meeting, Trotsky had used inflammatory language to urge revolution in the US. 'You anarchists here don't want any militarism or any government, which is of no help to the working class, and is always ready to fire on the workman. It's time you did away with such a government once and forever.'

A week later, Wiseman reported that Trotsky had sailed for Russia on board the SS *Kristianiafjord*, with '$10,000 subscribed by socialists and Germans to start revolution against present [Russian] government'. The port authorities in Halifax, Nova Scotia, where the ship was stopping off before crossing the Atlantic, were ordered to detain Trotsky, holding him in a camp for German PoWs, where the commandant said he very soon began preaching revolution and calling for an immediate peace agreement with Germany. 'He is a man holding extremely strong views and of most powerful personality, his personality being such that after only a few days stay here he was by far the most popular man in the whole camp,' the camp commandant said. But Claude Dansey, who at the time was still in MI5, dismissed the claims of an intended revolution. He examined the evidence against Trotsky and decided – despite the fact that MI5's own registry had Trotsky listed as 'a dangerous terrorist and agitator' and Wiseman's insistence that Pilenas was entirely reliable – that the Lithuanian was 'a Russian agent provocateur used by the old Russian Secret Police'. He ordered that Trotsky should be released at once. Dansey's orders were obeyed and Trotsky and his thirty-three fellow Bolsheviks sailed for Russia, taking with them the funds required to launch the Bolshevik revolution. After Dansey had transferred to MI1c to work for Cumming, MI5 discovered that Trotsky's return to Russia had been funded by the Germans.[16]

Wiseman's link with Edward Mandell House now made his involvement in the day-to-day intelligence operations difficult. With America having entered the war, Lawrence Grossmith, another British actor based in America, was co-opted from his work recruiting Americans for the British army and posted to the MI1c New York bureau. Like Thwaites, Grossmith was well connected in New York, having first arrived there in 1899 with Lily Langtry, the former mistress of the then Prince of Wales, later King Edward VII. But despite the reinforcements, it was clear by July 1917 that the pressure of Wiseman's liaison role with House meant taking a back seat away from the intensive agent-running operations. Both Wiseman and Thwaites returned to London for discussions with Cumming and it was agreed that Thwaites should take over day-to-day operations, with Wiseman as ex officio head. Wiseman, working from his Manhattan apartment, retained some specific areas of interest, such as Irish, Mexican and Russian issues.[17]

The main intelligence operation continued to be based in 44 Whitehall Street with Thwaites, Grossmith, William Boshell, Tom Furness and John Gillan joined by yet another actor, Captain Fred Lloyd, who looked after the files, and Frederick Hall, a 38-year-old officer in the Honourable Artillery Company, who arrived in September 1917. The changes instigated in MI1c headquarters by George Macdonogh and Claude Dansey made the US operation directly subordinate to Section V, the new political section.[18]

In the wake of the 1917 Bolshevik revolution, Frank Kirby recruited agents among New York's Russian community to go back into their homeland as British agents. Thwaites subsequently claimed to have personally talent-spotted and recruited the most famous British spy sent into Russia. This was Sidney Reilly, the self-styled 'master spy'. Despite his Irish name, Reilly was in fact born in Odessa in March 1874. He was a Russian Jew whose real name was Sigmund Georgievich Rosenblum.

He came to Britain in his twenties, acquiring a wife and, through her, a British passport in the name of Sidney George Reilly. He claimed to have an Irish father and a Russian Jewish mother. By the early 1900s, he was combining extremely dubious business activities with even more dubious espionage activities on behalf of a variety of governments. There have been suggestions that at one time or other between 1903 and 1917 he worked for the Japanese, Russian, German and British governments – in some cases simultaneously. There is certainly evidence that he was working undercover for British naval intelligence in Port Arthur in the Russian Far East in 1902 and 1903. By 1915 he was in Petrograd, where he had acquired a young Russian wife, while still married to his English wife, and was employed by the Russian government to procure weaponry. This took him, in July 1915, to America, where he again acquired a reputation for dubious business practices and, according to a banking source of Thwaites, made about two million dollars from Russian contracts by being 'entirely unscrupulous'. He also came under surveillance from the MI1c bureau as a possible German agent.[19]

Thwaites recalled that Reilly came to him in October 1917 and said 'he felt that he ought to be doing his bit in the war'. 'His appearance was remarkable,' he said. 'Complexion swarthy, a long straight nose, piercing eyes, black hair brushed back from a forehead suggesting keen intelligence, a large mouth, figure slight, of medium height, always clothed immaculately, he was a man that impressed one with a good deal of power. When later I knew him better, I discovered intellectual qualities of an unusual kind. He was a gambler by nature, whether in hazardous occupations or in games of chance.'

Reilly said he wanted to join the Royal Flying Corps so Thwaites sent him to Toronto where he was immediately given a commission.

But he was too valuable a find to be wasted as an equipment officer, to which department he was assigned. I reported to HQ at home that here was a man who not only knew Russia and Germany, but could speak almost perfectly at least four languages. His German was indeed flawless, and his Russian hardly less fluent. French and English he spoke with an almost imperceptible accent. Reilly was speedily summoned home to England. After an interview with C, the mysterious chief of hush-hush work, he was assigned to special duties in the Baltic and East Prussia. As he could pass equally well as a Russian or as a German he did work of the most valuable kind.[20]

There is one problem with this story. The actual message Thwaites sent to Cumming, signing it with his own initials, was far from a recommendation:

> With reference to your no. 206 of the 28th, Sydney Reilly is a British subject married to a Russian Jewess. He has made money since the beginning of the war through influence with corrupted members of the Russian purchasing commission. He is believed to have been in Port Arthur in 1903 as a spy for Japan. We kept him under observation 1916. We consider him untrustworthy and unsuitable to work suggested.[21]

The contradictions are typical of the entire Reilly story. But the derogatory report signed by Thwaites is backed up by an apparent request from Cumming to MI5 to monitor Reilly's movements once he arrived in London. The MI5 surveillance team failed to uncover any wrongdoing, although the assessment was probably based on little real evidence since Reilly easily lost them by jumping into a cab. Cumming seems at any event to have been very keen to have someone who could so easily merge into the background of Bolshevik Russia and took him on anyway. Despite the close relationship between MI1c and Vickers, Cumming was probably not too influenced by an excellent reference from one of the company's senior executives, who claimed to have known Reilly for thirteen years and 'never heard or known anything disparaging to his character'. The evidence from Cumming's diary suggests that he was aware that Reilly was a bit of a crook, but he seems to have believed that Reilly's Russian background outweighed the risks that he might cut and run, or even give the Bolsheviks the identity of Britain's secret service agents operating in Russia, and that given his opposition to the Bolsheviks his ability to duck and dive would be an advantage rather than a hindrance. Cumming records that Major John Dymoke Scale, one of his former officers in Petrograd who had just been appointed MI1c bureau chief in Stockholm, specifically to run agents into Russia, brought Reilly into Whitehall Court to meet him on 15 March 1918. Scale designated Reilly ST1, the first of the agents he ran out of Sweden, the ST standing for Stockholm, since Reilly was expected to operate not in Sweden but in Russia. Cumming sent him there immediately, with Reilly fuelling MI5's concerns by pestering Maksim Litvinov, the Bolshevik representative in London, to obtain travel passes. 'I was instructed to proceed to Russia without delay,' Reilly said. 'The process of affairs in that part of the world was filling the allies with consternation. My superiors clung to the opinion that Russia might still be brought to her right mind in the matter of her obligations to her allies.'[22]

It was to be a cause that was beyond even the extensive powers of Sidney Reilly. But whatever the origin of the doubts harboured by Thwaites, during Reilly's brief time working for MI1c, he appears to have deserved his self-styled image as a master-spy. Thwaites recounted how, during an intelligence mission in the Prussian town of Königsberg, Reilly allegedly dined with German army officers in their barracks and, despite the doubts Thwaites expressed in his report to Cumming, he was later full of praise for Reilly's ability as a spy. The Königsberg story was just that, a story, a piece of typical Reilly nonsense designed to reinforce the reputation he was determined to foster. But the simple truth is that it was Reilly's very dubious past and the techniques he had employed in earning his reputation that made him such a useful agent. As one senior MI1c officer said a couple of years after Reilly left the Service, no-one ever employed Reilly for his trustworthiness, he was taken on because he was 'of a certain use to us'. He was 'an intriguer of no mean class' with the 'means of finding out information all over the world'.[23]

Thwaites was appointed military control officer in March 1918, placing him under Vernon Kell, who moved to take over the entire New York operation as part of a turf war with Cumming over who should manage the 'military control' system once the war was over. A tense situation was not helped when Kell sent Edward Harran, still seething over his displacement as MI1c chief in Switzerland, to take over as MCO. William Boshell was assigned as Harran's deputy. But attempts by Kell, or perhaps Harran himself, to have the latter take over the entire British intelligence operation in the US came to nothing. Nevertheless, the row led to Lawrence Grossmith, now a captain, temporarily being made bureau chief. But in January 1919, Robert Nathan took control of MI1c operations in the US – largely collecting intelligence on IRA and Bolshevik activities – and brought Thwaites, now a lieutenant-colonel, back into the fold. When their cover was blown by a leaflet published in June 1919 by Irish republican supporters, Nathan returned to London to take over Section V, the MI1c political section. Thwaites, who was planning to get married to an American heiress and therefore had to stay in the US, remained briefly in charge of MI1c operations while Cumming fought the turf war with MI5 over the visa system. Cumming won the battle in September 1919. Harran was sent home and Captain Maurice Jeffes, who had served in France with the Intelligence Corps, was dispatched to the US to become chief passport control officer, the new cover for MI1c heads of bureau in the most important cities abroad, assisted by Captain Henry Maine. But the real secret service work was carried out by an official called A. W. James, who operated under the pseudonym Charles Fox. So successful were they that in a 1921 report on 'British Espionage in the United States', J Edgar Hoover, the then head of the US Justice Department's General Intelligence Division, and future head of the FBI, wrote that the British were 'much better informed on radical activities in this country, at least in New York, than the United States government'.[24]

NINE

Middle East adventures –
'Brigands and terrorists'

CUMMING'S operations in the Middle East and Mediterranean were initially low key, but in November 1914, he recruited 48-year-old Major Rhys Samson to set up an espionage system covering the region. Samson had been British consul in the Turkish town of Adrianople, from where he had been reporting on the poor state of the Turkish army and its lack of belief in the German military strategy. He was to be typical of the Turkish and 'Near East' experts drawn to Cumming's intelligence service in the region. They included a number of other members of Britain's Levant Consular Service; expatriates who before the war had been based in the Turkish capital, Constantinople, or other parts of Turkey; and a spattering of archaeologists and Arabists, of whom the most prominent were Gertrude Bell, David Hogarth and Leonard Woolley.

Samson was initially sent to Paris to work with the French Army's Deuxième Bureau, which traditionally had very good sources in the Levant. But as the British forces geared up for the Gallipoli campaign, it became apparent that there was a lack of first-hand reporting from Turkey and, in February 1915, Samson was sent forward to Athens together with a deputy, William Edmonds, a 32-year-old consular official who had also served before the war in Turkey, most recently as acting consul in Constantinople. Edmonds was described by one of his colleagues as 'quiet, grave, efficient, and extremely discreet'. Samson set up what would become the 'R' organisation – derived from his own covername, R for Rhys. His initial role was to support the

Mediterranean Expeditionary Force based at Salonika. He was assisted by Edmonds, Clifford Heathcote-Smith, who until war broke out was vice-consul in Smyrna (now Izmir), and Wilfred 'Ed' Lafontaine, an accountant in pre-war Constantinople who had moved to Athens on the outbreak of war. They were based at 4 St Dionysius Square, Athens, under cover of the British Refugee Commission, thereby attracting refugees from Turkish-controlled areas who might have something useful to report. As well as his own intelligence operation, Samson set up a small counter-espionage section run by Major George Monreal, a Maltese officer in the Wiltshire Regiment, who was assisted by Charles Tucker, an expatriate Briton whose family were sanitary engineers in Constantinople. Lieutenant Arthur Hill, RNVR, a former employee of the Standard Oil Company, ran a small commercial intelligence department in the legation tracking supplies to and from Turkey, and in particular German oil supplies.

Lafontaine was dispatched to Cairo to provide a link with the British military headquarters in the Egyptian capital and set up a number of outstations at various locations in Greece closer to the Turkish border, including Salonika, Cavalla, Dedeagatch (now Alexandroupoli) and the islands of Thasos, Chios, Samos and Lesbos, from where Heathcote-Smith was soon running agents into Turkey, deeply impressing the author Compton Mackenzie, who would take charge of Cumming's Greece-based counter-espionage operations a few months later. Heathcote-Smith looked for all the world like one of the British expatriate community in Turkey, although he was in fact the son of an English country parson. 'His fluency in Greek and Turkish, his soft voice, large moustache and big nose combined to suggest some ancestral link with this part of the world,' Mackenzie recalled. 'The dreamy earnestness of his gaze when he was expounding his scheme for the organisation and equipment of ten thousand Anatolian Greek irregulars to be turned loose on the Turks in Asia Minor, his childish sense of fun, his sudden, rapid denunciations of stupidity, his enfant terrible questions, and the way he somehow suggested one of the attractive heroes of the Arabian Knights, like Prince Camaralzaman, only reinforced this exotic image.'

Heathcote-Smith was in charge of all operations running agents into Turkey by sea from the Dardanelles round to Marmaris in the south-west. He had no trouble obtaining intelligence, recalled John Godfrey, a naval officer who would go on to head naval intelligence during the Second World War. 'The attitude of the ordinary Greek islanders towards us is one of friendly neutrality,' Godfrey recorded in his diaries. 'They hate the Turks wholeheartedly and will do anything to annoy them. Consequently our intelligence officer at Mitylene, Heathcote-Smith, has no difficulty getting news of the movements of Turkish vessels. The Greek fisherman remains at sea almost indefinitely in the hope of giving information and of course earning a reward. Thus we have an efficient lookout and intelligence system ready to hand. Heathcote-Smith employs a group of adventurers, Greek-British Levantines, who carry out small raids on the Turkish coast.' The adventurers operated from a 40-foot motor boat, the *Omala*, commanded by another of Cumming's local recruits, Lieutenant Charles Hadkinson RNVR, an Englishman who was a farmer in Macedonia before the war, and was 'a rosy apple-cheeked man of about fifty-five, who with his white hair and clear, vivid blue eyes might have been a Yorkshire farmer'. Hadkinson gave the Anatolian Greek irregulars who manned his ship the names of Robin Hood's men: Little John, Will Scarlet, Alan a Dale and Friar Tuck.[1]

Up until this point, most British reporting on the Middle East had come from liaison with the Russians and the French, but within days of his arrival in Athens Samson was sending Cumming a stream of extensive reports on the Turkish military from a number of agents. These not only included his own contacts inside Turkey but also those of James Morgan, the acting consul at Dedeagatch, who had agents inside the Turkish capital, Constantinople. By 25 March 1915, Samson was able to supply British commanders with the complete order of battle of the Turkish Army, giving the locations and strengths of all the various Turkish army corps. A number of agents were recruited from among the Turkish community in Greece to go back home and provide weekly reports, written in saliva or lemon juice on the back of apparently innocent letters. The reports were to be sent to a friendly shipping agency in

Salonika, marked for the attention of 'Alexatos', with a fallback address in Berne.[2]

At the same time, at the instigation of Blinker Hall, efforts were underway to try to bribe the Turks into pulling out of the alliance with Germany. Cumming had Edwin Whittall and George Eady, two of the British expatriate community in Constantinople, commissioned as junior officers in the RNVR and sent them to the Balkans to try to buy off the Turks with £4 million. Whittall saw the plan as 'a forlorn hope' and it foundered spectacularly when, on the very day that Eady opened negotiations with Talaat Bey, secretary-general of Turkey's governing Committee of Union and Progress (CUP), the Royal Navy began bombarding the Dardanelles. Although Whittall and Eady now reverted to more traditional intelligence work, the attempts to buy off the Turks continued throughout the war, largely through the maverick international arms dealer, and director of Vickers, Basil Zaharoff, who signed, and styled, himself as the mysterious Z, but also through the MI1c representatives in Switzerland where a number of opposition Turkish politicians lived in exile. Although Zaharoff's talks had little in the way of real success, they were yet another example of the Service's use of 'parallel diplomacy', secret talks to achieve a policy that the government of the day could not pursue openly, including subsequently talking to countries or terrorist groups with which Britain, publicly at least, had unfriendly relations.[3]

By the late summer of 1915, Cumming had a number of operations across the Mediterranean, including the Greek networks run by Samson in Athens, who had now moved to larger premises at 20 Academy Street, opposite the Greek armed forces general headquarters. There was an operation in Malta, where Cumming had a Royal Marine officer, Captain Edward Farmer, collecting naval intelligence; and in Rome, where Cumming's interests were looked after by Major Vivian Gabriel, a member of the Indian civil service who had been commissioned on the Army Special List in May and sent to the British military mission in Rome along with Eady to provide intelligence from the Italo-Austrian front. Cumming also sent a man out to Gibraltar to 'link up' with the

Admiralty's intelligence operation in Spain, which was run by a Royal Marine officer, Lieutenant-Colonel Charles Thoroton. The appointment of Thoroton had been the result of a power-grab by Hall, who decided that he should run secret service operations in Spain, although Cumming would have to fund them, a practice that naval intelligence subsequently admitted was wrong. The Gibraltar bureau's role was to collect intelligence not just from Spain but from French and Belgium refugees arriving there, at the same time talent-spotting potential agents who could be sent back home. It also ran operations into Morocco from Gibraltar. By mid-1916, Cumming had appointed a passport control officer, Captain Eddie Bryce of the East Lancashire Regiment, to look after his interests in Madrid. The Near East and Mediterranean desk at Whitehall Court was overseen by Francis Newnum.[4]

One of the most colourful of Cumming's officers was recruited by Samson in August 1915, having been sent to Athens to recuperate from an illness contracted during the Gallipoli campaign. Compton Mackenzie, already a famous author, would later become embittered and ridicule the secret service's, and Samson's, obsession with secrecy, but he was initially seduced by it all. Like Zaharoff, he hid behind the letter Z and confessed to being fascinated by Samson, 'a most lovable man' with a 'courtly grace of manner which sometimes reminded me of a French marquis and sometimes of a high-grade mandarin. He was a shortish man, very neatly dressed, with a round fresh face, a trim moustache and a pair of the largest tortoise-shell spectacles I had seen.'

Mackenzie agreed to run Samson's Athens-based counter-espionage service, which under George Monreal had been outwitted by the German secret service agents, partly from lack of funds and partly due to 'a sort of irresponsible credulity' on Monreal's part. 'The only difficulty is the money side of it,' Samson told him. 'C doesn't like spending money on *contre-espionage*, for after all, the real object of C's organisation is to obtain information about the enemy.' The main task was to counter the activities of the devious Baron von Schenck, the Kaiser's alleged master-spy in Athens, who was said to employ a bevy of ladies of ill repute to collect intelligence from Allied officers. It was an assignment the author saw as highly flattering. 'Nothing is easier for a novelist than to imagine himself a figure of considerably more importance than he actually is,' Mackenzie recalled. 'And I fear my sense of the ridiculous was at this moment lying dormant beneath the gaudy trappings of romance. Moreover, my personality was already feeling the effect of that subtle and sinister and perhaps not altogether unambitious initial Z.'[5]

His main assistant was the portly Tucker. 'There is often an inclination among thin men to find spiritual comfort in the society of fat men,' Mackenzie noted without any apparent malice. 'Charles Tucker was the best-tempered man I have met in my life and he had for a fat man an immense amount of energy. His father had had a sanitary engineer's business in Constantinople and he was at the present time a refugee in Athens with the rest of his family, of which Charles was the eldest son. Although Tucker spoke Greek, Turkish and French as fluently as he spoke English, there was nothing in his exterior to suggest the Levantine Englishman. He was typically the genial cockney businessman with a comfortable home in Ealing and a pride in his chrysanthemums. His cheeks were as pink as the eglantine, his full fair moustache was Saxon to the last hair. His main object in life was to feel that things were going smoothly and easily. His defects sprang from the qualities that made him such a good companion. He was apt to be too pliant and supple. A downright "no" would have saved him and me many a difficult moment.'[6]

Having got rid of Monreal, whose 'natural credulity and powers of invention were seriously militating against the efficiency of the work', Mackenzie moved the counter-espionage section to the British Archaeological School, where, apart from Tucker, his main assistants were Alberto Zanardi-Landi, a young member of an Italian aristocratic family, who liaised with Italian intelligence, was 'brave and chivalrous' and had 'thrown himself into secret service work with the passion of an artist', and 'Old' Weir, who had been a courier in Athens before the war and was employed to recruit and run Greek agents. 'He must at this date have been approaching seventy, a small man with a big grey moustache, apple cheeks, and bright sly eyes,' said Mackenzie. His father had been an Ulsterman and Weir himself looked 'just such as one you might see hanging about in the muddy market-place of some small town in northern Ireland gloating over the beat of the Orange drums on the melancholy anniversary of Boyne. It was fantastically surprising to hear from his lips a strong Greek accent instead of the Ulster brogue.'[7]

More of a hindrance than a help was Sergeant Henry 'Clarence' Cauchi. Half Maltese, half Greek, he was a shipping agent in Salonika before the war. Having been wounded on the Western Front and evacuated to London, Cauchi persuaded Cumming he was possessed of 'courage of a high order and an ability to keep his mouth shut' and was sent out to Athens, where he promptly proved himself possessed of neither. Mackenzie described meeting Cauchi for the first time in August 1915:

> I found the new agent in the bedroom at the top of a fly-blown little hotel. A great oval figure rose from the bed when I entered and crossed the floor with a heavy sliding motion to greet me. He offered me a hot damp hand and I heard for the first time that polyglot voice, saw those big dark animal's eyes gazing into mine and smelt that mixture of perspiration and musk. If I was under the sway of the mysterious enchantments of the secret service, Cauchi was absolutely drugged by them.

Sent on his first secret mission to lead an attempt to hold up the German diplomatic bag, Cauchi forgot the pseudonym under which he was to receive his instructions and spent two days cowering in a hotel toilet expecting the Greek police to arrest him at any minute.[8]

One key member of Mackenzie's team was Frederick Hasluck, who had been unfairly sacked from his post as assistant director and librarian of the British School in Athens. Hasluck, better known by his initials F.W., was an archaeologist and leading academic authority on the interaction between early Christian and Islamic societies in the Middle East, whose wife Margaret had been working for Cumming in Whitehall Court. Mackenzie described him as 'thin to emaciation with a finely carved nose above a straggling fair moustache'. He set up a card index of suspected German spies. 'The services of such an accurate, patient and logical mind put into shape the inaccurate, hasty and haphazard information that reached us about people, places and events,' Mackenzie said. 'We had differently coloured cards to indicate a rough classification. There were crimson ones for those whom we considered proved spies, yellow for those who had given us false information, green for those who had helped us, mauve for ladies of easy virtue, and white for the great indeterminate majority. We soon became less confident of being able to place people in categories, for the proven spy often turned out to be a perfectly innocent man, and the green friend a yellow traitor. So after a month or two we gave up the coloured cards and used none but white.'[9]

When Bulgaria entered the war on Germany's side, in October 1915, Samson set up another secret service bureau at Salonika with James Morgan as the head of the intelligence-gathering section and Hugh Whittall in charge of counter-espionage. Captain George Hill, a Canadian who had been brought up in Russia, was given a crash course in Bulgarian and sent to Salonika to run agents for Morgan, joining the Royal Flying Corps and learning to fly so that he could transport agents and pigeons behind the Bulgarian lines. Whittall, who would later serve in Switzerland, was another expatriate exiled from Smyrna and a cousin of Edwin – two other members of the Whittall family, Kenrick (known as Kenny) and Arthur, also worked for Cumming in Greece. Hugh Whittall's past career as a mining engineer – he had run Cecil Rhodes's gold mines in Rhodesia – no doubt appealed to Cumming. Whittall's cover was provided by a succession of commissions in the Royal Marines, the Army's General List and finally the RNVR, in which he was given the rank of lieutenant-commander. He was to play important roles in both the Balkans and Switzerland.[10]

Whittall's swashbuckling approach in his apprehension of the Greek police chiefs was typical of that taken by many of the officers based in Samson's outposts on the various Greek islands. John Linton Myres, who in peacetime was Wykeham Professor of Ancient History at Oxford, was based in Calymnos with a roving brief to collect intelligence around the

Dodecanese and launch small raids on the Turkish coast in his motor caique the *Ayios Nicolaos*. At the age of forty-six, and with a sinecure at Oxford, Myres might have been forgiven for seeking a desk job in London, but instead he adopted the role of an Aegean brigand who might have stepped from the pages of Homer, acquiring the nickname 'the Blackbeard of the Aegean'. Myres resembled an 'Assyrian king, with more than a suggestion of the pirate Teach,' said Mackenzie, whose previous encounter with him had been as a student at Oxford when Myres, then a junior proctor, fined him and a room-mate for throwing a shoe at a policeman. 'Few people could have helped feeling a slight astonishment at the violence of the change effected in a scholar in these changing times,' Mackenzie noted. 'Not so the Royal Navy which accepted Myres's feats of brigandage and terrorism on the coast of Asia Minor as the sort of thing any professor might do to whom a temporary commission had been recommended by their Lordships of the Admiralty. Those cattle raids of his on the Anatolian seaboard, when the Assyrian Myres came down like the wolf on the Turkish fold, were a delight to the wardrooms and gunrooms and they may have incommoded the enemy, though they were stopped in the end as doing more harm to the Greek population on the mainland than to their Turkish masters.' Meanwhile, the 20-ton cutter the *Valkyrie*, skippered by the Dorset farmer Lieutenant-Commander W. H. Rogers, ran the gauntlet of enemy patrols to land agents on the Turkish coast.[11]

While the former Levant consuls like Samson and Clifford Heathcote-Smith had some experience in intelligence collection and reporting, most of those they recruited had little if any previous knowledge of how to do the job and largely picked up what they could as they went along. J. C. 'Jack' Lawson, another Oxford don, whose knowledge of Greek and the Aegean owed more to his studies of Homer than any specialist training, was also sent to Souda Bay in Crete, from where he made a number of intelligence-gathering operations. He and Mackenzie had little regard for each other. Mackenzie called Lawson 'priggish and consequential' and complained that a book recalling his exploits exaggerated his role, a true case of the pot calling the kettle black. Lawson was more subtly disparaging of Mackenzie and his counter-espionage network, writing:

> My position as an intelligence officer involved a considerable amount of secret service work, particularly contre-espionage. Our politicians and journalists assure us from time to time that the British secret service is the best in the world. I do not know whether that is true, any more than I imagine do they; but if it is true, it must be the outcome of some natural genius in our people for such work and not of training or organisation; for the secret service work of the Aegean was conducted by amateurs and I for one never received one word of guidance.

Lawson's contribution to intelligence history also included an attempt to answer a perennial question about the British secret service which still resonates today. Did the British 'secret agent' have what would later be called a 'licence to kill'? Lawson's response summed up in broad terms the situation which, despite the prim protests which emanate from Whitehall whenever the issue is raised, remains true to this day. Certainly, in Lawson's view, in wartime at least, he did.

> His [the secret agent's] personal predilections in favour of keeping the ten commandments may be such that no act of his is likely to stain his country's good repute; but then an intransigent attitude towards moral standards in war-time will also impair his efficiency as an agent. 'Thou shalt not kill' does not veto the extermination of the enemy. What then is my conclusion? Roughly this, that the ethics of secret service in war-time do not permit the furtherance of schemes whose object is homicide, but neither do they prohibit enterprises from which the risk of incidental homicide cannot be excluded.[12]

Mackenzie and Samson, now also assisted by Stanley Garton, who had been sent out by London, communicated with Cumming using the 'U' code, which was employed by all the main British secret service bureaus abroad and was based on a small pocket dictionary with the system for its use, which relied on the use of rulers, changing monthly. According to Mackenzie, it was 'possessed of an infernal ingenuity' and 'would have furrowed the protuberant forehead of a senior Wrangler'. Throughout the late summer and autumn of 1915, Samson sent a stream of reports on Turkish military movements to London, Cairo, and the British commanders controlling the Dardanelles operations from the Greek island of Imbros. There were reports from reliable agents and correspondents in Constantinople and Smyrna on conditions inside Turkey; shortages of food, fuel and ammunition; German naval movements; military movements by rail from Turkish railway officials working with the British agents; the locations of British prisoners; and the number of Turkish casualties returning from the front at Gallipoli, showing that they were in fact considerably greater than the Allied losses. There was also a series of reports from British agents and the Russian, French and Italian vice-consuls in Dedeagatch on the massacres of Armenians. On 11 November 1915, Samson's agent number 10, based in Smyrna, reported widespread killings of Armenians in what would become one of the most notorious genocides in history with more than a million believed killed. 'At Buldur and Sparta, the Armenians have been nearly exterminated,' the agent said. 'A Christian conscript who has just returned from Adana said to me: "May God grant that I should not live to see such a sight again." He declares that the Turks, after killing the men, fell on the women, girls and children and after violating them flung them over the precipices into ravines or slaughtered and mutilated them.'[13]

At the end of 1915, with the focus of the war against Turkey moving from Gallipoli to Sinai, Samson, William Edmonds and Garton transferred to offices at 55 Avenue Alexandre le Grand, in the Egyptian city of Alexandria, fighting off an attempt by the army to grab control of Cumming's Near East operation and move it to Salonika. Samson was assisted in this fight by Sir Henry McMahon, the British high commissioner in Cairo, who told the Foreign Office:

Colonel Samson's bureau has recently come over to Egypt and he tells me that he finds that he can work here much more centrally, and usefully and in better perspective, than at Salonika or any other point on the outer perimeter of his sphere of action. I understand he is at the moment opposing an attempt to remove him from here elsewhere. I should be much obliged if you could let me know as early as possible that it is not contemplated to restrict or close this most valuable bureau.

A conference in Malta attended by Cumming in March 1916 led to the R organisation being formalised as the Eastern Mediterranean Special Intelligence Bureau (EMSIB) and the adoption of a policy expanding the use of 'intelligence yachts' to run agents into Turkish-controlled areas and collect their intelligence. Alongside Edmonds and Garton, Samson was also assisted by Lieutenant Everard Feilding, a barrister and secretary of the Society for Psychical Research, opening up interesting avenues for possible sources of intelligence. The area covered by EMSIB extended from Persia in the east to Tripoli in the west and included Bulgaria, Romania, Serbia, Montenegro, Greece, Turkey, Syria, Lebanon, Mesopotamia (Iraq), Palestine, Egypt, Sudan, Abyssinia and Eritrea, but Samson also had overall control over the operations in Switzerland that targeted exiles from the region, both for intelligence collection and secret talks aimed at dividing Germany from its Balkan allies. The scale of Samson's enterprise can perhaps best be appreciated by the fact that as at October 1916, some 300 agents were being controlled from Alexandria, a figure that does not include those run by Athens, Bucharest, Salonika and the various bureaux in Switzerland.[14]

Athens was nevertheless still the first stopping place for those seeking secret service in the Mediterranean or Near East, including the 53-year-old David Hogarth, a famous archaeologist and classicist, who was the keeper of Oxford University's Ashmolean Museum. Hogarth was recruited by Blinker Hall, commissioned into the RNVR as a lieutenant-commander and paid by Cumming, a not unusual combination for those Hall recruited for secret service. When Hogarth arrived in Athens in the autumn of 1915, looking for a role, Mackenzie suggested he go to Bucharest and set up a network of spies inside Bulgaria, but Hogarth was then called to Cairo, where he would be one of the founders of the Arab

Bureau, which also included T. E. Lawrence, and briefly Gertrude Bell and Leonard Woolley, among its number.

Lawrence had himself been considered by Samson as a possible expert on the Turkish armed forces but ultimately was the only one of the four never to work for Cumming. Bell was recruited by Hall at Hogarth's instigation in late 1915 and sent to Cairo. Like Hogarth, she was in fact paid by Cumming. She arrived in Port Said in November to be met by Woolley, who before the war had worked with Hogarth and Lawrence, at the excavations of a Hittite site at Carchemish in southern Turkey. Bell worked initially for the Egyptian military intelligence department under Colonel Gilbert Clayton, based in Cairo. 'For the moment, I am helping Mr Hogarth to fill in the intelligence files with information as to tribes and sheikhs,' she wrote to her mother. 'It's great fun and delightful to be working with him.'

Intelligence collection in the areas of the Middle East occupied by the Turks was complicated by rivalry between the British military authorities in France and India over areas of influence and, in March 1916, Bell was sent out to Basra to bring some sense to the intelligence operation there. 'None of these people from India know Arabic,' she complained in a letter to her father shortly after arriving there. 'What that means in an intelligence department I leave you to guess.' A senior army officer sent out to investigate intelligence in Mesopotamia wrote that Bell's 'great knowledge of Arabia is most valuable'. She was doing the work of a senior intelligence officer and 'ought to be officially recognised', he said, adding as if in complaint that 'she is at present being paid for by MI1c'. Bell was subsequently moved to Baghdad but continued producing detailed intelligence 'articles' for the 'War Office'.[15]

'Her first care was to synthesise and systemise the mass of detail regarding Arab personalities and tribes that poured into the civil administrative headquarters from every part of Iraq,' one of those who worked with her wrote. 'With unwearying diligence, she indexed and cross-indexed, collated and checked, wherever possible by personal interviews, every scrap of available information, making the dry bones live by her enthusiasm and the charm of her literary style. Her office-notes were vivid, accurate, but feminine withal. Her sympathy with the victims of "military exigencies" was tempered by common sense, her righteous wrath was mingled with a sense of humour, which never deserted her.' But her understanding of the nature of the organisation to which she was sending her reports appears to have been limited. Commissioned by 'the War Office' to write a series of 'articles' on the region, she protested over the failure to publish them, complaining that 'it's preposterous that I should take so much trouble to no end'.[16]

Woolley and Lawrence had been recruited into the Egyptian military intelligence department in December 1914 after assisting one of its officers in mapping out the Sinai desert and in obtaining the German plans for a railway line through Turkey linking Berlin with Baghdad before the war. There was a certain amount of free movement between Clayton's and Cumming's organisations and by the time Bell arrived in Egypt, Woolley was Samson's man in Port Said. One of his bravest agents was also the most timid, he recalled. The spy, a wizened and worryingly nervous Lebanese electrical engineer called Michel, offered to work for free in the hope that he would be given a British decoration at the end of the war. The would-be spy was landed on the Syrian coast and was swiftly arrested. He managed nevertheless to blow up a fuel dump for German submarines before making his way through Turkey, Bulgaria, Austria, Germany and Switzerland back to Port Said, carrying details of Turkish troop concentrations disguised as music. At the border with Bulgaria, he was stopped by Turkish guards, who suspected the notes were a code. Michel protested that he was a great musician on his way to Sofia to play a concert. The stationmaster at the border post played the piano, so he was asked to play the spy's music and 'prove whether it's music or not'.

Michel described how he sat in the stationmaster's sitting room fearing he was about to be exposed as a spy and shot.

> The stationmaster sat at the piano and he opened the first piece of music and he looked very puzzled and then lifted his hands and he brought them down on the keys and it was terrible. You never heard

such dreadful noises as came from that piano; and they all looked at each other and began to smile. Then the stationmaster went on to the second thing. The first thing had been the name of the town and the second thing was the number of guns there and I heard a very pleasant little chord; and the stationmaster looked pleased. The next thing was the number of troops. It was difficult to play but it sounded well, and then there was another place name and it was terrible, and the stationmaster tried and tried and at last he turned round and he said: 'This is too difficult for me.' I said: 'Of course, this is modern music. This is the new music, the stuff that I write. I am a great musician.' And they all took their hats and they bowed to me and I got safely through.

Woolley said Michel was 'the timidest and most naturally cowardly man I've known, who, at the same time, through sheer will-power, was one of the bravest fellows I have met'. This was saying something since Woolley was in touch with the Nili spy ring, a group of Zionists led by Aaron Aaronsohn, a prominent agronomist who ran an agricultural research station at Athlit in northern Palestine. Aaronsohn, his brother Alexander, sister Sarah and friend Avshalom Feinberg were the key members of the spy ring, which offered to provide the British with intelligence on Turkish activities in occupied Palestine, Lebanon and Syria. The first contact between Woolley and the ring came in late 1915, when Feinberg made his way to Port Said. Woolley immediately saw the value of the Nili ring, with its ability to gather a wide range of intelligence across occupied Palestine and Syria. He and Feinberg agreed how the ring should operate, what it should target and how to signal to the 'intelligence yachts' that it had an intelligence report to be collected or needed contact. The yachts, which were also used to land agents and couriers into Turkish-controlled territory, included a former German cargo ship, the 7,000-ton *Aenne Rickmers*, taken over by the British. It was renamed the *Anne* and used by Captain Lewen Weldon, a member of the Egyptian Survey Department commissioned into the army, to dispatch the EMSIB agents behind enemy lines. Feinberg was taken back to Athlit on the *Anne*, Weldon recalled.

The landing itself was without incident and I got back to the *Anne* safely. Our agent too, as it turned out, was safe enough at first. He was to arrange a regular system not only for obtaining information but also for handing it on to us. He did this thoroughly well, but unluckily we were unable to call and pick him up for some little time. The weather was against us and it was not until the 2nd December that I landed and tried to find him. But it was too late.

Feinberg and a colleague had tried to make their way by land to Port Said and were ambushed by a Bedouin gang. Feinberg was killed. 'He had got impatient and, taking another man with him, had tried to get through the Turkish lines to our own,' said Weldon. 'His friend, although wounded, reached the English trenches. But our agent had done a good job before he died. He had instructed some Jews on shore how to signal to us by hanging out, apparently without care, their sheets and blankets.'[17]

Woolley also used a steam yacht called the *Zaida* to land agents on the Palestinian, Lebanese and Syrian coasts. Many of the agents were recruited in Cyprus, where EMSIB rented a house just outside Famagusta. This was manned initially by an Intelligence Corps lieutenant, Vivian Hadkinson, who alongside his army rank was given cover as an RNVR lieutenant presumably to explain his work with the yacht. He was later replaced by naval lieutenants Herbert Salter and Walter Smithers, who also ran agents onto Turkey's southern coastline using a number of other ships, including the trawler *Veresis* and a former Channel ferry, the *Deveny*. Disaster struck in the late summer of 1916, when Woolley went out on the *Zaida* and the ship hit a French mine. Woolley and his crew were taken prisoner by the Turks, which led to a damaging break in the relationship with the Nili ring. Captain Ian Smith, an infantryman loaned by Clayton, took over in Port Said to handle the Zionist spies. Smith had a difficult relationship with Aaronsohn, who arrived in Alexandria in late 1916 quite wrongly convinced that he and his fellow Zionist spies were undervalued by the British. In fact, all the evidence suggests that they were regarded in Cairo as the best of the British agents in the region.

One British officer reported that Agent Mack, as Aaronsohn was known, was producing 'good stuff' and Cumming noted that he was considered 'very valuable' in Cairo, where he was ultimately seen as being a key factor behind the British military successes against the Turks in Palestine. Samson sought to reassure Aaronsohn, explaining the problems resulted from the fact that Woolley had not kept full notes of his contacts with his agents. Smith's inept handling of Aaronsohn poisoned the atmosphere between them, leaving Samson and William Edmonds struggling to repair the damage. But in February 1917, using a new intelligence yacht, the 16-ton *Managem*, Weldon landed Aaronsohn back at Athlit and contact resumed, with two of the Nili spies returning to Cairo with Aaronsohn to be debriefed. One of these was landed back into Athlit in March, returning with what Weldon called 'a good fat report about the enemy's movements'. He went back in April with Weldon to fetch more intelligence plus Aaronsohn's sister Sarah and Yussef Lizhansky, another key member of the Nili ring. They both returned to Athlit and throughout the summer of 1917 a number of successful operations to get intelligence out took place. But in September, with the British advancing through Palestine, the Turks began to dismantle the network. Sarah Aaronsohn was captured and tortured before managing to shoot herself to ensure she gave nothing away while Lizhansky gave himself up to protect other members of the ring and was hanged. 'He surrendered voluntarily and went to his own death rather than let his friends suffer,' Weldon said. 'Englishmen often talk about "playing the game", but even during the war, few Britishers played it to a finer finish than this Jewish girl and Yussef.'[18]

TEN

Middle East adventures 2 –
'The British Secret Service Gang'

RHYS Samson's departure for Egypt in December 1915 left another former Levant consul, 32-year-old William D. Matthews – described by Compton Mackenzie as a 'hot-tempered Ulsterman' – in charge of intelligence operations. Mackenzie's role was, in theory at least, restricted to counter-espionage, detecting German, Bulgarian and Turkish spies, and he still had little real idea of the extent of Cumming's organisation, or even indeed who the mysterious 'C' actually was. 'The initial of C was invoked to justify everything,' Mackenzie complained. 'But who C was, and where C was, and what C was, and why C was, we were not told.' Nevertheless, his good relations with the British minister, Sir Francis Elliot, and the increasing effectiveness of his agents and the intelligence they were obtaining enabled him to elbow Matthews aside, a process which may well have been the cause of the Ulsterman's 'hot temper'.[1]

Mackenzie named his agents after famous fictional or historical characters – one was called Jack Horner, another George Washington – but the best placed appears to have been the doorman at the German legation, who was recruited in December 1915 and given the soubriquet Davy Jones. 'From the first moment I saw the little man with his mousy hair and pale ragged moustache, his very pale blue eyes filmed with suspicion and furtiveness almost as if by an invisible cataract, I recognised in him the authentic spy, the spy by nature,' Mackenzie recalled. 'At that very first interview, it was evident that he was in a class apart. His character sketches of the legation staff were on a different level to any I had heard hitherto, and his physical descriptions were brilliant in their capacity to provide the essentials.' He spoke German well 'so he was able in passing through a room to pick up what was being said and he had such an accurate memory that I always received word for word what he had overheard without any embroidery. Thanks to Davy Jones, I learnt during the last week in December more about the German organisation of intelligence in Athens than we had learned in the preceding nine months.' Jones not only collected information he overheard, he also rummaged through the legation's litter bins to find valuable intelligence. It was the doorman's information that made Mackenzie's organisation an attractive partner for the newly arrived French intelligence officers, who forged an intelligence alliance with the British that was bolstered by Italian, Russian and Serbian intelligence officers.

Mackenzie embarked on the first of what was to be a series of attempts to create his own empire independent of Samson and was put very firmly in his place by Cumming, not least because the suggested changes were sent direct to Blinker Hall, bypassing both Samson and Cumming himself. Mackenzie ploughed ahead, determined to sideline King Constantine and return the former Greek Prime Minister, Eleutherios Venizelos, to power. King Constantine, whose sister was married to the Kaiser, was determined to keep Greece neutral, while Venizelos wanted Greece to come into the war on the side of the Entente. The myth of the ruthless 'British Secret Service gang' was in all probability created by Baron von Schenck, who was not in fact a master-spy but a propagandist whose material found a welcome audience in the Greek monarchist newspapers. The myth might well have been propaganda, but Mackenzie seems to have done his best to live up to it.[2]

The intelligence collected by the Salonika bureau was bolstered by the results of a German air raid on the city, which led to the arrest and expulsion of the German, Austrian, Bulgarian and Turkish consuls. Their offices were ransacked by Cumming's men for intelligence. But relations between the British secret service officers and Lieutenant-Colonel Frederick Cunliffe-Owen, the head of military intelligence at Salonika, were very poor. Hugh Whittall, who was involved in a series

of rows with Cunliffe-Owen, suffered a heart scare and was moved
to Switzerland. His replacement was Lieutenant Harry Pirie-Gordon,
RNVR, another archaeologist and Arabist, who had been working for
The Times and was coincidentally Mackenzie's accomplice in the Oxford
shoe-throwing incident for which the then junior proctor John Linton
Myres had handed out the fine. Pirie-Gordon was joined by Norman
Dewhurst, a lieutenant in the Royal Munster Fusiliers.

'I was kept busy getting agents to, and from, behind the German and
Bulgarian lines on the other side of the Macedonian plain,' Dewhurst
recalled. 'I had a special carrier pigeon service as pigeons were then the
only means of communication. Salonika at that time was a hotbed of
intrigue as it was the centre of the espionage services of all the warring
nations. The local meeting place of the various agents was the Café
Flocas. There while you drank your morning coffee, allied French agents
would be pointed out to you as well as those working for the Germans
and Bulgars.' Another favourite meeting place was the local brothel,
known as Madame Fannie's. 'This was a very select house and the girls
beautiful. Every time it was a case of combining business with pleasure
for I always came away with some useful information after my visit.'

It was by no means all pleasure. Even after Whittall's departure,
Cunliffe-Owen continued to object to the presence of the secret service
officers and made their life as difficult as possible. 'He was very jealous
of our organisation, which was independent of his control,' Dewhurst
recalled. 'The telegraph lines to London were frequently buzzing with
the battle that went on between the Foreign Office and the War Office
with regard to the liberty of action we enjoyed. What infuriated him the
most was that we got our reports to London quicker than he did.' More
worrying than the turf war with the British military was the brutality of
some of the local Balkan rivalries. Dewhurst described driving Geoffrey
Knox, the British consul in Cavalla, back to his house in the town. 'The
next morning when Knox opened his front door, he found one of his
agents cut to pieces in a sack, which was hanging from the door handle,'
Dewhurst said. 'I had a rather bad moment when I realised that what I
had just seen might become my lot.'[3]

Although Mackenzie's memoirs of his secret service work tended to over-play his own role, he was to be the architect of a system that was used by Cumming and his successors for the next three decades, both as a cover for their work abroad and a unique source of information. The system involved checking passports and issuing visas to anyone wishing to travel to British-controlled territory. It was to be overseen by military control officers in theatres of war, and elsewhere by civilian passport control officers. The basis for this system was drawn up by Mackenzie in the early summer of 1916, purely to deal with the flow of refugees through Greece, and involved stationing a number of men, mainly operating under what had become the standard secret service cover of a junior RNVR officer, at various points around mainland Greece and the islands to check the passports of anyone entering or leaving the country. This system also allowed them to talent-spot potential agents who might be in a position to obtain useful intelligence. Suspect travellers would not necessarily be refused visas. Their passports were simply marked surreptitiously to indicate that they were suspected spies. Explaining it in a signal to Cumming, whom he had still not met, Mackenzie said the comprehensive nature of his system was based in part on the good relations he enjoyed with the French and Italian intelligence organisations in Greece and his complete control over the work of the Serbian intelligence service, which had sub-contracted its Greek operations out to him. 'My duties as control officer keep practically all my agents busy day and night in making inquiries about people who propose to travel from Greece,' Mackenzie wrote in a memo in June 1916. 'I think this is a good plan because it gives all my known agents an official status and has enabled me to develop considerably a real secret service.'[4]

Typically, Mackenzie attempted to use the new system to cut out Samson and sideline Alexandria, which led to a series of rows involving not only Samson but also his deputy, Major Charles Ryder, who represented MI5 interests in the Near East; Sir Francis Elliot, who intervened on Mackenzie's behalf; and Cumming himself, who was forced to put Mackenzie in his place in response to Elliot's request on the novelist's behalf for more autonomy. 'There is no intention on

R's part to impose any obstructive control on Lieutenant Compton Mackenzie,' Cumming said at the beginning of July 1916. 'But he is in charge of the branch to which Athens belongs and responsible for the actions of his subordinate whom he appointed to do this particular work and Lieutenant Compton Mackenzie cannot be relieved of his [R's] control.' He also appointed Lieutenant Malcolm Maclachlan, a fluent Greek speaker and another exiled member of Smyrna's expatriate British community, to be liaison officer between Cairo, Athens and Salonika in order to improve relationships and reinforce the point that Samson, and not Mackenzie, was in charge.

At the same time, Cumming applied for funding for military control officers to be stationed in Alexandria; Athens, Christiania (now Oslo), Lisbon, Madrid, New York, Paris, Petrograd, Rome, Rotterdam and Stockholm. They worked to Cumming for intelligence reporting and to Vernon Kell for the reporting of possible German spies. Both Hanns Vischer, now working for both Kell and Cumming as the military control officer in Madrid, and the man sent to Lisbon – Lieutenant Windham Baring RNVR, later managing director of the Baring Brothers merchant bank – were to work closely with Charles Thoroton in Gibraltar. The Madrid bureau was subsequently supplemented by military control officers based in Barcelona, Bilbao and Vigo. Captain Philip Griffiths Pipon of the Indian Army was appointed as military control officer in Marseilles, an important port for travel in the Mediterranean, and was replaced shortly before the end of the war by Ernan Forbes Dennis, a captain on the army's General List. His wife, the American novelist Phyllis Bottome, recalled that Marseilles was 'an international hide-out for spies, who came and went from all directions, usually escaping recognition'. Relieved that her husband was no longer on the front line, she admitted not realising 'till much later that Ernan's new job had a dangerous "cloak and dagger" side to it, although even then, compared to the French front, it was a sheltered existence'.

The main role of Cumming's men in Spain was to talent-spot potential agents who could be sent into Germany. Despite the occasional tensions between Cumming and Blinker Hall, who had a penchant for taking too much control over secret service operations while at the same time still expecting Cumming to fund them, the relationship with Thoroton worked well and the only friction occurred when the military sent Captain Lachlan McEwen to Madrid. This was the same inept intelligence officer who had got himself into trouble with the Dutch police when Aylmer Cameron sent him to Flushing. Predictably, he upset both Cumming and Hall by attempting to run his own agents into Belgium from Spain, thereby endangering the fifty or so agents they already had there, and was recalled to France.[5]

Meanwhile, Mackenzie delighted in chasing German spies around the Greek countryside in an assortment of expensive cars and irritating the Foreign Office, who frequently protested to Cumming over Mackenzie's many overt attempts to get Eleutherios Venizelos re-elected Prime Minister and bring Greece into the war on the Allied side. When Cumming sent his former Danish agent Walter Christmas, a personal friend of King Constantine, to Athens, in the hope of persuading him to agree to go to war against Germany, Mackenzie was furious at the intrusion on his patch. 'Finally,' he said, 'Sir Francis [Elliot] protested against this irresponsible old man of the sea's sojourn any longer in Athens at the expense of the British government and he wandered off again.' What Christmas had to say about Mackenzie on his return to Whitehall Court was 'unrepeatable', recalled Frank Stagg. 'I took that most lovable man to the Hippodrome where Fay Compton was singing a song in which the last line of each verse was "I'll take a little more off". Christmas was getting more and more excited and clapping roundly. When at the height of his enthusiasm, I asked him if he knew she was Compton Mackenzie's sister, he looked tragic and said, "I'll take back everything I said about him. If only I had known he had a sister so lovely I should have made friends with him instead."'[6]

Despite Mackenzie's undoubted arrogance, or perhaps because of it, the few surviving documents in the SIS archives which deal with the First World War in the Near East and Balkans include a note that 'he did at times excellent work'. The most significant of his successes include the capture, in August 1916, of the German diplomatic bag, with Mackenzie's assistants and Greek agents intercepting the courier and persuading him to go with them because 'the British secret service' were out to kidnap him. Having then hit him over the head, they stole the mail, which was concealed in two cushions and included sketch maps of the British defences of the Suez Canal. It also included a letter from the Greek queen to her sister in Germany, the 'illegal' interception of which sent the Foreign Office into a state of panic since both sisters were cousins of King George V, as of course was the Kaiser himself, although this seems not to have been taken into account. Lord Hardinge, the permanent under-secretary at the Foreign Office, insisted that the letter be returned to the Greek queen by the British legation in Athens immediately and also ruled that no use could be made of the other contents of the illegally obtained bag. Mackenzie also dealt efficiently with both von Schenck and the real German master-spy, Captain Alfred Hoffmann, who were persuaded to give themselves up in early September 1916 amid a round-up of German and Turkish agents.[7]

The following month, October 1916, Mackenzie went back to Whitehall Court to meet Cumming for the first time and, with what he claims was some trepidation, was ushered into C's private room, which he described as

> tucked away under the roof, crowded with filing cupboards and shelves, and with the rest of the space almost entirely filled by C's big table. The dormer windows looked out across the plane trees of the Embankment Gardens to the Thames, over which twilight was creeping. I saw on the other side of the table a pale clean-shaven man, the most striking features of his face were a Punch-like chin, a small and beautifully fine bow of a mouth, and a pair of very bright eyes. He was dressed in the uniform of a naval captain. C paid no attention when I came in, but remained bent over the table, perusing through a pair of dark horn-rimmed spectacles some document.

Having originally intended to tear Mackenzie off a strip for all the problems he had caused, Cumming clearly took him to his heart, inviting him for dinner, introducing him to his wife as 'the man who had given him more trouble than anybody else in his service', and presenting him with his much valued swordstick. 'C had a passion for Compton Mackenzie,' said Stagg. 'The blighter used to send reports in blank verse which pleased the Old Man, but our people loathed CM because they had to unravel the rubbish – yards and yards of stuff that could have gone on a postcard.' While in London, Mackenzie also recruited the American playwright Edward Knoblock as his deputy. Knoblock already had experience of intelligence operations, having briefly taken over from Somerset Maugham as the Indian Political Intelligence man in Switzerland before Cumming assumed control there. Knoblock was educated at Harvard and spent his time between his flat in Albany in London's Piccadilly and a Paris apartment overlooking the garden of the Palais Royal. Originally known as Knoblauch (his father was half Dutch and half Hungarian), Knoblock changed his name because of the German connotations and by the time he was recruited by Mackenzie and Cumming he was a US citizen. None of this eased his recruitment as an MI1c officer, Mackenzie recalled:[8]

Knoblock wanted a commission, and I thought I could promise him a lieutenancy in the RNVR. C agreed, but no sooner had Knoblock hurriedly set about procuring a naval uniform than it was discovered that he could not be a lieutenant in the RNVR, because he was an American subject. 'However,' said C, 'I believe we can get him a commission in the RNAS.' So Knoblock dashed out and bought a woollen bird to sew on his naval uniform. No sooner had he equipped himself as a naval airman than he was told he might have to be a Second-Lieutenant in General Service. So Knoblock rushed off from those wonderful Regency rooms of his in Albany and equipped himself with a khaki uniform and the green tabs of an Intelligence Officer. As we were due to leave England on 3 November [1916] and as Knoblock's commission could not possibly be gazetted until long after that, we decided it would be safest to take all three uniforms out to Greece, and possibly dispose out there of the superfluous equipment when it was settled which service he was to join. In his enthusiasm, he even bought two swords, a naval and a military one.[9]

Eventually, Knoblock was commissioned in January 1917, as an 'Honorary Lieutenant' on the Army's Special List. By the time Mackenzie returned to Athens with Knoblock in tow, the political tension between the royalists and the Venizelos supporters was reaching boiling point and in early December, the royalists rampaged through the streets, attacking Venizelists and anyone connected with the British and French 'secret police'. They ransacked Mackenzie's house, with the apparent intention of killing him, but he was not there. The Foreign Office had by now lost its patience with Mackenzie's antics. 'He had, during the troubles in Athens, rather over-stepped the mark, by racing around the city in a car with armed guards standing on the running-boards and acting generally as a brigand,' said one of his officers. Mackenzie was ordered out of Athens and set up a base on the island of Syra, sending several dozen MI1c officers, most of whom wore the uniform of a junior RNVR officer, to run military control and intelligence-gathering bureaux around the Dodecanese islands. Mackenzie called this organisation the Aegean Intelligence Service (AEGIS) and sailed between his various bureaux in the *Avlis*, the former royal yacht of a Greek prince.[10]

By the spring of 1917, the emphasis was increasingly focusing on buying off Turkey and Bulgaria via secret talks held in Switzerland. Rhys Samson moved first to Paris and then to London, where he could have greater control of this process, touring the Swiss bureaux in order to reorganise the operation and make it more efficient. He took Captain Philibert Burlet, one of his assistants in Cairo, with him to Paris, installing him in charge of liaison with the French. Burlet was based at 18 Rue Chauveau Lagarde and had two 'letter boxes' in Rue Jacques-Callot, where letters could be left for him in the fictitious names M. Maurice Godard or M. Louis-Emile Bellon. William Edmonds was left in charge of the intelligence acquisition side of EMSIB HQ, now in Cairo. 'Edmonds was a most capable man and a charming fellow in every way, and had done an immense amount of invaluable work,' said Lewen Weldon. 'He was an exceedingly capable man, and had put in a lot of real hard work. He was one of the few people with whom I had dealings who seemed really to understand what my job was.'[11]

When King Constantine abdicated in June 1917 and Eleutherios Venizelos was reappointed Prime Minister, Mackenzie tried to return to Athens. But the change in political fortunes in Athens coincided with the recall to London of Mackenzie's two main allies at the British legation, the minister, Sir Francis Elliot, and the naval attaché, Commander Bill Sells. Mackenzie found his route back to Athens blocked by a combination of the new chargé d'affaires, Dayrell Crackenthorpe, and Captain Mark Astley Shute, whom Mackenzie had himself appointed to carry out military control in the Greek capital and saw as his subordinate. When Shute refused to accept his authority, Mackenzie sought unsuccessfully to have him sacked and although Shute would eventually be forced to go, so too was Mackenzie, with Crackenthorpe insisting he could not accept the novelist's return to Athens.

'I find my own task here interfered with by Captain Mackenzie's perpetual quarrels and intrigues and I earnestly hope that it may be possible to find some other employment for him in no way connected with Greece,' Crackenthorpe told Hardinge. Realising there was no way of keeping Mackenzie in place, Cumming moved Myres to Athens, ostensibly as liaison with the Greek general staff, and over the next few months gradually managed to have him take over from both Mackenzie and Shute, combining their two organisations. Meanwhile, he had the Foreign Office warn Crackenthorpe not to tangle with Myres since 'it must be remembered that he is a unit in a worldwide organisation which is centred in and controlled from London'.

Mackenzie retired on leave to Capri, claiming ill health, and did not work for Cumming again. He was in large part responsible for his own downfall, his arrogance leading him to make too many enemies among diplomats and military and naval officers who were all too ready to dismiss the work of Cumming's men. When one senior naval officer was told that C was 'very indignant' at the whole affair, he replied: 'I am sorry for C's indignation but I never had any information of any value from his organisation, which was a piratical crew who recognised – in a war area – no naval, military or Foreign Office authority, and brought the British name into disrepute at Athens, Syra, and Salonika and in addition expended a large amount of public money.' Knoblock returned briefly to London where he worked in 'Head Office' alongside Kennerley Rumford, a popular baritone, more famous as a result of his duets with his wife Clara Butt, the first singer of *Land of Hope and Glory*. He then moved to France, working from 'the Nunnery' in Pontarlier collecting reports from agents crossing the border.[12]

As the British advanced across Palestine in late 1917 and early 1918, new bureaux were set up there, with Vivian Gabriel, now a lieutenant-colonel, moving from Italy to take charge in Jerusalem, and Major Alec Kirkwood being appointed Cumming's man in Amman with the grandiose title of 'Chief British Representative'. Gabriel's replacement in Italy was Samuel Hoare, who would subsequently go on to become a prominent Conservative minister in the 1930s and who was in charge of operations for both Cumming and Vernon Kell. Based in offices in the Via Quattro Fontane, Hoare produced a plan to use the hapless Lachlan McEwen, now posted to Italy, to run agents through the enemy lines and recruited the young Benito Mussolini to run propaganda pieces on behalf of the British.

In Greece, Myres took charge of the intelligence-gathering operations while the counter-espionage section originally run by Mackenzie was taken over initially by Lieutenant Bruce Maclachlan, an Intelligence Corps officer, whose family, like the Whittalls, was also based in Smyrna. Lieutenant Arnold Gomme of the Army Service Corps, another authority on ancient Greece and later an eminent professor of Greek at Glasgow University, headed the political and economic intelligence section.[13]

Myres brought some order to the arrangements for recruiting agents, who were required to sign a contract laying out the requirements in detail. The 'confidential agent' was told:

> You must clearly understand . . . that your duties must be kept extremely secret and that you must use the greatest discretion in

obtaining information. Your value to us as an agent can only hold good so long as you are not suspected of being in our service, and it is only fair to warn you that should we hear from other sources that you are in our employ, your payment and employment will cease without notice.

The going rate for a Greek agent in the Greek city of Patras was 500 francs a month, suggesting that while the British provided the officers running the agents on the islands, the main French contribution was the cash to fund them. The duties in early 1918 of an agent in the southern city of Kalamata, run by Charles Tucker, who was now Patras bureau chief, were to keep him informed of 'everything concerning the following points':

1. All local suspects, enemy agents and their movements.
2. Information concerning submarines, signalling from the coast, possible landing of enemy agents, and communications with them. You will be careful in each case to give the approximate if not the exact time, the direction and all other details concerning same.
3. You will take note of all news and rumours which may be circulated by enemy propagandists with a view to creating dissension in the country and hamper the interests of both the Hellenic Government and the Allies. You should endeavour to ascertain the source of creation of these rumours and keep an active, but unostentatious, surveillance over local suspects.
4. You will endeavour to obtain all information regarding the sentiments of the inhabitants, and at the same time obtain a correct impression of what is likely to take place in the event of mobilisation taking place in your district. You should gather all information concerning anti-Venizelists, army officers and non-commissioned officers, unfriendly to the present regime, who may be sowing sedition amongst the soldiers.
5. All information concerning local politics and the situation from a political point of view in your district is also of interest.
6. All coast information from Messina should be regularly reported.

7. After studying local conditions for about a fortnight, you should return to Patras and confer with me with a view to improving upon the conditions of your work already lengthily discussed by us.

8. You should pay careful attention to all matters concerning the emigration of men of military age, the sea passenger service by steamers or caiques, whether the police enforce the passport regulations conscientiously, centres of smuggling and anything suspicious which you might hear of from the hinterland.

9. As soon as you have settled down in Kalamata you should let me have your correct address.

You will communicate with me in the manner already discussed between us. You should let me have a weekly report of your district. In case of anything urgent and of importance you should not hesitate to let me know by confidential messenger or by coming to Patras yourself. You will bear in mind that your duties are essentially of such a nature as to keep me correctly informed of all matters which concern the interests of both the Hellenic Government and of its allies and you should not hesitate to report anything suspicious concerning the conduct of any Government officials who do not appear to be acting correctly or loyally to the Government.

P.S. You should in case of emergency immediately burn this letter and all documents in your possession. You will endeavour to give every impression that your commercial vocation and occupations are entirely bona-fide.[14]

Redmond Cafferata was sent from Switzerland to take over the Athens counter-espionage operations from Maclachlan in May 1918, travelling via Italy to liaise with Captain Arthur Warden Baker, the military control officer in Rome. Cafferata was ordered by Claude Dansey to report on the state of the operation in Greece, including the abilities of both the officers and the agents. This appears to have been partly a result of the concern within Whitehall over the mess Mackenzie was assumed to have left behind and partly due to the constant attacks by the military intelligence section in Salonika, which, having managed to get rid of both James Morgan and Hugh Whittall, was making Harry Pirie-Gordon's life a nightmare, trying at one point to stop him sending telegrams in cipher because they insisted they should be able to read anything he sent out. Cafferata retained the covername of Zulu and was assisted by RNVR lieutenants Fred Parkinson and John Lewis and Royal Field Artillery lieutenant Henry Ormerod, plus a Greek translator and a Serbian liaison officer.

A request from Myres for more staff, coming as it did amid concerns within the War Office over the British secret service operations in Greece that were only exacerbated by the rows with Salonika, led Macdonogh and Blinker Hall to order an inquiry into the usefulness of the MI1c operation in Athens. 'That Commander Myres and his personnel work hard is quite realised,' Macdonogh said. 'But it is desired to know if their results lead to work of real use or if it is only secondary.' A conference of senior naval and military intelligence officers in the region, presided over by the British military attaché, Brigadier-General William Fairholme, initially suggested that military and naval intelligence should control the secret service operations. Commander Gerald Talbot, the naval attaché, was by far the most vociferous critic, engineering an order from the Admiralty that the entire operation should be handed over to the Greek police. Reporting back on the inquiry to Dansey, Cafferata was withering over 'the stupidity and danger of the proposal to abolish the SS [secret service] and hand us over body and soul to the tender mercies of the Greek police'. Despite his RNVR commission, Cafferata detected a naval conspiracy, pointing out that Vivian Gabriel – who also attended the conference – had warned Norman Dewhurst beforehand that the naval representatives 'were out on a wrecking expedition'. But throughout Myres appears to have kept his head, impressing all but Talbot that, far from being a waste of time and money that ought to be axed, 'the existing work should be extended' since 'they were not doing as much as they ought to do'. He revealed that they were running sixty agents and their operations cost about £2,000 a month and that he had 'the minimum staff with which anything like the desired results could be achieved'. He could not do without a proper number of agents. 'We are taking risks now that the French and Italians did not take and the services could not be really efficient without a larger staff,' Myres said. The inquiry ultimately agreed that he was doing good work and could do even better with more resources. Talbot demurred and sent his own 'opinions' to the Admiralty, informing them that 'I have personally seen no results which should justify the employment of the approximate number of sixty native agents mentioned by Commander Myres. No naval intelligence of any value whatsoever has come to me through this source and I consider that the activities of agents dealing with the Greek navy have produced most unfortunate results.'

In his report back to Dansey on the state of the Greek intelligence organisation, Cafferata dismissed the criticisms:

> That certain members of that conference came here with the intention of wrecking or snatching some part of C's organisation I have little doubt. If our organisation under Commander Myres has failed, and I cannot see that it has, it ought to be replaced by a larger and stronger service; if it has failed at all, this is only because it has been utterly understaffed; it seems to me that, having chosen a man of confidence to represent you here, and having that man as your chief, he should be loyally backed up by every means in your power. As a person of some considerable pre-war experience and not a little SS experience, I can only repeat that you have all you want in my chief. After all the good work that C has had in establishing a worldwide and successful SS organisation, I hope to God that he won't allow any part of his organisation to be wrecked by reports from certain members of the above conference who have not had the experience nor means of giving a considered opinion.[15]

Cafferata also had one of his agents from Switzerland, Jim de Teux – codenamed Walfisch – sent to Athens as a *Daily Mail* journalist for a specific undercover operation, the target of which is unclear. The

Mansfield Smith Cumming, the first 'chief' of SIS, from a painting by SIS officer H. F. Crowther Smith.

Ashley Mansions, Vauxhall Bridge Road, the headquarters of Britain's secret service between 1909 and 1914.

Walter Christmas, the Danish naval captain who insisted on being paid for his reports by a pretty young woman who was to meet him in a hotel in Skagen, northern Denmark.

Max Schultz, the British shipbroker who was jailed by the Germans for spying for Cumming. (Schultz family archive)

Hector Bywater, journalist and naval expert who spied for Cumming in pre-war Germany. (US State Department)

Walter and Edward Archer, aka Sage and Sagette, on board their yawl *Edirene* in 1914. (Alice Archer, Ryfylkemuseet)

Whitehall Court, the Service's First World War headquarters. 2 Whitehall Court is the section with the high tower on the right. (Nick Hiley)

WHITEHALL COURT, WESTMINSTER
ARCHER AND GREEN ARCHITECTS

Above left Captain Reginald 'Blinker' Hall, director of naval intelligence, 1914–19. (Getty Images)
Above Richard Tinsley, Cumming's Rotterdam bureau chief, as drawn by SIS officer H. F. Crowther Smith.
Left Brigadier General George Macdonogh, director of military intelligence, 1916–18. (© National Portrait Gallery. London)

Thomas Ralph Merton, the
Service's first 'Q'.
(AIP Emilio Segre Visual Archives,
W. F. Meggers Collection)

Henry Landau, who dealt
with the intelligence from
the La Dame Blanche train-
watching network.

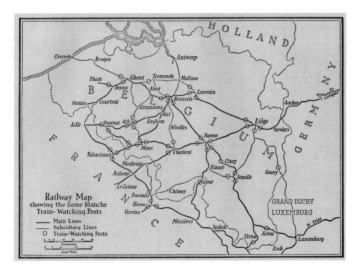

La Dame Blanche train–watching posts.

Park Mansions, South Lambeth Road, the location of
Pierre-Marie Cavrois O'Caffrey's air section.

Frank Stagg, who oversaw
Cumming's First World War
operations in Scandinavia.

Richard Carlyle Holme, First
World War Copenhagen bureau
chief, who ran operations into
Germany from Denmark.
(Henrik Sinding-Larsen)

Lawrence Grossmith, the British actor who briefly took over as New York bureau chief in 1918. (National Library of Australia)

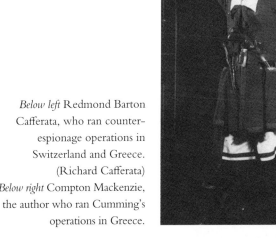

Below left Redmond Barton Cafferata, who ran counter-espionage operations in Switzerland and Greece. (Richard Cafferata)

Below right Compton Mackenzie, the author who ran Cumming's operations in Greece.

Sarah Aaronsohn, member of
the Nili spy ring, who shot
herself rather than give up her
colleagues.

Lewen Weldon on board *Anne*,
one of the yachts he used to run
agents into Turkish-controlled
territory.

West House, 1 Melbury Rd, Kensington, Cumming's house and SIS
headquarters from late 1919 to mid-1926.

cover was created in Paris by Philibert Burlet, now based at 6 Rue de Bellechasse and operating under the codename Rivoli. Burlet was himself an ex-journalist and had a number of contacts in his former profession but nevertheless had some difficulty arranging the cover, as he explained to Cafferata:

> The Associated Press of America refused to play and it is only on account of my cordial relations with the Paris [office of the] Daily Mail that I succeeded in obtaining the desired cover, which you will observe is quite good. Even then the matter had to be submitted to the decision of Lord Northcliffe – but please do not mention this to Jim. I trust that in return for the attitude taken by the D.M. in the matter, Jim will be able to do something for them in the business line, and above all 'j'espère qu'il ne fera pas de bétises' [I hope he won't do anything stupid], as I made myself responsible for his trustworthiness. I know that you will supervise Jim's stunts and so I merely mention this en passant.

In a separate letter, Staff Paymaster Percy Sykes, the MI1c administration officer, explained to Myres that in order to make him appear to be the genuine article, the *Daily Mail* was paying 'Walfisch' £15 a month 'to maintain his cover' and that Myres should pay the monthly balance of £20 from the bureau's funds.[16]

At the end of October, Dansey travelled out to the Balkans, meeting Myres in Salonika and closing down the Greek outstations, leaving just the passport control office in Athens under Myres himself. Dewhurst, who was one of the officers made redundant in this process, was purloined by Dansey to help him infiltrate three officers, Tom Masterson, Eddie Boxshall and Second-Lieutenant Henry Bowe into Romania behind the retreating Germans. Dewhurst drove them by road to Sofia and then train to Romania, the car journey taking them via the Roupel Pass. 'It was not without thrills,' Dewhurst recalled. 'News of the Armistice had not yet reached the Bulgars or our flyers and wholesale strafing was taking place with bullets whizzing around everywhere. We could see the Bulgarian troops being mown down on the other side of the valley, but the secondary road we were on received much less attention.' Masterson, Boxshall and Bowe all completed their missions, with Bowe subsequently making his way north across Russia to the Baltic.[17]

By now, EMSIB had been closed down and Rhys Samson was back at headquarters in charge of the political section, although he did briefly return to the Adrianople consulate at the end of the war before being recalled to London. He was subsequently sent out to Constantinople as bureau chief. With the war over, Colonel Charles French sent a signal to all military intelligence sections across the Middle East and the Balkans tasking them to 'secure good correspondents who will be of future rather than immediate use' for Cumming. They 'should work through me in close touch with MI1c in London as that section will be responsible for keeping up any correspondence they initiate.' French, the head of military intelligence, reiterated the concept of recruiting agents in one country to spy on the neighbouring country. 'It is conceivable that useful results may be obtained in the future by using one nationality to report on another,' he said. 'For instance Poles might keep us informed about Germany, Russia, Austria and Hungary.' The third-country rule, as it became known, was to be a key tenet of MI1c operations during the interwar years, but this certainly did not rule out operations inside the countries themselves, particularly when they remained as important as the first two French mentioned in his signal, Germany and Russia, an accurate prediction of the two main targets now facing Britain's secret service.[18]

'CUD' Thornhill stood on the bridge of the Mikhail Arkhangel as it headed towards the dockside in Onega. The ship was borrowed from the monks who lived on a lonely windswept island out in the bay. Thornhill, a colonel in the Indian army and the most senior British secret service officer in Russia, was on a dangerous mission. It was July 1918. British, French and American forces were waiting to land at Archangel, part of a three-pronged Allied intervention to halt the Bolshevik takeover. Thornhill and a handful of MI1c officers had been sent to take the port of Onega, a cluster of wooden huts and houses at the base of the White Sea. Thornhill's plan, more akin to special operations than secret service, was to create a diversion that would split off some of the several thousand Bolshevik forces in Archangel and allow the main Allied force to get ashore.

The Red Guards on the Onega dockside were relaxed as the Mikhail Arkhangel headed towards them, lulled into a false sense of security by the red flag flying from its mast and the tall authoritative figure in Russian uniform standing on the bridge. Thornhill's men, a mix of British, Serbian and Russian troops, were hidden below deck. He had been joined on the mission by his second-in-command, Captain J. J. Hitching, Captain Herbert Evelyn Lee and Second Lieutenant Charles Richards, all members of the Secret Intelligence Service, MI1c. They had travelled down by train from Murmansk to the White Sea port of Kem, where they were met by another MI1c officer, Captain Denys Garstin, in rags and exhausted after escaping from Moscow by foot, but insistent on joining the party. They took a trawler out to the island of Solovetsky, where the monks were known to be sympathetic to the anti-Bolshevist cause and happily lent Thornhill their supply ship.

As the Mikhail Arkhangel pulled alongside the pier in Onega and the crew began making fast, Thornhill leaned over the rail, chatting away in Russian to the four Red Guards, who were keen to know if the ship was bringing in food from the monastery gardens. Thornhill joked with the Bolsheviks, putting them completely at ease. Then suddenly, he ripped off his Russian Army greatcoat to reveal the uniform of a British officer and leaped ashore. The speed of his attack completely wrongfooted the Red Guards. One lunged at him with a bayonet, but the MI1c officer knocked it to one side and shot his assailant through the head.

By now, Thornhill's men were pouring up onto the deck to find him ready to take on three Red Guards single handed. One of the Bolsheviks raised his *gun to shoot Thornhill, but the MI1c officer's bodyguard, a giant ex-Russian army officer, leaped between them, taking the shot in his arm. The remaining Red Guards ran for their lives, pursued by the pistol-waving MI1c officers and their mixed band of troops. After five hours of street fighting, the Bolsheviks were overwhelmed and the town was in British hands, forcing Bolshevik commanders to send troops from Archangel and allowing the Allied forces waiting offshore to land. Thornhill received the Distinguished Service Order for what the citation described as his 'marked courage' during 'a most dashing attack', which 'inspired all ranks under his command'.*

ELEVEN

Murder and mayhem in Russia

AT the start of the war, Cumming attempted to set up a liaison operation with the Russian intelligence services, amid concern over the Tsar's commitment to the war. It was vitally important to the allies in the West that the Russians tied large numbers of German troops down on the eastern front. Cumming's strong desire for good liaison with his counterparts in the Tsarist military and naval secret services led to a suggestion that he should travel to Petrograd himself to cement relations. The Foreign Office rejected this proposal but, at the end of September 1914, did give him permission to set up a Russian bureau. He selected three officers, Major Archibald Campbell, Major Victor Ferguson, and Lieutenant Stephen Alley – who spoke fluent Russian, having been born and brought up in Russia – and sent them to Petrograd, seeing them off at King's Cross station.[1]

Ferguson was the administrative head of the 'British Intelligence Mission', as the bureau was to be called, with Campbell as the chief intelligence officer, but it was Alley who would prove to be the most important. He was born in 1876 in a village near Moscow where his father, a wealthy businessman, owned an estate. He was sent back to the UK at the age of fifteen to work in the family's mechanical engineering business, but fell out with his cousin and set up his own company on the basis of his invention of a patent tyre lever. He also joined the Surrey Yeomanry, a reservist unit, and qualified as an interpreter in Russian, French and German. But with his business on the verge of bankruptcy, he was forced to return to Russia to earn money, working for the

Maikop & General Petroleum Trust, a company owned by future US President Herbert Hoover, on a new oil pipeline being built to transport oil from the Maikop oilfields in southern Russia to the Black Sea. When war broke out, he was recruited into military intelligence and given his fluency in Russian was sent to see Cumming, who initially was reticent about recruiting him on the basis that his lack of medals would make it difficult for him to impress the status-conscious Russian officer class.[2]

> I was called up by the War Office to see Captain [Archibald] Wavell [later Field Marshal, the Earl Wavell] who was then in charge of intelligence, although he was only a captain. He was looking for an Officer to send to Russia and thought I might suit the job. I had met Wavell first in Russia when he was learning the language. He sent me to see C. I went over to his office, which was at that time in Whitehall Mansions, apparently he occupied the top flat, and personally he occupied the turret. I had to climb up very steep stairs to reach his room and he had apparently to lift a brick before you could open the door. I met C, who telephoned for his secretary to take notes. She popped up through a trap door in the floor and was present for the interview. C sent me to meet the Russian Military Attaché [Lieutenant-General Nikolai Ermelov] who occupied a flat in the same building. The only remark C made to me was that I might not fit the job as I had not any decorations, however at a second interview with [Ermelov] apparently my knowledge of Russian made him agree to my appointment. C's suggestion was that I should obtain some [fake] decorations from Clarksons, which however I did not do.

Campbell, who could not speak a word of Russian, was a poor choice as the main intelligence officer, but he was not helped by orders from Cumming that the MI1c bureau was to have no links to the embassy and to Colonel Alfred Knox, the military attaché, in particular. 'We were not taken to the British embassy, nor were we introduced to the British military attaché,' Alley later recalled. 'This was according to C's instructions and caused considerable trouble to us for a long time to come. It is impossible to imagine what was in the Old Man's head when he gave these instructions, he must have thought we were going to be on a secret mission.'

They set up their bureau in a room in the Russian general staff headquarters but wrote up their secret reports in Campbell's room in the Hôtel d'Europe. The initial reports had to be sent via the ambassador, which got the mission off to a bad start. Campbell's first report dealt with the main issue that dominated Whitehall's requirement for a secret service operation in the capital of one of its main allies – Russia's commitment to the war. In it he wrote:

> I have it from trustworthy source that strong influences are at work upon Russian Minister for Foreign Affairs in direction of proposals from Russian quarters to Germany for some kind of peace or mutual understanding regarding discontinuation or limitation of war, as between these two countries. Idea to be worked out in Rome between the two embassies. With this view, the counsellor of the Russian embassy is now in Petrograd. Referring to these German influences, Grand Duke Commander-in-Chief recently declared to Emperor in presence of other personages that he and army under his command could not conform to any such proposals. It is expected matter will shortly come out in the press. I can send names and other details if required.

The ambassador, Sir George Buchanan, was furious, sending the report but accompanying it with a far longer memorandum of his own, in which he denounced the claims as 'absurd'. He then added: 'I attach no importance to these reports although others have told me the Grand Duke of Hesse is urging the Empress to use her influence in favour of peace.'[3] There is no doubt that Buchanan was behaving as many other ambassadors had already done, and many more would do in the future, in objecting to secret service operations due to an instinctive distaste for such supposedly ungentlemanly activities and fear of potential embarrassment should they be publicly exposed. But if Alley's memories are anything to go by, Campbell did not help his own case:

Campbell, who was the sloppiest officer I had for some time, took charge of all the coding which was done and I had the sending off of his telegrams! All this work, i.e. coding and letter-writing was done in the hotel, and Campbell had some difficulty in destroying copies, which he put down the loo. My job, apparently, was to forward a summary of the Russian appraisal of the German troops facing them. I also had to send the latest news of the Navy, which meant sending a report about the *Göben* and the *Breslau*, which were very active in the Dardanelles. We were using a dictionary code and, after a short time, we had exhausted the amount of matter that could be coded, and letters had to be sent, which meant that one of us officers had to visit the embassy for these to be forwarded in the Bag. Campbell arranged a contact for himself and visited the embassy, still not having reported to the military attaché, Colonel Knox, which fact eventually brought trouble to us. He naturally resented our mission butting in and doing what he considered to be his job.[4]

Campbell's complete lack of social skills – he made it clear to Knox that his was a secret mission and that his bosses in London were insistent that he was to have nothing to do with the military attaché – ensured their relationship was always going to be difficult. The fact that his physical appearance was as slovenly as his operational procedure only added to the irritation Knox felt that he had no control over an officer, who as a mere major, was very much his junior. The position wasn't helped by the fact that following his initial report, which was no doubt received with interest in Whitehall, Campbell, by his own admission, failed to collect much intelligence of value. Given that he was attempting to set up his networks from scratch, this might not have been an issue for a few months, but it was overshadowed by a much greater problem in that both Buchanan and Knox objected violently, not just to Campbell but, to the presence of any British 'secret service' officers over whom they had no control, with Buchanan describing it as 'an intolerable situation' and denouncing their reports as largely 'political gossip' which had only 'added to my already heavy workload by rendering it necessary for me to contradict it'.

The problem appears to have been exacerbated by a plan to send British radio operators – known euphemistically as 'the technicians' – to Petrograd to control Russian military communications, a move apparently requested by the Russians, although there is more than a hint that the plan was devised by Cumming and Campbell before the latter went to Russia to monitor the Russian communications, and that it was first suggested by the British. Whatever the truth of the matter, Campbell's boorishness only served to make what was a substantial problem considerably worse and both Brigadier-General George Cockerill, the War Office Director of Special Intelligence, and Blinker Hall, who had just been appointed the Admiralty's director of Intelligence Division, advised Cumming to bring Campbell back to London in an attempt to end the rows. Campbell's approach had been 'the reverse of tactful' and 'it seemed doubtful therefore whether he was qualified to carry out this delicate and difficult task'.

Campbell returned home while his team of 'technicians' was put together, but he promptly set about upsetting everyone in the MI1c offices with grandiose plans for reorganisation. He was then sent back to Petrograd without the radio operators – the Russians having perhaps realised that the British would use them to monitor all their communications and changed their minds. Campbell was forcibly told not only to let Knox see everything he sent back to Cumming but 'to avoid in every possible way any cause for friction with the naval and military attachés and the discussion of questions which might create difficulties for the authorities at home'. Given the antagonistic attitude of both Buchanan and Knox to secret service activities, this would have been difficult for the most tactful of officers. It predictably proved completely beyond Campbell. Knox threatened to resign if he stayed, at which point the ambassador insisted Campbell and Ferguson be recalled, although Alley, whose knowledge of Russia and the language ensured him much better contacts than Campbell, was to stay.[5]

Alley noted that while both he and Ferguson visited the Russian fronts, Campbell declined to do so, apparently preferring to stay in Petrograd and argue with Knox. During a series of visits to the Caucasus in 1915 and 1916, Alley not only set up a number of useful contacts with Russian officers and local people, but also looked up some of the Russians he had known during his time working on the oil pipeline. At one point, he and a local guide found themselves heading straight for the Turkish lines.

> My guide suggested we turn back and go to the left, which we did, and eventually got into a cleft and proceeded along this until we were halted by a Russian who asked who the hell we were and where we were going. When told who we were, he informed us that he was in charge of a battery and invited us to spend the night there, which we thankfully did. The Russian officers were very pleased to see us, and produced a supper which was extraordinarily good. There was caviar and vodka, so after the meal, I produced a bottle of brandy, which I had put in my luggage with the intention of using it for my Russian friends. They pitched my tent in a position they said was all right, and we all went to sleep peacefully. At daybreak however, one of the officers woke me up, to say that I was in full view of the enemy, and would surely be shelled if I remained there. So I hurriedly moved. Later, we said goodbye to the battery commander and proceeded along the front on our return journey. It was along the top of the ride, and we were shot at all the way by the Turks who were on the other side of the Valley.[6]

Campbell's replacement as the head of Cumming's bureau in Petrograd was Major Cudbert Thornhill. 'Cud' Thornhill was born in Tibet, where his father was in charge of the British frontier station. 'Cud' was a highly impressive individual with a reputation as a great adventurer. A war correspondent for *The Times* who met him in Russia described him as 'one of the bravest men – and most silent – I have ever met'. Thornhill was 'a calm dignified, silent man, almost detached in his bearing, until the moment came for quick action; then the iciness would erupt like a volcano'. He followed his father into the Indian Army and became fluent in a number of languages, including Russian and Farsi, the main languages of the Great Game, the nineteenth-century battle between Russian and British intelligence officers for control over the countries of central Asia, in particular Iran and Afghanistan.

Thornhill fared better than Campbell, initially at least, repairing relations with Knox. His relationship with C is said to have become strained in mid-1916 after he resisted a move to Romania to improve intelligence on the Bulgarian and Serbian militaries, although just how strained is unclear and there is a feel of Cumming using the situation to his own advantage. He sent the MP for Chelsea, Sir Samuel Hoare, an acquaintance of Cumming's former deputy Freddie Browning and a Russian speaker, to take charge of the MI1c bureau, while Thornhill was made an assistant military attaché, controlling the collection of military intelligence, but with his reporting still controlled and circulated in London by Cumming.[7]

Hoare later described the depth of his surprise on meeting the chief of Britain's secret service:

'In all respects physical and mental, he was the very antithesis of the spy king of popular fiction. Jovial and very human, bluff and plain-speaking, outwardly at least, a very simple man, who would ever have imagined that this was the chief who . . . employed secret agents in every corner of the world? My first interview with him was typical of the man. I had expected to be put through an examination in the Russian language, and a questionnaire as to what I knew about Russian politics and the Russian army. I had imagined that I should have been almost blindfolded before being introduced into the presence of this man of mystery. Instead there were a few conventional questions in a very conventional room, a searching look and a nod to say that whilst it was not much of a job, I could have it, if I wanted it. In the space of a few seconds I was accepted into the ranks of the Secret Service.

Unusually, Hoare was given an extensive course in espionage work, probably because he was not the normal type of 'vagabond' Cumming employed on secret service and was therefore assumed to lack the natural abilities. There is little reference to any other of Cumming's men undergoing a training course, and frequent complaints over the lack of one. But Cumming clearly saw Hoare as a similar figure to his Washington bureau chief, William Wiseman, rather than one of the roguish spies he favoured for actual secret service operations on the ground. Cumming told Hoare to be tactful and firm in his treatment of both Buchanan and Knox. His representatives in Petrograd had been 'alternatively kicked and caressed by MA and embassy,' Cumming said, 'but at no time were they encouraged or given much assistance of any kind.' He told Hoare to keep on friendly terms with Knox, 'but resist any attempts on anyone's part to absorb mission, which as you well understand is integral and essential part of a complex and far-reaching system.'

Whatever his abilities, Hoare was not a Wiseman. He was a rather pompous, self-regarding man, but he was nevertheless someone whom the ambassador would see as being from 'the right class' and who could present a personable front for Cumming's mission while the secret service work was conducted quietly behind the scenes by others like Alley. Hoare never got on with Knox, who continued to try to take control of the mission away from Cumming, but with Thornhill acting as Knox's main intelligence officer the MI1c chief appears to have ensured that behind the scenes his men remained in control of the intelligence collection operation.

The limits on what Hoare knew of the real secret service work going on in Russia would later become clear, but despite the espionage course, Cumming appears to have been open about the role he wanted him to take. 'Being new, secret, and very indefinite, these [secret service] organisations were bound from time to time to come into collision with the ordinary missions of peacetime diplomacy,' Hoare said. 'It seemed well to the authorities in Whitehall to send out a new officer to join the British intelligence mission in Petrograd, whose first duty should be to smooth away some of the difficulties that had arisen.'[8]

Hoare had a budget of just under £2,600[9] and was given a firm brief on the duties of the Petrograd bureau, which were 'collection and forwarding of information on enemy fleets and forces; their progress; plans, success or failure; order of battle, movements and general military information on them'. He was also to collect intelligence on trade and breaches of the blockade, and the 'histories and movements of suspicious persons as are likely to be of interest to British authorities'. The instructions described Cumming as the chief of the secret service (CSS) and Whitehall Court as 'Head Office', two titles which are still in use today.

Most of the order of battle intelligence was collected by Thornhill. He was assisted by another MI1c officer, Captain Leo Steveni, a member of pre-war St Petersburg's British expatriate community – the city had been renamed Petrograd at the start of the war since St Petersburg was deemed to sound too German. Steveni's mother was the daughter of a Tsarist nobleman and minister. His father was a British citizen who before the war ran the largest firm of timber exporters based in St Petersburg and was a member of an expatriate community of some 2,000 Britons with their own shops, tailors, shirtmakers and an Anglican church. Steveni was commissioned on the Special List. The work he was doing at this stage was primarily concerned with intelligence on German army units based on the Eastern Front but also led to some important naval intelligence, particularly ahead of the British victory at the Battle of Dogger Bank in January 1915, for which Cumming received special thanks. This may be related to the Russian capture of the main German naval codebook, in late 1914, since British interception of the German naval wireless traffic by the Admiralty's Room 40 codebreakers is normally given the credit for the intelligence that was critical in winning the battle.

'To start with our mission was very under-staffed and we had to work really hard with long hours from 9 a.m. to 6 p.m. and from 8 p.m. to midnight, Sundays included,' Steveni recalled. 'Our work consisted primarily in obtaining from the Russian general staff German and Austrian army identifications secured on the Eastern Front, and as a quid pro quo we passed to the Russians similar information obtained on the Western Front from British and French sources. Prior to the evening session a member of our mission daily visited the Russian Admiralty to obtain their intelligence reports, the up-to-date location and movements of the German High Sea Fleet from Kiel and the North Sea naval ports. This was passed the same night by us by telegraph to London. The Russian naval intelligence in the early days of the war was regarded as first class. It can now be told that one of their reports gave the necessary warning to our Admiralty which enabled Admiral Beatty's battle cruisers to intercept and successfully engage units of the German High Sea Fleet off the Dogger Bank in 1915.'[10]

The intelligence operations going on in the background were run by Alley, Captain John Dymoke Scale, the subsequent recruiter of Sidney Reilly, and another MI1c officer, Lieutenant Oswald Rayner, who had been sent out in November 1915 with Major Henry Vere Benet to carry out an extensive 'censorship' of telegrams and mail examined in total collaboration with the Russian authorities, while sharing the intelligence it produced on a rather more selective basis. Some of the most productive material came on Scandinavian shipping companies taking goods into or out of Germany through the Royal Navy economic blockade.[11]

Rayner had been born in Smethwick, just west of Birmingham, where his father was a draper. He eventually got himself a job teaching English in Finland, which was then an autonomous grand duchy of Russia. He appears to have been adopted by a couple with whom he became friendly and who acted as his benefactors funding an education at Oxford, where he studied modern languages and made influential new friends, including Prince Feliks Yusupov, a member of what was reputed to be the richest family in Russia. A brief career as a junior Paris correspondent for *The Times* was followed by a move into the civil service as private secretary to Sir Herbert Samuel, the Postmaster-General, through whom he came to know David Lloyd George, a future Prime Minister, who was then Chancellor of the Exchequer. When war broke out, Rayner sought a commission in the army and with his fluency in French, German and Russian was swiftly recognised as having intelligence potential. He was commissioned into the Special List and assigned to Cumming. After a brief period working at Whitehall Court, he was sent to Russia where he shared an apartment with Benet and Alley.

Scale, a 6 foot 4 inch Indian Army officer, had been serving on the Western Front when his ability to speak Russian led to him being called back to England to escort a group of influential Russian parliamentarians, and ultimately to his recruitment by Cumming to advise Hoare on military matters and act as the link-man with Thornhill and Steveni. He was billeted in the Astoria Hotel, 'a fine five-storeyed building', with marble stairs, plate glass windows, brilliant brasswork and mahogany, thick red carpets and graceful palms, which gave it 'a glow of comfort unknown in any other hotel in Petrograd'. The Astoria was taken over by the government at the outbreak of hostilities and was now the 'official' hotel, open only to diplomats, officers and officials.

'Its salons ware kaleidoscopes of movement and colour,' Scale recalled. 'Cossacks, guardsmen, naval officers, in fact men in every Russian uniform imaginable, military and civil (most civilians in Russia wear uniform) sat at tables or stood in groups chatting with their women folk, often very beautiful women they were too in wonderful clothes and jewellery. Here and there among the throng officers in the uniform of one or other of the allied powers were conspicuous. No taciturnity or absence of smiles was noticeable here. In fact, one could hardly recognise the airs played by the military band so loud was the buzz of talk and laughter. A cheery, careless place was the Astoria (a happy hunting ground for enemy agents too!).'[12]

Scale worked across the intelligence system, assisting Thornhill as well as Hoare. Shortly after Scale arrived in Petrograd, Cumming set up the military control system, initially with two offices in Russia, one run by Alley in Petrograd, with offices at 19 Moika Embankment, and the second at Archangel, run by Malcolm McLaren, another of Cumming's officers. McLaren was another Briton who had worked in Russia's oilfields, although he is said to have previously been a sea captain and wore gold earrings that 'gave him the look of a pirate'. There were sub-stations at Torneå on the border between Sweden and Finland, where Lieutenant Harry Gruner checked people coming in and out of Russia; in the Far East at Vladivostok, where Lieutenant Leonard Binns RNVR was assistant military control officer; and across Russia's central Asian empire, where consuls issued visas under Alley's general supervision. Although the military control function was important, the primary role was of course to collect intelligence, and Alley later recalled sending his officers across Russia setting up agent networks: 'Collected a lot of suitable officers in Russia who really could speak the language, and popped them about to keep me informed as to what was happening.' They included Gerald 'Jim' Gillespie, working initially under consular cover and later as a sub-lieutenant in the RNVR, who used Petrograd for a base for trips around the Russian empire recruiting agents.

The staff at the Petrograd office were controlled by Ernest Boyce, who had worked with Alley in the Maikop oilfields. By 1916, those working there also included Winifred Spink, a 28-year-old female officer; Sidney Tomes, a civilian acting under consular cover; Maurice Mansfield, Alley's assistant from the Maikop days, who was commissioned as a lieutenant in the Army General List; and Frank Urmston, another expatriate brought up in Russia, where his father ran a Moscow-based engineering company. Urmston was given the standard MI1c cover of a commission in the RNVR, along with Lieutenant Harry Anderson and Sub-Lieutenant Frank Ball. As with many other MI1c officers, their naval rank was simply for convenience and they had no naval training whatsoever, Alley recalled.

> These officers were given commissions in the Royal Naval Reserve, and eventually obtained uniforms and had to be shown how to use their swords when an Admiral arrived from England and inspected them. They were very efficient at their jobs, but knew nothing of naval matters. Several of these officers eventually became quite important members of C's Staff.[13]

It was at this point, with concern growing that Russia might negotiate a separate peace with Germany, thereby releasing the seventy German divisions tied down on the Eastern Front, that Cumming's young service became involved in a gruesome and brutal operation aimed at determining the extent of the risk, and eliminating a man seen as being the most likely to persuade the Tsar to take Russia out of the war. The target was Grigory Yefimovich Rasputin, a so-called *starets*, or holy man, who had inveigled his way into the royal family's confidence, and particularly that of the Tsarina, by claiming to be able to control the haemophilia suffered by their son, the Tsarevich Alexei.

There were persistent rumours that a peace party under Rasputin's influence was working with Germany and a number of prominent Russians discussed plots to remove him from power. Hoare was approached by one of the plotters, Vladimir Purishkevich, a member of the Russian parliament, the Duma, in November 1916, and told that a plan existed to 'liquidate' Rasputin. 'At this time, the Russian word "to liquidate" was on everyone's lips,' Hoare later recalled. 'I had heard so much, however, of former plots and attempts to "liquidate the affair of Rasputin", and my friend's tone was so casual that I thought his words were symptomatic of what everyone was thinking and saying rather than the expression of a definitely thought-out plan.' Hoare appears not to have been aware that three of his own mission's officers, Alley (now MCO), Scale and Rayner, were in fact closely involved in the plan.

The murder of Rasputin has always been portrayed as an almost romantic attempt to rescue the Tsar Nicholas II and the Tsarina Alexandra from Rasputin's malign influence. In fact, it was without doubt one of the most brutal and ruthless incidents in the entire history of Britain's secret service. Alley and Scale were becoming increasingly concerned over the position of the German-born Tsarina, and in particular the role of Rasputin as her closest adviser. Such views were shared by many in Russia, where virtually anything that went wrong was laid at the feet of the so-called 'Dark Forces' that Rasputin was deemed to represent, and in London, where *The Times* described Rasputin as 'one of the most potent of the baleful Germanophil forces in Russia'. The deep suspicion with which he was regarded by the MI1c bureau in Petrograd is betrayed in Scale's own account of the period:

German intrigue was becoming more intense daily. Enemy agents were busy whispering of peace and hinting how to get it by creating disorder, rioting, etc. Things looked very black. Romania was collapsing, and

Russia herself seemed weakening. The failure in communications, the
shortness of foods, the sinister influence which seemed to be clogging
the war machine, Rasputin the drunken debaucher influencing Russia's
policy, what was to the be the end of it all?[14]

The key link between the British secret service bureau in Petrograd
and the Russians plotting Rasputin's demise was Rayner through his
relationship with Prince Yusupov, the leader of the Russian plotters.
Yusupov enticed Rasputin to his family's palace on the banks of the river
Neva in Petrograd for a 'party', with the prospect of sex apparently high
on the agenda. Yusupov told his wife Princess Irina, the Tsar's niece,
that she was to be used as 'the lure' to entice Rasputin to attend the
party, a suggestion that appears to have persuaded her to extend a holiday
in the Crimea so she was not in Petrograd at the time. Those known
to have been present for the 'party' in the Yusupov Palace, apart from
Rasputin, include Yusupov himself; the Grand Duke Dmitry Pavlovich,
the Tsar's second cousin; Purishkevich; Lieutenant Sergei Sukhotin,
a friend of Yusupov's; Dr Stanislaus de Lazovert, the medical officer
of Purishkevich's military unit, who was recruited as the driver; plus
Rayner.

Once there Rasputin was plied with drink and then tortured in
order to discover the truth of his alleged links with a German attempt to
persuade Russia to leave the war. The torture was carried out with an
astonishing level of violence, probably using a heavy rubber cosh – the
original autopsy report found that his testicles had been 'crushed' flat and
there is more than a suspicion that the extent of the damage was fuelled
by sexual jealousy. Yusupov, who is believed to have had a homosexual
relationship with another of the plotters, the Grand Duke Dimitri, is also
alleged to have had a previous sexual liaison with Rasputin. Whatever
Rasputin actually told the conspirators, and someone in his predicament
could be expected to say anything that might end the ordeal, they had
no choice then but to murder him and dispose of the body. He was
shot several times, with three different weapons, with all the evidence
suggesting that Rayner fired the final fatal shot, using his personal

Webley revolver. Rasputin's body was then dumped through an ice hole in the Neva.[15]

Hoare might not have been aware of his officers' involvement in the murder, but they kept him fully informed of the latest details of Rasputin's demise, allowing him to ensure that Cumming got the news first. He insisted that he was 'as greatly surprised as anyone' and, given the political machinations that led to his appointment as a 'front man' for Cumming's Russian operations, there seems no reason to disbelieve him. His first report back to Cumming, sent on 1 January 1917, began with the perceptive if unnecessarily extravagant words: 'In the early morning of Saturday 30 December, there was enacted in Petrograd one of those crimes that by their magnitude blur the well-defined rules of ethics, and by their results change the history of a generation.' Whatever Hoare had learned from the spycraft lessons before he left for Russia, it certainly did not include an understanding of how to write a concise intelligence report.[16]

There is some evidence that Alley, Scale and Rayner believed there was no time to waste, if they were to stop Rasputin and the Germans persuading the Tsar to pull his country out of the war, and that they had to act fast. Basil Thomson, the head of the Home Office Directorate of Intelligence between 1919 and 1921, subsequently claimed to have interviewed 'one of the persons principally concerned in the business' who told him that

all of those present were convinced that Rasputin was engaged in a plot to persuade the Tsar to make a separate peace with Germany and just before Christmas, Rasputin is said to have revealed the whole plan in a burst of confidence. The separate peace was to be proclaimed on January 1, 1917.

The most likely source of Thomson's information is Alley, who in 1919 set up the Bolshevik Liquidation Club, an informal lunch club for British intelligence officers concerned at the communist threat. Its members included not only Thomson, but also the two most famous

MI1c officers to spy inside Russia, Sidney Reilly and Paul Dukes. It was clear that both the Tsar and Sir George Buchanan suspected Rayner's involvement while Scale's position was such that it was thought convenient to ensure that he was out of the country at the time of the killing. He was sent to Romania to assist in an operation run by George Macdonogh through Cumming to prevent the advancing Germans making use of the country's oilfields and stocks of grain.[17]

When Romania entered the war on the side of the Entente in August 1916, Cumming had four officers in Bucharest, including his former clerk Captain Tom Laycock, who was sent out in November 1915 to act as a 'letter box' for reports from an agent in Constantinople which were written in secret ink on the inside of newspaper wrappings. Laycock was joined by Bertie Maw, who collected intelligence from local customs officials on German goods passing through on their way to Turkey; W. A. Guthrie, the bureau's cipher clerk; and Second-Lieutenant Eddie Boxshall, who was half German and had been born in Bucharest, where his father ran an iron works. They were soon running a couple of dozen agents against Bulgaria but without producing the level of intelligence required on the Bulgarian and Serbian military.[18] The German invasion of Romania, which followed the latter's entry into the war, led Cumming to send the former adventurer and mining engineer turned Unionist MP Lieutenant-Colonel Jack Norton-Griffiths of the Royal Engineers to the oilfields at Targoviste and Meroni in the south of the country 'with the express object of endeavouring to effect the most complete possible destruction of the oil industry' and preventing it falling into German hands. Meanwhile, with the Germans advancing on Bucharest, Laycock and Boxshall set up a military mission based in the temporary Romanian capital of Jassy as cover for their continued espionage operations, while Maw was withdrawn and sent to Lausanne. Norton-Griffiths travelled via Petrograd, arriving in Bucharest in mid-November 1916, with the German troops advancing on the oilfields. He immediately sent a CX telegram to Macdonogh via Cumming, asking for two officers from Petrograd, one of whom was Scale. A few days later, Norton-Griffiths dispatched a second telegram to London, recommending the total destruction of the oilfields. When the two biggest oil companies, the Americana and the Astra, and the Romanian government all declined to assist him in his plans, Norton-Griffiths approached Harry Mejor, the general manager of the British-owned company Romanian Consolidated Oilfields, explaining the plan. 'He had now come to the conclusion that this was all too slow,' Mejor recalled. 'The Germans were rapidly advancing, and he was afraid the whole petroleum industry and possibly even the stocks would fall into their hands, which would be a calamity for the allies, and he wanted our company's permission to destroy our stocks, plant, etc. first and to begin at once.' Norton-Griffiths told Mejor his bosses in London were insistent that 'money is no object if the destruction can be prompt and complete'. Mejor accepted the promise and some of the company's British engineers agreed to help destroy their wells and equipment as well as those of all the other companies. Norton-Griffiths commissioned two of them, Tom Masterson and John Hayward, there and then as lieutenants in the Army Special List, while Philip Simpson, a Briton working for another Romanian-based oil company, was also commissioned in the field as a lieutenant. Over the next several days and nights, Norton-Griffiths and the rest of his team barely stopped. During a ten-day period of complete mayhem, they worked their way across the oilfields, destroying the wells, pumping stations and oil stocks, with machinery smashed or dynamited and the oil and the wells set on fire. The Romanian authorities tried to stop the destruction, arresting Guthrie briefly, but it was too late. The devastation caused by Cumming's men in Romania was described later by Scale in an account of how he and Simpson destroyed the giant refinery at Campina, north-west of Ploesti:

> Everything was enveloped in dense smoke, a sea of crimson, as towers of flame with deafening roar rose hundreds of feet into the air above our heads. Monstrous clouds threatened to crush us as they sank slowly blotting out everything. The heat was suffocating, there was no wind, but hot blasts of air took one's breath away, while the black oil splashed down like rain. Tremendous concussions, shaking everything,

followed each other in quick succession, as the heated tanks exploded and hurled their blazing contents a thousand feet upwards. Huge sheets of crumpled iron shrieked overhead, and came to earth with sickening thuds, while a continual shower of smaller objects rattled around. A fleeting view of crimson hills, through a vista of smoke, was a refreshing reminder that the world was still intact a few miles away. I could hardly believe that this inferno was of our making, it seemed as if we must have roused some sleeping volcano to angry eruption.

The final report by Norton-Griffiths gives a bleak picture of the scorched-earth policy the British officers pursued:

Time alone can balance the gain, as against the loss and destruction with which it has been the mission's painful duty to lay waste the land. I venture to think that where we have passed a deep impression of what war should be has been made. It certainly has been a revelation from the highest to the lowest that our conception of obstructing the enemy means sacrificing the individual and the fruits of the earth, at no matter what cost to either, to accomplish our ends.

After the war, Romanian Consolidated Oilfields attempted to claim £1,270,724 13s 7d in compensation on the basis of the signed agreement between Mejor and Norton-Griffiths, but were surprised and angry to find that the government had no knowledge of such a deal and no intention of honouring it. Given that Norton-Griffiths was knighted, Masterson and Scale were made Companions of the Distinguished Service Order, and both Hayward and Simpson were decorated with Military Crosses for their roles in the destruction of the oilfields, it was perhaps unsurprising that the company found it difficult to accept the government's attempts to distance itself from the affair.[19]

Scale returned to Russia, having recommended that the Royal Flying Corps base a squadron of aircraft on the Romanian border to bomb the Romanian oilfields repeatedly and thereby ensure the Germans could never make use of them. Back in Petrograd, he found that the city had been swept by what Hoare called 'a crop of wild rumours about British participation' in Rasputin's murder. 'The fact that I was known to have been in relation [*sic*] with Purishkevich, and that my office was notoriously well informed about Russian affairs, gave a ready excuse to father the plot and even the murder on me and my staff,' Hoare exclaimed indignantly. 'I knew nothing of this outrageous charge until Sir George Buchanan told me of the rumours that were reaching him. Though the story seemed incredible to the point of childishness, the British ambassador had solemnly to contradict it to the Emperor at his next audience.'

Meanwhile, Stephen Alley had sent Scale a note making clear that the story was very far from childish nonsense. There had been no response so far to Scale's proposal to bomb the Romanian oilfields, Alley wrote. He then went on to refer quite clearly to Rasputin's murder:

> Although matters here have not proceeded entirely to plan, our objective has clearly been achieved. Reaction to the demise of 'Dark Forces' has been well received by all, although a few awkward questions have already been asked about wider involvement. Rayner is attending to loose ends and will no doubt brief you on your return.[20]

TWELVE

'The Ace of Spies'

THE Rasputin operation and the agent networks set up by Stephen Alley and his military control officers give the lie to an internal MI1c summary, written in 1924, which states that 'no real SS [secret service] work was done in Russia until the coming of the Bolshevik regime in the Autumn of 1917'. Alley took over from Samuel Hoare, who returned to Britain 'for reasons of health' a few weeks before the February Revolution, so-called despite taking place in early March 1917, because Russia was still using the Julian calendar, which was thirteen days behind the more widely used Gregorian calendar. The unpopularity of the war and of the Tsarina, in part a result of Rasputin's previous influence over her, added to poor conditions and food shortages to fuel the February Revolution. The revolution led to the abdication of the Tsar and the setting up of the Provisional Government, initially under Prince Georgy Lvov but eventually run by the socialist Alexander Kerensky.[1]

A list of 'special duties' officers working in Petrograd from around this time, all of whom appear to have worked for Cumming, included Alley, John Scale, Leo Steveni, Malcolm McLaren, Frank Ball, Harry Anderson and Frank Urmston, as well as Captain Bill Hicks of the Liverpool Regiment; Captain Claude Bromhead of the London Regiment; Captain Charles Parker Schwabe, who was on the army's General List; Lieutenant Denys Garstin of the 10th Hussars; Lieutenant Herbert Lee, army General List; and Lieutenant Leopold Hodson RNVR. There were also a number of civilians: Herbert Grant and Lionel Reid, who were on the staff as civilians but were subsequently given the protection of being commissioned as lieutenants in the RNVR; and Frank Hayes and Albert Hodson, both also recruited as civilians but subsequently given emergency commission as lieutenants on the army's Special List. Another civilian in the office, Lawrence Webster, who looked after the office accounts, was given an RNVR commission in April 1917 and sent to Kiev as K1, Cumming's representative in the Ukraine. His naval medal card records that he 'was in Kiev when it was bombarded by the Bolsheviks and was there throughout five days of fighting. When the Germans entered Kiev [in March 1918], he hid from them and carried on our work.'[2]

Cumming also appears to have made use of one of his nephews, the Russian-speaking academic Professor Bernard Pares of Liverpool University, who initially received Foreign Office backing for secret service work as the official correspondent of the British government on the Russian Front. When they grew edgy, after he revealed the true extent of the Russian casualties, Pares switched to George Macdonogh for backing, presumably on his uncle's advice. 'I went over to the War Office and offered my services to General Macdonogh, director of military intelligence, my first introduction to that great master in the field,' Pares said. 'No-one else had a standing invitation from a Russian field commander and they [his services] were readily accepted. There could not be any salary, as I could not have a commission; and if I had had one, I couldn't have gone at all in this irregular way. "May I write for the *Daily Telegraph*?" I asked. "Certainly," said Macdonogh. I told its proprietor, Lord Burnham, I couldn't telegraph except in case of a Russian victory, which, by the way never came; but he offered me one thousand pounds a year, which was just double what I had received from the Government.' Pares, who was also involved in running the International News Agency, an MI1c propaganda operation, was subsequently knighted for his secret service and propaganda work in Russia.[3]

Scale and Thornhill spent much of June 1917 in Romania, compiling assessments of how prepared Russian troops were for a German attack. 'Russian offensive on this front should not be relied on,' Scale wrote. 'There is no confidence in success among men.' There was a shortage of ammunition and men, with the latest reinforcements arriving from Russia only causing more damage to general morale. 'Enemy have superiority in aircraft and artillery,' Scale continued. 'If offensive starts it can only be short-lived as supplies are wholly inadequate for continued action.' The second half of 1917 saw anti-war feeling growing steadily in Russia, fuelled by food shortages and general discontent.[4]

Vladimir Ilyich Lenin, the Bolshevik leader, had spent much of the war in Switzerland, where his activities came under close observation from Cumming's officers on the ground. But with the Tsar's abdication he decided to go back to Russia to take advantage of the new political situation and using Swiss socialists as intermediaries began negotiating with the German government to allow him and other Russian revolutionaries based in Switzerland to travel back to Russia through Germany by sealed train. The Germans saw clear political advantage in assisting the Bolsheviks with their policy of 'peaceful defeatism' aimed at ending the war and had been secretly providing them with funds. They agreed to allow the train to go through Germany without any customs checks or other interference. A CX report sent back to London by MI1c's Berne bureau noted that Lenin had agreed to a German demand that he guarantee that all those travelling back to Russia on the train were 'partisans of an immediate peace', a stipulation with which it was not difficult to comply. Alerted by the Berne bureau that Lenin was on his way back to Russia, Alley personally tipped off the Provisional Government's counter-espionage department while Harry Gruner strip-searched the Bolshevik leader at the Torneå passport control office but was unable to prevent his entry into Russia. The Berne and Geneva bureaux both warned that the Bolsheviks were not only receiving German funding but were also acting with the Germans to sow discord and dissent within the Russian armed forces. The increasing prospect of the Bolsheviks taking a leading role in the government, with the inevitable expectation of official Russian policies on the war that were directly counter to British interests, led the MI1c bureau to start consolidating its agents. Meanwhile, Alley travelled across Russia firming up the various agent networks recruited initially by himself and subsequently by the military control officers he had been 'popping about' to gather intelligence.[5]

Cumming, charged by his bosses in London to shore up the increasingly precarious position of the Provisional Government, asked William Wiseman in Washington to use his close contacts with Frank Polk, the head of the US State Department intelligence service , to establish joint US–UK intelligence missions into Russia that might prevent it leaving the war. Wiseman wasted no time in persuading Polk to set up a joint mission to Russia, with the US and the UK each providing $75,000 in funding – around $1.2m each at today's prices. It was to be led by the British author Somerset Maugham, who was related to Wiseman. Maugham was to make contact with Professor Tomáš Masaryk, the head of the Czech National Alliance. Masaryk, a future president of Czechoslovakia, had gone to Russia to organise the Czech legions, who were fighting the Germans alongside Russian troops, into a Czech national army. Maugham took four Czech émigrés with him, including Emanuel Voska, the US head of the Czech National Alliance and at least later, and probably already, a US military intelligence officer.

'The Germans have got a great start on us, and have no doubt a very complete organisation,' Wiseman said. 'We may never be able to equal them in efficiency. This should not deter us from making the attempt, and we have found by experience that German Secret Service methods can even be defeated by the more honest, though possibly less efficient, means which we adopt.'

Maugham would later describe his mission in some detail, neatly sidestepping the Official Secrets Act – and any blame for his naïvety – by having his fictional and highly cynical spy Ashenden undertake the same mission. But in his autobiography, Maugham admitted that his own approach was far from cynical:

The long and the short of it was that I should go to Russia and keep the Russians in the war. I was diffident of accepting the post, which seemed to demand capacities that I didn't think I possessed, but there seemed to be no one more competent available at the moment and my being a writer was very good 'cover' for what I was asked to do. I set off in high spirits with unlimited money at my disposal and four devoted Czechs to act as liaison officers between me and Professor Masaryk who had under his control in various parts of Russia something like 60,000 of his compatriots. I was exhilarated by the responsibility of my position. I went as a private agent, who could be disavowed if necessary, with instructions to get in touch with parties hostile to the government and devise a scheme that would keep Russia in the war and prevent the Bolsheviks from seizing power.

Maugham was not of course to know – as he went off on the mission – that it was to be a total failure. He arrived in Petrograd in early September 1917 with orders to set up a Slav press bureau that would publish propaganda aimed at encouraging support for the more moderate, and anti-German, Mensheviks, while at the same time acting as a cover for a 'special secret organisation' run by Voska and aimed at 'unmasking German plots and propaganda' in Russia. A few weeks after arriving, Maugham sent a telegram to Wiseman accurately predicting that Kerensky would not be able to hold on to power for much longer. But a couple of days later, in an assessment that must rank among the least prescient ever made by one of the Service's representatives, he said the situation looked 'more hopeful for the future'. The people of Petrograd were 'heartily sick' of the Bolsheviks, whose next bout of 'agitations . . . may be anticipated to be their last'. Wiseman telegraphed back warning him that he must not at any cost reveal his mission or the relationship with the Americans to the other British intelligence officers working in Russia. Wiseman reported the nub of Maugham's views back to London, giving only the accurate assessment of Kerensky's position and omitting his over-optimistic prediction of the Bolsheviks' future chances. A week later, Maugham was even more convinced that the Bolsheviks were unlikely to take power. Kerensky had strengthened his position and 'will retain power because his enemies have no-one with whom to replace him', he said.

Strangely, or perhaps only with the benefit of hindsight, Ashenden had a different point of view:

It seemed to Ashenden that it was critical and if anything was to be done it must be done quickly. He had at length devised a plan of campaign. It took him twenty-four hours' hard work to code a telegram in which he put his scheme before the person who had sent him to Petrograd. It was accepted and he was promised all the money he needed. Ashenden knew he could do nothing unless the Provisional Government remained in power for another three hours, but winter was at hand and food was getting scarcer every day. The army was mutinous. The people clamoured for peace. Plans were drawn up. Measures were taken. Ashenden argued, persuaded, promised. He had to overcome the vacillation of one and wrestle with the fatalism of another. He had to judge who was resolute and who was self-sufficient, who was honest and who was infirm of purpose. He had to beware of treachery. He had to humour the vanity of fools and elude the greed of the ambitious. Time was pressing. The rumours grew hot and many of the activities of the Bolsheviks. Kerensky ran hither and thither like a frightened hen.

Maugham was called back to London in early November to report to the British Foreign Secretary, Arthur Balfour, and US President Wilson's close aide Colonel Edward Mandell House, who was coming over with Wiseman for talks. They arrived in Falmouth on 7 November, the day the Bolshevik revolution put Lenin and Leon Trotsky in charge, ending Maugham's mission. 'It is not necessary for me to inform the reader that I failed in this lamentably,' he later admitted. Nor did he expect acceptance of his view that it was 'at least possible that if I had been sent six months before I might quite well have succeeded'.[6]

The new Bolshevik government agreed an armistice with Germany in mid-December 1917 and a week later began peace negotiations. On 7 January, amid fears that Petrograd was too vulnerable to a German attack, Sir George Buchanan, the British ambassador, took the bulk of the British war mission home, leaving behind only a skeleton staff at the embassy. The Bolshevik government moved out of Petrograd to Moscow and, with armed resistance from former Tsarist forces swiftly turning into civil war, began hasty attempts to reconstitute the armed forces, which had been ripped apart by the anarchy of soldiers' committees overturning any decision made by a 'bourgeois' officer. The resulting chaos saw Red Guards given authority they were often incapable of using sensibly. Harry Gruner, who by now probably regretted the decision to strip-search Lenin, was arrested and sentenced to be shot in January, despite his status as vice-consul at Torneå, only to be reprieved shortly afterwards. Cudbert Thornhill, 'the hero of many exciting adventures in Petrograd during the revolution', had been forced at one point to leave under threat of arrest. But by January, he was back, reporting that the new Bolshevik army would be formed from munitions workers, since these were deemed to be better educated than simple peasants. By late February, Ernest Boyce was telling Cumming that a Socialist Volunteer Army, which included 'a good proportion of officers', was being formed, a few days later he reported that General Mikhail Bonch-Bruevich, the head of the Supreme Military Council, had been 'authorised to form a new volunteer army with officers, no committees, and with strict discipline' and that he was making preparations for the defence of Petrograd and Moscow. Former officers were being re-engaged, albeit temporarily, to reinforce discipline. Robert Bruce Lockhart, who had been sent out by the Foreign Office to act as the British representative in Moscow, reported that Trotsky, now the Commissar for Army and Navy Affairs, was trying to row back on the Bolsheviks' destruction of the officer corps, insisting that 'we must create a real fighting army well disciplined with officers and generals'. The anarchy caused by the soldiers' committees had to end. 'Now we must have discipline.'

There was a clamour from the War Office for more detail on the structure of the armed forces which C's officers – now based in Moscow as well as Petrograd – struggled to satisfy. Moscow claimed, improbably, that 70 per cent of the army was still intact and fit to fight, whereas Charles Schwabe had a long interview with the Russian general in charge of Petrograd military district, who said, with some justification, that the Red Army, as it was to be called, was 'merely a paper organisation' and suggested, with misplaced optimism, that if it were ever to become an effective force it would be used not to defend the Bolshevik government but to bring it down. The differences reflected a large degree of confusion over the truth of the matter, with secrecy hampering operations.[7]

With the future unclear, Cumming sensibly decided to centre his anti-Bolshevik operations in Sweden as a fallback in case it should become impossible to run a bureau inside Russia. John Scale returned to the UK to begin preparing to take over the Stockholm office, with Oswald Rayner assisting him. Raleigh le May, another member of Russia's pre-revolution British community, was appointed as vice-consul in Helsingfors [now Helsinki] to run the bureau there, under Scale's direction, and assisted by Harry Hall, a former British businessman in Latvia who was so assimilated he had played for the Latvian national football team. Scale was appointed assistant military attaché in Sweden on 12 March 1918 as cover for his new post and three days later took his first new recruit, Sidney Reilly, into Whitehall Court to see Cumming. 'Major Scale introduced Mr Reilly who is willing to go to Russia for us,' Cumming wrote in his diary for 15 March. 'Very clever – very doubtful – has been everywhere and done everything. Will take out £500 in notes and £750 in diamonds, which are at a premium. I must agree tho' it is a great gamble as he is to visit all our men in Vologda, Kief, Moscow etc.' Cumming wisely took Reilly's 'valuables' as collateral.[8]

Reilly appears to have been handed a wide brief, dealing with the half-dozen MI1c bureaux across Russia in Petrograd, Moscow, Vologda, Kiev, Murmansk and Vladivostok. Given his dubious reputation, particularly when it came to financial matters, Cumming's willingness to provide him with £1,250 of service money, the equivalent of around £50,000 today, seems like madness. But Reilly's contacts on the ground were to be invaluable and there is a strong argument that in the coming months he more than repaid the investment. His time as an MI1c officer, with the code-number ST1 – the first 'travelling agent' recruited by Scale in his new role as head of the Swedish bureau, with the ST standing for Stockholm – was brief but productive.

It did not have an auspicious beginning. Reilly left the ship he was on at Murmansk, which had been occupied by Royal Marines a couple of weeks earlier, and was arrested by the British naval authorities. Fortunately, Stephen Alley was on his way home – he later claimed that he had been sacked by Cumming for refusing to assassinate Joseph Stalin. This is more credible than it might at first seem, given that it would probably have tipped the balance in the Bolshevik leadership in favour of continuing the war. Cumming certainly wanted to get rid of Alley at this point, although why is unclear. Alley's departure, temporary as it turned out, left Boyce in charge in Petrograd. Alley was taken to see Reilly to check his credentials. The new British spy produced a microscopic code from under the cork of an aspirin bottle, which Alley immediately recognised as genuine, and Reilly was released.[9]

He travelled to Petrograd, where he tapped into his network of friends and associates. 'I knew Petrograd as a man does know the city in which he has lived from childhood to middle age,' he said. 'I was returning home after an absence of only two years. I had many friends in the city. I knew where I could go when I arrived there. I knew upwards of a score of people on whose co-operation I could implicitly rely.'

Reilly lived with a pre-war acquaintance, Yelena Boyuzhovskaya, on Ulitsa Torgovaya, posing as a Turkish merchant and adopting the covername Konstantin Markovich Massino, using the maiden name of his second wife, Nadine. He initially spent a month in the city and was horrified at the extent to which it had changed since the Bolsheviks had taken over:

> Petrograd, which once could challenge comparison with any city in the world, bore a ruinous and tumbledown aspect. Houses here and there lay in ruins. There was no police except for the secret police which held the country in thrall, no municipal administration, no sanitary arrangements, no shops open, no busy passengers on the pavements, no hustle of traffic on the roads. The place had sunk into utter stagnation and all normal life seemed to have ceased in the city. The great mass of the people was starving. Everybody I passed avoided my glance and shuffled by with obvious suspicion and terror. Petrograd was in a state of panic. Slowly the atmosphere of horror, exuded from the very walls

and pavements, seemed to grip at my heart, until I was in a mood to start at a shadow.[10]

Reilly sent his first report on 16 April, acknowledging that the Bolsheviks were in complete control, their power enforced by the secret police of the Chrezvychaika, the Extraordinary Commission against Counter-Revolution, better known as the Cheka. Nevertheless, he argued, there was a growing opposition which if supported would eventually be able to overthrow the new rulers. 'Our action must therefore be in two parallel directions,' he said, 'firstly with the Bolsheviks for accomplishment of immediate practical objects; secondly with the opposition for gradual re-establishment of order and national defence.' The immediate objectives should be the safeguarding of the northern ports of Murmansk and Archangel and the removal of the ammunition and weapons from Petrograd before it fell to the Germans. Typically, he asked for 'an expenditure of possibly one million pounds' some of which 'may have to be expended without any real guarantee of ultimate success'. It was a typically audacious request for funds from Reilly, a master of sharp practice. But Cumming, no doubt used to some of the devious characters he loved to employ asking for large sums of operating cash – although almost certainly never before on such ambitious lines – sensibly ignored the request.[11]

One of the first people Reilly got in touch with was his former lawyer in Petrograd, Aleksandr Grammatikov, an associate of Lenin and ostensibly a Bolshevik supporter. The Soviet leader had intervened to protect Grammatikov from allegations – which, unbeknown to Lenin, were true – that he was an informer for the Okhrana, the old Tsarist secret service. Grammatikov arranged for Reilly to meet Bonch-Bruevich, an important contact given the concern in London to know the full scale of the plans for the Red Army. Bonch-Bruevich, who was deeply aware that his demoralised forces would need Allied support if they were to hold off the Germans, arranged a pass for Reilly to travel to Moscow. He arrived in late April, painting an even more depressing picture of the city than that with which he had portrayed Petrograd:

Moscow was a city of the damned, paved with desolation, filth, squalor, fiendish cruelty, abject terror, blood, lust, starvation. Everywhere was starvation, food queues that had forgotten to be clamorous, dearth, stagnation; and over all silent, secret, ferocious, menacing, hung the crimson shadow of the Cheka. The new masters were ruling in Russia.[12]

Reilly sent a report from Moscow on 30 April, detailing a speech made by Trotsky two days earlier in which he outlined the plans to set up the Red Army. 'The bourgeoisie must never again be allowed to come into the possession of arms,' Reilly reported Trotsky as saying. 'The Red Army is formed for the only kind of justifiable and honest warfare, namely civil war on the bourgeoisie and all revolutionary armies not in agreement with the Bolsheviks. The employment in the army of officers of the old regime will be purely temporary and they will be dispensed with the moment sufficient numbers of proletariat officers have been trained. The 1 May celebration is to be the clarion call to the world announcing the victorious Russian proletariat revolution and the doom of the ruling classes. The burden of the speech was uncounted appeals for merciless class war. Any mention of the political situation was avoided. Neither the Allies nor the Germans were mentioned. The territorial losses of Russia were dismissed as mere scratches on the map which will be obliterated with the advent of the International Proletariat Revolution. The present economical chaos was boldly characterised as the legacy of the former bourgeois regime.'[13]

A week later, Reilly went to the Kremlin trying to get in touch with Bonch-Bruevich, an act subsequently used to reinforce the popular view of the audacious British master-spy. Robert Bruce Lockhart claimed that Reilly marched up to the door of the Kremlin in his RAF uniform and demanded to see Lenin. 'Asked for his credentials, he declared that he had been sent specially by Mr Lloyd George to obtain first-hand news of the aims and ideals of the Bolsheviks,' Lockhart wrote. 'The British government was not satisfied with the reports it had been receiving from me. He had been entrusted with the task of making good the defects.'

Reilly met Bonch-Bruevich's brother Vladimir, a military adviser to Lenin. Told of the incident by Lev Karachan, a senior Bolshevik foreign affairs official, Lockhart was furious:

> That same evening, I sent for Boyce, the head of the Intelligence Service, and told him the story. He informed me that the man was a new agent who had just come out from England. I blew up in a storm of indignation and the next day the officer came to me to offer his explanation. He swore that the story Lev Karachan had told me was quite untrue. He admitted, however, that he had been to the Kremlin and had seen Bonch-Bruevich. The man who had thrust himself so dramatically into my life was Sidney Reilly, the mystery man of the British secret service and known today to the outside world as the master spy of Britain. My experiences of the war and of the Russian revolution have left me with a very poor opinion of secret service work. The methods of Sidney Reilly, however, were on a grand scale which compelled my admiration. He was a man of great energy and personal charm, very attractive to women and very ambitious. I had not a high opinion of his intelligence. His knowledge covered many subjects, from politics to art, but it was superficial. On the other hand, his courage and indifference to danger were superb.[14]

The truth behind the now legendary visit to the Kremlin seems more likely to be that Reilly was simply looking for his sponsor, General Bonch-Bruevich, and as a result was taken to see the general's brother. However, it was certainly true that Lockhart was not trusted by the Foreign Office, where he was himself seen as a dangerous maverick, and it seems likely that Reilly would have made use of this in his attempts to secure his own access. At any event, a couple of days later, Reilly had the first of a series of interviews with the general himself, who seems to have taken something of a shine to the new British officer, seeing him as someone who might be able to influence his government on Russia's behalf. Bonch-Bruevich was angry at the terms imposed on the Bolsheviks by the Germans during negotiations for the treaty of

Brest-Litovsk – and the concessions agreed by Georgy Chicherin, who had taken over from Trotsky as Commissar for Foreign Affairs – and was keen that the allies should fight alongside his demoralised forces if the Germans attacked.

'Bruevitch received Grammatikov and myself very graciously,' Reilly recalled. 'Grammatikov introduced me by my own name, informing him that, although English by nationality, I had been born in Russia and lived there all my life, and was in fact to all intents and purposes Russian. I corroborated this story and added that I was very interested in Bolshevism, the triumph of which had brought me back to Russia. Bruevitch listened to this declaration, which after all was quite true, with great complacency, and in response to my request gave us every facility for studying Bolshevism in its cradle. Nobody could be more officious on our behalf than Bruevitch.'[15]

Given the conflicting evidence thus far on the creation of the Red Army, Reilly's ability to obtain a series of interviews with Bonch-Bruevich could only have enhanced his reputation in London. The information Reilly obtained added little to that already being circulated, but coming as it did from the mouth of the man charged with setting up the Red Army, described by Reilly at one point as 'the brain centre' of the new Russian military, it had far greater credibility. At one point, Bonch-Bruevich read his proposals over the phone to Trotsky in Reilly's presence, even asking the British spy if there was anything else he thought he might do.

Bonch-Bruevich's approach throughout was an attempt to persuade the Allies that they should promise the Bolsheviks military support should the Germans invade. 'He considers that a marked change for a more rational and common sense outlook among the Bolshevik leaders is noticeable,' Reilly reported from his first interview on 9 May. 'Regarding the reorganisation of the army, he has drawn up a plan, more or less on the old military lines. The elective principle – the chief cause of the destruction of the old army – he insists should be abolished and regimental committees are to have a say only in matters of supplies, entertainments and recreation.'

Unfortunately, as Boyce and Cudbert Thornhill were both reporting, the Bolsheviks were split, with much of the government opposing Trotsky's decision to restore officer control of the army. This was not reflected in Reilly's reporting, the main thrust of which was Bonch-Bruevich's appeals for Allied military support. 'General constantly referred to necessity of Allied recognition on basis of national resistance to Germans,' Reilly reported in his fifth interview, during which Bonch-Bruevich announced that he had received Lenin's and Trotsky's official authorisation to supply the British with military intelligence. Bonch-Bruevich ranted against Chicherin, suggesting he must have been bribed by the Germans to agree some of the concessions granted during the peace talks at Brest-Litovsk. 'He was in a desperate frame of mind, and said that the only means to counterbalance German dominion was an immediate understanding with the Allies,' Reilly said, before quoting Bonch-Bruevich as pleading: 'Cannot the Allies see that by keeping aloof, they give a free hand to Germany, that they are abandoning us, the officers, who alone can save the situation?'[16]

Another British intelligence officer who arrived in Moscow in the March of 1918 was Captain George Hill, a War Office agent who had been brought up in Russia and had earlier served in Salonika, flying agents across the Bulgarian lines, before moving back to Russia. While operating in western Russia, in the city of Mogilev, now in Belarus, Hill found himself being followed by two German agents.

Unfortunately, my way took me into an ill-lit street and here it was that my followers started to put on speed, and I suddenly realised that two thugs were after me. Just as they were about to close with me, I swung round and flourished my walking stick. As I expected, one of my assailants seized hold of it. It was a swordstick, which had been specially designed by Messrs Wilkinson, the sword makers of Pall Mall, and the moment the attacker had the scabbard in his fist I drew back the rapier-like blade with a jerk and with a forward lunge ran it through the gentleman's side. He gave a scream and collapsed on the pavement. His companion, seeing that I was not unarmed, took to his heels.

Hill went back to his hotel and stopped on the stairs to examine the blade 'anxious to know what it looked like after its adventure. I had never run a man through before. It was not a gory sight. There was only a slight film of blood halfway up the blade and a dark stain at the tip.'

Shortly after Hill arrived in Moscow, swordstick in hand and accompanied by two of Cumming's agents previously based in Odessa, he went to see Trotsky, who, in a measure of the reasonably good relationship enjoyed by British officers on the ground with Russia's new Bolshevik leadership, made him inspector for aviation, with the role of advising him on the creation of a Russian air force. Hill also helped the Bolshevik military set up an intelligence section with agents based on the Eastern Front who could identify German units and report on their movements.

> Within a few weeks, we had a complete net of agents working in all the eastern territories occupied by the Austro-German army. Identifications came to me every day, and a copy of them was telegraphed to London. Time and again, I was able to warn London that a German division had left Russia for the Western Front.[17]

The amount of material had been increased by the influx of German diplomats and military officers following the Brest-Litovsk agreement, with German telegrams from Russia to Berlin being intercepted and sent back to London disguised by various means, including being described as stolen German documents supposedly found in waste-paper baskets. The rapid increase in the number of intelligence officers in Russia and the existence of so many different organisations, co-operating to varying degrees with the Russians, led to a good deal of confusion. Denys Garstin, who was working with Thornhill, complained that C had sent in Frank Urmston 'with orders to get into touch with no-one officially' – effectively preventing him from obtaining any intelligence at all – while Hill was collecting and reporting intelligence to London entirely independent of anyone else. Garstin lamented that 'this lack of co-ordination seems to be cause of unnecessary duplication, confusion at home, and mistrust among Russians'. It was agreed that Hill should amalgamate his organisation with the MI1c operations now run by Boyce, assisted by an army staff officer, Captain Victor Small; Lionel Reid; and Urmston. Hill's reports on German units were to be sent to Cumming rather than George Macdonogh. Other MI1c officers in Moscow during this period included Lawrence Webster, who had eventually been forced to escape from Kiev during the German occupation, and Second Lieutenant Henry Bowe, who had made his way to Petrograd after the journey through Bulgaria and Romania with Claude Dansey and Norman Dewhurst.

Cumming also continued to make use of the 'natural cover' afforded by businessmen, agreeing to pay the expenses of Henry Armitstead, the Russian representative of the Hudson's Bay Company, who travelled across Russia in mid-1918 on a 'special trade mission'. In a letter to the company's deputy governor, Charles Sale, Cumming said that since Armitstead 'has with your kind permission temporarily placed his services at my disposal for a journey through Russia, I wish to put on record that I will refund you for all Mr Armitstead's expenses on the journey from the time of leaving London until his return.'[18]

THIRTEEN

'Deception, dirt and mean behaviour'

THE British intelligence officer who worked most closely with Sidney Reilly was George Hill, who having originally come to Petrograd working for military intelligence subsequently switched to work for Cumming. Hill shared Reilly's predilection for recruiting female agents whose 'relationships of trust' with their agent runner were not solely focused on espionage.

'I first heard of Sidney Reilly as a cipher and knew him only as ST1, his secret service name,' Hill said. 'He had been sent out to tackle the new situation which had arisen with the advent of the Bolsheviks. Next I heard of him under one of his assumed names, and finally was introduced to him as Sidney Reilly. He was a dark, well-groomed, very foreign-looking man, who spoke English, Russian, French and German perfectly though, curiously enough, with a foreign accent in each case. At our first meeting, we took a liking to each other. I found that he had an amazing grasp of the actualities of the situation and that he was a man of action.'[1]

The assumed name Hill first heard was not Massino, Reilly's Petrograd persona, but an entirely different identity that he used in Moscow, that of a Greek businessman, a Mr Constantine, living in the apartment of Aleksandr Grammatikov's actress niece, Dagmara Karozus, whose flatmate, another actress, 22-year-old Yelizaveta Otten, was soon sleeping with Reilly.

Hill was busy setting up a large network of agents and safe houses with couriers ready to take his reports north to Cudbert Thornhill, who was on a special mission for the war cabinet collecting intelligence on the prospects for an Allied intervention. Thornhill had been setting up agent networks across the north between Murmansk and the White Sea port of Kem to warn the British of any Bolshevik advances. The British, French and Americans were planning to land forces at Archangel as part of a three-pronged intervention from the north, south and east of Russia, designed ostensibly to prevent the Germans taking control of Russian weapons, ammunition and supplies and to assist the Czech forces still in Russia to reopen the Eastern Front against the Germans, although the motivation in some quarters was very definitely to assist the former Tsarist generals who were trying to remove the Bolsheviks from power. Thornhill was allocated as the force's chief intelligence officer, and a number of MI1c officers worked with him, including Denys Garstin, one of the Hodsons, Victor Small, Lieutenant Guy Tamplin of the Royal Garrison Artillery, Captain John 'JJ' Hitching of the London Regiment, Captain Alfred Hill of the Royal Highland Regiment and Captains William Calder and Walter McGrath of the Royal Engineers. Calder, who transferred to the RAF in March 1918, and also had the additional cover of a commission in the RNVR, was military control officer in Murmansk, where yet another MI1c officer, Second Lieutenant Lawrence Collas of the Middlesex Regiment, was also active. Leo Steveni was sent to the Far East, monitoring the progress of the Russian, Czech and Cossack forces there, travelling by train in his own private carriage for several thousand miles across northern China, the Russian Far East and Siberia from Vladivostok to Chelyabinsk. Cumming's irritation at the way in which so many of his officers had been suborned by the War Office to take part in the intervention was not helped by attempts to take Ernest Boyce, Malcolm McLaren and Herbert Lee as well, and by George Macdonogh's insistence that Stephen Alley, despite his point-blank refusal to involve himself in murder, was being sent to Murmansk as part of the intervention force and was to continue to be paid out of MI1c funds. Alley was soon cabling home to Claude Dansey that he needed more MI1c officers to exercise proper military control measures and an increase in funds to £1,000 a month. Thornhill would explain the details when he returned to London.[2]

'The full story of Thornhill's work with that expedition would make a book of adventure that would thrill every youth of an adventurous spirit,' wrote one of those who was with him. 'He had the map of north Russia imprinted on his brain. He knew every village, every trait of the Russian. It seemed to me that he didn't need the assistance of a dossier to check the history of a suspect brought before him, one look from the pale blue eyes told him all there was to know. Thornhill's job just now was to keep an eye, not only on the acknowledged prisoner spies we had captured, but on the suspects in our Russian ranks. Contradictorily, his most faithful officer at that time was a Russian, a man of six foot four and immensely strong. He used to amuse us with a feat that few might emulate, making the sign of the cross with a 56-pound weight in his right hand. Thornhill and this Russian giant had adventures in other parts of the continent. The story told to me, but not by the colonel, was that the two had saved the life of each other in turn when it was necessary to say goodbye to Petrograd in a hurry immediately after the outbreak of the revolution.'[3]

It seemed inevitable that the intervention would lead to British intelligence officers based further south, in Moscow, Petrograd and Vologda, being forced to leave the country. At a meeting with Boyce and Reilly in early July, it was agreed that if and when their colleagues were forced to leave, Reilly and George Hill should stay behind and go underground. It was also agreed that alongside his courier and agent networks, Hill should put men on the major train stations to watch troop movements; set up a special operations 'destruction gang'; and create a section to forge identification documents for Hill, Reilly and their agents.[4] Hill subsequently said:

> At a conference with Lieutenants Boyce and Riley [sic], I agreed to stay behind and: arrange the courier service; take charge of coding; continue to use my own channels of information; run a small destruction gang; continue to keep in touch with the Air Force; and work in with

2nd Lieutenant S. Riley[sic] RAF, who was receiving very excellent information from all possible sources. I considered that Lieutenant Riley knew the situation better than any other British officer in Russia and as he also had the more delicate threads in his hand, I therefore agreed to co-operate with him, and leave the political control and our policy in his hands.

The courier service began operating on 8 July, when the first couriers left for the north via two separate routes, one going through Nizhny Novgorod, Viatka (now Kirov) and Kotlass, and the other through Petrograd and Petrozavodsk, Hill said.

I estimated that twenty to twenty-five couriers would be sufficient to carry on constant communications with the army in the north. Results proved that more would be required. Courier 1 [using the Nizhny Novgorod route] returned after twelve days. He reported a difficult passage north, was twice arrested and searched. He returned by trickery direct from Archangel by train and so cut the journey in half. He said the nervous strain was very great and a good rest would be needed after every journey. Courier 2 went on the Petrozavodsk route. He was away twenty days and had a similar experience to No. 1: His journey was however more expensive as he had to use horses in certain places.[5]

With the intervention imminent, there was a series of meetings with Boyce and Lawrence Webster to iron out the details of the way in which Reilly and Hill would operate, during which Boyce authorised their plans and their estimates of how much it would all cost. Hill's main base was to be a house in Ulitsa Pyatnitskaya, one of the old city's pre-revolution shopping streets, where he surrounded himself with young women, including his secretary, who was 'au courant with all the work'.

Evelyn was partly English, but had been educated in Russia, and besides English and Russian she knew German, French and Italian perfectly. She was a brilliant musician and could turn her hand to anything which required skill. It was essential that the people about us should be entirely trustworthy. Evelyn and I discussed the matter and decided to ask two friends of ours, girls of English birth but Russian upbringing, to join our organisation. Sally and Annie both jumped at the chance. They had brothers, one in the machine-gun corps and the other in the tanks, fighting on the Western Front. Both had been wounded, but were back in France and the sisters were aching to do something. Sally was one of the most beautiful girls I have ever seen. She had raven-black hair, a peach-like complexion and the most sensitive, pale, transparent hands. Annie, her sister, was not so good-looking but was a plump, merry, good-natured soul. We had decided that Sally should become cook to this establishment of ours, and do all the housework, cooking and buying what was necessary. Annie would start a dressmaking business. We wanted another ally to run messages for me and deliver the parcels to Annie's customers. After a good deal of thought between us we decided to enrol a young Russian girl we knew, an orphan who had just reached the mature age of seventeen. Vi was a tall blonde with blue eyes, and the most appealing ways, and time proved she was also full of pluck.

Hill's chief courier, a Russian cavalry officer codenamed Z, rented two rooms in the flat of a prostitute, 'a rather good-looking woman' working on Ulitsa Tverskaya, 'the Bond Street of Moscow'. The prostitute was the widow of one of the chief courier's fellow officers who was killed early in the war. 'For reasons best known to herself she had taken to the oldest living in the world,' Hill said. 'What was more natural and our weary couriers could rest in safety in one of the rooms there.' They used six other safe houses scattered across the city, plus a house at Kuskovo, 10 miles outside Moscow, and 'a small wooden country residence forty miles away, which was to be a final retreat and refuge if Moscow grew too hot for me or any of my agents'.[6]

Reilly continued to come up with proposals for how the British government could spend large sums of money, no doubt channelled through him, in order to win influence in the region, asking for two and a half million roubles to allow two Russian publishing companies to buy the main Ukrainian newspapers.

> The firms' ready cash resources have all been tied up by the Bolsheviks and the proposal now is that the British government or the allied governments should advance a short-term loan of up to two-and-a-half million roubles. The policy of the papers would be determined and conducted in close agreement with representatives of the allies. In the present critical stage of Russian history each factor which contributes to the unification of Russia (and a united Russia can and must only be an independent Russia) acquires special value. It ought to be comparatively an easy thing to establish a common line of action with the papers in Petrograd, Moscow and in other Russian towns. Should the Soviet power continue to stifle the Russian press, tens of thousands of copies of the Ukrainian press will find their way over the border and the idea of the Union of Russia will be upheld and kept alive.

Section V passed the idea on to the Foreign Office, which queried how it might work given that the Germans had annexed the Ukraine, but certainly did not quibble with the sums of money requested by Reilly.[7]

The first elements of the Allied intervention force landed at Archangel on 2 August 1918, just 1,500 strong and made up of British and French troops, although it would eventually be reinforced by another 10,000 men. The Bolsheviks reacted by temporarily closing the British and French embassies.

'The situation for some days had been very critical and the allies were not received by any of the Soviet officials,' Hill reported. 'Our agents informed us that the Soviet was divided into two very strong parties.' The first wanted all British and French officers arrested and expelled, the second, led by Karl Radek, wanted them publicly shot over what were in fact false reports of the shooting of some Soviet commissars in Kem. A number of British and French officials were briefly arrested, including Robert Bruce Lockhart, Boyce and Webster. Reilly's empty flat was raided by agents from the Cheka and he and Hill went underground. Reilly reverted to his Massino and Constantine personae while Hill burned all his British clothes and re-emerged in typically Russian clothing as Georg Bergmann, actor. 'It had previously been arranged that our go-betweens would be women, and each of us had a member on our staff, who had been selected for this work,' Hill said. 'Our go-betweens had commenced their services and things seemed to be running very smoothly. Meetings took place as a rule in the public gardens.' Reilly was soon reporting on the morale and plans of the Russian navy.[8]

By now, few of the Allied representatives in Russia saw any value in backing the Bolsheviks, although Lockhart, to the irritation of the Foreign Office and indeed many of the British intelligence officers in Russia, had managed to advocate virtually every possible option at one point or another. The primary aim was not to bolster the Bolsheviks but to subvert them, or even overthrow them entirely, and what appeared to be an ideal opportunity to do the latter had emerged. Two Latvian soldiers made contact with Captain Francis Cromie, the British naval attaché in Petrograd, asking for British support for the anti-Bolshevik underground. The two 'walk-ins' were sent to Lockhart, who asked to meet their senior officer, a Colonel Eduard Berzin, before passing all three on to Reilly.

The full extent of Lockhart's involvement is far from clear. His own published account seeks to distance himself from the whole affair – and indeed from anything but the most insubstantial involvement in espionage and covert operations – but his reports to the Foreign Office portray a different picture, recording various attempts to fund and support the anti-Bolshevik underground. Although not actually a member of MI1c, Lockhart was certainly not averse to mounting covert activity that trampled all over their territory. Since the Latvian regiments were being used to police Moscow, Reilly saw them as a potential weak link and held a series of meetings with them, trying to persuade them to help overthrow Lenin and install a provisional government, with his old friend Aleksandr Grammatikov as Interior Minister. Lockhart, who admitted discussing the plans with his French counterpart, claimed to have 'categorically turned down' any such suggestion. 'Reilly was warned specifically to have nothing to do with so dangerous and doubtful a move,' Lockhart later claimed. But he was in fact present at a number of meetings with the two Latvian walk-ins, and insisted on meeting Berzin before handing the project over to Reilly, making his attempts to distance himself from the affair somewhat improbable, although Reilly was certainly quite happy to claim the conspiracy as his own.[9]

> When I had sounded Berzin and entirely satisfied myself with regard to him, I unfolded some of the details of the conspiracy and asked him whether the collaboration of his Lettish [Latvian] colleagues could be secured. Our meeting took place at the Tramble Café in the Tverskoy Boulevard, and I stressed the money side of the question, promising large sums to the commandants and proportionate rewards to the lower ranks. Berzin assured me that the task I had set was easy, that the Letts were full of disgusted loathing for their masters, whom they served only as a pis aller [last resort]. In consideration of my princely proposals he could positively guarantee the future loyalty of his men to me. Thereupon I handed him over some of the earnest money instructing him to divide it with his fellow commandants, and from that point Berzin dipped regularly into our exchequer.[10]

How far the 'conspiracy' planned to involve British intelligence in yet more killings is difficult to judge, although the evidence points strongly towards the intention to murder. The Bolsheviks subsequently claimed the plan was to kill Lenin and the rest of the Bolshevik leadership. Hill insisted that Reilly only intended to humiliate the Bolshevik leaders and had been 'very firm' in dissuading Berzin from assassinating them. 'He impressed upon the Colonel that the policy should be not to make martyrs of the leaders but to hold them up to ridicule before the world. He proposed to march them through the streets of Moscow bereft of their lower garments in order to kill them by ridicule, and then to intern them in a prison in Moscow from which they could not escape'. But the MI1c willingness to get involved in the murder of Rasputin, Alley's claim of orders from London to murder 'Stalin', the reality of the situation on the ground, and Reilly's own account all suggest that the murder of Lenin and Trotsky, if not the entire Bolshevik leadership, was indeed on the agenda. 'Lenin and Trotsky were Bolshevism,' Reilly wrote. 'Once they were removed the whole foul institution would crumble to dust, but while they lived there could be no peace in Russia.'[11]

There are similar question marks over the claim, now widely accepted, that Berzin and his two fellow officers were part of a Russian 'sting' operation that set out from the start to entrap the British. The evidence of what actually happened at the time suggests otherwise and the main details supporting the claims that it was a Cheka 'sting' from the very start did not emerge until the 1960s, by which time the KGB was engaged in a full-scale propaganda war designed to use the Cambridge spies, and in particular Kim Philby, to build up its own reputation at the expense of its British counterpart.[12] Whether or not the Latvian 'walk-ins' were originally agents provocateurs or genuinely angry that the Russians had handed their country over to the Germans, the Cheka were soon well aware of what was going on and able to take control of the operation, because they had their own spy in the Allied camp.

Subsequent post-mortems within the Service concluded that the plot began to unravel after Lockhart brought in the French and US consuls. Lockhart was not himself present at a conference called at the US consulate on 25 August to allow Reilly to meet the French and US intelligence officers who were also planning to stay in Moscow. The meeting was attended by the US consul-general, De Witt C. Poole; the French consul-general, Fernand Grenard; the head of the US intelligence network, the businessman Xenophon Kalamatiano; and the head of French intelligence in Moscow, Colonel Henri de Vertement. Grenard brought with him René Marchand, the Moscow correspondent of the French newspaper *Le Figaro*, who was also gathering intelligence for the French. Reilly admitted to a strange feeling of concern before the meeting:

I had an uneasy feeling (such as one frequently gets in dangerous situations, when one's nerves are constantly on the 'qui vive') that I should keep myself to myself and not go to the meeting which had already been arranged for me. But in the end I allowed myself to be persuaded. The meeting took place for safety at the American consulate, the only one which had not yet been raided by the Bolsheviks. Monsieur Grenard, the French consul, introduced me without naming me to de Vertement, who of course knew who I was, and then to my surprise to René Marchand, whom he described as a confidential agent of the French government and here it was that the uneasy feeling, which had haunted me all along, became acute. I was by no means favourably impressed with Monsieur Marchand, Moscow correspondent of the Paris *Figaro* though he was, and discreetly drew de Vertement into another room and arranged with him some details about liaison. To do so, I had to disclose him some details of our conspiracy. The room in which we were was long and badly lighted. In the midst of an animated discussion, I suddenly became aware that Marchand had crept in to the room and no doubt overheard a large part of our conversation.[13]

Reilly was right to feel apprehensive; Marchand was a double agent and was passing everything he learned from the French on to Felix Dzerzhinsky, head of the Cheka. Marchand reported back the precise details of Reilly's plans, revealing that Reilly and his conspirators intended to mount an armed attack on a session of the All-Russian Congress of Soviets due to be held three days later at the Bolshoi Theatre, with the whole Russian leadership in attendance. The attackers, armed with pistols and hand grenades, would hide behind the stage curtains waiting for a signal from Reilly, at which point the Latvian troops would close all exits and cover the audience with their rifles, while Reilly leaped on the stage and seized Lenin, Trotsky and the other leaders.[14]

The Congress of Soviets was immediately postponed, strongly suggesting that it was not until this point that the Cheka knew precisely what was going on. Then on 30 August, in two unrelated attacks, socialist revolutionary opponents of the Bolsheviks shot dead Moisei Uritsky, the head of the Petrograd Cheka, and attempted to assassinate Lenin, who was badly wounded, with one bullet only just missing his heart.

The Bolsheviks launched what was to become known as the Red Terror, with thousands of suspected opponents arrested and hundreds executed. The British embassy in Petrograd was attacked by armed members of the Cheka. Cromie resisted, firing his pistol at the attackers, and was shot dead. The MI1c offices on Moika Embankment were also raided and Ernest Boyce, Sidney Tomes, Bill Hicks, Guy Tamplin, Lawrence Webster and Charles Schwabe arrested along with Lockhart and a number of other British officials and citizens. The party newspaper *Pravda* announced the discovery of a widespread Anglo-French conspiracy to overthrow the Bolsheviks, shoot Lenin and Trotsky, and set up a military government allied to the West and hostile to Germany. Lockhart had provided a total of a million roubles to fund a counter-revolution, *Pravda* said. 'The intention of the allies as soon as they had established their dictatorship in Moscow was to declare war on Germany and force Russia to fight again.'

Those arrested as a result of the exposure of the plot included Reilly's mistress, Yelizaveta Otten, who insisted that he had never discussed his 'political motives' with her. When the 'repression against British officers began', Reilly had fled, telling her he was leaving Russia forever, she said. It was not until her arrest that she had discovered that Reilly 'had been foully deceiving me for his own political purposes, taking advantage of my exclusively good attitude to him, and by his seeming departure from Moscow he wanted to veil a change of his attitude towards me, intending to move to one divorced lady he had promised to marry'.

The 'divorced lady' was Olga Starzheskaya, a Bolshevik party secretary, who had also been seduced by Reilly. She was also arrested, telling the Cheka that she had genuinely believed the man she knew as Konstantin Massino was a Russian and a supporter of the Bolsheviks. She had been deeply in love with him and intended to share her life with him, she said. 'I had no doubts he was Russian. I believed him and loved him, regarding him as an honest, noble, interesting and exclusively clever man, and in the depths of my heart I was very proud of his love.' She was horrified when the truth came out, she said. 'The deception, dirt and mean behaviour of this man pained me enormously.'[15]

Like Reilly's mistresses, Lockhart was also busy distancing himself from the whole affair, but with far less justification. The MI1c post-mortem held him largely to blame for the collapse of the scheme. 'He very quickly involved the French and there seems little doubt that the French then brought in a French correspondent who was actually in touch with the Cheka,' a former intelligence officer who had studied the files said. 'In a sense, Reilly was landed in it by Lockhart. I think Lockhart was very glad to have got away and not get tarred with Reilly's brush as it were. There is a slight smell around that whole period. The French were probably the culprits in that they were very slack about security and they produced this correspondent who was supposedly working for them but was also working for the Russians. It all came unstuck then.'[16]

Reilly and Hill went underground while the arrested Britons were eventually taken to the Peter & Paul Fortress, where they were crammed into small cells. Schwabe managed to escape, swimming across the Neva and, according to information passed by the Americans to John Scale in Stockholm, set up 'a working organisation' the aim of which was 'blocking all supplies to enemy powers by destruction and terrorism'. Eventually, Lockhart, the MI1c officers and a number, but not all, of the other Britons were freed in exchange for Maksim Litvinov, the Bolshevik representative in London, who was seized by the British in response to the Moscow and Petrograd arrests. The spell spent in jail was not totally unproductive for the Service. While there, Boyce met Nikolai Bunakov, a former Russian Army officer arrested for being 'politically unreliable', and recruited him as a long-term British agent – with the designation ST28. Bunakov was to play a prominent role in operations against the Soviet Union well into the Second World War.[17]

Jim Gillespie took control of the intelligence networks and began setting in place a fallback plan under which they were handed over to John Merrett, who owned the Petrograd-based engineering firm Merrett and Jones and was a longstanding member of the city's British expatriate business community. Gillespie gave Merrett 200,000 roubles to fund the networks before getting out to Finland, where he was to take over the British passport control office in Torneå, providing the 'letter box' for British secret service couriers coming into Finland from Russia. He then passed their reports back to Scale in Stockholm for reporting on to London. Merrett soon found himself not just running the intelligence networks but also using the courier routes as escape lines to get British citizens out of Russia, and having to bribe Cheka officials to provide decent treatment and food for Boyce, Tomes and the other Britons incarcerated in the Peter & Paul Fortress.

'I had assisted Mr Gillespie, the last of the intelligence officers, and on its becoming too dangerous for him to remain longer, I undertook at his request to keep on foot the various organisations started by Captain Cromie and other British officers,' Merrett later said. 'These organisations, although formed originally for political and other work, were utilised by me for obtaining the release of those in difficulties, and getting them across the frontier in a variety of ways. The regular routes had become impossible. The work entailed considerable danger to myself, and involved my actual arrest on one occasion by the Red Guards. Fortunately, I succeeded in escaping on my way to prison, and was thereafter only able to avoid rearrest by adopting disguises and sleeping in ever-changing and out-of-the-way quarters.'

William Murray-Campbell, of the Anglo-Russian Bank, described how he was helped to escape by Merrett, 'at no little danger to his personal safety', and confirmed that Merrett 'was the means of obtaining valuable information with regard to the doings of the Bolsheviks, which information was supplied to His Majesty's Military Attaché in Stockholm [Scale] through various channels including myself'. Meanwhile another, who described Merrett as a 'Scarlet Pimpernel', told a senior Foreign Office official:

I asked Mr Merrett how he dared the risk of being arrested at every moment, he laughingly replied that while the Bolsheviks were busy arresting him on the Moika, he was to be found in the country and when they were after him in the country, he was to be found somewhere else.[18]

Gillespie was not in fact the last British intelligence officer. Cumming also had Captain Franklin Clively and Major George Goldsmith in the Caucasus. This was the same Baron George de Goldschmidt who had worked for him in Brussels during the run-up to the war, having since changed his name to remove the Teutonic resonance. He had been sent by George Macdonogh and C with orders to collect intelligence and to set up a band of Kurds and Armenians who would mount raids on Turkish lines. Goldsmith was provided by MI1c with six incendiary bombs, which he used to destroy stores of rubber tyres ahead of the German and Turkish advance. Clively was Goldsmith's chief Russian expert and they were joined by Colonel Harry Rowlandson, an Indian Army officer and fluent Russian speaker who worked across the Caucasus over the next two years, in various disguises, but the American engineer he claimed to be was soon spotted as a fraud by a Bolshevik counter-espionage officer and he and Clively had to make their way through the lines to India. In mid-1918, with a Turkish 'Army of Islam' marching on the Caspian city of Baku, Goldsmith found himself making an unlikely alliance with the local Bolsheviks that brought out a rare show of unity between British Prime Minister David Lloyd George in London and Trotsky in Moscow, both of whom ruled that it would be better were the Turks to control the city than risk losing it to the Bolsheviks in Lloyd George's opinion, or the British in Trotsky's. The latter's decision was rejected by the local soviet, who voted to ask for British assistance, with the Bolsheviks losing control as a result. The local Bolshevik leaders, led by the Armenian Stepan Shaumyan, left the city, only to be captured and shot by anti-Bolshevik forces, with another British intelligence officer, Reginald Teague-Jones, then of the Indian Political Intelligence, but later himself a member of the Service, falsely blamed for their demise. Teague-Jones was also forced to change his name, but in his case for fear of retribution by Cheka agents. Back in London, Goldsmith was 'very indignant' to find himself hauled over the coals by Cumming for the decision to work with the Bolsheviks, the ticking off no doubt largely due to it having been the unfortunate Macdonogh who was forced to break the news of the local deal to a furious Lloyd George during a meeting of the war cabinet.[19]

Even in northern Russia, in Petrograd and Moscow, Reilly and
Hill were still operating underground and both evaded capture until the
beginning of November when, with Cumming having found a less tainted
replacement, they made their way back to Britain on false passports. But
more than a dozen of their Russian agents were less lucky and were captured
and shot. Both Reilly and Lockhart were sentenced to death in absentia.

Shortly after Hill arrived back in the UK, he was summoned to
Whitehall Court for a meeting with Cumming. 'His offices were at the
top of a London building overlooking the Thames,' Hill recalled. 'The
various rooms, corridors, entrances and exits were so like a rabbit warren
that it was some time before I really knew the geography of the place.
The Chief, a short, wire-haired, square man, with penetrating eyes and
lips which looked stern, but could in a second take on a humorous curve,
was in naval uniform. He was sitting at a desk on which were three or
four telephones. Other telephones were attached to automatic brackets
on the wall. For half a minute, he leisurely surveyed me and I have never
been so thoroughly looked over before or since in my life. Then he came
forward, shook me by the hand and asked me to make a verbal report
on my last work. It was curious to think that I had come into the secret
service by chance and not by design, that until that morning, although I
had worked for the last year on nothing but secret service work, I did not
know the Chief or have any official existence in his department. I think
one of the most pleasing recollections of that meeting was the Chief's
approval and unqualified admiration and praise for the work I had done.'

Reilly and Hill were awarded the Military Cross on C's
recommendation. Hill, as the senior officer, was also made a Companion
of the Distinguished Service Order. The citation stated:

> He has since early December 1917, been constantly working between
> the north of Russia and Romania and southern Russia. He has attended
> Bolshevik meetings at night when street fighting was at its height,
> passing back and forth through the Bolshevik fighting lines, and has
> been almost daily under fire without protection. He has conducted
> himself with courage and coolness and rendered valuable service.

They were then sent into southern Russia, under cover as British merchants, in order to provide intelligence on which British policy might be based during the Paris peace conference. Reilly dispatched a stream of reports backing the anti-Bolshevik forces and urged that they receive substantial British backing both financially and in terms of supplies, again no doubt to be passed through him. He also took a swipe at Major-General Frederick Poole, the head of the British military mission, over his relationships with not just one, but two Russian women, 'Gen still fooling about with Mme P and Tundukoff. Bad impression. Never saw such ugly women . . . Everyone disgusted Gen P's carryings on with Mme P.' The hypocrisy of such criticism, given Reilly's own behaviour and the clear implication that had the women not been ugly, it would have been perfectly acceptable behaviour, does not appear to have occurred to Reilly, although it certainly must have been apparent back at 'Head Office', where his personal file contained details of his female 'contacts' in Russia and a series of pleas from his wives to be told where their errant husband was.[20]

Despite his Military Cross, Reilly soon found that he was no longer held in high regard either by the Foreign Office or even by Cumming. His rampant anti-Bolshevism, his apparently unconditional support for Boris Savinkov, a former left-wing terrorist turned White Russian leader, and his taste for *Boy's Own* schemes made him at best unreliable, at worst dangerous. Reilly applied for a full-time post with MI1c, telling Lockhart, 'I venture to think that the state should not lose my services. I would devote the rest of my life to this wicked work.' But his dubious practices had left him with too many enemies among the 'swells' in Whitehall and by the beginning of May 1920, when he left the RAF, he was, officially at least, no longer employed as an officer by MI1c. In fact, he continued to work for the Service for some time, sending reports and attempting to use the influence he evidently still believed he had to push for covert action to overthrow the Bolsheviks. Despite his subsequent reputation as a dangerous maverick, and his undoubted sleight of hand where money was involved, Reilly's usefulness and his ability as a spy are not in doubt, according to one former member of the

Service who made a detailed study of Reilly's files. 'He's been written off by historians by and large,' the former officer said. 'But he has been greatly under-rated. He was very, very good – a very able agent and a far more serious operator than the impression given by the myth. Historians do have this tendency to write off something that has been made to appear glamorous. He was unusual but I don't think he was glamorous. He was a bit of a crook, you could almost say, certainly [guilty of] sharp practice. But as an agent he was superb.'[21]

FOURTEEN

Red dusk

CUMMING wasted no time in sending in another leading exponent of
espionage to Russia to relieve John Merrett and set up more permanent
reporting structures. Paul Dukes, a fluent Russian speaker, had already
been in contact with the intelligence services while working in Petrograd
as a member of the Anglo-Russian Commission, a British propaganda
organisation. A few months before the October Revolution, he was asked
by Tsarist intelligence chiefs to provide them with as much information
as possible on the Bolshevik leaders. In order to spell out to officials
back in Whitehall precisely what the Russians did and did not know,
Dukes filed two heavyweight reports on the leading Bolsheviks, derived
from information provided by the Russians and the French. These added
significantly to what MI1c and MI5 knew and almost certainly had an
impact on Cumming's subsequent decision to select him for the secret
service mission in Russia.[1] After the revolution, Dukes remained in
Russia, working in the south, ostensibly with a relief mission funded by
the American YMCA. Called back to England in the summer of 1918
by an 'urgent' telegram from the Foreign Office, Dukes arrived by Royal
Navy destroyer at Aberdeen and was put on a train to London's King's
Cross station where a car was waiting to pick him up.

> Knowing neither my destination nor the cause of my recall, I was
> driven to a building in a side-street in the vicinity of Trafalgar Square.
> The chauffeur had a face like a mask. We entered the building and
> the elevator whisked us to the top floor, above which additional

superstructures had been built for war-emergency offices. I had always associated rabbit warrens with subterranean abodes. But here in this building, I discovered a maze of burrow-like passages, corridors, nooks and alcoves, piled higgledy-piggledy on the roof. Crossing a short iron bridge, we entered another maze, until just as I was beginning to feel dizzy I was shown into a tiny room about ten-foot-square where sat an officer in the uniform of a British Army colonel. 'Good afternoon, Mr Dukes,' said the colonel. 'You doubtless wonder that no explanation has been given to you as to why you should return to England. Well, I have to inform you, confidentially, that it has been proposed to offer you a somewhat responsible post in the Secret Intelligence Service. We have reason to believe that Russia will not long continue to be open to foreigners. We wish someone to remain there to keep us informed of the march of events.'

The colonel, Frederick Browning, took Dukes to Cumming's office to meet the chief. 'From the threshold the room seemed bathed in semi-obscurity,' Dukes recalled. 'The writing desk was so placed with the window behind it that on entering everything appeared only in silhouette. A row of half-a-dozen extending telephones stood at the left of a big desk littered with papers. On a side-table were maps and drawings, with models of aeroplanes, submarines, and mechanical devices, while a row of bottles of various colours and a distilling outfit with a rack of test tubes bore witness to chemical experiments and operations. These evidences of scientific investigation only served to intensify an already overpowering atmosphere of strangeness and mystery. But it was not these things that engaged my attention as I stood nervously waiting. My eyes fixed themselves on the figure at the writing table. In the capacious swing desk-chair, his shoulders hunched, with his head supported on his hand, sat the Chief. This extraordinary man was short of stature, thick-set with grey hair half covering a well-rounded head. His mouth was stern and an eagle eye, full of vivacity, glanced – or glared as the case may be – piercingly through a gold-rimmed monocle. At first encounter, he appeared very severe. His manner of speech was abrupt. Yet the stern countenance could melt into the kindliest of smiles, and the softened eyes and lips revealed a heart that was big and generous. Awe-inspired as I was by my first encounter, I soon learned to regard "the Chief" with feelings of the deepest personal admiration. In silhouette, I saw myself motioned to a chair. The Chief wrote for a moment and then suddenly turned with the unexpected remark, "So I understand you want to go back to Soviet Russia, do you?" As if it had been my own suggestion.'[2]

Dukes was given the designation ST25, as he was to be run by John Scale in Stockholm. Cumming told him that he had to find Merrett and pick up the reins of the agent networks set up in Petrograd and Moscow by Stephen Alley, Ernest Boyce, Scale and Jim Gillespie, as well as those run by the now-dead naval attaché Francis Cromie. 'The words Archangel, Stockholm, Riga, Helsingfors recurred frequently, and the names were mentioned of English people in all those places and in Petrograd,' Dukes recalled. 'It was finally decided that I alone should determine how and by what route I should regain access to Russia, and how I should dispatch reports. "Don't go and get yourself killed," said the Chief in conclusion, smiling. Three weeks later, I set out for Russia, into the unknown.'

When Dukes arrived in Petrograd, using a false identity as a Ukrainian member of the Cheka, Merrett's flat was his first point of call, only for him to be told that Merrett was in prison and his flat sealed up. Dukes took lodgings with a friendly Russian couple and a few days later, one of the Russian agents Dukes was in contact with arrived at his lodgings with 'a huge fellow, whose stubble-covered face brimmed over with smiles beaming good nature and jollity. This giant was dressed in a rough and ragged brown suit and in his hand he squeezed a dirty hat.' The scruffy giant was introduced to Dukes as Merrett.

'I thought you were in prison,' Dukes said.

'Not quite,' Merrett replied. 'I had a larky getaway, slithered down a drainpipe outside the kitchen window into the next yard as the Red Guards came in at the front door.'

Merrett's wife Lydia had been arrested as a hostage in an attempt to get him to give himself up but he had shaved off his beard, changed from his previous good clothes into his scruffy Russian attire and continued running the spy networks and escape lines. But amid fears that Lydia had been broken during a seven-hour interrogation in the Cheka's Gorokhovaya headquarters, Merrett was himself smuggled out and Dukes bribed a Cheka official to obtain the release of Mrs Merrett before taking her down the escape lines set up by her husband to freedom in Finland. He spent Christmas 1918 in Stockholm with Scale, where he handed over a first batch of reports before returning overland to Petrograd.[3]

'Mr Merrett was certainly acting under circumstances of grave personal danger,' Dukes later told a senior Foreign Office official. 'When I arrived in Petrograd I found him continuing the work of Mr Gillespie, who had been compelled to quit the country. At the same time he was engaged in enabling allied subjects, particularly British who were in difficulties and whom the Bolsheviks refused passes, to find means of crossing the frontier unobserved. I found him in hiding, changing his abode every night, in various disguises, and hotly chased by the agents of the Extraordinary Commission. I formed the judgement during those days that Mr Merrett was actuated partly, perhaps, by a love of adventure, but mainly by a sense of duty towards the British colony in Petrograd. There was at that time absolutely nobody left who was attending to the material wants or discovering means of communicating abroad. Mr Merrett, I believe, felt that he could not leave Petrograd until someone arrived, or some arrangements were made for the continuation of the various activities for which he temporarily, voluntarily assumed the responsibility. Very little is generally known of the great services he rendered in the autumn of 1918.'[4]

The first reports arrived in Whitehall Court on Christmas Day and were worthy presents for Cumming, being top secret memos between Leon Trotsky and the Bolshevik navy's commander-in-chief, Admiral Vasily Altvater, a senior Tsarist naval officer who had been persuaded by the Commissar for War to work with the Bolsheviks for the good of the country. Altvater detailed the dire state of the Bolshevik navy and suggested that the entire fleet might have to be placed on a state of permanent reserve. The correspondence also revealed that Russia now saw Britain as the main threat to its territory with the main argument against placing ships in a state of permanent reserve as being 'the possibility of an attack by England and her allies on Petrograd by sea'. Altvater warned that the Bolshevik fleet did not have enough sailors to man all its ships or enough coal to maintain any 'operations taking any length of time'. He also accurately predicted that the Royal Navy could occupy the Estonian capital, Reval (now Tallinn), 'at any moment' – by the time the report reached London, the Royal Navy had already placed the city 'under British protection'. From information gathered in the naval dockyards, Dukes said the Russian sailors would not be prepared to fight the Royal Navy. 'In the summer they were, on the contrary, in the majority pro-ally, especially the crews of the torpedo-flotillas and mining divisions, the latter openly declaring their intention of going into the White Sea and fighting on the side of the British.'

The reports from Dukes were backed up by an agent run by Hastings Taylor, Cumming's man in Christiania. The agent, N63, reported in mid-January that the Baltic fleet effectively consisted of only two ships, the cruiser *Oleg* and the battleship *Andrei Pervozvanny*, while there were only enough food stocks in Petrograd to last three weeks. Dukes reported that all the Russian submarines were in such a poor condition they were unable to put to sea and that sailors in Petrograd were opposed to the Bolsheviks, largely because they were so poorly fed. He also described how the refusal of Russian sailors to put to sea to take on the British at Reval had led a hysterical Fyodor Raskolnikov, the Commissar for Naval Affairs, to take the fleet out himself, ending in defeat for the Russian ships and his capture by the Royal Navy. The detail of the reports from Dukes was such that he was able to pass on the full minutes of a stormy meeting of naval Bolshevik representatives attended by Raskolnikov's wife, who had taken over as Naval Commissar. Dukes described how Trotsky had become so annoyed at reports of officers being forced by junior ranks to clean the lavatories that he smashed an ink well with his fist, declaring: 'I dare not call this sort of thing by its right name as there is a lady present.'[5]

Dukes worked with a number of Russian agents, including Nadezhda Ivanovna Petrovskaya, a doctor and former revolutionary,

who was a genuine member of the Bolshevik Party and had known
Lenin well enough to have visited him in prison as his fiancée when
he was arrested in St Petersburg in December 1895. Petrovskaya,
who used the covernames Mariya Ivanovna Semyonova and Mariya
Ivanovna Smirnova, was Dukes's mistress and, once Merrett left, his
chief assistant. Funding came from another expatriate businessman,
George Gibson, who was winding up the affairs of the family shipping
company and agreed to bankroll the operations since it was impossible
for Cumming to get money into Russia. Gibson lent Dukes 200,000
roubles to pay the agents and cover his own expenses. Dukes sent
his first reports out in early December 1918 with two couriers,
one of whom was Pyotr Sokolov (ST65), previously a Russian
international footballer, who was recruited by George Hill. He was,
in all probability, talent-spotted by either Harry Hall or by a member
of the Charnock family, expatriate Britons living in Russia before the
revolution and very close to the embassy. Harry Charnock, a close
friend of Lockhart, had set up the first Russian football league and
Sokolov was a 6ft 4in central defender for the national champions, St
Petersburg Unitas.[6] The reports were passed via the frontline MI1c
post at Terijoki (now Zelenogorsk) on the Finnish–Russian border,
where Hall was the vice-consul, to Gillespie in Torneå on the border
between Finland and Sweden and then up to Scale in Stockholm
before being forwarded on to London.

   After being released from captivity at the end of the war, Conrad
O'Brien-ffrench was summoned to the War Office in January 1919
to be met by Catherine Mann, the pretty War Office secretary to
whom he had sent reports hidden behind secret ink. She introduced
him to 'a youngish colonel in the uniform of the Life Guards. It was
Colonel Stewart Menzies, later referred to by those who worked for
him as S.M.' Menzies offered O'Brien-ffrench a 'highly secret' job as
assistant military attaché in Stockholm working with Scale. O'Brien-
ffrench was to replace Lieutenant Ernest Michelson, another old Russia
hand. Michelson, whose family owned a Petrograd-based engineering
company, was being sent to Christiania, having won the Military Cross

for his work for MI1c in Russia. Michelson had escaped from Petrograd under cover as the correspondent of the *Daily Chronicle*.

When O'Brien-ffrench arrived in Stockholm, he was met by Scale, his wife and his secretary Oohna Stewart, all preparing to go skiing and with a pair of skis for him. With his luggage yet to appear, O'Brien-ffrench was forced to ski wearing the dark overcoat, bowler hat and spats in which he had arrived.

> I got covered in snow as, of course, I fell repeatedly. The other skiers who saw me floundering about in such a manner could hardly believe their eyes; but I joined the major's party in laughing until none of us could stand up. The next morning at the office, I was busy reading files and getting up-to-date with what was going on. Most of the important information about Russia seemed to come from an agent working under several assumed names, but known to us as Paul Dukes, secret agent ST25. My designation was ST36. Paul Dukes was the answer to a spy-writer's prayer. He had knocked about Tsarist Russia as a boy, spoke the language perfectly, although he had a slight accent, had a flair for journalism, a keen sense of the dramatic and a sensitive nose for important information. Above all, he was intelligent, courageous and good-looking. My superior Major Scale was tall, handsome, well-read, intelligent, with a debonair manner which endeared him to everyone.[7]

Within weeks of O'Brien-ffrench arriving in Stockholm, the courier links between Dukes and Finland were broken by a series of Cheka arrests. Dukes was forced to make his own way out, travelling across the ice between Petrograd and Terijoki in the sleigh of a Finnish smuggler before a Bolshevik patrol on horseback bore down on them, forcing him to abandon the sleigh and walk across the ice to Finland clutching his reports. Once there he found that while Sokolov had successfully brought back one batch of reports, the other courier had failed to return. Dukes had to reconstruct the reports that had never been delivered from memory. Scale came down to question him and ensure they got as much from his presence in Terijoki before sending him back again by land.[8]

Cumming returned to his naval roots to find a way to keep the reports from Dukes coming into the UK. He spoke to Captain Wilfred French, who operated a small flotilla of coastal motor boats (CMBs), based on Osea Island in the estuary of the river Blackwater in Essex, ideal for creeping out unnoticed into the North Sea. The fast, light, three-man boats, 55 feet long and equipped with one or two torpedoes and Lewis machine-guns, were designed for lightning strikes against larger warships and had been used against the naval base at Zeebrugge. But Cumming had a different use for them, as he explained to Lieutenant Augustus Agar, who had volunteered for 'special service' in the Gulf of Finland.[9]

He said there was a certain Englishman – unnamed, and with regard to whom no details were given – who had remained in Russia to conduct intelligence, whose work was regarded as of vital importance, and with whom it was essential to keep in touch. It was necessary to help him to get out alive, as he was the only man who had first-hand reliable information on certain things which was required by our government. There had been, C explained, a kind of secret link or courier service between this man via Finland and Estonia, but latterly the couriers had been captured and nothing now came through. The proposal was that I should go out with two CMBs and endeavour with their speed to land fresh couriers on the coast whence they could reach Petrograd, deliver messages to this man, and bring back his reports. I would be transferred to the Secret Service and adopt a civilian occupation. Officially, the British Government would know nothing whatever about me. I should choose a picked band of young men for my crew, who would also to all appearances be private individuals. The chief then proceeded to explain to me his system of contacts. These contacts represented men in his Secret Service work. Each contact had a number. I myself would be given one and would be known only by this number, with which I was to communicate with headquarters. As the head of the area in which I would be operating had his headquarters in Stockholm, I would henceforth be known as ST34. Similarly, the unnamed Englishman in Petrograd with whom it was my immediate mission to establish contact was designated as ST25.[10]

Agar and his men based themselves at a small yacht club in Terijoki. It was opposite the Russian naval base at Kronstadt, just 10 miles away. The courier selected to go in and assist Dukes was Pyotr Sokolov. Agar and his men took Sokolov, carrying dispatches for Dukes, across the channel to Petrograd, leaving him in a rowing boat off the Russian island of Krestovsky, at the mouth of the river Neva, and forty-eight hours later going back to pick him up.

'We were soon at the mouth of the river opposite Krestovsky island,' Agar said. 'We could see the dark line of rushes which fringed the shore a quarter of a mile away, and waited anxiously for the pre-arranged signal of three short flashes. Nothing appeared but after about five minutes I thought I saw a flickering of light which might, at that distance, be the flash of an electric torch. We went ahead to close this light and yes, there was no doubt now, it was Peter's signal. I stopped and waited while I gave the reply signal, exactly in his direction. A few minutes later we heard the sound of oars, followed very shortly by a low hail. I heard my name called. I called out in reply, "*khorosho*" – "all right" – and Peter was alongside. We shook hands and away we went at full speed on the return journey. Peter was just about dead beat, as well he might be after the strain of the last forty-eight hours. We didn't speak at all. Hampsheir gave him some biscuits and rum and I think he went to sleep.'

Back at the yacht club in Terijoki, there was a good deal of celebration that the first part of the job was over. All that needed to be done now was to extract Dukes at a later date once he had gathered the additional intelligence asked for in the dispatches from London. Sokolov explained that Dukes was not ready to come out but had given three alternative dates, on one of which he would be at the rendezvous waiting to be picked up. The documents, all written on tissue paper, were handed over to Raleigh le May (ST30) for transmission to London. 'We sat up until well into the hours of the morning discussing with Peter the state of affairs in Petrograd, and I listened with horror as he recounted experience after experience during his last forty-eight hours and of his dramatic meeting with ST25 in broad daylight in a public park.'[11]

Agar and his men were left with little to do while they waited for the dates on which it had been arranged they should try to extract Dukes. But with the Bolshevik warships in Kronstadt harbour bombarding the fort at Krasnaya Gorka, which had been captured by the anti-Bolshevist White Army, they were reluctant to stand idly by. Agar passed a message back to Cumming via le May's deputy, Harry Hall, asking permission to attack the Russian warships. The response from London read: 'Boats to be used for intelligence purposes only. Stop. Take no action unless specially directed by SNO [Senior Naval Officer] Baltic.' Cumming's reluctance to countermand an order from an admiral, in this case Rear-Admiral Walter Cowan, allowed Agar the leeway he needed to pursue the action. On 17 June, Agar took two boats out of Terijoki and headed for Kronstadt, intent on sinking some of the Russian warships that were pounding Krasnaya Gorka. One of the boats suffered engine failure and had to turn back but Agar, his deputy, Sub-Lieutenant John Hampsheir, and his chief motor mechanic, Hugh Beeley, managed to get their motor boat close to the Russian cruiser *Oleg*, which had carried out much of the bombardment.

Throwing all caution to the winds, I put on full speed and headed straight for the Oleg, which was now clearly visible. In a few moments we were nearly on top of her. I fired my torpedo less than five hundred yards away, just as the first shot from her guns was fired at us in return. The torpedo hit just abaft her foremost funnel, throwing up a high column of water and a huge column of black smoke reaching up the top of the mast. Either this gave the alarm or else we were observed as fire was directly opened on us from all quarters. I quickly put the helm over, turning almost a complete circle, and with the sea now following us, headed back westwards across the same direction from which I had approached and passed between two destroyers at full speed, who also opened fire.

There followed a hair-raising trip across the Gulf of Finland with Agar twisting and turning his boat to avoid the Bolshevik gunfire. He was awarded the Victoria Cross and promoted to lieutenant-commander. Hampsheir received the Distinguished Service Cross, and Beeley the Conspicuous Gallantry Medal. The notification of the medal awards in the *London Gazette* lacked detailed citations because the Bolsheviks had put a price on the head of those responsible, but Agar's name, and the key point of the citation, that the medal was 'for most conspicuous gallantry, coolness and skill', did appear.[12]

After several failed attempts at extracting Dukes, the motor boats went back to Kronstadt to mount a further attack, combining forces with other elements from the Royal Navy's Baltic Squadron, and this time doing even better, sinking three more Bolshevik warships, the battleships *Andrei Pervozvanny* and *Petropavlovsk* plus the key submarine supply ship *Pamyat' Azova*. If Altvater's reports to Trotsky were correct, the only serviceable ships of the Russian Baltic Fleet had been destroyed, while there was a further intelligence haul when Bolshevik sailors who swam ashore in Finland were interrogated by Lawrence Webster, who was now attached to Cowan's staff.[13]

Two more VCs were awarded for this second operation, one to Commander Claude Dobson, who led the attack, and the other to Lieutenant Gordon Steele, the second in command of the boat that torpedoed both the *Andrei Pervozvanny* and the *Petropavlovsk*. Steele saw his commander shot dead, hauled him off the steering wheel, steadied the boat and torpedoed the *Andrei Pervozvanny* at 100 yards range, the citation said.

> He had then a difficult manoeuvre to perform to get a clear view of the battleship Petropavlovsk, which was overlapped by the Andrei Pervozvanny and obscured by smoke coming from that ship. The evolution, however, was skilfully carried out, and the Petropavlovsk torpedoed. This left Lieutenant Steele with only just room to turn, in order to regain the entrance to the harbour, but he effected the movement with success and firing his machine-guns along the wall on his way, passed under the line of forts, through heavy fire, out of the harbour.[14]

Agar and three other officers received the Distinguished Service Order and six other officers the Distinguished Service Cross, while the Kronstadt raid was lauded in the press. 'The Royal Navy has achieved yet one more hazardous feat of arms which might well have been considered unthinkable and impossible had it not been done,' *The Times* said. 'How many more than a score of gallant lives might have been paid for so great a success had not the operation been admirably planned, accurately timed and perfectly executed?'[15]

Further attempts by Agar and his men to get Dukes out failed, and eventually, in August 1919, he made his own way across the Latvian border, assisted by an agent in the Cheka. Aleksandr Nikolalevich Gavrishenko, a former Imperial Navy commander and a member of the anti-Soviet organisation Yedinaya Velikaya Rossiya (United Great Russia), had managed to penetrate the Cheka, putting him in an ideal position to smuggle British spies in and out of Russia. Dukes only just escaped execution by White Russian soldiers who, seeing him cross the border without problems, took him for a Bolshevik spy. Agar returned to the UK, landing at Hull and taking the train to King's Cross before going on to Whitehall Court to present his final report to C.

Once more I traversed that labyrinth of corridors in the building near Whitehall which was familiar to me before I left London. Once again, I ascended the last flight of steps leading to the top floor and C's sanctum. The pretty lady secretary was still there and genuinely pleased to see me back. She said that I was expected but would have to wait a few minutes, so I waited in the passage outside. Presently another door opened and a man came out carrying a dispatch case. He was tall, dark-haired and lean. Something about him and his manner arrested my attention and seemed to me to be familiar, but whether it was the eager look in his eyes, or a certain tense expression in his face, I cannot say. I looked at him again and then in a flash of intuition a thought came to my mind. 'Yes,' I said to myself. 'It must be him.' I was the first to speak.

'Are you Dukes?'

'Yes,' he replied.

'Well,' I said, 'how strange that we should meet at last like this, and here of all places. I suppose you know I am Agar.'

He laughed. 'C has a habit of arranging these little matters like this.' At which we both laughed and shook hands and entered C's office together.[16]

During his relatively brief ten-month mission to the Soviet Union, Dukes had masqueraded under the false identity of the Cheka, and had managed to join both the Red Army and the Bolshevik Party. Undoubtedly the most important part of his work was stitching together the agent networks left behind by Jim Gillespie and carefully tended by John Merrett. These were led by Albert Hoyer, a Danish sea captain who spoke fluent Russian and English and had worked for the Russian naval attaché in Copenhagen during the war. He was subsequently loaned to Stephen Alley in Murmansk before working for MI1c in Kirkenes, on the border between Norway and Russia. Hoyer was 'a man of extraordinary physique who could easily pass for a prizefighter', one British official said. After the revolution, he claimed to be a Bolshevik by persuasion and took a job as a ship's captain with the Russian merchant navy, the Sovtorgflot, using it as an opportunity to set up an agent network in Petrograd, focusing on naval, military and air force intelligence. By September 1919, Hoyer was already reporting, via John Scale, on the fate of the British sailors captured during the raid on Kronstadt as well as the low fuel stocks in Petrograd, plus full details of the damage to the Russian fleet. The great advantage of the Hoyer network was that, as a ship's captain, he was able to travel abroad frequently, carrying the agents' reports with him, passing them on during port stops in Reval or Helsingfors. The close co-operation between SIS and Finnish intelligence ensured the Finnish authorities hampered his ship's departure from their ports to give him the necessary time to pass on reports, discuss any issues that had arisen with the network, and receive any messages or additional tasking from Head Office. On at least one occasion, a ban on his ship leaving the Finnish port of Viborg was used to allow him to go to Reval 'to arrange matters', providing an opportunity to talk to the MI1c bureau chief in Reval, Lieutenant-Colonel Ronald Meiklejohn of the Royal Warwickshire Regiment, who was a veteran of the Russian intervention. The stream of reporting from Hoyer and a number of other agents, including first-hand reports from Russian naval officers that were highly valued by the new director of naval intelligence, Rear-Admiral Hugh Sinclair, continued well into the mid-1920s.[17]

Nadezhda Petrovskaya had been tasked to collect agent reports and pass them to Sokolov whenever he got into Russia. She was funded by a further 200,000 of George Gibson's roubles, but both she and Gibson were arrested a few months after Dukes got out. Petrovskaya was sentenced to death. Shortly afterwards Gavrishenko was arrested and shot. Gibson was eventually released while Petrovskaya was held prisoner until 1922 when she was given an amnesty. The journalist Kürz-Gedroitz was then arrested and sent to a prison camp. He was released after a few years, but was shot during the Stalinist purges of the early 1930s. Although it seems likely that, under what must have been intense pressure, Petrovskaya named Kürz-Gedroitz, she never gave up the members of the Hoyer network who had been left in her care by Dukes and were subsequently run by Nikolai Bunakov (ST28), who was now based in Finland and was in charge of getting reports out of Russia, with Sokolov as his main courier. Bunakov operated under cover of a commercial trading company, AB Ekonomic, selling British goods, including Kiwi boot polish, into Finland and providing a 'letter box' for reports from SIS agents.[18]

Alongside his work stitching the British networks back together, Dukes might be reasonably credited with inventing what was to become a standard piece of tradecraft for the secret agent, placing incriminating evidence in a waterproof bag and hiding it in a lavatory cistern.

> I wrote mostly at night, in minute handwriting on tracing-paper, with a small caoutchouc [latex] bag about four inches in length, weighted with lead, ready at my side. In case of alarm, all my papers could be slipped into this bag and within thirty seconds be transferred to the bottom of

a tub of washing or the cistern of a water closet. In efforts to discover arms or incriminating documents, I have seen pictures, carpets, and bookshelves removed and everything turned topsy-turvy by diligent searchers, but it never occurred to anybody to search through a pail of washing or thrust his hand into the water-closet cistern. Only on one occasion was I obliged to destroy documents of value, while of the couriers who, at grave risk, carried communications back and forth from Finland, only two failed to arrive and I presume were caught and shot.[19]

Not for the last time, the government was anxious to use the secret intelligence procured by the Service to justify its involvement in a foreign intervention. 'We understand that Mr Dukes, who recently returned to England after a stay of several months at Petrograd and Moscow, has placed at the disposal of the Government valuable information upon the situation and outlook in Bolshevist Russia,' *The Times* reported. 'In some official quarters, it is felt that this information should not be withheld from the public. The issues involved are held to be far too grave to justify final decisions by the Government without the support of an accurately informed public opinion.' As a result, Dukes wrote a long series of highly publicised articles in the newspaper, thereby ensuring that he could never be used for real secret service missions again, but far too late to prevent the public pressure for withdrawal of British troops becoming irresistible.[20]

At the same time, Scale found himself embroiled in another tale of torture and murder when it emerged that one of his agents, an anti-Bolshevik Russian from central Asia, Mohammed Bek Hadji Lashet, was running a gang of Russian émigrés who were using pretty, young women to lure Russian Bolsheviks to their deaths. Female members of the group – there was a White Russian blonde and a dark-haired 'exotic' central Asian woman to cater for different tastes – targeted Bolsheviks based in, or passing through, Stockholm, luring them to a lakeside villa on the outskirts of the city, where they were tortured to provide any information they had, and killed in a variety of equally unpleasant ways.

The long-running police investigation into the murders both frightened and fascinated the Swedish public, with bodies turning up all over the countryside around Stockholm and the involvement of White Russians in the 'Murder League' feeding into xenophobic concerns over the number of expatriate Russians in Sweden. The authorities were even less happy when the full scale of Lashet's involvement with British intelligence emerged. He was not only one of Scale's agents, he had worked with the Anglo-Russian Commission in Petrograd before the Bolshevik takeover, and so was also linked to Dukes. After the revolution, he moved to Stockholm, where he offered intelligence to the American embassy. The US officials were so worried by what he was prepared to do on behalf of the anti-Bolshevik cause that they suspected he was a Bolshevik agent provocateur and as a result turned him down. He and fifteen other Russian émigrés were eventually arrested and charged with the murders of four Bolsheviks, two of them embassy officials. The court was told that Nikolai Ardashev, a Bolshevik commercial agent, was enticed to the villa on a lake north of Stockholm by a beautiful sixteen-year-old Russian girl who took him there in a large chauffeur-driven car. Dagmara de Gysser was in fact the daughter of a White Russian general and she swiftly became the femme fatale and central character in the whole affair. The villa was owned by the Swedish operatic star Lily Strindberg, whose sister was Lashet's mistress. She and her lover moved in and it swiftly became renowned within the local Russian community for the regular orgies that occurred there. Ardashev's sexual expectations were, however, swiftly dashed on arrival at the villa, where he was overcome by members of the 'Murder League', chained to a wall and left for twenty-six hours, before being brought before a 'court-martial' of gang members, interrogated and condemned to death. He was promised a reprieve if he signed a number of cheques, which he did to no avail. Having signed the cheques, 'the doomed man was blindfolded, gagged and garrotted to death,' the court heard. 'While he was being slowly strangled, the young woman watched his dying struggles calmly, cigarette in mouth.' In an attempt to distance themselves from Lashet, British officials subsequently leaked material to the British press suggesting that he was a mercenary prepared to sell his information to the highest bidder, which in all probability was true, and that he was involved in plots to subvert British rule in India. Lashet and his fellow members of the 'Murder League' insisted to the last that the murders were motivated by anti-Bolshevik beliefs. An American official writing in the *Washington Post* hinted loudly at the British involvement:

> The whole affair is a combination of Bolshevik provocation and Monarchist plots against the Bolsheviki and ordinary robbery and murder. It is practically certain that all the criminals were in the pay of some higher powers. Were they obeying orders or acting on their own initiative? This will soon be known.

If it was, it was never made public, but both the Swedish, and indeed the British, authorities were in no doubt as to the links between Lashet and the British secret service, causing some difficulties in relations and, a few weeks after the trial came to an end, John Scale was moved to Helsingfors.[21]

During this period, Cumming was also continuing to use his nephew Professor Bernard Pares to collect intelligence in Russia, paying him £666 6s 8d – around £25,000 at today's prices – for information collected from two journeys across Russia in the spring and summer of 1919. Pares was very much of an anti-Bolshevik bent, while another MI1c agent active in Russia around the same time, the *Manchester Guardian* journalist W. T. Goode, appeared at least on the face of it to be rather too close to his Russian hosts. Goode courted controversy while travelling around Russia and the Baltic republics by allegedly acting as an intermediary between Lenin and the Estonians, who were less than grateful. Arriving in Reval, Goode was arrested and put on a Royal Navy destroyer, where he found himself being lambasted by Rear-Admiral Cowan for courting the 'goodwill of the Bolsheviks'. In a report passed to the war cabinet, the British naval commander in the Baltic lamented such behaviour: 'Whether he is a Secret Service agent or not, I consider it most undesirable that he should have further freedom of action out here.' The lack of understanding of what Goode was actually doing rather than appeared to be doing was to be a recurring factor with SIS operations during this period, sometimes even within the Service itself. It is not clear if Goode and Pares were aware they had been working for the same organisation, but back in London they became engaged in an unseemly and embarrassing spat in the pages of *The Times* over their respective positions on Bolshevik Russia.[22]

FIFTEEN

'A very useful lady'

THE extent of the material that the British obtained on Trotsky during the first two years of Bolshevik control in Russia was in part the result of his importance within the regime and the fact that his areas of influence, initially foreign affairs and subsequently military and naval matters, coincided with the interests of Cumming's main customers. But it was also the result of a remarkable post-revolutionary MI1c operation against the Bolsheviks, only the first of many similar operations carried out by the Service in Russia throughout the twentieth century. The operation centred around another journalist seen by a number of British officials as being far too close to the Bolsheviks. Arthur Ransome, later author of the popular children's book *Swallows and Amazons*, but then Russia correspondent of the British liberal newspaper the *Daily News*, had links to MI1c dating back to before the revolution, when he reported directly to Cudbert Thornhill and was a key player in a British-run propaganda organisation, the International News Agency. This organisation, which aimed to place pro-Russian stories in British newspapers and vice versa, was regarded as Ransome's 'brainchild'. He personally proposed the idea to the British ambassador, Sir George Buchanan, in mid-January 1916. Two days later, it was given to Thornhill to control. The British journalists taking part included not just Ransome, but Morgan Philips Price of the *Manchester Guardian*, Hamilton Fyfe of the *Daily Mail* and Guy Berenger of the Reuters news agency. The enterprise was far from a success, but the relationship between Ransome and MI1c had been established and would prove far more valuable later in the year. He was also closely associated with John Scale, who was enthusiastically dreaming up propaganda ideas for the International News Agency, and Ransome was in no doubt as to the British officer's role, later recalling that he and Scale had spent an evening 'fixing up a paper announcing the fall of Baghdad either the night this happened or perhaps the night before'. He was even given a pass by Samuel Hoare authorising him to collect information on behalf of the 'British Intelligence Mission', the official name for the MI1c bureau. Previously keen to join up to fight on the Western Front, Ransome was also provided by Thornhill with a letter exempting him from any military service. He was deemed far too valuable to MI1c for his information-gathering ability, although at this stage it was not clear how valuable he would eventually turn out to be.[1]

The October Revolution did not at first sight appear to back up Thornhill's confidence in Ransome. The *Daily News* correspondent made the classic journalistic mistake of missing the big story, returning home to England three weeks before the revolution and having to comment from England on what was happening rather than reporting from the front line. He only returned to Russia in mid-December, but within weeks was to meet the woman with whom he would share the rest of his life and who would provide him, and by extension MI1c, with access to the inner workings of the Bolshevik leadership and government 'such as no other foreigner enjoyed'. The full details of the operation were 'redacted' from the MI5 personal file on Ransome released to the British national archives, but the first hint of her importance to Britain comes in June 1918, with an 'extremely urgent' telegram from Robert Bruce Lockhart to the Foreign Office requesting permission to put 'a very useful lady' on Ransome's passport as his wife.

A very useful lady who has worked here in extremely confidential position in a Government office desires to give up her present position. She has been of the greatest service to me and is anxious to establish herself in Stockholm where she would be centre of information regarding underground agitation in Russia in the event of Bolsheviks being overthrown by the Germans. Not only have her services to the allies been considerable but it would be highly important for us to have inside information of future movement. Lady is not Bolshevik, but is known to all leaders of the movement. In any case, she promises to take no part in political agitation work. In order to enable her to leave secretly, I wish to have authority to put her onto Mr Ransome's passport as his wife and facilitate her departure via Murmansk.[2]

Ransome was already married but effectively, if not officially, separated from his first wife Ivy. The new supposed 'wife' was Trotsky's highly trusted secretary, Yevgeniya Petrovna Shelepina, whom Ransome had met at the end of 1917 while interviewing her boss, then still the Foreign Affairs Commissar. Ransome fell deeply in love with Shelepina, 'a tall jolly woman' unlike any he had met before, as Ransome's friend, the MI1c officer George Hill, recalled:

She must have been two or three inches above six feet in her stockings. At first glance, one was apt to dismiss her as a very fine-looking specimen of Russian peasant womanhood, but closer acquaintance revealed in her depths of unguessed qualities. She was methodical and intellectual, a hard worker with an enormous sense of humour. She saw things quickly and could analyse political situations with the speed and precision with which an experienced bridge player analyses a hand of cards. I do not believe she ever turned away from Trotsky anyone who was of the slightest consequence, and yet it was no easy matter to get past that maiden unless one had that something. She was a glutton for work; morning after morning she would be at the office at nine o'clock and not leave it until well past midnight.[3]

Shelepina provided Ransome with good reason, and the excuse, for spending a lot of time in Trotsky's offices in the Commissariat of Foreign Affairs, based opposite the Winter Palace in Petrograd. As they became increasingly close during the early part of 1918, the British saw an opportunity to use their relationship to their own advantage. Lockhart and the British chargé d'affaires, Sir Francis Lindley, went out of their way to encourage Ransome to get close to the Bolshevik leadership in order to obtain intelligence that could assist in their reporting back to London. It would be naïve to imagine that Shelepina was unaware of the risks she ran in passing documents to Ransome, who then passed them on to Lockhart, Lindley or Ernest Boyce, another MI1c officer who was to become a close personal friend of the reporter. It is clear that the identity of an agent is being protected by the redactions in the official files and that agent is in fact Shelepina. Putting her on Ransome's passport was a fallback plan to ensure that she could get out of Russia, should the Bolsheviks begin to suspect quite how much assistance she had been giving the British.[4]

While Ransome was undoubtedly sympathetic to the aims of the revolution, and to many of its architects, he was not in fact as sympathetic to its actual results – the anarchic fallout and in particular the Red Terror – as is commonly believed. But it was essential that it appeared to the Bolsheviks that they were the ones gaining from his close relationship with Shelepina, and his resultant good friendships with Trotsky and Bolshevik propaganda chief Karl Radek. As a result, Ransome filed a number of reports praising aspects of the Bolshevik government that, privately, he freely admitted to detesting. One British intelligence officer noted that 'many of his articles were written in order that he would not be compromised with the Bolshevik leaders'. The operation had to be kept so secret, with knowledge of it held within a very tight circle of officials, that back in London the plan to put Shelepina on Ransome's passport raised eyebrows among middle-ranking Foreign Office and MI5 officials who had not been briefed on what was going on. 'I gather that the Ransome referred to is Arthur Ransome, correspondent in Russia to the *Daily News*,' one MI5 officer noted. 'His articles have been, I consider, most detrimental as he has frequently applauded the Bolshevik government and one is forced to the conclusion that he has become a Bolshevik himself. I can hardly believe that Ransome's official wife is going to do useful work in Stockholm as anti-Bolshevik. It is a long journey and she might be corrupted.'[5]

Lockhart was later scathing about this attitude among a large number of British officials but particularly within MI5. Ransome was not a member of his mission but was, nevertheless, 'something more than a visitor', Lockhart said. 'Ransome was a Don Quixote with a walrus moustache, a sentimentalist, who could always be relied upon to champion the under-dog, and a visionary, whose imagination had been fired by the Bolsheviks and frequently brought us information of the greatest values. An incorrigible romanticist, who could spin a fairy-tale out of nothing, he was an amusing and good-natured companion. As an ardent fisherman who had written some charming sketches on angling, he made a warm appeal to my sympathy, and I championed him resolutely against the secret service idiots who later tried to denounce him as a Bolshevik agent.'[6]

These 'secret service idiots' were not among the majority of Cumming's men in Russia, but they certainly were in the ranks of MI5 back in London. Although Ransome's favourable reporting of the Bolsheviks' activity was seen as near treason by many in Whitehall, among the intelligence officers operating in Petrograd and Moscow, some of whom had been involved in his recruitment to work for MI1c before the revolution, there was clearly a much more nuanced view. Hill, whose room in the Union Hotel was close to Ransome's, was 'constantly in touch' with the *Daily News* correspondent.

He himself interested me even more than I expected him to do. He had radical views which he never hesitated to express, and he was not exactly persona grata with British officials in Russia. This was partly due to a trick he had of entering into an argument and deliberately exciting the anger of his opponent – I suspect because he found this was one of the easiest ways of getting at the truth, and Ransome was pre-eminently a journalist out for the news. He was extremely well informed, intimate with the Bolsheviks and masterly in summing up a situation. He was a tall, lanky, bony individual with a shock of sandy hair, usually unkempt, and the eyes of a small inquisitive and rather mischievous boy. He really was a lovable personality when you came to know him. He lived on the same corridor as I did, but had no bathroom attached to his bedroom and so used to come in early every morning to take my suite. Our profoundest discussions and most heated arguments took place when Ransome was sitting in the bath and I wandering up and down my room dressing. Sometimes, when I had the better of an argument and his feelings were more than usually outraged, he would jump out of the water and beat himself dry like an angry gorilla. After that he would not come for his bath for two or three days, then we would meet and grin at each other, I would ask after the pet snake which lived in a large cigar box in his room, and the following morning he would come in as usual, and we would begin arguing again, the best of friends.[7]

When the British-led intervention force landed at Archangel on 2 August 1918, Ransome left for Sweden, having persuaded one of his Bolshevik friends, the diplomat Vatslav Vorovsky, to take Shelepina with him on a trip to Berlin as his secretary. From there she joined Ransome in Stockholm, where despite their previous friendship, and his role running operations into Russia, John Scale was initially suspicious of the reporter.

'It certainly ought to be understood how completely he is in the hands of the Bolsheviks,' the MI1c bureau chief reported a few weeks after Ransome's arrival in Stockholm. 'He is living here with a lady who was previously Trotsky's private secretary, spends the greater part of his time in the Bolshevik Legation, where he is provided with a room and a typewriter, and he is very nervous as to the effect which his present attitude may have upon his prospects in England. I also know that he informed two Russians that I personally am an agent of the British government and said that he had this information from authoritative sources, both British and Bolshevik. He seems therefore to be working pretty definitely against us.'[8]

But passing through Stockholm on his way home, after being released in exchange for the Bolshevik representative in London, Maksim Litvinov, Lockhart briefed Scale on what Ransome was doing. Scale spoke to Ransome again and sent a fresh report to Cumming, retracting his previous assessment. He now believed that the reporter had been 'badly handled' and that 'he is quite loyal and willing to help by giving information, and that this appearance of working against us is due to his friendship with the Bolshevik leaders, not by any means to any sympathy with the regime, which the Terror has made him detest.' MI5 were meanwhile told by Cumming to lay off Ransome, who had been given the agent designator S76, the S standing for Sweden. 'We expect to get a lot of most valuable stuff from him,' MI1c said. 'It is hoped that you will see your way, so to speak, to leave him alone for a bit and give him a chance.'[9]

Now it was the turn of the new head of military intelligence, Major-General William Thwaites to try to get action taken against Ransome. Thwaites had just taken over from George Macdonogh. Incensed by a report from Petrograd in the *Daily News*, he became convinced that Ransome was 'a Bolshevik agent' and that his reports were 'nothing but Bolshevik propaganda'.

'Personally, I cannot understand the *Daily News* or any other paper being prepared to pay for the rubbish he telegraphs,' Thwaites said in a letter to Major-General Sir Frederick Maurice, a recently retired officer who had exposed lies told to Parliament by Lloyd George and therefore had the ear of a number of newspaper proprietors. 'The publication of highly coloured accounts of the peace and order prevailing under the Bolsheviks is bound to have bad effect in this country,' Thwaites told him.[10]

The report from Stockholm that had so provoked the military's ire was in fact merely an interview with Litvinov, one of Ransome's closest friends in the Bolshevik leadership and its leading expert on the UK. It was therefore full of information that ought to have been of the greatest interest to British military intelligence and certainly must have been well received in its more detailed CX version in Whitehall Court. Far from having any slant, it merely reported what Litvinov was saying and while it therefore no doubt exaggerated the extent to which the Bolsheviks were in control, and certainly downplayed the scale of the killing during the Red Terror, putting the total of executions at only 400, it all came from Litvinov's mouth rather than that of Ransome, so could scarcely be called inaccurate reporting.

Far more importantly it provided critical information on the Bolshevik willingness to make concessions in return for an end to the intervention and the economic blockade. The immediate repayment of Russia's debts to Britain was impossible, Litvinov said. But the Bolsheviks were prepared to discuss concessions for gold and forestry in return for British machinery. He also talked reassuringly about the condition in which the British citizens still held by the Russians were living.

The CX version of the report went further, answering the specific point that Scale had briefed Ransome to put to Litvinov. How would the Bolsheviks react to an ultimatum that they must allow Allied forces to occupy Russia and would in return be given a complete amnesty? Litvinov's response was unequivocal. 'To agree to such a proposal would, from the point of view of the Bolshevik leaders, be saving their own lives at the expense of the Revolution, and their own lives do not with them enter into the question at all,' Ransome reported him as saying. Litvinov admitted that the revolution faced difficulties and he appeared to be pinning his hopes for the future on a successful revolution in Germany, but he warned that if the Allies tried to occupy the entire country, the Bolsheviks would unleash 'a new period of terror in Russia'.[11]

Meanwhile, unaware of what was going on behind the scenes, Maurice approached the proprietor of the *Daily News*, George Cadbury, the head of the famous British chocolate company, who confessed to being somewhat confused by the contradictory attitudes emerging from Whitehall's corridors. 'His position is that he doesn't like Ransome's stuff any more than you do, and takes your view that it is not worth paying for,' Maurice told Thwaites. 'But some little time ago, Lockhart came to see the editor and begged him to keep Ransome in Russia, or at least in Stockholm, on the grounds that he was the only Englishman who knew what is going on.' Despite Lockhart's pleas, the *Daily News* editor, A. G. Gardiner, decided that Ransome had 'gone native' and twice attempted to recall him, only to be contacted by someone else, this time representing 'the War Office', who 'implored' him not to bring Ransome home. The man from the War Office was in fact the actor turned spy Harley Granville-Barker, now a senior MI1c officer.

Gardiner told him that the paper was not getting its money's worth from Ransome's presence in Stockholm. Granville-Barker was so anxious to ensure that Ransome was kept in the field that he agreed that MI1c would fund part of the cost of keeping him in Stockholm. 'So you see the situation is that the *Daily News* wants to get Ransome back,' Maurice told Thwaites. 'But they are keeping him there in deference to what they believe to be the insistence of the War Office and the Foreign Office.'[12]

No doubt somewhat embarrassed by this clear case of the left hand not knowing what the right hand was doing, Thwaites spoke to Cumming and was himself finally briefed on the operation, leaving Ransome free to continue to file reports that were highly sympathetic to the Bolsheviks, albeit again, following Maurice's intervention, under pressure from Gardiner to moderate his pro-Bolshevik stance.

But reporting from Stockholm on conversations with Bolsheviks based there, or passing through on their way somewhere else, was all very well. The British needed Ransome to get inside the Kremlin and find out for himself what the views and intentions of Lenin and Trotsky were, and what the future held for the British citizens still jailed in Butyrka prison. The problem was that the Bolsheviks might now be quite reasonably suspicious of the motives of both Ransome and Shelepina, or might even have realised the extent of Ransome's links with Scale. Sending them both back in was therefore fraught with difficulty. Ransome made a secret trip to England in mid-December, with MI1c warning MI5 some days beforehand. They gave limited details of his work on their behalf, adding what seems at this distance to be a touch of ironic humour designed to mollify the continuing MI5 irritation, although it might have had more practical origins. 'There is of course no objection to an ordinary search when he arrives,' MI1c said. 'We cannot guarantee him, but it is suggested that there is no fear of his bringing in secret ink, so the more trying methods might be omitted.'[13]

Scale persuaded the Swedish authorities to put 'Ransome, Arthur, with wife' on a list of thirteen Bolsheviks who were to be expelled, and Lockhart arranged a prominent talk at King's College, London, where he denounced Ransome's reporting and 'the mischievous

character of statements which were calculated to create an entirely
false impression among Labour and Liberal opinion in this country'.
His reputation as an 'out-and-out Bolshevik' restored, Ransome went
back to Moscow with Shelepina. But while she was to stay there, for
the medium term at least, he was to come back out after six weeks to
make his report. So, before Ransome left, he and Scale arranged two
different coded signals, each with its own specific meaning, which
could be sent by wireless to indicate to Ransome that he should
return to London, while suggesting to the Bolsheviks that he was
coming home for purely personal reasons. The deadline the two men
agreed for his departure was 3 March 1919. Scale waited a week and,
when Ransome did not arrive, sent a message to London asking that
the Foreign Office dispatch a wireless telegram to Georgy Chicherin,
the Bolshevik Commissar for Foreign Affairs, with a pre-arranged
coded message intended for Ransome.[14]

Amid continued concern within MI5 and the Foreign Office at the
prospect of the 'dangerous Bolshevik' Ransome returning to the UK,
Clifford Sharp, an MI1c officer operating under 'natural' journalistic
cover, was asked to explain the true situation in an attempt to persuade
the Whitehall doubters. Sharp was a genuine journalist, in fact a
renowned editor of the *New Statesman*. He was called up in 1916 and
sent to Stockholm, ostensibly as a special correspondent for *The Times*,
for whom he did indeed report, keeping back the more detailed material
for his bosses at Whitehall Court. Briefly back in London from his base
in Stockholm, he provided a memorandum outlining the real position,
written using his secret service designator S8 to disguise his own identity.

'S76 [Ransome] is not a Bolshevik,' Sharp said. 'His association with
the Bolsheviks was begun and has been continued throughout at the
direct request of responsible British authorities. He was first asked to get
into the closest possible touch with them by Mr Lindley when he was
chargé d'affaires.' There then followed a brief explanation of around
fifteen lines – redacted by the Service in 2004 to allow the memo to be
released to the National Archives – in which Sharp presumably described
Ransome's role. Sharp then added:

I am myself convinced that while he has personal ties with several Bolsheviks he has never in any single instance been disloyal to the British authorities or British interests. S76 may be regarded as absolutely honest. If you ask him any questions about his numerous activities in Russia, you will get the exact truth. His reports about conditions in Russia may also be relied upon absolutely with only the proviso that his view tends to be coloured by his personal sympathies with men like Litvinov and Radek. He will report what he sees, but he does not see quite straight.[15]

Ransome arrived back in the UK on 24 March determined to advocate an end to the trade embargo 'as otherwise the Bolshevik government will collapse and Russia will be in state of complete anarchy'. He was interviewed first by a suspicious Victor Cavendish-Bentinck of the Foreign Office before being sent to see Sir Basil Thomson, the director of Criminal Intelligence at Scotland Yard.

'Thomson, extremely grim, looked very hard at me,' Ransome later recalled. 'After a moment's silence, he said: "Now, I want to know just what your politics are." "Fishing," I replied.'

The journalist had already admitted to having been concerned over the 'considerable risk of detection at the hands of the Bolsheviks' that he had run on behalf of the British secret service and he told Thomson that the appearance he gave of being pro-Bolshevik was a completely false one. 'He declares that he himself is absolutely anti-Bolshevik,' Thomson said. 'But he thinks that if something is not done soon, Russia will slip into a state of anarchy, which will be far worse than the present situation. He appears to have been very closely in touch with all the Bolshevik leaders, and is perfectly frank about what they told him.'[16]

Ransome reported back to Ernest Boyce at Whitehall Court that same afternoon, full of information and with a large bundle of Bolshevik documents having been taken by courier from Newcastle to London before him. The mission had been a great success. He had interviewed Lenin three times, and had a number of other meetings with Trotsky and leading Bolsheviks. 'I even got a letter from Lenin authorising all the

Commissars to give me whatever information I might ask for,' Ransome said. 'I was entirely uncontrolled and went to meetings where I heard the liveliest of opposition to the Bolsheviks, both from the right and the left.'

He attended sessions of the Bolshevik's executive committee, the party leadership, and was allowed into Butyrka prison to see the English officer prisoners alone, telling them that he was a 'secret service officer' and offering to pass messages back to London, a move that in at least one case occasioned disbelief and a deep suspicion by the prisoner that Ransome was part of a Cheka provocation. The Bolsheviks had been completely open, Ransome said in his report, with only one exception. This was the conference held to set up the Communist International, better known as the Comintern, the group of international communist and socialist parties which was created to provoke worldwide Bolshevik-style revolution, with British left-wing parties taking part and British rule over India one of the primary targets. The Comintern was to be one of MI1c's main enemies during the years between the two world wars. The first three days of the conference, held from 2 to 6 March, were secret sessions, Ransome said.

> I knew nothing of it until the evening of the first day when a friend told me about it and asked why I had not been there. I then at once telephoned to Litvinov and said that of course if they did not wish me to know what was going on there I would not ask to go, but that otherwise I should of course be interested. Litvinov pretended that he had merely forgotten to tell me and I was admitted forthwith.[17]

At the end of 1919, Litvinov met British officials to hammer out a deal under which the British, seen by the Bolsheviks as one of their most important potential trading partners, would drop their embargo on trade with Russia. The talks, held on the neutral territory of Copenhagen, were ostensibly between Litvinov and the British MP and former trade unionist James O'Grady on obtaining the release of British prisoners still held in Russia, but while this was undoubtedly an important issue that both sides wanted to resolve, the real aims were to find a way of normalising relations following the damaging intervention. O'Grady had taken with him 'two friends who are accompanying him by his desire'. These 'friends' were in fact Robert Nathan, who had now taken over from Rhys Samson as head of Section V, the MI1c political section, and Nathan's Russian expert Lionel Gall. During the critical period of the talks, held over Christmas 1919, O'Grady did not take part, leaving the two MI1c officers to work out the secret side of the arrangement that would lead not only to an exchange of prisoners but also to a resumption of trade between the two countries, with the Service once more reinforcing its ability to hold secret talks and make covert deals that the government could not afford to be seen to make. A few weeks after the O'Grady talks ended, Lloyd George announced talks aimed at a resumption of trade with Russia, a move he could not have afforded to do publicly without knowing that the real deal had already been thrashed out by Nathan and Gall. Nathan was knighted in the middle of the O'Grady–Litvinov talks, although this seems more likely to be connected to his work against Indian and Irish extremists in the United States than as a result of his dealings with the Bolsheviks.[18]

By the beginning of May 1920, Ransome was increasingly concerned about Yevgeniya Shelepina. The civil war was going badly for the Bolsheviks. The White Army, backed by the allies, were pushing forward towards Moscow from the south and Petrograd from the west, making a collapse of the regime a distinct possibility and putting her in danger from the anti-Bolsheviks, while Ransome remained deeply worried that the Bolshevik leadership might have realised what had been going on. He, Robert Bruce Lockhart and MI1c began preparing the way for Shelepina's 'extraction' from Russia, with Lockhart writing to John Gregory, an assistant secretary at the Foreign Office, to ask that Ransome be given an official passport that included Shelepina as his wife. Gregory was one of the British officials who had expressed concern over Ransome's reporting and perceived opinions, so Lockhart's letter was undoubtedly necessary. Ransome was 'most anxious to see you with regard to the extraction from Russia of Miss Shelepina,' Lockhart wrote. 'I should be extremely grateful if you could do anything to help her as she has been of considerable service to us on many occasions.' Lockhart added a much longer, informal note, explaining that Ransome and Shelepina had worked together on behalf of MI1c.

> During the Autumn of 1918, and the winter of 1919, she was working with Ransome [brief passage redacted from file by SIS] and was incidentally instrumental in getting out of Russia the numerous Bolshevik papers and literature which Ransome sent on to you. In February of this year, she returned to Russia with Ransome [brief passage redacted from file by SIS]. She is now in a difficult situation and exposed to danger from two sides (1) from the reactionaries who no doubt would like to hit at Ransome through her and (2) from the Bolsheviks in the not unlikely event of their turning suspicious of Ransome. The latter is most anxious about her fate and considers herself morally responsible for her safety. He would be extremely grateful if the Foreign Office could aid him in this matter and grant her a visa for England where he is quite prepared to guarantee her political nonexistence. From personal knowledge of the lady, I think we can safely do this.[19]

Ransome wrote to Boyce, proposing that he go into Russia, not just to 'extract' Shelepina but also to collect further intelligence. 'It seems to me to be blazing madness for us to have no-one in Russia capable of getting first-hand news at the top of the progress of Soviet Russia,' Ransome told his friend. 'There is no-one else who can keep in such close touch with affairs there as I can. I am just as friendly with the leaders of the other parties inside Soviet Russia as with the Bolsheviks.' C. P. Scott, editor of the *Manchester Guardian*, was willing to fund the trip 'although he knows that he will get very little for his paper. I think I could also get out written reports of the state of affairs generally, if we arranged beforehand how I should address them to ensure their reaching the right hand. The main point is that whatever British policy may be, it will be an advantage to us to have somebody in there, and it would be ridiculous to throw away all the work I have done in getting the ability to be in there.'

Scott also gave an undertaking to those government officials concerned over the effect of Ransome's reporting that he would not put anything in his newspaper that would be detrimental to the government's interests. With funding from the *Manchester Guardian*, Ransome travelled to Reval via Stockholm, where he picked up a document signed by John Scale and designed to get him past any British officials. Armed with this, the passport containing Shelepina's name and his letter from Lenin, he set off from the Estonian capital for Moscow. Despite Lenin's letter, Ransome was threatened with being shot as a spy as he crossed the lines into Bolshevik territory. He then made his way to Moscow where Shelepina eventually succeeded in persuading the Bolsheviks to let her leave, although the quid pro quo appears to have been that she take out more than a million roubles worth of precious gems to be used to fund foreign left-wing parties that were part of the Comintern. What happened to these gems and how much Ransome, or indeed MI1c, knew about the deal is unclear. It seems likely, given the need to balance the various assurances provided by Ransome and Shelepina, and the fact that they continued to live happily in exile, that the gems were delivered to the satisfaction of the Comintern, and that both Ransome and MI1c were aware of their existence, allowing British intelligence to track the delivery of the gems and identify the Comintern representatives who received them. The first of a series of operations targeting top Soviet officials had ended in complete success, with Shelepina 'extracted' successfully by Ransome. But with his wife Ivy refusing to divorce him, it was impossible for Ransome and his mistress to go to England to live. So he used Estonia as a base for his reporting assignments for the *Manchester Guardian*. He remained in contact with his friends in MI1c until at least 1922, providing them in mid-1920 with a list of former Tsarist officers serving in the Red Army, and presumably potential targets as agents, and in September 1922 meeting up with Boyce, now passport control officer in Helsingfors, during a trip around the Baltic in his new yacht, *Racundra*. Arriving in Helsingfors in early September, a day later than planned, Ransome hurried ashore to meet some friends, who included Boyce. 'I wasted all that day in friendship,' Ransome wrote. 'But early next morning there was a coughing and spluttering and spitting alongside and I tumbled out to find that . . . Commander Boyce had brought his little motor-boat, *Zingla*, to take me for a run round the harbour to show me the way through the buoys and out into the fairway.' The journey, and the meeting with Boyce, was recorded in Ransome's book *Racundra's First Cruise*. Two years later, finally divorced and free to marry Shelepina, he took her to the UK.[20]

THE little caravan of four men on small long-haired Persian ponies picked its way carefully over the Kopdagh mountain range that separated the north-eastern Iranian city of Meshed from the Soviet border. Indifferent to the snow and rocks, the ponies climbed the steep narrow pathways with the agility of mountain goats. Two of the four men, obviously foreigners, had hunting rifles slung across their backs. The other two were guides, provided by a friendly Persian official in the border town of Lotfabad to help the foreigners, both Russians, evade the clutches of the Soviet secret service, the OGPU. The smaller of the two Russians was Boris Bazhanov, the most prominent Soviet official ever to defect to the West; the other was his OGPU minder, Arkady Maksimov, who having failed to prevent his charge from crossing the border was left with the stark choice of defection or firing squad.

Bazhanov had set out from the very first to infiltrate the Soviet system, turning himself into a high flier. He had succeeded spectacularly, serving as secretary to both Stalin and the Politburo. If he had stayed inside the system, he could have been promoted to the very top. But the OGPU were already suspicious, sensing a Western spy, and Bazhanov had twice tried, and failed, to get out to Scandinavia, from where the British secret service ran its operations inside the Soviet Union. With that route closed to him, he quit Moscow for a top job in the capital of the Turkmen Soviet Socialist Republic, Ashkhabad, close to the Persian border. Early on 1 January 1928, with the frontier guards in a drunken stupor after seeing in the New Year, Bazhanov and Maksimov slipped across the border into Persia.

Now the defectors were headed for Meshed. In a replay of the Great Game, the nineteenth-century battle between the Tsarist and British secret services for control over central Asia and the gateway to India, their latter-day counterparts were already involved in a tug-of-war over Bazhanov, each side trying to persuade the Shah to give them the defector. Bazhanov was a major prize. He knew all the secrets of the Soviet leadership, all of the skeletons in Stalin's cupboard. The British wanted to get him to India, where they could debrief him at their leisure. The OGPU simply wanted him dead. They already had a hit squad waiting for him in Meshed. The British secret service had dispatched Major Leo Steveni, an old Russian hand, to the city post-haste, under guise of military attaché, his sole task to debrief the defector before the OGPU got to him, to get as much intelligence on Stalin and the Soviet leadership out of Bazhanov as possible, just in case he never made it to India.

SIXTEEN

Post-war operations — 'Fantasy and intrigue'

AT the end of the war, both the Admiralty and the War Office pushed for a single intelligence service, combining foreign intelligence-gathering, domestic security and counter-espionage. This was rejected as 'utterly unworkable' by Cumming. He was backed up by Vernon Kell and the mandarins at the Foreign and Home Offices. The Foreign Office was insistent that it must be able to control all secret service operations carried out abroad, and eventually a decision was deferred. When a cabinet sub-committee on secret service met in January 1919, there was general agreement that the war had seen a highly successful use of 'secret service'.

'The conditions of war led to a large expansion of secret service in every direction,' the committee said. 'The main expansion took place in the Foreign Office service in which there was an enormous growth in all kinds of secret operations abroad, involving the expenditure of very large sums of money. The Committee have good reason for believing that heavy as this outlay has been, it has been thoroughly justified by the results and that the information thus placed at the disposal of the British Government has been equal, if not superior, to that obtained by any other country engaged in the War.'[1]

The decision to retain a post-war secret service collecting intelligence abroad led to the need for a proper name for the organisation. It could not continue with the wartime staffing of army or naval officers while at the same time being a civilian organisation run by the Foreign Office. 'Secret Intelligence Service' had been around since 1915, but had not been in general use. 'MI1c' was no longer sufficient, although it remained the title of the War Office liaison section until the Second World War and would continue to be used as a convenient covername for the Service during the inter-war years. Titles put forward during 1919 included the Special Intelligence Bureau, but the final decision was that it should be called the Secret Intelligence Service (SIS), the title it retains to this day, with Cumming taking the formal title of Chief of the Secret Service (CSS), more commonly reduced simply to the initial C, originally from Cumming's name, but now standing for Chief. An official charter gave the Service's role as: 'to supply all authorised Government Departments with any information that they may require which is not readily obtainable through other official channels.'

In the late summer of 1919, the SIS moved to a new base, Cumming's new home at 1, Melbury Road, West Kensington. This was originally planned to double as Cumming's personal home and a safe house, an annex away from the Whitehall headquarters, where secret matters could be discussed and secret operations run. But the Treasury anxiety for a peace dividend put paid to such plans and it also became the Service's new headquarters, with other offices at 1 Adam Street, off Strand, close to Whitehall, providing facilities for liaison with other government departments, most notably the Treasury. Cumming's basic budget was initially cut to £30,000, a drastic reduction from £80,000 a month at the end of the war, but a hard-fought rearguard battle earned a reprieve. Initially, it was agreed that this would be doubled to £60,000. This was still far less than the £250,000 Cumming claimed he required and it took a typically robust intervention from Winston Churchill, the then Minister of War, to force the Secret Service Committee to rethink the extent of the cuts. Churchill insisted that reducing the amount spent on secret service at a time when both Russia and Germany were in turmoil would be foolhardy.

I think it well to let you know that I for one could not consent to any reduction at present and indeed go farther to say that it may be necessary to increase the funds in order to take advantage of the opportunity presented by an open door into Germany and Austria. It is imperative from the

military point of view that the secret service organisations working in and
in connection with Germany, Austria and Russia should be maintained at
least at their present level. No-one can foresee what the next few months
may bring forth and it is vital to see that there is no diminution in the
quality and quantity of information now being supplied.'

The committee accepted, in view of Churchill's letter and the
evidence put forward in his own claim by Cumming, that £60,000
would be 'entirely inadequate' and agreed to put forward an estimate
of £310,000, including the £250,000 budget submitted by Cumming,
whose total spending for the financial year 1919/20 would eventually
amount to £205,200.[2]

The SIS headquarters staff in late 1919 comprised a couple of dozen
officers plus a similar number of supporting staff. In part to save money,
but also as a means of creating a web of bureaux that could prevent or track
Bolsheviks coming into Britain and the Empire, Cumming continued the
passport control system, taking total control of it, absorbing the MI5 staff
who previously administered it, and expanding it to cover thirty-nine cities
in twenty-five countries. Since anyone coming into Britain and the Empire
from potential enemy countries like Russia or Germany required visas, the
passport control officers could check the background of anyone applying
and thereby either weed out suspected spies and subversives or mark their
visas secretly to ensure they were tracked when they did arrive on British
soil. The total annual outlay was £117,000, but this was offset by around
£80,000 in income from visa charges, making the net cost £37,000.
Cumming, however, only received a £20,000 supplement for running
the system and had to absorb the rest of the costs from the SIS budget.
Wherever possible, arrangements were made either through Scotland Yard
or directly with local authorities for the passport control officers to liaise
with the local police to share information on criminals, communists and
spies seeking to travel to the UK, with the main emphasis on preventing
the spread of Bolshevism. Cumming overcame his aversion for counter-
espionage operations to appoint a number of counter-Bolshevik officers in
European capitals to keep track of the communist threat. The war cabinet

backed the move, ruling in August 1919 that 'in view of the unsettled conditions in Eastern and Central Europe and of the known activities of Bolshevik agents, and the widespread nature of Bolshevik propaganda a system of visa control in allied and neutral countries over alien passengers desiring to come to the United Kingdom should be maintained for the present and probably for a period of two years.'[3]

But the passport control officers were far from being the only officers deployed abroad; a number of countries were covered by SIS officers working in completely different occupations and, as in Bolshevik Russia, a number of genuine journalists and businessmen also worked for Cumming, under 'natural cover', producing intelligence reports. Nor was it just journalistic or business posts that were used. Professor Arthur Cotter taught in Helsingfors in the immediate years following the First World War while reporting back to Cumming, and Ernest Michelson operated in Christiania as the owner of an import–export agency, subsequently a popular cover for fictional spies. When the Treasury insisted on closing down the Service's Buenos Aires bureau, run by Captain Connon Thomson, Cumming found someone in the Argentine capital 'who will work for us gratis'. Patriotism and the sheer adrenalin rush of being a spy were powerful recruiting sergeants to those with other means of income. A number of other bureaux also closed. Politicians, unaware of the secret work carried out by the passport control system, and angry at the continuation of visas, particularly in how it affected their own ability to travel to France and Belgium, railed against their continuance in peacetime, and one Whitehall meeting heard that there was 'considerable agitation' among MPs over the issue. The Foreign Office representative conceded the difficulty of going to Parliament and defending the system on the grounds that 'it gave us an opportunity for carrying out secret service work abroad without entailing expenditure'. Cumming worried that lifting visas for France and Belgium might be 'the thin end of the wedge' that would see large numbers of his bureaux axed. This was certainly a Treasury ambition, and while more senior officials were surely aware of the real role the bureaux carried out, this did not seem to extend to some of the middle-ranking officials who were looking for cuts.

The anger over the cuts extended to the bureaux overseas with the entire Vienna office, including its new chief, Ernan Forbes Dennis, resigning en masse in protest at retrospective pay cuts imposed in the spring of 1920. The strike was successful, forcing the cuts to be repealed. Dennis was in charge of passport control and SIS operations not just in Austria but in Hungary and Yugoslavia as well. He was assisted by a former Intelligence Corps officer, Carlisle Aylmer Macartney, and by Margery Bates, who had spent the war mounting counter-espionage operations in Switzerland.[4]

Throughout the 1920s and 1930s, both the SIS and the Foreign Office would find themselves defending the passport control system against Treasury officials who had no idea that the organisation they were trying to cut was in fact at the heart of Britain's intelligence operations overseas. 'The abolition of our Passport Control Offices will cause embarrassment and expense to our SS [secret service] which will anyhow be serious and will vary in magnitude according to the number and locality of the controls that are abolished,' the Foreign Office protested, to no avail. One Treasury official complained in early 1921 that the main work of the passport control officers appeared to be chasing down adulterous husbands and wives.

> My personal opinion is that a lot of the work which you state is done by examiners is not really work proper to the Passport Office at all. I am somewhat surprised that you find it necessary or desirable to make these somewhat inquisitorial investigations into the private affairs of husbands who are attempting to desert their wives and wives who are running away from their husbands. And if a lady wishes to earn an honest living in Valparaiso, why is it your affair what she calls herself?

The Foreign Office lamented that the Treasury proposals appeared designed 'to destroy the scheme entirely' and expressed astonishment at the naïvety of its officials.

> It seems quite clear that they still have no idea of the nature of the work of the officer or the value that attaches to the possession of a British

Stephen Alley, who ran
operations in Russia during
the First World War and was
allegedly sacked for refusing to
take part in the murder of Stalin.

Oswald Rayner, who worked
first in Petrograd and then in
Stockholm and oversaw the
torture and murder of Rasputin,
firing the last shot.

William Somerset Maugham,
sent to Russia by SIS to try
to prevent the Bolshevik
revolution. (Time & Life
Pictures/Getty Images)

Sidney Reilly, the so-called
'Ace of Spies', a brilliant secret
service officer flawed by his
anti-Bolshevik obsessions.

John Dymoke Scale *right*, bureau chief in Stockholm 1918–19,
with his secretary Oohna Stewart and Conrad O'Brien-ffrench *left*.

George Hill, who worked with
Reilly in Russia.

Ernest Boyce, Petrograd bureau
chief in 1918.

Jack Norton-Griffiths, who led Cumming's operation to destroy the Romanian oilwells and corn stores ahead of the advancing German army.

'Cud' Thornhill, SIS officer who ran intelligence operations during the Allied intervention in northern Russia in 1918 and 1919. (© National Portrait Gallery, London)

Paul Dukes, the British agent who went into Bolshevik Russia to pull together the SIS networks left behind in 1918.

Augustus Agar, the coastal motor boat commander sent to Finland to extract Dukes from Russia.

Pyotr Sokolov, one of the couriers for the SIS agent networks in Bolshevik Russia.

Robert Bruce Lockhart, British representative in Russia who worked with Reilly and Ransome. (Getty Images)

Arthur Ransome, the left-wing journalist who worked for SIS in pre- and post-revolutionary Russia. (Getty Images)

Yevgeniya Shelepina, Trotsky's secretary, who provided Ransome with intelligence on the Bolsheviks. (© Arthur Ransome literary estate/Brotherton Collection, Leeds University)

Harley Granville Barker, SIS officer who paid the *Daily News* to keep Ransome in Moscow so that he could run Shelepina. (Getty Images)

Wilfred 'Biffy' Dunderdale, who ran espionage networks in the Ukraine before becoming Paris bureau chief.

Desmond Morton, head of SIS production from 1919 to 1931. (© National Portrait Gallery, London)

Claude Dansey, who reorganised SIS on behalf of the War Office in 1917 and went on to run the Z Organisation.

Broadway Buildings, the Service's headquarters from 1926 to 1964.

Below left Hugh Sinclair, who became 'C' on Cumming's death in 1923.
Below right Valentine Vivian, who ran counter-espionage operations.

Norman Dewhurst, who served in Salonika during the First World War and joined the Z Organisation in the 1930s.

Boris Bazhanov, secretary to Stalin and the Politburo, who defected to the British.

Frank Foley, SIS bureau chief in Berlin during the 1930s.

Jonny de Graaf, agent inside Soviet military intelligence run by Foley. (FBI)

Stewart Menzies, effectively Sinclair's deputy during the 1930s, who succeeded him as C when Sinclair died in 1939.

Lawrence Grand, head of D Section, the special operations section set up ahead of the Second World War.

passport as proof of nationality and identity. Otherwise they would not make such an extraordinary comment on the case of a lady who wants to go to Valparaiso in an assumed name. They appear to discredit the information given them as to the functions performed by the Passport Office and wish to dictate to the Foreign Office the nature of its duties. We should press for the acceptance of the scheme in its entirety. The thirty-seven posts asked for, which were regarded as the minimum necessary at the present moment, have been reduced to twenty-six.[5]

Cumming requested a budget of £126,000 for the financial year 1921/2 and was forced to make do with £100,000, much to the irritation of the Army general staff, who complained that 'should it suddenly be found necessary, owing to a change in the political situation, to reintroduce secret service agents into a new country, it will probably be found that the service is ineffective at first, as it often takes years to build up an efficient service. This would become a matter of prime importance should there be a change in the relationship between England and France.'

The following year, Cumming was offered just £65,000, but after criticism from the service departments that this was inadequate, and the production by Stewart Menzies of charts showing that cutting the budget to that extent would mean the closure of twenty-one bureaux across Europe, including those in Finland, Sweden, Latvia and France, plus the complete loss of any representation in Latin America, it was raised to £85,000. Churchill protested that Cumming needed £132,000 if he was to do his job properly. 'The reductions proposed would ruin an organisation which had proved efficient and useful and would result in the waste of money already expended,' Churchill said. 'It is considered vital that the money available for SIS should remain constant; if agents get the idea that they may be thrown over at any moment, we cannot expect to find them, while to confine SIS activities to certain limited areas only so impairs the general efficiency and reliability of the SIS as to render it to a large extent ineffective.' As a result, Cumming's budget was raised to £90,000, with an acceptance that this would mean cuts in coverage.[6]

The headquarters was reorganised in the aftermath of the war with SIS split into two separate branches, circulation, or liaison, and production, each sub-divided into a number of different sections. The circulation sections remained essentially as they had been following the reforms devised by Claude Dansey in 1917, with Section II passing reports to, and receiving requests for information from, the Air Ministry; Section III dealing similarly with the Admiralty; Section IV with the War Office, including MI5; Section V with the Foreign Office and the Board of Trade; and Section VI liaising with the Home Office Directorate of Intelligence, which performed the domestic civilian counter-espionage operations that would later become the responsibility of MI5. In 1923, Section I became the political section, dealing with the Foreign and Home Offices, and the Board of Trade, and Sections V and VI were temporarily abolished. The new production department, headed from April 1919 by Major Desmond Morton, was split geographically and run by so-called 'G officers', with G1 covering central Europe, G2 northern Europe, G3 southern Europe, G4 Spain and South America, G5 the Near East, G6 the Far East, and G7 North America. A separate unit, N Section, set up sometime during the 1920s and run by David Boyle, intercepted the diplomatic bags of embassies in London, a process that had its origins in a British tradition of reading diplomatic mail dating back to the fourteenth century. The contents of the bags were carefully opened, copied and resealed in an operation known as Triplex. N Section employed a team of thirty seamstresses to sew the diplomatic bags in a way that would ensure no-one knew they had been opened. By 1923, the total budget for Head Office was £26,000 a year.[7]

The bureaux around the world were split into seven geographical groups, including both those using the passport control cover and those operating under other types of cover, such as consular officials, businessmen or journalists. The staff of those bureaux that were based around a passport control office was made up of a bureau chief, or SIS 'representative' – usually a passport control officer, but in smaller bureaux an assistant passport control officer working to a bureau chief in the capital or even another country in the region. The bureau chief was assisted by passport examiners, some of whom did secret service work and some of whom did not, plus clerks and secretaries, who were also split into those who did, and those who did not, have involvement in secret service work. Under the 'third country rule', the bureaux supposedly only engaged in secret work in target countries outside their own base, co-operating with the local police and security services on counter-espionage. So the bureau in Berlin would operate against Poland or Czechoslovakia but would not operate against Germany, and would in fact actively co-operate with the German state security organs against Soviet operations. However, this was not an immutable rule, with Berlin in the 1930s following the rise of the Nazis being one example of where it was ignored.

Each geographical area either had an inspector travelling round the region overseeing their work or a chief passport control officer, who performed a similar supervisory function for the smaller bureaux. By 1923, there were SIS representatives in Germany, the Netherlands, and Belgium, an area designated 'the German Group', which had a budget of £21,500 a year. The Swiss Group covered the SIS bureaux in France, Switzerland, Italy and Spain, from where agents were also run in Portugal, and cost £16,450 per annum. The Central European Group comprised the bureaux in Austria, Hungary, Czechoslovakia, Bulgaria and Romania, and was relatively cheap at £9,510. The Scandinavian group, with an annual budget of £11,510, included Poland as well as Norway, Sweden and Denmark. The Baltic Group comprised Estonia, Finland, Lithuania and Latvia and cost £15,750. The Near-East, at £20,000 per annum, was made up of bureaux in Turkey; Egypt, which also covered Palestine, the Hejaz (the Red Sea coast of Saudi Arabia), Syria and Jordan; Greece; and southern Russia. This was still not entirely in Bolshevik hands but coverage was subsequently taken over by a new passport control office in Constantinople when British forces withdrew from occupation of what was then the Turkish capital in September 1923. There was a surprising large Far Eastern Group, an area in which SIS was widely regarded as being poorly represented, with bureaux in Vladivostok, where Frank Blyth Kirby was now in charge, Tokyo, Harbin, Shanghai, Canton,

Singapore, Hong Kong and Vancouver, and with a budget of £18,200 a year, this included an £1,800 contingency fund for emergencies. The bureau in New York, which alone cost £8,520 a year, did not fall within any of the geographical groups.[8]

The main targets for the Service were dictated by the War Office, the Admiralty and the Foreign Office. The Army's priorities in the immediate post-war period were Germany, Russia, Japan, America and Turkey, in that order, while the Admiralty priorities were for the first four of those, but in reverse order, largely because America and Japan posed the main threats to the Royal Navy's domination of the world's oceans, while Germany and Russia only threatened operations in the Baltic, Black Sea and the Mediterranean. The Foreign Office said the areas it wanted covered by secret service activities were 'Asia-Minor and the Caucasus, Bolshevism, and the activities of the German Socialist Party.'[9]

The heads of the overseas bureaux were sent regular detailed questionnaires on the areas of interest, listing all the questions to which the customer departments required answers. SIS headquarters also issued instructions, spelling out the need to provide details of their sourcing.

> Allot numbers to every source from which you obtain information, whether that source is a paid, unpaid agent or even an unconscious source which you constantly tap. We shall require full particulars of any other agent or source that you make use of in order that we may card them up. You should send the name of the individual, his nationality, social position, abbreviated past history, probable qualifications for employment, what lines he may be likely to be best on, and why, etc. In sending in these particulars, all names and other information likely to lead to the identification of the individual in case your letter got into the wrong hands should be put into code. We should like to get this list at the very earliest opportunity so that when your reports [come] in, we shall at once understand who the author or authors are.

Similar instructions were sent out to the bureaux on the ideal format for reports, in a memorandum headed, possibly with previous experience of Mackenzie and Samuel Hoare in mind, 'Brief Hints on the Form of Reports':

At the head of your report, put your serial number, the town from which it is written, and the date. In the centre of the page underneath put a concise title explaining the substance of the report. On the left-hand side, put the number of the source who obtained the information. Commence by stating how the information was obtained, or if this does not fit in with the remainder of the report attach a covering letter explaining this. At the end of the report, typewrite, or write, if you are the final authority responsible. At the end of the report, at the bottom left-hand corner, [set] out the distribution, so far as you are concerned. Get the report typed out in paragraphs in as clear a manner as possible.[10]

The best reports were graded from A1, signifying that SIS 'regarded them as of primary importance' and that they were based on 'original documents actually in the possession of SIS or to which a representative of SIS has had access'. A1 denoted: 'Statements by agents of exceptional reliability, in which the SIS repose especial confidence for peculiar reasons.' A2 was applied to reports 'which, for various reasons, cannot be classified as A1; but which are of importance, both as regards subject matter and reliability'. B was used for reports 'of less importance, but the interest and reliability are such to justify their being used'.[11]

The most important passport control offices were in the Baltic, Scandinavia, Poland, Germany and the Balkans, from where Bolshevik Russia could be monitored, and in France and New York, where there were large Russian émigré communities. France, Poland and Scandinavia were also important for working against Germany, as were Switzerland, Belgium and the Netherlands, from where Richard Tinsley continued to operate agents inside Germany. Thornley Gibson, a classical singer and former Irish Guards officer based in Switzerland, was providing influential reports obtained on concert tours inside Germany. Clifford Sharp was going into Berlin from Stockholm to talk to his socialist contacts there a few weeks after the war came to an end. He was sent to Berlin to investigate the situation inside a defeated and demoralised Germany, reporting back via the MI1c bureau chief in Stockholm, under the agent designator S8. But his report was treated with some suspicion, largely because it rightly played down the likelihood of success for the left-wing revolution that had followed the armistice. 'It will be noted that it is practically identical with the reports which appeared in *The Times* from their special correspondent at Stockholm, who was in fact sent into Berlin at our special request,' an intelligence officer in London wrote, adding a rider that it was clearly coloured by conversations with the moderate socialists with whom Sharp had been in contact throughout the war. Given that all Britons, including journalists, were prevented from travelling to Germany, *The Times* was no doubt pleased with its series of scoops. But while there were some similarities, the newspaper version contained none of the considered analysis of Sharp's report, which – despite the concerns in London – was essentially correct in suggesting that for many the revolution had by now lost its popular appeal and that economic hardships caused in large part by the continuing Royal Navy blockade were more of a potential problem. It was this that might result in the revolutionaries led by Karl Liebknecht and Rosa Luxemburg regaining momentum, Sharp warned.

I consider political situation entirely satisfactory, whilst economic situation is dangerous in the extreme, especially in view of Liebknecht's policy of abandoning politics for industrial agitation. I feel it impossible to over-estimate necessity for extreme situation in Germany, which, failing economic supplies, is literally desperate. Continuation of blockade without explanation or promises for the future creates a fatalistic spirit of helpless fear. In the minds of those who should be endeavouring to prepare for reorganisation of economical life, this increasing possibility of irrevocable disaster is only slightly less damaging to us than to the Germans. If bare economic necessities can be secured so that industry can be started and wages paid, a strong moderate government is in my belief assured, failing this chaos is inevitable.' The revolution did indeed peter out, but it took another four months before the British blockade was finally lifted.[12]

Tinsley's operations monitoring German military operations led in July 1919 to the arrest of two of his agents in Berlin and a complaint from the German delegation to the Versailles peace conference. 'The Espionage Bureau organised by Mr Tinsley of the Uranium Steamship Company Rotterdam, has, since the end of last year, developed great activity in Germany, with the object of gaining an insight into her present military organisation,' the German delegation complained. The two arrested agents, both Belgians, were Arthur Caenepenne and Frederic Promper, who had been running a network of a dozen 'first-class agents' inside Germany. Their bureau in Berlin was raided by the German police, who found incriminating papers showing that they had succeeded in recruiting forty-two German soldiers to supply intelligence in response to 'shopping lists' of questions the British wanted answered. 'The information supplied by these men, in accordance with careful instructions and in reply to a detailed list of questions distributed to them, was worked up by Caenepenne into reports which he dispatched regularly every fortnight to Tinsley in Rotterdam,' the Germans complained. 'The organisation employed in its work the methods of common criminals. Promper was in possession of a whole parcel of excellently made skeleton keys.' One letter to Caenepenne from London sent with 'quantities of morphia, opium and cocaine', and seized by the German police, explained how to use the drugs to doctor cigarettes or drinks to make the German soldiers more talkative. 'We are very far from thinking that the proceedings of these agents can correspond to the intentions of the Allied and associated Governments,' the Germans said. 'Apparently these irresponsible subordinates think to acquire merit in the eyes of their country if they procure information on military questions even by employing reprehensible means. To our great astonishment, we think we see signs that the allied and associated governments imagine that we are trying to hide something in this connection.' It is unclear whether their easy access to drugs assisted Tinsley's agents in obtaining the information that allowed them to burgle some of the safes in the German War Office, 'to the great advantage' of its British counterpart, but he would continue working for Cumming until the end of 1923 – by which time his budget was at £5,500, the largest by far of the individual bureaux. This made him a prime candidate for the Treasury bean counters, who forced his departure. Tinsley was promoted to captain in the RNR on retirement 'in recognition of services rendered during the war.'[13]

SIS had a number of officers across Germany. The passport control office in Berlin, initially headed by Major Timothy Breen, with Henry Landau controlling the intelligence operations, had sub-offices in Cologne, Frankfurt and Hamburg. The Bolsheviks were setting up a centre for the infiltration of agents into western Europe in Berlin, giving Breen and his staff a tough job ensuring that those who did get through were known about. The first stops were inevitably the Directorate of Intelligence blacklist of suspicious aliens and the files of the Berlin police, Landau said.

> As to the traveller's purposes, and the usual commercial information, it was not only obtained through recognised business channels such as banks, but in many cases the applicant was watched for a long time by our agents. Every movement was followed. I often laughed over the indiscretions of some of the individuals. In the hands of their wives, the information would have been devastating.

There were also SIS officers working at the headquarters of the British Army of the Rhine in Cologne, monitoring military and political activity on both the extreme left and right, as well as German compliance initially with the terms of the armistice and subsequently with the Versailles Treaty. They soon found much of their time taken up with countering French attempts to set up a separatist movement that would espouse the cause of a buffer state, a so-called independent Rhineland Republic. 'The British Intelligence Service in Cologne was proving a thorn in the side of its former ally,' Landau said. 'It was no use for France to pretend that she was not sponsoring the separatist movement, for all her intrigues and plans were being uncovered by British agents.'[14]

With some of the new passport control officers struggling to work out how to obtain the intelligence that was expected in Whitehall, Paul Dukes, Sidney Reilly, Malcolm McLaren (now back in London to take over Russian coverage, as a Lieutenant-Commander in the RNVR), and Vladimir Orlov – a White Russian associate of Reilly's, who was just as fond of 'sharp practice', if not more so – toured Europe in late 1920, establishing contacts that might lead to future intelligence on Bolshevik activities, including exchanges of information with the intelligence services of the countries they visited and, in the case of Dukes, at least, advising Cumming's representatives on how to go about their job. There had in fact already been an only partially successful attempt by SIS to set up 'anti-Bolshevik' links with European intelligence services. Reinforcing the reasoning behind these efforts on the ground was no doubt useful, but the grand tour produced little real intelligence, indeed, as Desmond Morton's biographer notes, 'one might be forgiven for thinking that the fact that these four rogues were all involved in the planning and execution of the scheme should have been enough to consign it immediately to the realms of fantasy and intrigue'.

McLaren defended the wisdom of the mission in a report to Morton:

> We had as our aim the investigation of the possibility of forming an anti-Bolshevik intelligence service, which should be able to work at the highest possible pressure of all those engaged by the intelligence services of the governments interested in the combating of Bolshevism and yet be run at a minimum cost. We endeavoured to convince all those who were at the head of the intelligence services that the episodic character of the struggles for Bolshevism which are being carried on today by each government independently without any co-ordination between the activities of their anti-Bolshevik service and those of others was absolutely harmless to the Bolsheviks. For various reasons, [they] could not decide on their own initiative to officially enter into an agreement with us. At the same time, they are quite willing to assist us to the best of their ability.[15]

By the early 1920s, the frontline of SIS reporting on Russia was via the passport control offices in Finland and the Baltic republics, from where a number of the agents left inside Russia were run. The main SIS officers in the region during this period were all old Russia hands, with John Scale supervising operations in the region until March 1921 when they were taken over by Ronald Meiklejohn. Nikolai Bunakov and Pyotr Sokolov were still in Terijoki, going in and out of Russia, running the agents and bringing back reports. Meiklejohn was based in Reval as chief passport control officer for all three Baltic republics, controlling the operations at the smaller passport control offices in Kovno [Kaunas], the then capital of Lithuania, the Latvian capital, Riga, and the western Latvian port of Libau [now Liepāja]. Arthur Macpherson, another prominent British expatriate in Petrograd before the war, was in charge in Libau and Henry Bowe was in Kovno. The sub-passport control office in Riga was run by Harry Hall, but there was a separate Riga bureau run initially by Harry Pirie-Gordon, assisted by Norman Dewhurst, and later led by Dewhurst, with Lawrence Collas as his deputy. Dewhurst's cover was initially deputy assistant commissioner and later head of the British political mission, in which role he had the happy duty of informing the Latvian government in January 1921 that their country had been recognised by Great Britain. At this point, SIS representation in Riga became more formal, with 43-year-old Raphael Farina, who had been born in Switzerland of a British mother and Italian father and had learnt Russian working as a mining engineer in Siberia, switching from his post in MI5 and taking over as passport control officer, covering both Latvia and Lithuania.

The Reval office was run, under Meiklejohn, by S. G. Goodlet, also a member of the pre-war British community in Russia, and between 1920 and 1922, by Stephen Turner, whose real name was Sydney Tomes, under which name he had previously worked for MI1c in Petrograd and Torneå. He was one of the MI1c officers arrested and imprisoned in Butyrka prison. Turner/Tomes's background and what is known about his subsequent life bear all the hallmarks of an undercover intelligence operator. Before the war, he had been the foreign sales representative for the Leicester-based textile company Faire Brothers, operating in France, Germany, the Netherlands, Belgium, Switzerland, Denmark, Norway, Sweden and Russia, and a perfect candidate for Cumming's pre-war group of travelling businessmen. Given that he was sent to work for MI1c in Russia, it seems likely that he was already known to Cumming. He spoke German, French and Russian fluently and, after spending two years working for Meiklejohn in Reval, quit to set up a business in the Baltic which apparently involved the transport of goods along the coast via fast motor boats, an ideal operation to allow the infiltration and exfiltration of agents into and out of Soviet territory. He is also known to have been working for SIS, alongside Bunakov, during the Second World War. The other SIS staff working in Reval included Sydney Steers, under cover of vice-consul, and a Russian agent-runner Arseni Zitkov. Meiklejohn left in September 1926 and was replaced by Captain Alexander Ross, who had worked as an intelligence officer during the First World War. Both his wife and mother were Russian. He was replaced in 1930 by Captain Chester Giffey, an army officer seconded to the Foreign Office, who remained bureau chief, assisted by Steers and several agent-runners including Alexander McKibbin and Frederic Aurich, right up until the outbreak of the Second World War.[16]

The Service used every opportunity to infiltrate its officers into Russia, both to collect intelligence and to set up agent networks. During 1920, Lawrence Webster travelled across the Baltic republics as the head of a relief mission sent in by Lady Muriel Paget, a prominent humanitarian. The British trade mission in Moscow, sent there in 1921 and upgraded to a diplomatic mission in 1924, provided cover for intelligence operations and a postbox for messages to and from agents. It included several known SIS officers, two old Petrograd hands, Collas and Oswald Rayner, and Gerald Fitzwilliams, who had been assistant passport control officer in Vienna. One of the leading members of the mission, Edward Charnock, a former businessman in Petrograd, who served as the mission's commercial attaché, was issued with special passes allowing him to travel to areas not normally open to foreigners as a direct result of his family's role in setting up the Russian football league. Charnock would subsequently be accused by the Bolshevik authorities of helping to run Boyce's network of spies inside Russia and, given his privileged access, it seems unlikely that they were wrong to do so.[17]

Inevitably, given the difficulty of operating inside the Soviet Union, there were a number of duds. The first is said to have come in 1921, when

Meiklejohn's agent BP11 produced a series of reports allegedly from messages sent between Moscow and Reval obtained by an agent inside a Bolshevik mission in Reval. They showed that the Comintern was stirring up anti-British feeling on the Indian sub-continent, as well as in Afghanistan, Persia and Turkey, leading Lord Curzon, the British Foreign Secretary, to demand the Soviet government end this 'flagrant breach' of the Anglo-Soviet Trade Agreement signed earlier that year. There was no doubt that the Russians were trying to subvert India, and that it breached the agreement, but the Russians questioned the details of the instances cited by Curzon, claiming that one of the Bolshevik officials named was in jail at the time of his alleged offence. The result was a series of post-mortems within SIS and the British intelligence community at large in which the Government Code and Cipher School, the peacetime successor to Room 40, questioned the existence of a radio link, since it had no intercepts of messages between Reval and Moscow. This ought in itself to have been no surprise since such a link would have been difficult to intercept from the UK, but more to the point the messages were just that – messages; it was perfectly possible that they had been sent by landline. Meanwhile, Basil Thomson, director of intelligence at the Home Office, questioned the accuracy of BP11's reports of Comintern cash funnelled to Sinn Fein subversive 'germ cells' in Ireland, although why is unclear, since previous evidence of this had already crossed his desk. Thomson, a vigorous anti-Bolshevik not averse to exaggerating both the potential threats and his own importance, may well have been irritated not to have come up with the idea himself. However, the Sinn Fein links to the Comintern were well known and the Bolsheviks were attempting to subvert the authorities across western Europe so there was no reason to suppose they might not be doing so in Ireland in support of Sinn Fein. Shortly afterwards, Thomson was forced to resign after losing the confidence of the Prime Minister, Lloyd George. Whether this had any connection to his criticism of SIS reporting is unclear, but he was a man who made enemies easily and was prone to behaviour that left him vulnerable to retribution. SIS continued to defend BP11's reports since 'the genuineness of the same source has been proved by subsequent events'.[18]

SEVENTEEN

The Zinoviev letter

CUMMING was not there to see the main successes of his prescient willingness to put a good deal of his limited funding into setting up agent networks in Russia. He died in June 1923, sat on the sofa in his office at his Melbury Road home, having quite literally given his heart to the organisation that was his pride and joy. Cumming was due to retire and his successor had already been selected, apparently according to a tacit agreement between the Admiralty and the War Office that the director of MI5 should be a soldier and the chief of SIS a sailor. Cumming's designated replacement, the director of naval intelligence, Rear-Admiral Hugh 'Quex' Sinclair, took over immediately. He kept the title C, now standing for 'Chief' rather than Cumming, and the idiosyncratic use of green ink to sign all his memos and letters, understanding, as an admiral, that according to naval tradition its use signified the writ of the man in charge. Sinclair had a reputation among his friends as a man with a taste for the high life. He acquired the nickname Quex after the title character in Arthur Pinero's then highly popular play *The Gay Lord Quex*, who was supposedly 'the wickedest man in London', and preferred flamboyant clothes to naval uniform. One of his officers recalled meeting him for the first time:

'I was put in a small room and left. Shortly, in came the most unusual person I had ever seen. He was a short man with a Jewish face and keen eyes. He had a hard-brimmed hat in his hand and below a blue suit with a red tie he had light brown shoes. My first impression was that how clever the authorities were to head their SS [secret service] with an Armenian gangster.[1]

Sinclair was an inveterate empire builder. He was appalled to find that the SIS headquarters staff had been reduced to just thirty-five and set about a major reorganisation and a highly aggressive attempt to expand his empire. One of his first acts was to call a conference of the Service's regional inspectors and chief passport control officers and point out that they were allowing too many poor reports to get through and not producing sufficient material of really good quality. Despite his complaint that they were 'specially created in order to relieve the pressure of work on Headquarters, and to prevent information of little or no importance being forwarded' and yet were not doing their job, the sub-text of this appears to have been doubts in Sinclair's mind as to whether they were actually necessary. He also warned them that they were failing in one of their main roles, preparing a 'scheme for maintaining their services and communications in their respective areas in the event of war'. Sinclair told them that 'it was desired to maintain a nucleus organisation in each country which bordered on any of those which were likely to go to war, even if it was only a single agent in any country. This nucleus should be kept up to date and revised frequently.'[2]

Having made clear to his officers abroad that there was a new man in charge, Sinclair set out to take all Britain's intelligence organisations under his control. He had, like Blinker Hall and William Thwaites at the end of the First World War, long believed that all the intelligence and counter-intelligence operations should be under one roof and controlled by one man. The only difference, if there was a difference, was that he had very firm ideas who that man should be: him. He began by taking over the Government Code & Cipher School (GC&CS), which had previously been under his control as director of naval intelligence, and then set about attempting to sweep up the other secret service operations, including MI5. He secured backing for this proposal from the directors of intelligence of all three services, who wrote to the Foreign Secretary, Lord Curzon, arguing that an amalgamation of SIS and MI5 as a single Secret Intelligence Service under the control of the Foreign Office would produce 'greater efficiency and economy'. Bolstered by this support, Sinclair announced to the Prime Minister's Committee on Secret Service that 'the whole organisation of the British Secret Service was fundamentally wrong. There was no central control of policy, but a serious lack of co-ordination and co-operation which resulted in overlapping and a waste of time.'

Sinclair's aim was nothing less than an amalgamation of SIS; GC&CS, which he already controlled and which was the largest of the post-war intelligence departments, with seventy-three personnel; Indian Political Intelligence; MI5, which had only thirty-three staff; and Special Branch. 'All the different departments ought to be placed under one head and in one building in the neighbourhood of Whitehall, and to be made responsible to one Department of State, which ought to be the Foreign Office.' There was constant 'overlapping' between SIS and MI5 and between SIS and SS1, the secret service liaison branch of Special Branch; 'indeed, he [Sinclair] had gone to the pains of keeping record for the last three weeks, in the course of which twenty-five cases of overlapping had been noticed. It was known that this lack of liaison resulted in agents being paid twice for the same thing by different people.' Sinclair dismissed arguments from the head of Indian Political Intelligence against a merger with SIS as 'flimsy', adding that 'its continuance as a separate entity was a farce'.[3]

Sinclair was absolutely right, but over-played his hand. While the civil service mandarins who made up the committee undoubtedly thought he had a point, and were impressed by the industrious way he set about making his case, they were shocked by his blunt honesty and were reluctant to allow so much power in the hands of one man, particularly when he was as willing to act in such a brutal fashion to achieve his aims. The committee noted in its report that there was merit in amalgamating the various intelligence services under one chief and that at the start of their investigation and interrogation of the various officers in charge of the intelligence services, there had been 'a mild predisposition' on the committee in favour of amalgamation.

With one exception, these officers expressed general satisfaction with existing arrangements. It is only right, however, to record that the remarkably efficient chief of the Secret Intelligence Service strongly urged an amalgamation of all branches under one head. In his view, there should be a single organisation, installed in a single, centrally situated building with the Passport and Passport Control Offices under the same roof to provide camouflage. The main body of opinion represented by the other witnesses was more conservative in character. Generally speaking, they appeared satisfied with the existing order of things.

It was a view with which, given their concerns over such power being in the hands of one man, the committee concurred, although it admitted: 'We have no hesitation in saying that if there were today no British secret service of any kind and we were called upon to organise one *ab ovo*, we should not adopt the existing system as our model.' It was scarcely an endorsement of the status quo.[4]

Sinclair may not have been happy with the size of the Service he inherited but the extensive network of 'representatives' around the world put in place by his predecessor was certainly producing some exceptional material. The extent of intelligence being obtained from inside Russia was impressive, particularly on the two key military areas of interest: chemical and bacteriological weapons, and military co-operation with Germany. The Russians were allowing the Germans to train on their territory and co-operating on the production of chemical weapons, enabling the Reichswehr to get round the strict limitations on military activity, in particular the production of chemical weapons that had been imposed by the Treaty of Versailles. The use of gas during the First World War had led to an arms race, with the British, Germans and Russians all experimenting to find the most efficient chemical and bacteriological weapons and the most practical defences and antidotes.

During the early 1920s, SIS sent out a series of extraordinarily detailed and well-informed reports on Soviet preparations for chemical warfare, addressing both defensive and offensive operations and based on multiple strands of reporting. A fifteen-page summary of information obtained by SIS about the Soviet chemical weapons capability was circulated to customers in March 1924 – a similar report had been circulated the previous year. The new summary was issued by Section III, the SIS naval section, possibly because the agent was a Soviet naval officer. It reported that the Soviet chemical weapons programme had been reorganised under the leadership of Vladimir Nikolaevich Ipatiev, then one of the country's, if not the world's, leading scientists. The reorganisation, in the autumn of 1923, was the result of consultation with German chemical weapons experts, the SIS report said, detailing the negotiations that led to the Russo-German co-operation. These included the sale of poison gases direct to Russia by at least one German company, in breach of the Versailles Treaty, and an inter-government agreement to send German engineers to the Urals to maximise the amount of chemicals obtained using the country's own mineral resources, in return for a proportion of the produce.

The report gave an extensive picture of Soviet preparations for both offensive and defensive chemical warfare, describing the growth in Russian expertise in chemical warfare, assisted by German scientists, detailing the various chemicals in use, an extensive list of laboratories and factories involved in the testing and production of chemical weapons and the military and air force bases where chemical weapons were stored. It listed all the poison gases in use or under examination by the Soviet armed forces, primarily the pulmonary agents phosgene, chlorine and chloropicrin, and the blister agents lewisite and yperite (mustard gas). It also gave details of four new poison gases invented by Soviet scientists and revealed that 'trials with gas in the field have been carried out and have led to many casualties, which have been hushed up'. The report provided information on Soviet research into ways of defending troops against the attacks, including the concept of releasing a counter-cloud of antidote to certain gases, to which it added the caveat that this last was not thought workable. It also described the gas masks in use by Soviet forces. The contents of the report, which came from four different sources, were given added authority since SIS was able to send the report to the

British chemical weapons experimentation centre at Porton Down, near
Salisbury in Wiltshire, together with an example of the main Russian gas
mask then in use, the Zelinski–Kaumant respirator.[5]

The summary led to a series of questions about the specific gases and
scientists involved and the SIS agent responded with precise formulae
and details of the gases plus what information they were able to provide
on the scientists. The source subsequently named a member of the Soviet
trade delegation who was responsible for collecting similar intelligence
on the British chemical weapons programme and reported that scientists
and mining experts from the leading German chemical company Bayer
AG were in Russia, assisting the Soviet programme.[6]

By November 1924, the SIS network was reporting on Soviet
work on 'germ' warfare, which focussed on the use of encephalitis and
anthrax. The work was being carried out in Leningrad (as Petrograd had
been renamed, although the SIS reports still used the previous name) by
Professor P. R. Maslokowitz, who appeared to be a strong candidate for
the soubriquet Doctor Death, and whose experiments were aimed not
just at producing bacteriological bombs but also ampoules for Comintern
agents to use to infect individuals or groups of people in enemy countries.
Most chillingly of all, the report revealed that Maslokowitz was using
human guinea pigs, political prisoners taken from Petrograd prisons,
where some Britons still languished.

Work on the production of bacteriological bombs is done by the
professor of the biological chair of the Petrograd Medical Institute
(former Women's Medical School), P. R. Maslokowitz, who is working
under the personal direction of the initiator of this form of bomb,
Professor Zlatorogov, a very prominent bacteriologist. The seat of work
of Maslokowitz–Zlatorogov is the bacteriological laboratory of the
Medical Institute and a pavilion of the Veterinary–Zoological Institute
[at 5 Chernigovskaya Street] has now been assigned in addition, where
experiments are made not only on animals, but also on people, placed
at the disposal of the bacteriologists by the Military Authorities (who
subsidise the above-mentioned research) from the Petrograd prisons.

Doctor Maslokowitz is a profoundly learned man, but mentally not quite normal, being entirely absorbed in hatred of humanity as a whole. He was the first to obtain permission to experiment on live persons, this occupation of his – pure vivisection – having already given him notoriety among the prisoners, mostly political, from among whom the necessary human specimens for his research are selected. Maslokowitz worked for a long time in Port Alexandrov on plague research and on his instructions work is being conducted on the production of ampoules of pulmonary plague bacilli ordered by the Secret Section of the Comintern for unknown purposes. These ampoules are, however, not suitable for application in bombs.

A few weeks later, the same network provided a six-page report on experiments with anthrax bombs dropped on a herd of cattle which proved that 'humans would not remain immune' to its effects. The report gave extensive detail of the results of the effect on the cattle obtained by constant monitoring and post-mortem examination as well as detail of how the Soviet bacteriological bomb itself was constructed and operated. 'They are prepared and stored at the laboratory of Zlatorogov-Maslokowitz at Petrograd, Tchernigowskaya Street, 5,' it said. 'There are now in storage not less than fifty bombs of this sort, so far as is known loaded with anthrax and encephalitis.'[7]

A further report on Soviet preparations for biological warfare circulated in September 1926 revealed that they were stepped up during 1925 with the construction and isolation of a new test site on the Ochakov peninsula on the Black Sea. 'The more important test work, on a scale approximating real warfare conditions, was transferred to this place,' the four-page report noted. It gave details of the tactics that would be used, the use of bacteriological agents in artillery shells and reiterated that the Soviets were concentrating on two types of bacteriological agents, anthrax and encephalitis.

The bacilli most suitable for application under European conditions are the bacilli of epidemic encephalitis (B. epid. encefal.). Trials of this

yielded extremely favourable results and in case of war mobilisation
expenditure for the production of suitable aeroplane bombs has been
approved. The bacilli of epidemic encephalitis are suitable of reaction
on the personnel of the enemy army and for spread in the rear in his
administrative and factory centres. These bacilli may be used in two
ways: by means of aeroplane bombs, and secondly, by agents spreading
them in the enemy's rear by means of a special kind of small bombs,
with pulveriser action, in outward appearance reminiscent of thick
coloured pencils or some other article of general use. Articles of this
sort will be distributed in a crowd when they will go off, others will be
picked up casually and the bearers will become the involuntary carriers
of further infection. These articles are being made in the workshops of
the military authorities.[8]

The Naval Section's reports on the Soviet chemical warfare
programme continued during the same period, with a number of
'confidential agent' reports of new gases invented by the Russians,
complete with details of their formulae and properties. This included the
use of akrolein in hand grenades, mustard gas and chloropicrin in artillery
shells, and details of the chemical agent stocks and production levels. By
the beginning of 1925, Soviet factories were producing between 20 and
30 tons of mustard gas every month. The main chemical agent factories
were all in what is now the Ukraine, at the Azotte factory in Donetsk,
which was producing 9.8 tons of phosgene a day, but had the capacity
to produce up to 84 tons a day; the Alkali Works, Slavyansk, which was
producing just under a ton a day but could increase this to 4.9 tons; and
the Banduzhinsky Chemical Works at Bakhmut (now Artemivsk), which
was producing 4 tons of chloropicrin, 3.2 tons of phosgene and 1.2 tons
of mustard gas a day. The Soviet Union's chemical weapons stocks as at
1 December 1924 were: chlorine gases, 1,590 tons; phosgene, 568 tons
and mustard gas, 495 tons.[9]

At least one of the agents providing information on the Soviet
chemical weapons programme, a naval chemical weapons expert called
Eugen Kunitzin Neradov, was a member of the Hoyer network. The

network was run out of Helsingfors by Ernest Boyce, assisted by Harry Carr, whose father was managing director of a group of Russian timber mills before the revolution. Carr, who was born in Archangel, was recruited amid an expansion of the Helsingfors bureau, then run by Raleigh le May, in order to handle the Hoyer network and other agents inside Russia. Boyce, who had spent the previous fifteen months in London working in the SIS political section (Section V), after being freed from Butyrka prison, took over as passport control officer for Helsingfors in early 1920, with le May becoming his deputy. Carr was recruited at the same time, via a friend of his father's, to be the assistant passport control officer.

I was told to go to an address near Charing Cross station in London. So I went to the address, and to my surprise I saw in the window sacks of coal. But I walked in and an elderly man was sitting behind a table and he said to me: 'Oh, go into the room just behind here, and someone will be coming in a minute or two to interview you.' Well, I went to that room and shortly afterwards a man with greyish, whitish hair walked in and introduced himself as Commander Boyce. After hearing me speak Russian and interrogating me about my background, Commander Boyce said that I seemed a suitable candidate for the job they had in mind in Finland. Arrangements were then made for me to go out to Helsingfors. I travelled to Helsingfors via Norway and then after arriving there and reporting to Raleigh le May, I found that I had to sit in room at the Legation. Raleigh le May himself was at the Passport Control Office premises, and it was when I was translating that stuff that came into the room where I was sitting that I really began to realise that I was translating something really secret. It was clear that the things were reports that were coming in from some kind of secret agents. Then I was moved from that room to the passport control premises under Raleigh le May and began, of course, translating and typing there. It was not long afterwards that Commander Boyce turned up and took up the post of Passport Control Officer in Helsingfors.[10]

Despite the high standard of the reports coming out of the Soviet Union on chemical and bacteriological warfare, the most influential reports by far were coming from Ronald Meiklejohn in the Baltic Republics, specifically from Riga, where SIS were running a number of sources into the heart of the Soviet Communist Party and government, with at least one agent either present at meetings of the Politburo or with access to the minutes of their discussions. It was the reporting of this 'trustworthy agent' that allowed SIS to conclude that the Politburo was the Soviet Union's leadership, a fact previously unknown to the outside world. He also revealed that Moscow was funnelling thousands of pounds in hidden subsidies to the Communist Party of Great Britain; that the Comintern was mounting intense operations to subvert British rule in India; and that the Soviet leadership were determined to keep trade links with Britain open at any cost. The network run from Riga also included, crucially as it would later turn out, an agent with access to what proved to be 'surprisingly accurate' intelligence from inside the Comintern leadership, including letters from Grigory Zinoviev to the leaders of communist parties in a number of Western countries, encouraging them to stir up trouble and subvert the existing political systems. It led the Swedes, with whom Meiklejohn was sharing his intelligence along with the Poles, presumably on a reciprocal basis, to describe the British reporting as 'exemplary'.[11]

The British were also receiving good intelligence on Russian diplomatic intentions, in particular on the attempts to subvert India, from the interception of Moscow's messages to its agents abroad. This and the seizure of a Hull trawler and its crew enraged the cabinet to the extent that they authorised the Foreign Secretary, Lord Curzon, to issue a warning to Moscow in which he was to use the messages between Moscow and its agents abroad that had been intercepted by GC&CS. Since the Russians knew the British were intercepting their messages, 'the advantages of basing the published British case on actual extracts from the dispatches which had passed between the Soviet Government and its agents, outweighed the disadvantages of the possible disclosure of the secret source from which these despatches had been obtained,' the cabinet members ruled. It does not seem to have occurred to anyone that the Russians might well know that the British were intercepting the messages, but certainly did not know that they were deciphering them as well, or they would have changed the ciphers, which is what they did the minute they received the ultimatum.[12]

A very highly placed British source inside the Soviet Communist Party now provided MI1c with a series of groundbreaking reports on the response to what swiftly became known as 'the Curzon Ultimatum'. The first was from the 'trustworthy Moscow agent', reporting on a 'stormy' joint meeting of a number of members of the Politburo and the Soviet of People's Commissaries – effectively the Russian cabinet – called immediately after the British note was handed over. The meeting, held at Georgy Chicherin's home because he was ill, also included Leon Trotsky; Joseph Stalin, by that stage Communist Party general secretary; and Lev Kamenev, the Soviet premier, who with Stalin and Zinoviev formed the troika that was effectively ruling Russia as a result of two serious strokes suffered by Lenin.

The SIS report was given a rating of A2, only because the source had not sent the actual minutes. It quoted the Commissar for Foreign Trade, Leonid Krasin, as complaining that he had warned that they should not interfere in India or the Middle East, and that this was bound to cause problems with the British, but he had been accused of being 'a petty provincial' by the party theoretician, Nikolai Bukharin. Trotsky responded by saying that Bukharin was right.

> As long as we work against England's interests in the East and India, London will take us into account. India, Afghanistan, Persia, Egypt constitute Great Britain's heel of Achilles and we would be great blockheads if we did not wound her there. The note is unpleasant, but it must be made ineffectual and any break with London must be avoided.

The agent's report revealed the leadership's decision that Krasin should go ahead with the vital trade talks and promise that Moscow would not attempt to undermine Britain in India and the Middle East while at the same time the subversion should continue. Krasin subsequently returned to London where he met Lord Curzon, who was of course aware from the agent's report that the Russians intended to continue their propaganda against India and the Middle East. Curzon insisted that if the anti-British propaganda did not cease, then the trade agreement would be suspended. Soon afterwards, two MI1c representatives abroad reported that the Soviet leadership had ordered open propaganda against the British in the Middle East and India to cease and told agents abroad to send all future communications by courier.[13]

Then in early June, the Service received some astonishing material, the full minutes of meetings of the Soviet of People's Commissars (Sovnarkom), shortly before the delivery of the ultimatum, and a full meeting of the Politburo two weeks later, which discussed the British demands. The SIS report which accompanied the minutes of the Sovnarkom meeting of 5 May 1923, and was graded A1, noted that they showed that it already had a good idea of the contents of the British note from the Russian trade delegation in London. Trotsky's response during the meeting was defiant, even belligerent.

Trotsky denounced 'British imperialism' for resorting to blackmail as the only way to overcome communism. 'The ruling classes in England see how the class struggle is beginning to undermine the vast edifice of the British state,' he said, 'how this is beginning to give way and crumble under the pressure of the growing self-consciousness of the working class. These classes see with horror that the peoples of the East are beginning to emerge from under the guardianship of England, that either today or tomorrow India may be lost to British rule.' The independent foreign policy of the Soviet Union and its patronage of 'the oppressed nations of the East' had 'aroused extreme wrath among the British imperialists and led them to the thought of again taking up the devil's work against the revolution'. The Politburo had documents showing that Britain and Romania were working together against the Soviet Union and 'that England has long been meditating an attack upon south Russia. British imperialism will live to rue the day that saw its bloody attempts to strangle Soviet Russia.'

The Politburo minutes, from a meeting held in the Kremlin on 19 May 1923, were even more important in that they demonstrated for the first time to the British that it was the Politburo which ruled the Soviet Union and that both the Soviet of People's Commissaries and the Comintern was directly subordinate to its command. The SIS report on the meeting was an early attempt at the 'Kremlinology' that was to dominate both Cold Wars, the detailed analysis of the way the different members of the Soviet leadership behaved, even down to their respective positions on the podium at events held in Red Square, to determine who was 'in' and who was 'out'. The SIS analysis, which accompanied the minutes and was again graded A1, noted that 'in Lenin's absence, Trotsky is the chairman of the Politburo, and as such is the most influential personage in Russia'; that Bukharin and Zinoviev were the most powerful influences on foreign policy, directing what Chicherin did; that the Comintern was used by the Politburo as a means to further the interests of the Soviet state; that the Soviet Union was reaching out to Turkey, Afghanistan and Persia in order to undermine Britain's position in the region; and that, critically, the Soviet leadership was desperate to keep the trade links with Britain open at virtually any cost.

Much of this was correct, to the point that it now seems odd that no-one in Whitehall already knew that the Politburo was in charge of the Soviet Union, but the assessment that Trotsky was in charge in Lenin's absence was in reality misleading. That certainly appeared to be the case from the Sovnarkom minutes, but it is not clear why the SIS analyst writing the report felt the more important Politburo minutes also showed this to be the case. In fact, the troika of Stalin, Zinoviev and Kamenev effectively ruled the Soviet Union in Lenin's absence while, over the long term, Stalin was inexorably positioning himself to take complete control, a situation that the Politburo minutes portend, with Stalin opening and directing the discussions. While his colleagues in the Soviet leadership saw his position as Central Committee general secretary as a boring bureaucratic party post, Stalin recognised it as a unique means by which to take power and had already used it to appoint his own people to key regional party posts, a move that would eventually make him all-powerful within the Central Committee and ultimately the Politburo. To be fair to SIS, it was not alone in failing to spot that Stalin was the real successor to Lenin. Trotsky and Stalin's fellow troika members, Kamenev and Zinoviev, also managed to deceive themselves on that point, a failure that was ultimately more damaging to them than the SIS misinterpretation was to British foreign policy-making. Not one of those three died peacefully in their beds.[14]

While genuine minutes of Politburo meetings were a rarity, the Service was receiving other high-level political reports from Moscow. During the first half of 1923, SIS had at least three well-placed agents based in Moscow, and run from within the Baltic republics, who were providing A1 intelligence on the minutes and communiqués of secret meetings of the Comintern, the People's Commissars (effectively the Soviet cabinet); and even top secret Soviet security reports on the extent of anti-Bolshevik activity in the interior of the newly created Soviet Union, revealing the extent of the problems facing the communist leadership. These reports, which also showed the first signs of major splits within the party ahead of Lenin's death, were backed up by intelligence provided by sources run from Paris and Berlin.[15]

Northern Europe was not the only area from which the Service monitored the activities of the Bolsheviks. The Foreign Office priorities in Asia Minor and the Caucasus were watched from a large intelligence network based in Constantinople. Since the Middle East, the Caucasus and central Asia were at the time seen as the preserve of Indian Political Intelligence, this came under the control of a British Indian police officer, Major Valentine Vivian, in a joint operation with SIS. Initially, the SIS bureau chief was Samson, then in 1921 Captain Louis Christie. They were assisted by Harold Gibson, an expatriate Briton who had been born and brought up in Moscow, where his father ran a chemical works. 'Gibbie', as he was know, had previously been on the Service's staff in Russia.

The situation in Russia was also being watched closely from the south, via a naval intelligence operation featuring Lieutenant Wilfred 'Biffy' Dunderdale RNVR, the 'Biffy' deriving from his time as an amateur boxer. His mother was the Russian Countess Demidov and his father a wealthy businessman, and representative of Vickers, in Constantinople before the First World War. Dunderdale was born and went to school in Nikolaev in the Ukraine and, as a result, spoke fluent Russian. He was studying naval engineering at Petrograd University when the revolution broke out and was swiftly recruited by the Royal Navy's intelligence operation in the Black Sea. Based initially in Sebastopol, and using pre-revolutionary contacts, including former school-fellows from Nikolaev, he set up a network of agents extending deep into the Caucasus, reporting mainly on the Russian Black Sea Fleet and coastal defences, but also intercepting and expelling German agents. Dunderdale's agents also included Odessa-based fishermen who could pass through the Russian fleet without suspicion. Dunderdale intercepted Bolshevik wireless transmissions, picking up a series of messages urging the ships of the Black Sea Fleet, many of which were initially under the control of the White Russians, to mutiny against their officers. Dunderdale's expertise as an agent runner, his fluency in Russian and his highly detailed reports swiftly ensured that he came to the notice of Hugh Sinclair, then still director of naval intelligence, who ordered that his name should be removed from all but the most tightly controlled reports to protect those of his agents who had been connected to him prior to the revolution.

Dunderdale's reputation and status was hugely advanced by an incident in April 1920, in which his agents warned that nine members of the crew of a submarine, the *Utka*, which was being handed over to the allies, were about to mutiny, disarm the rest of the crew and give themselves up to the Bolsheviks. This intellignce enabled the Royal Navy to step in and pre-empt the action, resulting in Dunderdale being appointed MBE. In late 1920, he discovered that the British consul in Sebastopol was conducting 'amateur intelligence work' and complained that it was hampering his own efforts, insisting that it was 'essential that only one person should be in charge of secret intelligence in one town'. The consul was in fact acting on Gibson's orders, but he was duly called off the search for Bolshevik and German agents and, a few months later, Dunderdale and his agent network were recruited into SIS. 'Biffy', an immensely sociable man, full of amusing anecdotes from his life as a

British spy, always maintained that his first job for the Service involved paying off the foreign members of the harem of Turkish leader Sultan Muhammad with gold sovereigns and having the Royal Navy take them back to their countries of origin. The Constantinople operations were clearly well regarded in Whitehall. When the Allied occupation of Constantinople came to an end in 1923 and the Indian authorities decided that Vivian was needed back on the sub-continent, SIS recruited him too and after three months working in Production, he was sent to Cologne as the inspector for the central European bureaux.[16]

Amid all of the successes in Russia, there continued to be failures. One of the main problems with human intelligence is verifying that what an agent says is correct. Tasking of agents, such as the questionnaires issued by SIS on specific subjects during this period, focuses the agent's mind on what is required but also provides less scrupulous agents with a 'shopping list' they can exploit for cash or influence. Even the most honest of agents can provide incorrect reporting. This might be for a variety of reasons, many perfectly innocent. The relationship between agents and the intelligence officer handling them needs ideally to be a 'relationship of trust'. This will sometimes induce an agent who is anxious to please to produce the material the handler requires without proper checks, to be too trusting of their own sources of information, or simply to get it wrong. Gathering intelligence on issues that others are trying to keep secret will often be difficult, even the most careful and honest of agents will occasionally make mistakes.

Vladimir Orlov was neither the most careful nor the most honest of agents. After touring Europe on behalf of SIS, drumming up support for intelligence that would assist in the war on Bolshevik terror, Orlov moved his base from Paris to Berlin, where, with the support of both SIS and the German authorities, he set up an anti-Bolshevik intelligence network, taking £500 of start-up funding from Cumming, as well as an annual subscription of £5,000. He was also heavily subsidised by the German police, who provided his office accommodation. Cumming agreed from the start that Orlov should be able to pass the intelligence to anyone, although SIS must get a copy of every report, but was nevertheless naïvely surprised to discover that it was also being passed to the Germans, apparently not realising that Orlov had used the grand anti-Bolshevik tour to feather his own nest rather than that of SIS. Cumming and Desmond Morton were initially very pleased to have access to the information Orlov could supply, assuring him that they would 'give him the freest hand possible in all matters'. This was to turn out to be at best naïve. Orlov very soon proved himself to be an inveterate liar and, in January 1923, he was officially dropped.[17]

On 8 October 1924, SIS received a copy of a letter supposedly sent by Zinoviev to the Communist Party of Great Britain. It called for the mobilisation of sympathetic forces in the Labour Party and the intensification of 'agitation-propaganda work in the armed forces'. The letter, which appeared to confirm a widespread belief that the Labour Party was soft on Bolshevism, came at an opportune moment. The idea that Labour was not prepared to be tough with the Soviet Union had been fuelled by the signing by James Ramsay MacDonald, the Labour Prime Minister, of two treaties with Russia – one of which, aimed at settling Russian debts, was dubbed 'Money for Murderers' by the popular press – and by the decision not to prosecute John Campbell, a Communist journalist accused of preaching sedition to the armed forces. MacDonald's government was defeated on 8 October 1924 and he went to the country, telling the King that he saw the row as 'one of the moves in the game which made our position for further fighting intolerable'.

That very day, SIS received an intelligence report from Riga which appeared to be an English version of a letter from Zinoviev to the Central Committee of the Communist Party of Great Britain, dated 2 October 1924 and seeking to play on the divisions caused by the 'Money for Murderers' treaty, which was due for ratification by Parliament. 'It is indispensable to stir up the masses of the British proletariat,' the letter said. 'It is imperative that the group in the Labour Party sympathising with the treaty should bring increased pressure to bear upon the Government and parliamentary circles in favour of ratification of the treaty.' It was sent to the Foreign Office with a note pointing out that 'the document contains strong incitement to armed revolution and constitutes evidence of intention to contaminate the Armed Forces; and it constitutes a flagrant violation of Article 16 of the Anglo-Russian Treaty, signed on 8 August'. The note added that 'the authenticity of the document is undoubted'. There is no doubt that the hurried circulation of the letter was unusual. Given the issues at stake, Morton was asked by the Foreign Office for 'corroborative proofs' of its authenticity. He got what he needed from an SIS agent in place inside the Communist Party of Great Britain, who Morton claimed was able to confirm that the party leadership had discussed a letter from Moscow instructing them on how to force Parliament to ratify the treaty and warning them against trusting the Labour Party, although it later transpired that the agent never mentioned a letter, a surprising omission had one really been received. To be fair to Morton, he was right to claim that the letter was not in any way different to other letters from Zinoviev previously sent to other Western communist parties and passed to SIS by its agents within the Soviet bureaucracy. It was the election that made this letter different, not its contents.[18]

It was political dynamite and with a cabal of former senior intelligence officers, including Freddie Browning and Blinker Hall, now Unionist MP for Eastbourne, aware of its existence, it was inevitable that it would be leaked to the press. The *Daily Mail* splashed it across its front page, with banner headlines: 'Civil War Plot by Socialists' Masters; Moscow Orders to Our Reds; Great Plot Disclosed', five days before the general election, which took place on 29 October. The leak forced the government to lodge an official protest, to which the Russians responded with a denunciation of the letter as 'an impudent forgery'. Despite the fact that leak was clearly aimed at discrediting the Labour Party, its real effect on the election is uncertain. The Conservatives were always expected to win; indeed, the letter arguably did more damage to the Liberal Party, whose natural supporters turned in huge numbers to the Conservatives, thereby beginning a long period during which the Liberals were the third party in British politics.

There is now little doubt that the letter was fake, not least because the Russians made such determined efforts to find out who forged it.

They concluded that the most likely source was a White Russian forger who was based in Riga and was heavily linked to Orlov, having supplied him with a number of fake documents to order in the past. Reports from three separate Bolshevik intelligence officials, sent to the Lubyanka, headquarters of the Cheka's successor, the OGPU, in November 1924, all agreed that the letter was produced by Ivan Dmitrievich Pokrovsky, a member of the White Russian intelligence organisation based in Riga. Pokrovsky 'has in his possession Comintern stationery and made it up from extracts of Zinoviev's speeches with something extra added', according to an OGPU report.

The most comprehensive of the three accounts of the letter's origin came from Aleksandr Gumansky, a Bolshevik agent who infiltrated the White Russian movement in Berlin. 'It was fabricated in Riga by a certain Pokrovsky, a really talented person, who worked for the British since 1920,' Gumansky claimed. Pokrovsky said he had been asked by a leading Russian émigré based in England for material that could be used against the British Labour Party in the forthcoming election, although there was a general belief that the Russian émigré was Orlov. Gumansky's report had added credibility since it included a verbatim account of the affair in Pokrovsky's own words. 'My chief, Captain Black, suggested that I should compose a letter addressed to the British communists,' Pokrovsky said. 'I drafted it out on proper paper and without a signature, not knowing how it would be used. This was before the general elections.' Pokrovsky was paid a total of £1,360 for the letter, which was subsequently sent to the Bolshevik representative in London, Gumansky said.

Further evidence to back up the story that it was forged in Riga comes in the memoirs of Leslie Nicholson, who took over as SIS head of bureau in the Latvian capital in 1934. Nicholson described how Artur Schmidkoff, the head of the Latvian political police, was fond of boasting to him that he had uncovered the man who forged the Zinoviev letter.

With a squad of men, he had raided the flat of a known ex-British agent and had discovered carbon copies of what he described as 'the original

Zinoviev letter'. These carbon copies had certainly been produced on the agent's typewriter, which was found in the flat. Although I tried to question Schmidkoff further, he refused to be drawn. All he would tell me was that he personally was convinced that the man was indeed the originator of the letter and he implied that it had been fabricated and passed to a 'British organisation' for financial gain.[19]

In the middle of the acrimonious row between Moscow and London over the letter and its provenance, another old conjurer of intelligence reappeared. During a terse conversation over the letter between an unhappy and perplexed MacDonald and an equally bemused Soviet envoy, Christian Rakovsky, the latter pointed out that such fakes were not unusual. He himself had received a letter only the previous week from a Mr Singleton, promising to show him 'some important documents' that would compromise 'various left-wing groups in the Labour movement in Britain and on the Continent'. What Rakovsky did not tell MacDonald, possibly because it seemed unlikely to improve the tone of the conversation, was that Singleton had also offered to give him the names of all the British secret service personnel operating in Moscow. The offer had at any event been dismissed out of hand. Singleton was in fact none other than Cumming's 'very noted international spy' Enrique Lorenzo Bernstein, who had apparently been acting as an agent for Orlov's fake document production line and had previously sold the Russians forged documents, until they too realised that he was just 'an unscrupulous rascal'. MacDonald's investigation of the letter also included a farcical interview with Major Malcolm Woollcombe, the head of Section I, now the SIS political section, in which Woollcombe was sat in one room and MacDonald in another, with Sir Eyre Crowe, the permanent under-secretary at the Foreign Office, stood in the doorway, relaying the questions and answers between the two men.[20]

SIS soon realised that the Zinoviev letter was a fake, with Morton telling MI5 on 27 November that 'we are firmly convinced this actual thing is a forgery'. Unfortunately, a committee set up by the incoming government and chaired by the new Foreign Secretary, Sir Austen

Chamberlain, concluded that 'there was no doubt as to the authenticity of the letter', with SIS, not for the last time, shaping its reports to provide what its political masters wanted to hear. Despite Morton's previous firm convictions that the letter was a fake, he drafted a report for the cabinet providing 'five very good reasons' why the letter was genuine. SIS subsequently claimed that 'we now know the identity of every individual who handled it from the first person who saw Zinoviev's copy to the day it reached us. With the exception of Zinoviev himself, they were all our agents.' There was no truth whatsoever in that statement; indeed, so far is it from the truth that it could only have been a deliberate, and somewhat desperate, attempt at deception. The conclusions of an internal inquiry into the letter's provenance – mounted in the late 1960s by Millicent Bagot, an experienced MI5 officer and Sovietologist – remain as incisive now as they were when they were first written:

White Russian intelligence services were well developed and highly organised, and included the operation of a forgery ring in Berlin. It seems likely that they asked either those forgers, or their contacts in the Baltic States with similar skills, to produce a document which would derail the treaties and damage the Labour government. Because of British intelligence links with Berlin, information about the proposed forgery would have reached certain members of the British Intelligence agencies who were on the look-out for opportunities to further the Conservative cause in Britain, and to discredit the Labour Party in the process. Anyone in that position, and with a wide net of contacts in London, was well placed not only to vouch for the authenticity of the letter but also to encourage its dissemination in quarters where profitable – and mischievous – use might be made of it.[21]

EIGHTEEN

Moscow rules – 'A very risky game'

WHILE there were undoubted successes for SIS in the 1920s, particularly in the Soviet Union, there were also plenty of failures other than the Zinoviev letter, including several very public embarrassments. The first came in an appropriately timed article in *The Times* of 1 April 1924. Percy Sykes was going through a messy divorce, which left his wife Annie so angry and vindictive that she had taken a number of 'books' belonging to the SIS paymaster and hidden them, initially suggesting to both Sykes and the court that she had sold them and was not prepared to say to whom. It was not clear what the 'books' were, but the effort to which the courts, and Sykes and his lawyers, went to get them back, the accompanying costs in court time and legal charges just to retrieve them, not to mention the extent of the newspaper's interest, all suggest that they were the Service's accounts, which Sykes had taken home with him, giving his wife the opportunity to wreak her revenge in the most embarrassing method possible. Eventually the court jailed Annie Sykes for a month, much to her estranged husband's discomfiture, before she finally consented to disclose where the books were, apparently perfectly safe. Ordering her release, on 6 May 1924, Mr Justice Hill noted: 'If this silly woman had given the information on 31 March, which she has now furnished, there would have been no trouble.'[1]

While that could have had very serious consequences if the books had fallen into the wrong hands, it was ultimately merely embarrassing. The second incident was far more serious. Sidney Reilly had by now dropped out of use by the Service, but in January 1925, Ernest Boyce wrote to him, suggesting he test the reliability and usefulness of a White Russian organisation known as 'the Trust' by meeting some of its representatives in Paris. Reilly was convinced of their sincerity and agreed to meet the organisation's leaders on the Finnish–Russian border, but what neither he nor Boyce knew was that the Trust was in fact an organisation set up under the control of the OGPU and heavily infiltrated by its agents. Reilly went to the border and was enticed to cross over by two OGPU agents masquerading as opponents of the regime. He was then taken to Moscow, where he was arrested and incarcerated in the Lubyanka. The Soviet government newspaper *Izvestia* carried a report suggesting that Reilly had been shot dead after crossing the border, but an SIS report obtained from Russian émigré sources described how he was, in fact, shot in the back at Stalin's insistence after days of being interrogated in the Lubyanka, the OGPU's Moscow headquarters. 'The Bolsheviks wished to conceal his arrest, but the English found it out, and the Bolsheviks, in order to escape the possible demands by the English of his release, murdered him,' the report said. Four OGPU officers took him to woods north-east of Moscow on the evening of 5 November 1925. On their way they stopped, claiming that the car had broken down. All four OGPU officers, together with Reilly, got out of the car to stretch their legs. One of the OGPU officers, named only as Ibrahim, lagged behind the party and then 'put several bullets into Reilly'. He fell but was still alive and another officer fired the shot that killed him. SIS was pursued by two of his wives for compensation. But although Reilly was clearly acting in conjunction with Boyce, to the extent that the latter was recalled to London to be 'carpeted' by Sinclair over his role, it insisted disingenuously that 'all Reilly's activities after 1921 were his own private affair' and, given Reilly's 'somewhat complicated matrimonial tangles', it had no intention of paying up.[2]

The third major embarrassment came just a few days after the government committee on the Zinoviev letter declared it genuine. John Leather, the Paris representative of the Burndept Wireless Company, the company's two other Paris-based staff and two young Frenchwomen were arrested by French police and charged with espionage. The French press revelled in the sensational story of the British spies and their two French

Mata Haris, who were tasked by Leather and his assistant William Fischer to befriend French officers and obtain intelligence about French military aircraft and bases. One of the two women, a 24-year-old artist's model called Marthe Moreuil, had been seduced by Fischer, while the other, a dancer named Andrée Lefebvre, was run by Leather himself. He, Fischer and their colleague Oliver Phillips all denied espionage, but it emerged in the French press that both Leather and Fischer had served together in the British Army's Intelligence Corps in Cologne in the immediate aftermath of the war, Leather as an officer and Fischer as an NCO. They then denied any continuing involvement in intelligence work but Leather's insistence that he had resigned his commission more than a year earlier was somewhat undermined by the fact that he was still named as a serving Intelligence Corps officer in the 'Army List' of officers published each year by the War Office. The British government meanwhile insisted that 'no department of His Majesty's Government is in any way connected with or has any knowledge of the activities of the firm in question', sidestepping the awkward fact that it was not the company, but the employees, who were being accused of working for British intelligence.

The deliberately misleading denial did not fool a number of British Members of Parliament, not least because it was well known within the British establishment, and probably the French counter-espionage service as well, that Leather was a cousin of Desmond Morton, the SIS head of Production. Hugh Sinclair had little chance of keeping the Service's embarrassing involvement in spying on a major ally quiet. His empire-building had made him too many enemies, most notably Sir Wyndham Childs, the assistant commissioner in charge of Special Branch, who was warned by the Prime Minister's Secret Service Committee that his job was on the line as a direct result of his poor relationship with Sinclair. Clearly well briefed, the Labour MP Ernest Thurtle told the House of Commons that the denial, issued by his fellow MP, the Foreign Secretary, Sir Austen Chamberlain, was a 'diplomatic falsehood'. Told by the Speaker that he must withdraw the remark or be suspended for that day's proceedings, Thurtle replied: 'I have very great respect for the Chair, but I have equal respect for truth, and I cannot withdraw it.'

He then marched out of the House to rousing cheers from the Labour benches. Leather was sentenced to three years in jail and a 3,000-franc fine, Fischer and Phillips received two-year jail sentences and 2,000-franc fines and the two women lesser sentences of six months and 500-franc fines each. The Foreign Office subsequently made it very clear to Sinclair that it had made 'a gentlemen's agreement' with its French counterpart that neither country should spy on the other again.[3]

Having failed to gain control over MI5, Sinclair set up his own counter-espionage section, Section V, headed by Valentine Vivian, responsible for counter-espionage, although liaison with MI5 remained via Section IV, the military section, until 1931. Section I remained the political section, liaising with the Foreign and Colonial Offices and with the Board of Trade. Sinclair also moved SIS back from the remote reaches of West Kensington to St James's, close to Whitehall and his clubs. In June 1926, he took a 21-year lease for two floors of 54 Broadway, opposite St James's Park Underground station. The Government Code and Cipher School and SIS took over the third and fourth floors of what was known as Broadway Buildings.[4]

During the 1920s, SIS not only operated abroad but also tracked Bolshevik agents once they arrived in the UK. In the immediate aftermath of the war, MI5 had been limited in its operations to countering subversion of the armed forces, with the Home Office Directorate of Intelligence taking over counter-subversion and counter-espionage at large. This led to a situation in which SIS ran agents against the Bolsheviks, while MI5 had none at all and was therefore grateful for the material it was provided by Morton on what was happening in the various Soviet offices across London. One particular area of interest was the All-Russian Co-operative Society (ARCOS), based at 49 Moorgate, with SIS running agents against it from the moment it began its operations in October 1920 and sharing the intelligence freely with the MI5 officer compiling its Bolshevik Black List, initially Raphael Farina, whose understanding of Russian led swiftly to him being recruited as bureau chief in Riga.[5]

SIS continued to share its intelligence on ARCOS with MI5, and the British knowledge of the activities of the Russians was bolstered by the work of the GC&CS codebreakers, who had managed to break the substitution tables used for enciphering Soviet diplomatic telegrams. But in May 1927 there was a major disaster brought about by a poor relationship, not between MI5 and SIS, but between the intelligence services and the police, and in particular between Sinclair and Childs.

In October 1926, Bertie Maw, now back in London, went to Sinclair and told him that a neighbour of his in Wimbledon, an accountant, worked at ARCOS and was willing to provide information on what was going on there. In view of the tensions surrounding SIS anti-Bolshevik operations in the UK, Sinclair said the accountant should go to Scotland Yard, which he did, but Chief Inspector James McBrien, who interviewed him, appeared not to take his offer seriously. Maw's neighbour 'was apparently not enthusiastically received and commented unfavourably upon the treatment meted out to him,' Sinclair said. The SIS chief then told Maw to let his accountant neighbour know that if anything else happened, he should go to Sinclair, who would ensure that people listened to what the accountant had to say. At the end of March 1927, the accountant gave Maw a copy of the front page of a classified army document, which had been copied at the ARCOS offices. He told Maw that a disaffected worker in the ARCOS photostat department, a Mr Langstone, had been dismissed and had taken the photocopy with him, handing it to the accountant to deal with. Given that it was a War Office document, the responsibility for investigating the affair clearly fell to MI5 and so Sinclair passed it on, at which point MI5 began their own investigation, with an officer meeting both the accountant and Langstone on 9 May. The evidence they gave convinced Vernon Kell that some sort of action needed to be taken.

Quite why things tumbled out of control from this point on, without SIS having a hint of what was about to occur, is impossible to explain other than in the context of the now venomous rivalry between Sinclair and Childs. There was no apparent urgency for any action and the British authorities now had an agent inside ARCOS, who was well placed to assist them with a number of sensitive operations that SIS, MI5 and GC&CS were mounting jointly, including one tracking a senior ARCOS official called Jacob Kirchenstein, otherwise known as Johnny Walker, who was believed to be one of the Comintern's main agents in Britain. Other current investigations into Soviet espionage that might have been assisted by the new source included one into Wilfred McCartney, one of Mackenzie's former officers, who was now spying for Moscow, and another into a network of agents run by William Ewer, the foreign editor of the *Daily Herald*.

The potential damage from the Ewer network was discovered a year later by MI5, which realised that two Special Branch officers were tipping Ewer off about investigations into Soviet networks and that Ewer had a team of agents watching the SIS and GC&CS headquarters, tracking officers entering and leaving the premises. The dangers inherent in the Soviet ability to monitor SIS activity were not lost on Vivian, with Section V issuing a memo warning that 'it seems hardly necessary to point out that, through such items of information and with the assistance of his foreign correspondents, it would be simple for Ewer to trace the representatives and agents of SIS abroad as it has been for him to trace the headquarters organisation in London, and with the information so gained he would be in a position to embarrass, or damage the credit of, the Government at home as seriously as to gull, betray and cripple SIS organisations abroad.'[6]

Kell was of course unaware of this in May 1927, but the potential use of Maw's accountant friend as an agent inside ARCOS to uncover the Soviet networks ought to have been obvious to him. There is little sign that it played any part in his subsequent thinking. Two days after the interviews with the two informants, Kell showed their testimony to Sir Archibald Bodkin, the Director of Public Prosecutions, who confirmed that copying the document was an offence under the 1911 Official Secrets Act. The MI5 director then attempted, without success, to discuss the issue with Sir John Anderson, the permanent under-secretary at the Home Office, and Field Marshal Sir George Milne, the chief of the Imperial General Staff, before showing the evidence informally to Childs. Apparently desperate to talk to someone about the case, and having failed to speak to any of the senior civil servants who might have taken a more considered view, Kell finally explained it to the Secretary for War, Sir Laming Worthington-Evans, who arranged a meeting for him with the Home Secretary, Sir William 'Jix' Joynson-Hicks. 'Jix', a fanatical anti-Bolshevik, took the evidence to the Prime Minister, Stanley Baldwin, who was discussing a separate matter with Chamberlain. All three agreed that the police must raid the ARCOS offices the following day.[7]

It is very hard to conceive of a more foolish thing to do in the circumstances. The ARCOS offices were in the same building and to all intents and purposes inseparable from the Soviet Trade Mission. The raid was bound to have serious side-effects for the British mission in Moscow, which was certainly collecting intelligence and would at the very least have been acting as a letter box for the SIS networks, if not actively running agents. The various operations against the ARCOS offices, which might well have progressed successfully with the assistance of the accountant, allowing MI5, SIS and GC&CS to track the Soviet agents operating in Britain, would inevitably suffer irreparable setbacks. It would be tempting to assess the potential damage to intelligence operations against the Russians that was likely to be caused by the raid as being as bad as it could possibly be, had the politicians who ordered it not somehow contrived to make it far, far worse.

Neither Childs nor Kell discussed the raid, or its potential side-effects, with Sinclair beforehand; there was no attempt to raid any other Soviet premises at the same time, which might have ensured the maximum chance of obtaining evidence and preventing intelligence being passed back to Moscow; SIS was in fact only informed less than four hours before the raid, when Childs asked for either Sinclair or Morton to come to a pre-raid briefing at Scotland Yard; and Chamberlain failed to mention the decision to order the raid to any senior Foreign Office official. It is hard not to suspect that Childs deliberately organised the briefing for lunchtime knowing the clubbable SIS chief was likely to be dining in the Savoy or the Army and Navy. 'Quex' was indeed out of the office on a long lunch and was only informed at 3 p.m. when he returned to Broadway Buildings of what was by now due to take place ninety minutes later. He immediately rushed over to the Foreign Office to ensure 'the conveyance of a suitable warning to our people in Moscow' only to find senior Foreign Office officials as ignorant of the raid as he had been only minutes earlier. They swiftly discovered that Chamberlain had agreed to the raid the previous evening and not bothered telling any of his staff. Sinclair's concern over the damage done to the work of his officers in the mission in Moscow was to be more than justified and his anger at Kell, and in particular Childs, is not difficult to understand.[8]

If anything the raid itself was even more inept than the decision-making process that preceded it, presenting a passable imitation of Hollywood's Keystone Kops. Morton, who had gone to the Scotland Yard lunchtime briefing, went along on the raid with Childs. Arriving together with a number of Special Branch officers ahead of the City Police, who because of jurisdictional boundaries had to carry out the raid, they just stood around outside the offices affecting to be ordinary passers-by. That this would have given the ARCOS employees time to get rid of any really damning evidence is probably irrelevant, since two Special Branch officers were Soviet agents, and no doubt tipped the Soviet handlers off to the impending raid anyway. When it actually took place, it appeared to Morton that no-one seemed to know what they were doing. There were no Russian-speaking officers capable of deciding what was and was not suspicious, while according to the one police officer, ARCOS staff were continuing to burn 'decoded telegrams' even as the Special Branch officers carried out their search. 'No-one seemed to be in charge, there was no-one to appeal to for orders or to organise the search,' Morton noted. 'Carter [a Special Branch officer] was busy arguing with the chief officials of ARCOS regarding the opening of the safes; the City Police were on duty guarding the rooms and the rest of the SB [Special Branch] appeared to be wandering about and wondering what to do next.'[9]

Despite this fiasco, the ineptitude of the entire affair was yet to reach its zenith. The failure to find any convincing evidence sent the politicians into a panic, and despite Sinclair's insistence that, with the damage already done, they might as well now raid all the Soviet premises in London to gather as much evidence as they could, no-one was prepared to act. Childs was by now desperately trying to distance himself from the whole affair and refused to ask Joynson-Hicks to authorise further raids, while insisting that anyway the entire issue was the responsibility of Kell, who argued, with some justification, that his men could not carry out police raids and it must therefore be entirely down to Childs.[10]

A week later, Baldwin announced the 'results' of the raid – which were published in a Government White Paper – and the decision to break off relations with Moscow. Given the lack of incriminating material captured in the raid, the 'evidence' was bolstered by the text of six telegrams that had been deciphered by GC&CS. The following day, it emerged that the raid had uncovered a classified British document which could have been used to demonstrate the mission's wrongdoing, making the use of the deciphered telegrams unnecessary, but it was too late. Two days after Baldwin's announcement that he was breaking off relations with the Soviet Union, Chamberlain and Joynson-Hicks read the text of some of the messages to MPs, in order to make the government's case that it had no choice but to order the raid, with the Home Secretary describing ARCOS as 'one of the most nefarious spy systems that it has ever been my lot to meet'. The Russians were not slow to get the message, dropping the cipher systems the British had broken and replacing them with the one-time pad system, which if used properly was impossible to break. The codebreakers were horrified. Very soon the decipherable Soviet diplomatic messages dried up, along with the intelligence they provided.[11]

Over the coming weeks, Sinclair used the debacle to argue his case that there should be a single unified intelligence organisation. 'The value to all Departments of Government of this particular type of information and the extreme delicacy of its source of origin need no emphasis,' he complained. 'The publication of the telegrams automatically stops their source of supply for some years at least. It was authorised only as a measure of desperation to bolster up a case vital to Government, which had the facts been fully known at the time, needed no such costly support. If the three branches of secret service had been united under one chief, there could have been no breakdown in the machinery such as had occurred on this occasion. From a secret service standpoint, the raid took place without due consideration either of the probable issues or of the further action which might be required to deal with such issues. Even the officials of the Foreign Office (with the exception of the Secretary of State himself) were totally unaware that the raid was contemplated until informed by SIS. Consequently, HM Representatives at Moscow had not been informed, a state of affairs that conceivably might have led to most serious results.'[12]

Sinclair spoke too soon. He may well have been lulled into a false sense of security by a Soviet announcement on 9 June 1927 that it had arrested and shot twenty 'British spies' and the subsequent execution of a naval officer based at Kronstadt, who was said to have spied for the British. While some of those shot may have had links to SIS, many were former Tsarist officials or Russians who simply had friends in the British mission; one man, Vladimir Evreinov, who worked for a Moscow bank, appears to have been denounced simply because he once lived in England, had a British wife and occasionally attended bridge nights in the mission, scarcely the behaviour of a spy or of someone trying to disguise his connection to the British. The Foreign Office denounced the executions. Sir Robert Hodgson, the senior British diplomat in Moscow until relations were broken off, specifically dismissed several cases, including the allegation that Edward Charnock had been in touch with a Red Army officer who worked for the Revolutionary Military Council. The officer's wife was an old schoolfriend of Charnock's wife and he was, Hodgson admitted, 'doubtless in a position to procure information on matters of military importance'. As a result, Charnock 'avoided any dealings with him that might conceivably compromise him,' Hodgson said. 'He met him in all some four or five times during the five and a half years the Mission was in Moscow and then only in company. On no occasion did he discuss military matters with him.' This did not of course rule out that information was passed between them via their wives, but the bulk of the executions appear to have had no real connection with espionage.[13]

A month later, the Service suffered a devastating blow. The Russians announced on 10 July 1927 that in a series of operations since the break in relations they had arrested 'more than twenty-three persons employed in the British Intelligence Service under Boyce, formerly officially attached to the British Mission at Helsingfors, and later at Reval'. *The Times* correspondent in Riga reported that 'the OGPU's fantastic conclusions would be laughable if they did not serve as a pretext to execute a number of Russians'. But this time, the claims of 'British spies' were genuine. The bulk of the Hoyer network had been rounded up, including Albert Hoyer himself; Eugen Kunitzin Neradov, a naval chemical weapons expert; Professor Nikitin, 'a poison gas expert'; Afanasy Khlopushkin, a member of the OGPU; and Vladimir Valitsky, a former Red Guard who worked in the Moscow office of Sovtorgflot and provided details of movements of troops and military equipment.

Hoyer was originally arrested a year earlier. The OGPU released Hoyer for 'lack of evidence' and then mounted a surveillance operation on him and his contacts, only waiting for the right moment to swoop. At some point, he had visited the embassy claiming Ernest Boyce had failed to pay him and asking that they write to him seeking the payment. Whether this was under OGPU control is unclear, but it seemed likely, and he was sent away. At any event, the OGPU scarcely needed to get more evidence of British espionage. They knew all about the Terijoki bureau. They knew about Pyotr Sokolov and Nikolai Bunakov, putting them on trial in absentia along with Boyce, and they knew that Hoyer had been in touch with Paul Dukes in 1919. Hoyer admitted that the priorities for his network were to collect intelligence on Russian military, naval and air forces, with particular interest in Soviet military co-operation with Germany. His admissions to the OGPU were carefully designed to deceive their counter-espionage experts, in what appears to have been the standard response recommended by SIS to its chief agents if they were caught and were unable to deny involvement with any espionage activities. Hoyer admitted knowing Boyce since before the revolution, when the pre-revolutionary Russian Navy loaned him to the British, but claimed that he had persistently refused to spy for Boyce until 'a love feast in Reval' in 1925, at which he promised the British 'spymaster' that he would organise an agent network in Leningrad. Messages from SIS were sent in to him via Ronald Meiklejohn in Reval, the court heard. The couriers bringing messages in confirmed their identity 'by pulling out a watch stopped at 6 o'clock', while agent reports were normally sent out by courier to Finland for Boyce. Nine of those charged were sentenced to death, including Hoyer, Neradov, Khlopushkin, Valitsky and a woman named only as Shorina. Professor Nikitin, the poison gas expert, who claimed that he gave the British 'only harmless information' because he 'liked his wife to have silk stockings', was jailed for a year.[14]

Another spy trial in mid-October saw Charnock and Hodgson again being accused of espionage, with some evidence that the charges were genuine this time. 'From the outset of their arrival in Moscow certain members of the British mission, utilising their diplomatic immunity, carried on spy work to collect information as to the Red Army and Fleet and the aviation industry,' a Soviet military tribunal was told. 'The most active collaborator of the head of the British mission in organising spy work was Secretary E. V. Charnock, who recruited spies among the employees of the War Department.' Charnock was being supplied with secret Soviet War Ministry documents by Vladimir and Kirill Prove, the tribunal was told. The two brothers, both sons of a pre-revolutionary millionaire, first met Charnock at the house of an uncle four or five years earlier. They obtained secret Soviet War Ministry documents via another relative, who had worked as a lawyer in the War Ministry, and from two other War Ministry officials. The brothers regularly handed over various secret documents, plans and sketches to Charnock, whom they met apparently innocently in public places. They were paid anything between £5 and £25 for the documents. The court heard that they had told their interrogators they had repeatedly tried to stop working for the British but Charnock had 'fiercely threatened' them, telling Vladimir: 'If you leave us, we shall destroy you; our arm is long.' While this appears to have been a case of the OGPU interrogators gilding the lily for domestic consumption, the rest of the allegations were entirely credible. The two brothers and their lawyer relative were shot while two other War Ministry officials were sentenced to two years' imprisonment.

The timing of the arrests of the Hoyer and Charnock spy rings might have had nothing to do with the ARCOS raid, although this seems unlikely. Whatever the case, British control over the agents was put in jeopardy by the withdrawal of the mission, with the British intelligence officers given little opportunity to implement emergency measures that might allow them to keep their agents in place, as had occurred after the break that followed the Lockhart plot. Charnock said that after the ARCOS raid, 'the mission building in which we lived was surrounded by secret police. Even when we went to town in our motor cars we were followed by mysterious fellows in sidecars. Not a movement that we made, no matter how innocent, escaped their observation.'[15]

The level of intelligence reporting from inside Russia, particularly on chemical and biological warfare, dropped off completely once the Hoyer network was wound up. Much less intelligence now got through. The Politburo and Central Committee minutes had also stopped coming in so regularly as they were in the period 1923–5, almost certainly because the main agent providing them resigned from his official post in 1925. It is impossible to prove beyond a shadow of a doubt that Boris Bazhanov, who was secretary to both Stalin and the Politburo, was a British spy, but there is a great deal of evidence to suggest that, from the very moment he joined the Communist Party in October 1919, he was a British agent in place, attempting to climb as high in the Soviet communist hierarchy as possible, and doing so with spectacular success. In his original memoirs, *Avec Staline dans le Kremlin*, published in Paris in 1930, two years after he fled the Soviet Union, Bazhanov said that once the Bolsheviks took over the Russian empire, fighting communism from outside the system became impossible; 'it had to be undermined from within'. Bazhanov described himself as a 'Trojan horse' infiltrated into 'the communist fortress', using 'a mask of communist ideology' to disguise his real intentions. 'The game was very risky, but I could not allow myself to be deterred by the thought of risk,' he said. 'I had to keep constantly on my guard. I had to watch my every word, every move I made, every step I took.'[16]

Boris Georgievich Bazhanov was born in 1900 in the Ukrainian village of Mogilev-Podolsky. During the period of the Russian Civil

War (1918–21), fighting between the Bolsheviks and the Ukrainian
nationalist forces, led by Simon Vasilievich Petlyura, meant that the area
in which Bazhanov lived changed hands repeatedly. Bazhanov appears
to have been recruited in the summer of 1919. There are three main
candidates for the British intelligence officer who recruited him, all with
particular expertise in the Ukraine. The first is George Hill, who had
been creating a network of agents and saboteurs in the region before he
went to Moscow in 1918 and who spent part of the summer of 1919
in the Ukraine together with Harold Gibson, another MI1c employee.
Gibson himself is the second possibility. He had worked in the Petrograd
office as a secretary but was to become one of the Service's best Russian
agent-runners, a dominant figure among the SIS representatives in
Eastern Europe during the 1920s and 1930s. The third possible candidate
is Wilfred Dunderdale, who although a member of naval intelligence
in 1919, was mounting secret service operations into the Ukraine from
Constantinople. Whoever did recruit Bazhanov, from the point at which
he actually joined the party he behaved like a classic entryist, swiftly
getting himself elected to a succession of party posts. During the period
after he joined the party, power changed hands several times, he recalled.
'The Bolsheviks came, then left again. In the summer of 1920, the town
of Yampol was again in Soviet hands and I was appointed member and
secretary of the town revolutionary committee . . . Mogilev was occupied
a month later. I was transferred there and again elected secretary of the
party district committee.'[17]

Having established a history and base within the party, Bazhanov
moved to Moscow in November 1920 to study engineering at the
Moscow Higher Technical School, the country's leading technical
university. Like all Soviet universities, it had a communist party cell, but
since it was 'basically inactive', Bazhanov recalled, it was 'no bother' for
him to get himself elected party secretary once again. His leadership roles
in various party organisations were to be invaluable to him when, in late
1921, he eventually obtained a job working for the Central Committee,
where he began endearing himself to top party officials. The first official
he targeted was Lazar Kaganovich, a close ally of Stalin. Impressed by

Bazhanov's assistance, Kaganovich promoted him to a post checking the Central Committee minutes and ensuring they made sense. Acting on his own initiative, Bazhanov then redrew the party statutes, deliberately wording them so that they could be misused to assist an unscrupulous politician to gain power. He showed them to Kaganovich, who took them in turn to Vyacheslav Molotov, another prominent Soviet politician and protégé of Stalin. Molotov took Bazhanov and his proposed new statutes to Stalin. 'Stalin looked at me long and hard,' Bazhanov later recalled. 'He understood, as I did, that my statutes represented an important instrument for using the Party apparatus to gain power.'[18]

Stalin put the proposals to Lenin, who agreed they should be discussed by the Politburo, which sent them to be looked at by a commission. It was headed by Molotov, with Bazhanov as its secretary. He was now on good terms with a number of future senior Soviet politicians, including Molotov, Kaganovich and Georgy Malenkov, who briefly headed the Soviet Union after Stalin's death. Molotov and Kaganovich appointed Bazhanov to various posts where he was careful to press their interests, and by extension those of Stalin. Bazhanov had access to reports crossing their desks, including the top secret minutes of the Politburo. At the end of 1922, he became secretary to the Orgburo, the Central Committee's main administrative body, which dealt with all the documents emanating from the various bodies and commissions associated with the Soviet Communist Party Central Committee, including the Politburo. He immediately instigated a complete reorganisation of the files, ensuring that he had access to any document he wanted at any time. Bazhanov's career was at its peak in August 1923, when he was appointed secretary of the Politburo itself, at the same time becoming Stalin's main secretary. Bazhanov later said of this promotion that as 'a soldier of the anti-Bolshevik army, I had imposed upon myself the difficult and perilous task of penetrating right into the heart of the enemy headquarters. I had succeeded.'[19]

Bazhanov already had complete access to all the minutes of Central Committee, Sovnarkom (cabinet) and Politburo meetings, as well as a wealth of reports and data from sub-committees. His new job ensured he was privy to every single top secret report emanating from within the Politburo. 'The Politburo was the principal repository of power in the USSR,' he said. 'It was responsible for all major decisions respecting government of the country, as well as all questions of world revolution. All segments of the government which had matters to submit to the Politburo sent them to me.'[20]

The OGPU was already highly suspicious of Bazhanov and the pressure soon began to tell. Bazhanov made a brief visit to Finland, Sweden and Norway in December 1924, ostensibly to buy skates for the Soviet national ice-skating team, although given subsequent events it may well have been to tell Ernest Boyce that he could no longer continue. The OGPU now went directly to Stalin, telling him that Bazhanov was a 'hidden counter-revolutionary'. Bazhanov managed to persuade the Soviet leader that the accusation was the result of his having won an argument with the head of the OGPU, Genrikh Yagoda, during a committee meeting. Shortly after stepping down from the post of Politburo secretary, Bazhanov managed to get himself sent to Norway as the captain of the Soviet skating team. He arranged for his girlfriend to be sent to Finland at the same time, intending that they should defect together. Yagoda attempted to stop Bazhanov going, without success, but had little difficulty blocking the girlfriend's trip to Finland. If Bazhanov defected now it would have been obvious that his girlfriend was going with him and she would have been in serious trouble, so he had no choice but to return home at the end of his visit to Norway. When Bazhanov subsequently broke off the relationship with the girl, she denounced him to the OGPU. He survived an investigation, but was now under suspicion from Stalin as well as Yagoda and the Soviet leader blocked him from going abroad. Realising any attempt to cross the European borders was now impossible, Bazhanov worked out a plan to get himself appointed to a senior party job in Ashkhabad, the capital of the central Asian republic of Turkmenistan and only 30 miles from the border with Persia, but with Yagoda convinced he was a counter-revolutionary, he had to be tracked at all times by an OGPU minder.[21]

Bazhanov and his minder, Arkady Maksimov, crossed the border into Persia on the pretence of a hunting expedition in the early hours of New Year's Day 1928. Maksimov was unarmed. Bazhanov had the bullets for the hunting rifles, so the OGPU man had little choice but to go with him, since if he stayed he would in all probability be shot for failing to prevent his charge from leaving. Bazhanov deliberately chose to leave on New Year's Day, knowing that the Soviet border guards would all be sleeping off hangovers from the previous night's celebrations. The British seem to have been unaware that he was coming, but Leo Steveni, who had been working as an intelligence reporter for the Indian Army's codebreaking organisation at Simla in the Himalayas, was swiftly sent to the Iranian town of Meshed as British military attaché to make an initial debriefing and ensure he got to Simla, with Lieutenant-Colonel Frederick Isemonger, the head of the Indian police, and therefore Indian Political Intelligence, in North-West Frontier province, sending the Viceroy's train to collect Bazhanov and bring him to his debriefing.

Steveni later said that, as a result of the Meshed mission, he 'acquired an entrée into certain circles specialising in that particular racket', the most prominent of whom was Stewart Menzies, by now a lieutenant-colonel and effectively Hugh Sinclair's deputy. Steveni recalled that Menzies 'never received me in his office, but always made a point of meeting me at one of his clubs. Looking back I was inclined, at that time, to gauge my standing with Menzies by the club he invited me to lunch at, estimating that my stock was at its zenith when the luncheon appointment was fixed at White's, but not quite so high when at the Travellers.'[22]

Once safely in India, Bazhanov was extensively debriefed by Isemonger and Colonel Harry Rowlandson, whose Russian had been honed on secret service across the Caucasus and Central Asia. Bazhanov produced a series of papers on every aspect of the Soviet Union. Given that he knew every detail of the way in which the Soviet Communist Party and the country's government operated and was able to provide intimate details of Stalin's rise to power, together with a breakdown of his strengths and weaknesses, it was no surprise that the material he produced was regarded in London as gold dust. He was then taken not to London, but to Paris where Wilfred Dunderdale was now SIS bureau chief. Bazhanov later said this was his choice, and given the large Russian expatriate community in Paris that is entirely possible, but it is clear that, while he was in Simla, there were months of extensive efforts by SIS to get him to London, which were blocked on the basis that it would be a severe embarrassment to the government of Ramsay MacDonald. The British asked the French to give Bazhanov asylum on the basis that the material he produced would be shared with them. Dunderdale oversaw a further debriefing of Bazhanov, producing an extensive report on the workings of the Politburo and the Soviet secret service. Whether or not Wilfred Dunderdale was involved in Bazhanov's recruitment, this made good sense. Dunderdale spoke perfect Russian. He was gathering material via the Russian expatriate community in Paris and Bazhanov would be ideally placed to assess the sources. He continued to monitor Soviet newspapers, analysing the situation in the Soviet Union for both SIS and its French counterpart, the Section de Renseignements of the Deuxième Bureau.[23]

Both Dunderdale and Valentine Vivian regularly visited him to discuss new material on the Soviet Union, providing a measure of control over fraudulent or inaccurate reporting, a move that paid dividends when he identified a new series of Politburo minutes and official Soviet documents obtained by SIS in Riga as clearly faked. The intelligence was being supplied by the OGPU's resident in the Latvian capital. It is unclear if the move was, as Bazhanov suggested, a purely mercenary attempt to make money or a deliberate Soviet deception operation.[24]

Bazhanov continued providing SIS with reports until at least 1936 when he was contacted as a potential source by the Polish Intelligence Service. Bazhanov told the Poles that he was analysing the Soviet press and compiling reports on military, political and economic matters in the USSR and that he was paid £5 a report by SIS, around £200 at today's prices, which seems to have been the going rate at the time for agent reports. Bazhanov told the Poles that he was providing two Western intelligence services with reports. He complained that his main customer (SIS) was 'too cautious and terribly bureaucratic. Sometimes, they ask very trifling questions, cavil at every word etc.' This fits with the profile of Valentine Vivian, whose training in the Indian police made him careful to check even the smallest point of detail. 'VV was much maligned as a fusspot,' one former SIS officer said. 'But he had the policeman's eye for detail and note-taking that proved extremely useful.' Bazhanov told the Polish intelligence officer that he would very much like to get rid of his role with SIS, although this claim seems more likely to have been a negotiating ploy rather than a real threat to the supply of reports to SIS. Shortly, afterwards, Polish intelligence also began receiving what they described as Bazhanov's 'excellent reports'.[25]

NINETEEN

The Jonny case – 'A very valuable agent'

REMARKABLY, even under the supposedly more efficient Sinclair regime, the Service still had no proper training for new officers on how to recruit and run agents when Leslie Nicholson was appointed SIS bureau chief in Prague in the summer of 1930. Nicholson pinned his hopes of learning how to do the job on a briefing he was to receive from Captain Thomas Kendrick, the SIS representative in Vienna. It was to be a major disappointment.

> Nobody at any stage gave me any tips on how to be a spy, how to make contact with and worm vital information out of unsuspecting experts. I was granted a temporary respite, however, at the end of my communications course. I was not to go straight to Prague and set up shop, but to go instead for two or three weeks' holiday in Vienna. Here I was to meet our man, who was one of the most experienced in the business and he would give me some on-the-spot advice. My mentor was a man of great charm, a keen sense of humour and with an air of middle-aged respectability, which I found reassuring in view of his stories. 'Could you give me some idea of how to begin?' I asked him imploringly. 'Are there any standard rules? Or could you give me any practical hints?' He thought for a bit. 'I don't think there are really, you'll just have to work it out for yourself. I think everyone has his own methods and I can't think of anything I could tell you.'

In reality, Nicholson later insisted, an SIS representative abroad was 'a very normal, frustrated, hard-working, ordinary person, most of the time. He is hedged about by the rules and regulations, bombarded with boring questions, interminable reports and assessments of his own reports. Officially, he must lead a normal and discreet kind of life; he has to keep up a suitable front job and that means doing the job in addition to the intelligence work. The biggest headache of my years in the Service was the necessity of accounting for every single penny and trying to justify the expenses we had to render monthly. The whole system was ruled over by a retired naval paymaster known to everyone in the Service as "Pay". He treated public money as if it were his own and seemed almost to begrudge every penny we spent. We all complained about him bitterly and an outsider might logically have assumed that he was indeed an ill-tempered, tight-fisted old miser, but this was hardly the case. I lunched with him when I was in London and these occasions were always most enjoyable. If our accounts were rather a trial, the fault was certainly ours, though Pay was a stickler for detail which, in some cases, we would have preferred to gloss over.'

Nicholson said Percy Sykes rarely left his London office and as a result 'had the most exaggerated picture of the sort of life we led'. This was not helped by a visit to Prague during which Nicholson took Sykes to dinner and on to a couple of nightclubs, where he proved to have 'expensive tastes' that belied his fastidious accounting. 'He was a gay old dog and liked to "put up his eye-glass at the girls",' Nicholson recalled. They ended the night in a small nightclub with an 'intimate cabaret' designed to make full use of the Sykes eye-glass.

The main act was provided by pretty Hungarian twins who, in unison, performed a rather sexy striptease. Pay's monocle rose and fell with regularity as his eyebrows lifted in approval or astonishment. After the performance, the girls came along to drink in the bar and went from table to table, drinking freely of champagne or anything that happened to be available. After some time, the alcohol began to excite their Hungarian temperaments and to liven things up they started throwing empty glasses at the walls after downing the drinks. Soon most of the customers were under the tables with glass splinters flying everywhere. Pay and I were sitting on the carpet with our table held up in front like a shield and he was enjoying himself enormously. 'By gum,' he kept turning to me and shouting above the racket. 'You fellows certainly see life.' Pay duly moved on to his next port of call with profuse thanks to me for making his stay so enjoyable. I couldn't help thinking that I had done very little to disillusion him about the way outside agents carried on en poste.[1]

Despite the Treasury cutbacks, Hugh Sinclair attempted to improve coverage by expanding into the Caucasus, Iran and central Asia, an area that, despite George Goldsmith's 1918 mission, was traditionally covered by Indian Political Intelligence. During the late 1920s, the loss of the Soviet intercepts and the agents inside Russia drastically cut the amount of material the British were getting on Moscow's intentions. Pressure mounted on SIS from British forces based in Baghdad and concerned at the lack of intelligence they had on Soviet activity in the region. The senior air officer in Iraq, Air Vice-Marshal Edward Ellington, warned in June 1927 that 'our intelligence preparations need strengthening now against Bolshevik activities both in north-western and south-western Persia'; he also wanted better intelligence on Palestine, Egypt, Syria, the Hejaz and Aden, an area that MI1c had covered from Egypt since the First World War. The Air Ministry replied that SIS was being asked to expand its operations into Baku, the capital of Azerbaijan, and the Persian regions of Tabriz and Khuzestan, an area that would be covered by an alliance with the Anglo-Persian Oil Company (APOC).

'It is quite realised that information regarding Soviet schemes and plans, whether emanating from Moscow or Baku, is at the present time very meagre,' one senior RAF officer told Ellington. 'SIS are doing their utmost to better this information and are now attempting to spread their influence eastward from the Black Sea so that in due time they will cover both Tiflis [Tbilisi] and Baku.' Valentine Vivian was sent on a tour of the Middle-East to devise a plan to set up new bureaux across the region. The network he proposed would be based on Cairo, where there was already an SIS bureau, with sub-bureaux at Bushehr in Iran, Jeddah in Saudi Arabia and Port Sudan, in north-east Sudan. He estimated that it would cost around £3,500 a year to run but there were no funds and so alternative plans were made. SIS developed an exchange relationship with APOC under which the oil company's officials in Persia provided intelligence on what was happening locally, both on their own initiative and in response to specific requests from SIS in London, while they in turn would be fed information relating to the oil markets. The liaison in London was between Vivian and Colonel Henry Medlicott, a senior APOC executive. 'Since the government hold 80 per cent of the Anglo-Persian shares, it was arranged that Colonel Medlicott should be placed in direct touch with SIS, in order that such information as might become available from time to time from government sources, and which might affect the position of the Anglo-Persian Oil Co., might be unofficially transmitted,' noted one senior British intelligence official. This reciprocal information-sharing process with British companies was to become a common method of obtaining intelligence in places like the Soviet Union. Strapped for cash, SIS attempted to reinforce this ad hoc intelligence collection by persuading the RAF to base an officer in Basra who would run agents for both SIS and the military. But the problems inherent in operating in countries like Persia, where it was relatively easy to corrupt officials, became apparent when Georgy Agabekov, a senior OGPU officer working in the Middle-East defected to France. Agabekov, who defected after falling in love with his English teacher in Constantinople, revealed that the Russians were intercepting the intelligence reports sent back to London both by the Anglo-Persian officials in south-west Persia and by Leo Steveni in Meshed.[2]

SIS was not just searching for intelligence on Soviet activity abroad. Throughout the 1920s and into the early 1930s – with MI5 hampered by the rules confining its role to armed forces security and Special Branch operations seen as inadequate – the Service took the lead role in hunting down Soviet agents in the UK, recruiting its own sources and co-operating closely with a small Metropolitan Police radio intercept operation run by Harold Kenworthy, a Marconi employee on indefinite loan to the police. It operated out of the attic at Scotland Yard, employing a number of ex-naval telegraphists to intercept illicit radio stations, and first worked alongside SIS and its agent runners during the 1926 General Strike, in what turned out to be a somewhat embarrassing operation.

GC&CS had deciphered Soviet diplomatic messages showing that Moscow was encouraging industrial unrest in the UK, subsidising striking miners to the tune of £2 million, so the Metropolitan Police operators were on the lookout for any illicit Comintern radio messages. When an unusual radio link, using apparently false callsigns, was found to be operating somewhere in London, there were inevitable suspicions of Soviet subversives. Sinclair called in the GC&CS radio expert Leslie Lambert, better known as the BBC 'wireless personality' A. J. Alan, and together he and Kenworthy constructed a miniature direction-finding device small enough to fit into a Gladstone bag to track down the radio transmitter.

'The portable set was put to good use,' Kenworthy recalled. 'Influence by Assistant Commissioner and SIS made it possible to get access to roofs of buildings in the vicinity of the suspected source of signal which had been roughly located by taking a completely empty van and sitting on the floor with the Gladstone bag. It was gratifying that the work put in was finally rewarded by actually "walking in" from the roof tops into the top of a building housing the transmitter whilst the operator was using it. The result was an anti-climax as the transmitter had been set up by the *Daily Mail*, who thinking that Post and Telegraph personnel would be joining the strike at any moment decided to try and be ready for a "coup". The call sign AHA was derived from [the newspaper's proprietor] Alfred Harmsworth. As a matter of high policy nothing was ever published about this exploit.'[3]

Desmond Morton recruited a number of agents to hunt down Bolshevik spies and saboteurs, linking up with a private right-wing intelligence agency financed by the Federation of British Industries to gather information on left-wing subversives and employing a number of 'casual' agents himself. His operations inside the UK were backed by Sinclair, who told the Secret Service Committee that it was 'impossible to draw the line between espionage and counter-espionage' operations since both related to the intelligence activities of foreign states which SIS was mandated to monitor. The most notable of these casual agents was

Maxwell Knight, the former director of intelligence at the British *Fascisti*, who had set up his own network of intelligence agents and had links to Vernon Kell. An eccentric man with a passion for natural history, Knight would later present a BBC radio programme for children as 'Uncle Max', but his fame within the intelligence services was based on a willingness to wait years for the 'sleeper' agents he placed inside the Communist Party to gain positions of influence. 'The secret of his success was his uncanny ability at getting on with people,' one former intelligence officer said. 'He could persuade them to do things they didn't want to do, which is the secret of being a good agent runner.'[4]

By 1929, Morton was clearly concerned that Kell might persuade Knight to work for MI5 and persuaded Sinclair to take him on the SIS books to hunt down communists and subversives linked to the Comintern and Moscow. But the Service's UK operations soon became untenable and SIS became embroiled in a major row with Special Branch over Morton's operations inside the UK. In the early summer of 1931, the Secret Service Committee was forced to intervene, transferring Knight and Morton's other 'casuals' to MI5 and restoring the latter's right to control all UK-based counter-espionage and counter-subversive operations. Henceforward, the responsibilities of SIS and MI5 reverted to the pre-First World War divisions as originally defined by Kell and Cumming, with SIS only operating abroad and MI5 responsible for security in the UK and the colonies. Although, SIS continued to intercept the diplomatic mail of embassies based in London and in the mid-1930s set up Section X to intercept their telephone communications.[5]

By now the system of identifying agents had changed from the original use of letters, indicating the bureaux which controlled them, to an only slightly more covert format under which every headquarters section and foreign bureau was allocated a digraph identifier and every officer and agent was given a five-figure number beginning with the digraph of the section or bureau to which they worked. So for example, Harold Gibson was bureau chief in the Latvian capital, Riga, in the early 1930s, when the system was first introduced. The Riga bureau chief's designator under the old system was FR, or FR/0. Under the new system, Latvia was allocated the digraph designator of 31, while Gibson's personal designator became 31000. Agent designators were similar with the first two figures identifying the bureau running the agent and the last three figures the agent, eg, Victor Bogomoletz, a Russian who ran intelligence operations into the Soviet Union for Gibson, was agent 31109. The system was also used for reference numbers on CX reports, with the first two digits indicating the target country and the third digit indicating the subject area, using the number of the section interested in that area. So a five-digit CX serial beginning 314 was a report about Latvia covering a military topic and therefore interesting Section IV, the military section, with the last two digits as a running serial.

Bogomoletz was a former Tsarist officer who was both anti-Bolshevik and pro-British, but whose primary motivation for working for SIS was money. He ran some very valuable agents inside Russia. Bogomoletz had been recruited by Gibson when the latter was based in Constantinople and as a result under the previous agent designation system was known as HV109, with HV being the bureau designator for Constantinople, hence the direct transfer to agent 31109. When Gibson moved to Bucharest in December 1922, where he operated under journalistic cover as a local correspondent for the *Daily Telegraph*, Bogomoletz went with him – where high-value agents developed a personal relationship with their controllers, they tended to work to the same officer throughout their tenure, a practice that continues to this day. Gibson and Bogomoletz ran a number of agents across the newly created Soviet Union, including one in the Sevastopol naval base, with other agents inside the Red Army in the Ukraine and Siberia.

Possibly because he was believed to have been compromised by the time they moved to Riga, Bogomoletz did not attempt to run operations into the Soviet Union across the Latvian border. Instead, using an early agreement with Polish intelligence, a precursor to what would become an exceptionally close relationship during the Second World War, Bogomoletz inserted his agents via Poland. Although there were a number of trusted Russian émigrés working for SIS – either on the staff like Bogomoletz, Pyotr Sokolov and Nikolai Bunakov, or on a more occasional basis as with Boris Bazhanov in Paris – the Service was extremely wary of Russian émigré sources, largely as a result of the activities of the Trust and the Sidney Reilly affair. They were regarded as 'consciously or unconsciously, the channel both for true information and misinformation or disinformation,' one SIS officer said in the early 1930s. 'We treat practically all reports from White Russian circles in the same way, namely, on the assumption that they are partly, or wholly, inspired by the GPU and we leave them severely alone.'[6]

The Treasury cuts had reduced the number of passport control offices to just nineteen across Europe at the beginning of 1931, and while these still included the important bureaux covering Germany and the Soviet Union, they left whole swathes of the world to be covered by other means.[7] SIS bolstered its overseas operations by persuading the employees of a number of companies working abroad to use this 'natural cover' to mount espionage operations. It developed good relationships with a number of British firms, such as Vickers, Shell, British American Tobacco, the Hudson's Bay Company and APOC, under which the companies' employees would be encouraged to collect intelligence. As part of these exchange relationships, the companies themselves would be kept up to date on the activities of rivals or local situations. The Service relied more heavily on Vickers for assistance than on any other company, with its representatives around the world offering an extension to the coverage provided by the SIS bureaux, particularly in areas where the Treasury cuts limited the Service presence, such as Latin America and Africa. Even in Europe, Eddie Boxshall, the SIS man in Romania, funded his official work through his 'natural cover' as the local Vickers representative.

Romania became an important bureau following the loss of the networks in Russia, with the British setting up a liaison arrangement with Romanian intelligence under which the two agencies ran joint operations into Russia, thereby disguising the British involvement.[8] The loss of the networks in Russia and the frailty of the intermittent diplomatic presence there meant that although by 1932 there was briefly a passport control officer based in Moscow, the Service's operations inside Russia now depended heavily on Britons working there under the 'natural cover' of jobs in ordinary businesses such as the forestry industry and engineering. The Metropolitan-Vickers Electrical Company, which provided equipment and maintenance for a number of Soviet power stations and was part owned by Vickers, was an obvious vehicle for such 'natural cover' operations. The staff included a number of former officers who had served in Murmansk, most notably the UK-based managing director, Charles Richards, who as an intelligence officer had taken part in Cudbert Thornhill's raid on Onega.

Richards was tasked to gather intelligence via Allan Monkhouse, the company's Russian manager, and some of his staff, who paid the locally employed Russian staff extra to collect information, but by the beginning of 1933 the operation had over-reached itself. An investigation ordered because Stalinist officials believed the company was deliberately making equipment go wrong to boost its profits uncovered the intelligence-gathering operations and six of the Metropolitan-Vickers British staff plus a dozen of its Russian employees were arrested and charged with espionage and sabotage. While there was no evidence at all to back up the sabotage charges, during the investigation at least one British manager appears to have told an OGPU informant that in the event of war the company would destroy its plant. More to the point, the Russians admitted receiving money for gathering intelligence.

The Metropolitan-Vickers court case, following as it did on a series of Stalinist show trials which ended in the innocent victims being shot, attracted mass interest around the world. The courtroom was packed with hundreds of news reporters and photographers, including a young Reuters reporter, Ian Fleming, who would subsequently make the father of his espionage hero, James Bond, an employee of Vickers who spied for SIS. As with the Bond books, the main female character was a beautiful young Russian blonde, Anna Sergeevna Kutuzova, who told the court that she overheard Richards giving Monkhouse and another employee, Leslie Thornton, both of whom also worked as army interpreters during the British intervention, instructions on what information to collect.

Given the OGPU's propensity for extracting evidence for the show trials that bore no resemblance to the truth, the world's press understandably looked on the case with a jaundiced eye, accepting the absolute insistence by John Simon, the British Foreign Secretary, that while Richards had worked in intelligence in Russia in 1918–19 it was never a matter of 'secret service' and he had not been in contact with any British intelligence official for fourteen years. The OGPU predictably persuaded all of the arrested Russians to admit to accepting money for intelligence ranging from the state of other Soviet factories, rail movements of troops and munitions, the quality of shells produced in a factory close to one of the company's power stations in the Urals and the quality of the metal used in constructing Soviet aircraft, but none of the watching news media believed it.

In fact, like the Special Branch investigators who raided the offices of ARCOS six years earlier, the OGPU had stumbled across what for them must have been a novelty, a genuine case of espionage, but had failed to find the documentary evidence, which was written down in Thornton's diaries. These had been sent back to the UK at the end of 1932, when it first became apparent that the company was under investigation. Thornton and another of the British employees admitted collecting information, although they argued that they did not see this as intelligence-gathering, and both Thornton and Monkhouse struggled to explain several large sums of money paid to some of the Russian employees, which began as loans and ultimately became gifts, including in one case the money for a new apartment paid in sterling rather than roubles, which Thornton openly admitted having handed over, an admission which failed to appear in the British press.[9]

The Russians did not get the absolute confirmation of the British use of Metropolitan-Vickers to gather intelligence they were seeking until the end of the Second World War when Kim Philby, the so-called Third Man and a Soviet agent-in-place inside SIS, sent them an internal memorandum examining ways of developing 'natural cover' operations inside the Soviet Union. The memo, entitled 'Penetrating Russia', noted that 'natural cover has served us well in Russia in the past – indeed, right up to the Metropolitan-Vickers affair, which was due entirely to our own carelessness'.[10]

The Service was not left completely without sources in the Soviet Union. Harold Gibson was using Bogomoletz to run an old schoolfriend from Russia, a Communist Party member disillusioned with the Soviet system, who provided extremely high-grade reports during the 1930s. But the identity of 'Gibbie's spy' was passed to Moscow by the Soviet spy Anthony Blunt when he joined MI5 in 1940.

One of the Service's best agents was a member of a secret Soviet military intelligence unit attached to the Comintern. Johann Heinrich de Graaf, or 'Jonny X', was a walk-in, a Soviet agent who volunteered his services to Frank Foley, the Berlin bureau chief, in June 1933. Born in Germany in 1894, de Graaf was one of the socialist leaders of a mutiny on board the German battleship *Westfalen* in 1917. He subsequently joined the German Communist Party and in 1930 was recruited to be part of a special section of Soviet military intelligence, then known as the Fourth Department of the Soviet General Staff. The section worked with the Comintern, ensuring Communist Party activists in other countries around the world followed the party line and teaching them how to bring about world revolution. De Graaf was sent to the Frunze Military Academy in Moscow.[11]

After graduating, in April 1931, he was sent first to Romania and then, four months later, to the UK, where the Communist Party of Great Britain was under pressure from Moscow over its failure to capitalise on the rising unemployment and hunger marches. De Graaf entered the UK using the cover of Ludwig Dinkelmeyer, a Hamburg wine merchant. He worked with George Aitken, the British Communist Party official responsible for communist infiltration of the UK armed forces, to subvert British sailors and troops. De Graaf was present in the UK during the Invergordon mutiny of September 1931, when sailors of the Atlantic Fleet went on strike after learning on arrival at the naval base at Invergordon in Scotland that their pay was to be cut by 10 per cent. Nevertheless, he returned from the UK highly critical of the work of the British Communist Party and the issue was raised in an angry debate between de Graaf and Harry Pollitt, the British communist leader, at a Comintern meeting in Moscow in 1932. By now, de Graaf was disillusioned with the Soviet communist system and while on his way back to Moscow, he had approached the US vice-consul in Cologne asking for political asylum, but had been rebuffed. Following his criticism of Pollitt, he was sent back to Britain in 1932 to sort out the party's propaganda efforts and push for further reform.[12]

Prior to the Nazi crackdown on communists, Soviet agents sent into the West, and many going to other points around the world, travelled first to Berlin, where the Comintern's secretive International Liaison Department (OMS), which administered Comintern underground operations around the world, providing the agents with their new 'legend', or cover, and supplying supporting documents, including passports. They similarly returned to Moscow from their assignments via Berlin, exchanging their fake documents for their originals. De Graaf returned from his mission to England via Berlin, where he approached the US embassy and, having again been rebuffed by the Americans, then went to the British. He met Frank Foley, who because of the Comintern activity in Berlin was already regarded within the Service as something of an expert on Soviet operations in the West, and offered him detailed information on communist activity inside the British armed forces and the UK generally. De Graaf demanded a one-off payment of 2,000 Reichsmarks (around £7,200 at today's prices) plus a monthly retainer of 500 Reichsmarks. Under standard SIS procedure, Foley should have contacted Head Office and asked for directions as to how to handle de Graaf, but instead he bided his time, debriefing the new agent carefully and checking him out with the old German socialists who were still on the Service's books from the First World War attempts to provoke mutinies and strikes inside Germany. Satisfied de Graaf was genuine, Foley persuaded him to stay in place inside the system and work for the British, rather than seeking asylum immediately. Foley gave de Graaf the codename 'Jonny X', which would invariably be shortened to Jonny. Once de Graaf had agreed to act as a British agent-in-place, Foley sent a coded telegram to London, in which he said: 'Am in touch with Johann, who is Comintern and can supply full breakdown of British and other communist parties... Consider this most important contact I have yet made and convinced genuineness. May I continue negotiations?' The message caused consternation at Broadway, with urgent discussions between Sinclair and Valentine Vivian leading to the latter being sent to Germany to investigate. 'Head Office sent Vivian to Berlin immediately to find out what was going on,' a former SIS officer said. 'Jonny had visited the UK in 1931 and 1932 and there was a lot of excitement about it all because of this.' Vivian confirmed Jonny's value to the Service and retrospectively backed Foley's unilateral action. The Berlin bureau chief then debriefed Jonny extensively, sending back a series of reports on various aspects of Soviet underground operations, which formed the basis for two comprehensive handbooks on communism produced by Vivian. The first report was twenty-eight page account of 'Communist Disintegration Work Within HM Forces'. Jonny's ability to detail the organisation, structure and leadership of the Communist Party of Great Britain was regarded as particularly valuable, a former senior SIS officer said, adding: 'Details were passed to MI5 who took executive action on the basis of information supplied by Foley.'[13]

Later that year, the Comintern sent Jonny to China. Despite its lack of resources, SIS had a number of officers based in the Far East, with Godfrey Denham, ostensibly Deputy Director, Central Intelligence of the Indian Police in Shanghai, but also acting as its first chief representative there and warning that Bolshevism was spreading in China and was 'a very real danger to the British Empire in Asia'. Cumming gave Denham 'a mandate to be in charge of all our work in Japan, China, Tibet and Siberia and southern Asia'. Denham was replaced in 1923 by two consular officers, Harry Steptoe in Peking and Arthur Blackburn, in Shanghai. But by the end of 1928, Steptoe had moved to Shanghai to take sole control of SIS operations in China with no actual consular duties, although his cover remained the post of vice-consul. He was assisted during the early 1930s by another consular official, George Kitson, and by Frank Hill, the new SIS man in Peking. Steptoe was not highly respected among the British administrators in China, with Sir Frederick Dreyer, the British commander-in-chief, describing him as being 'in the habit of talking too much. He is anxious to impress everyone in the Far East with his importance; in fact he behaves in a manner which I should imagine was the exact opposite from that which one would wish secret service agents to adopt.'

Moscow had made concerted efforts to turn China into a communist state, but had suffered setbacks, first in April 1927, when the Chinese authorities raided Soviet offices, seizing large numbers of incriminating documents which detailed Soviet operations in China. The raid appears to have been carried out in tandem with the British. Certainly, Steptoe led the investigation into the documents. It sparked the attempted defection to the British of Yevgeny Kozhevnikov, a Soviet agent operating under the name of Eugene Pik. He demanded a substantial sum of money. Captain Jack Shelley, an officer on the Shanghai Defence Force who liaised with SIS and MI5, telegraphed London saying that the Russians already knew he was trying to defect and that he could not therefore be used as an agent in place. 'His value as an agent to be employed by us is nil,' Shelley said. 'He would be useful for identifying Soviet agents and Communists arriving in Shanghai or elsewhere in China but his price is high and we have not the money to pay him.' Unable to get any money from the British for his revelations, Kozhevnikov/Pik defected to the Nationalist Chinese, and the British obtained the intelligence he provided anyway. He also began writing for the *North China Daily News*, revealing that the operations in China were carried out by a military arm of the OGPU known only as 'OO' – tantalisingly reminiscent of the James Bond 'Double-0' designator – and that they had now relocated from Peking to Hankow. Given the former Soviet agent's willingness to talk to all and sundry about his former occupation, Shelley noted acerbically: 'I shall be surprised if Pik dies a natural death.'

The second blow for the Russians came in June 1931, when as a result of information obtained by an SIS representative, who appears to have been Foley, the Chinese authorities in Shanghai, aided by the British, arrested Hilaire Noulens, the head of the Far Eastern Bureau of the Comintern and seized the bureau's secret archives. Although the documents were enciphered, the British were soon able to break the cipher and read details of how the Soviet agents operated abroad. A substantial report by Vivian on the results of the investigation into the documents suggests that

Foley already had an agent inside the OMS in Berlin, providing details of Comintern attempts to set up communist movements across the Far East.[14]

The documents seized following Noulens's arrest provided a groundbreaking picture of Soviet attempts to spread communism and subvert the West. Once deciphered, they gave a complete picture of the scale, methods and aims of communist activity in China, Japan, Formosa, Korea, Malaya and the Philippines, Vivian said.

> It is to be noted that the Noulens papers afford a unique opportunity of seeing from the inside, and an unimpeachable documentary evidence, the working of a highly developed Communist organisation of the 'illegal' order, covering a considerable geographical area, one, moreover, which, according to later evidence, is still in operation in spite of the set-back administered by the arrests and seizure of archives.

The papers included the Far Eastern Bureau's accounts, allowing Vivian to 'follow the money' to track the organisation and its cover operations. This led to SIS being able to compile a complete breakdown of the organisation and the leading members of the Chinese Communist Party. The documents also showed 'the conscious exercise of control by the Comintern over events in a foreign country' with the intention of turning it into a Soviet satellite and demonstrated beyond any question that the Comintern was 'actively concerned with the development of every phase of communist activity and with the organisation of labour unrest, in China, Japan, and her dependencies, Indo–China, Malaya and the Philippine Islands.'[15]

Jonny's mission to Shanghai, under cover as a soya bean merchant, promised further timely detail of an organisation that had managed to rebuild itself to good effect. The city, the world's fifth largest, included international settlements controlled by the British, French, American and Japanese. It was China's most industrialised city and was famous for its scandalous nightlife dominated by White Russian women who, having fled the Bolsheviks, had settled in the French quarter of the city, turning Frenchtown, as it was known locally, into the city's red-light district. Shanghai was also the centre for communist attempts to take over the country. The Chinese Communist Party had gone underground in the face of 'elimination campaigns' waged against it by the Nationalist leader, Chiang Kai-Shek. Communist rebels, led most notably by Mao Zedong, were out in the provinces fighting against the Nationalist troops, but the party's underground headquarters was in Shanghai. The Comintern had a very strong presence there, based around the offices of *Shanghai Life*, a Bolshevik newspaper, and the Russian Co-operative Society, Tsentrosoyuz.

'The offices of *Shanghai Life* act as a meeting place and a cover for the disaffected residents of Shanghai and the various agents that visit the place,' said one British intelligence report. Grigory Semeshko, who was rumoured to be 'a former Orthodox priest dismissed for drunkenness', was seen as the most important Comintern agent in Shanghai. He and other 'leading spirits in *Shanghai Life* are regularly visited by Bolshevik agents from Vladivostok and Peking'. Many of the Comintern's more famous members were in Shanghai at various times in the early 1930s, including Richard Sorge, the prominent American communist Agnes Smedley and Arthur Ewert, a leading member of the German Communist Party. Soviet military intelligence officers like Jonny and Sorge were sent into Shanghai to advise the communist rebels both in political subversion and military tactics.[16]

Initially, Jonny was to make a brief reconnaissance trip to China. Arriving in Mukden (now Shenyang), in northern China, after a journey across Siberia, he sent a postcard to Foley, with the coded message: 'On my way home, J.' Jonny then made his way to Shanghai, where he made initial contact with Kitson and, a few weeks later, he was back in Moscow. He returned to Shanghai via Berlin and Paris, where he arranged to meet Foley. Back in China, Jonny operated under the *nom de guerre* of Comrade Chung, instructing Chinese Communist guerrillas in how to produce bombs and carry out sabotage and terrorist operations. His main role was to assist Ewert in these instructions, but they did not get on and were recalled to Moscow in the spring of 1934 after a series of arrests among the Chinese Communist activists. Jonny explained the arrests away by blaming Ewert, who, he said, had been reckless, meeting openly with the widow of the Chinese Communist leader Sun Yat-

Sen, who was under police surveillance. Ewert had also engaged in a
damaging row with Manfred Stern, the senior military adviser, during
which Ewert drew his revolver in order to persuade the commander
to hand over some documents. The arrests resulted from a break-in at
Ewert's safe house when a large amount of money was stolen from a desk
in which Ewert also kept the addresses of his Chinese co-conspirators,
who were arrested shortly afterwards, Jonny said. The arrests brought a
temporary end to the Comintern's presence in Shanghai.[17]

Harry Steptoe, still SIS chief representative in China, was clearly
speaking with the experience learned during this period when he
subsequently advised the British police commissioner in Shanghai on
how to counter Comintern activity.

> I would point out that the members of the Comintern are all highly
> trained and hand-picked men, sent out on their various missions only
> after intensive training. Their number is not legion; the Comintern
> is concerned with guarding their identity and their functions. If
> their identity can be discovered, personal descriptions obtained (and
> photographs where possible), their value to the Comintern is lessened, in
> fact it may become nil. If their functions on the spot can be ascertained,
> then knowledge of their method of work becomes available, the
> ramifications of the apparatus known, and the chances of being able
> adequately to provide for internal security are enormously increased.[18]

Jonny's next major mission was to South America. The Soviet leaders
decided in the early 1930s that the experience gained in China could be
transferred to Brazil. Moscow believed it could stage a military uprising
there which would create a Soviet satellite state inside Latin America.
The establishment of a Soviet-style regime in Brazil would disrupt Anglo-
American influence in South America and act as the catalyst for further
revolutions that could see communism sweep from South and Central
America into the US and Canada. Jonny's role in aborting the communist
coup in Brazil was probably his greatest success. Brazil was chosen not
just because it was the largest country in South America but because it

had a recent history of turmoil and a relationship between landowners and peasants that in many ways appeared to mirror that of China, where, despite the setbacks suffered by the Comintern, there was increasing support for the communist cause. Best of all, the Comintern controlled a Brazilian leader around whom the discontented masses would rally.

Luis Carlos Prestes, the so-called Knight of Hope, had become a national hero in Brazil after the abortive Lieutenants' Uprising of 1924. When the revolution failed, he led a ragged band of little more than a thousand rebels on a 15,000-mile march across the country's impoverished heartland. A few years later, the US government approached him, offering him the Brazilian presidency if he would back a coup aimed at installing a government more favourably disposed to the Americans, but Prestes, who was already secretly in contact with Moscow, declined the US offer. He went instead to Russia, where he was carefully groomed to lead a new Communist-backed revolution in Brazil. His presence in Moscow was kept completely secret, Jonny said. 'He studied intensively both military affairs and politics and became a committed member of the Communist Party.'[19]

In late 1934, a number of Comintern agents were infiltrated into Brazil. They included Jonny, whose ostensible role was the team's explosives expert and guerrilla tactician, but whose real role was to watch Ewert, who was organising the coup although under suspicion following the China failure. Ewert was travelling on an American passport in the name of Harry Berger. Jonny's cover was as Franz Paul Gruber, an Austrian businessman. The Comintern's International Liaison Department (OMS) had moved initially to Copenhagen after the Nazis came to power. So Jonny had to go there from Moscow to pick up the Gruber travel documents and arranged to meet Foley in the Danish capital to brief him on the intended Communist coup and his own intended role. After Jonny's explanation, Foley went to the British passport control office and sent an enciphered telegram to London to get Valentine Vivian's views and then met Jonny again to explain that he must destroy the coup from within. Jonny arrived in Brazil, accompanied by his mistress Lena Krüger, who was to act as the group's secretary and as driver for Prestes.

Jonny was run from London by Vivian, who went out to Brazil to set up arrangements. He went to Jonny's lodgings and rang the doorbell. 'A Negro servant opened the door, screamed and shut it in my face,' Vivian reported. He rang the bell again but having received no response he went round the side of the house and climbed through an open window. 'As I scrambled in and fell down the other side, an enormous arm protuded from a curtain levelling a .500 automatic Colt [revolver] at me.' Fortunately, the 'enormous arm' belonged to Jonny. Vivian also set up a link for Jonny with the SIS representative in Brazil, Alfred Hutt, who worked under 'natural cover' as a senior executive of the local electricity company.

The Comintern team set about creating an opposition force for Prestes to lead, carefully concealing the fact that it was actually a communist front. The Aliança Nacional Libertadora (ANL) was a coalition grouping of socialists, liberals and communists designed to shape the platform for the triumphant return of the 'Knight of Hope' to Brazil. In fact, Prestes had already been secretly brought back to Rio de Janeiro and was living in a safe house on Rua Barão da Torre. Under the Comintern plan, ANL supporters inside the Brazilian armed forces would seize power in the north of the country on a popular mandate. Once the northern provinces were secured, the revolution would move to the capital. The ANL, with Prestes at its head, was to remain in government until the situation had stabilised, Jonny told Foley. The Comintern team would then remove all non-Communists from power, completely get rid of the socialists and liberals in the ANL, and impose a Soviet-style regime with Prestes as party leader and head of state.

Next would come the Sovietisation and complete appropriation of the property of the landowners and bourgeoisie, then the distribution of land among the population. Once the northern provinces had been made Soviet, there would be a breathing space to allow communist influence to spread over the remainder of Brazil and the other states of south America. The process of Sovietisation would continue until it covered the whole of Brazil.

The Comintern propaganda experts skilfully manipulated the media to portray Prestes as a liberator waiting for the right moment to return to rescue his countrymen. His letters from 'abroad' were read out at alliance meetings to rapturous applause and the movement grew rapidly. The British tipped the Brazilian government off in early 1935. A few months later, clashes between ANL supporters and fascists gave the Brazilians the excuse they needed to ban the alliance and force it underground. The Americans were also brought into the picture, agreeing to fund Jonny's disruption of the Comintern operation to the tune of $40,000. As the military expert on the team, Jonny was well placed to ensure that the carefully planned revolution failed. His main tasks for Moscow were to spread subversion among the junior army officers who would ostensibly lead the revolution and to train the local Communist activists in revolution. 'It was my job to organise the army for revolution and train party members accordingly,' Jonny said. 'Through careful planning, I worked it so that half the army was in favour and half opposed.' He succeeded in working those in favour of the coup up to such a pitch that they started the revolution ahead of orders, successfully taking over garrisons in the key northern cities of Natal and Recife, thereby ensuring that Jonny would look as if he had done his job. Prestes and Ewert brought forward the parallel revolution in Rio de Janeiro, but with Jonny having ensured that a majority of army officers in the capital were ANL opponents, and Hutt ensuring power to the barracks was cut off at precisely the right time, it soon failed. Officer cadets infiltrated into the army by the alliance took over an infantry barracks in the fashionable suburb of Orca, at the foot of the Sugar Loaf Mountain. The local population collected on the mountain to watch as troops loyal to President Getúlio Vargas assembled on the Copacabana beach before bombarding the barracks with artillery fire and retaking it with ease. More than a hundred people were reported killed and several thousand were taken into custody.

Prestes, Jonny, Krüger and Ewert were all arrested, along with a number of other members of the group, while the remainder fled abroad. The safe in Prestes's house, which contained all the documents detailing the Comintern plans, should have been protected. As the team's explosives expert, Jonny was supposed to have rigged it up with a booby trap so that anyone attempting to open it without the combination would have been killed and all the secret documents destroyed. However, although Jonny constructed what the Rio de Janeiro police later described as an 'infernal machine' inside the safe, he ensured that the impressive combination of TNT and dynamite would not blow up if the safe was opened. This allowed the police to recover documents, letters, maps and notes incriminating hundreds of people involved in the planned coup. In fact, they already had most of the names of the ANL contacts. Krüger, working under the covername of Erna Gruber, had made herself invaluable, not just to Prestes in particular, but to other members of the group and their Brazilian co-conspirators, who knew her as *Alemãezinha*, the German girl. She knew the names and addresses of virtually all the Communist activists and sympathisers, both in the political organisations and in the Brazilian armed forces.[20] Hutt intervened behind the scenes to get Jonny and Krüger released and they were subsequently sent by an unsuspecting Comintern official to Buenos Aires on another mission, to train Communist rebels in the use of explosives and guerrilla tactics. Jonny used the visit to uncover the complete organisation and leadership of the Argentinian Communist Party, passing the details on to the British, who in turn handed them to the authorities in Buenos Aires.

Following the collapse of the Brazilian revolution, the entire mission was the subject of an intensive investigation in Moscow under a senior official, Stella Blagoeva, a close associate of Dmitry Manuilsky, Stalin's man on the Comintern Executive Committee. In an atmosphere of mutual denunciation, Jonny found himself being blamed in Moscow, accused not of being a British agent, but of being in the pay of the anti-Bolshevik White Russians. There were clear grounds for suspicion. He had after all, like Ewert, been involved in both the Chinese and Brazilian arrests and, unlike Ewert, he had managed to escape Brazil and was living with Krüger in Buenos Aires.

There was also something very strange about his wife's sudden emergence. Neither the Comintern nor the Soviet Communist Party had any record of Krüger; indeed no-one seemed to know who she was.

On 22 November 1936, Manuilsky himself sent a telegram to Jonny, recalling him to Moscow immediately. The OMS had now relocated to Paris. Jonny and his wife were to go there first to hand over their fake documents and then go from there to Moscow. Jonny returned alone, meeting Valentine Vivian and Foley in Paris for a debriefing and to discuss what he should do. They both tried, without success, to persuade him not to go to Moscow. It seemed certain to end in his execution, but Jonny was confident he could see it through. He arrived in Moscow on 5 March 1937, explaining Krüger's absence by claiming that she had committed suicide in Buenos Aires. This was in itself highly suspicious. There were no news reports of her death in the Argentinian newspapers. Jonny had not reported her death to anyone in the party or the Comintern until his arrival in Moscow. Those who had met Krüger had reported that she was a clever, vivacious and highly resourceful woman, not the kind to commit suicide. Even more importantly, Jonny claimed to have reported her death to the Argentinian police and to have remained in Buenos Aires to sort out all the official formalities. Blagoeva clearly had problems accepting that the Argentinian authorities, who had an extradition agreement with Brazil, had allowed Jonny to leave the country unimpeded, even though he was still using the same name by which he was known in Brazil, where there was a substantial reward out for his arrest.

Jonny had also travelled back to Europe on board a British ship, in contravention of the basic rules for members of the Fourth Department. Jonny excused his departure from his orders by explaining that he had to break the news of Krüger's suicide personally to her family in Berlin. It was a plausible excuse. But he could hardly tell Blagoeva the truth, that he was being debriefed by British intelligence officers, with Foley doing his damnedest to try and persuade him not to go back to the Soviet Union. During his time in Moscow, Jonny was put up in Room 670 of the Novaya Moskovskaya hotel, which was used by the Fourth Department for officers being debriefed after foreign trips. It was here that he typed up his report on the operations in Brazil, the arrests and the reasons behind them, and also on his 1934 confrontation with Ewert in China. At the same time, he repeatedly tried to persuade Blagoeva and other Comintern leaders to send him back to South America, preferably with large amounts of money with which, he claimed, he could obtain the release of Ewert and Rudolfo Ghiodli, the head of the South American section of the Comintern activists, who like Ewert had been arrested in Brazil. They and Prestes should be the ones explaining why the coup failed, Jonny told Blagoeva. 'For the Comintern, the problem is very important and in my view can only be settled by the comrades in South America themselves,' Jonny said. 'These comrades can say why the plan in the north-east wasn't followed and they can analyse the political occurrences in Brazil. If the Comintern gives me a free hand and enough money I am 90 per cent certain that I can free Ewert and Ghioldi and bring them back to Moscow. I can't guarantee this at the moment with Prestes. That would require a careful study of his situation.'

Blaming those who were arrested and offering to bring them back to Moscow was not the only ploy the resourceful Jonny tried. He also claimed to be able to put Soviet military experts in touch with an Argentinian scientist, allegedly a committed member of the party, who had invented an 'electric cannon' which worked without smoke or noise. If he were sent back to Buenos Aires, he could obtain blueprints for the cannon and also continue his work providing Communist training – 'where it is urgently needed' – inside the Argentinian armed forces. An unsurprisingly suspicious Blagoeva did not believe a word Jonny said and called in the NKVD, the Soviet security and intelligence service, to investigate. They placed Jonny under 24-hour observation. Suspicions mounted when a maid found a revolver in his room while another hotel employee reported that a woman was visiting the German at night. People who had come into contact with Jonny were taken into custody and questioned about their association with him, but eventually he managed to convince the NKVD and his bosses inside the Comintern and the Fourth Department that he was innocent. He was no doubt helped by his former instructor at the Frunze Military Academy, who described him as 'a born terrorist' and told the NKVD that if they found that he was not to blame for the Brazilian debacle, he should be sent abroad as soon as possible so he could take over pro-Soviet disinformation and terrorist activities. Given that this was the height of the Stalinist purges and that many innocent people were being executed, Jonny's escape was an astonishing tribute to his resourcefulness and powers of persuasion. However, although his efforts had ensured that the revolution in Brazil failed, he could argue quite honestly, as he had to Foley and Vivian, that 'the real causes of the failure were lack of support from the civilian population and the disregard of certain Brazilian officials, who in spite of their agreement to help sat on their hands'.[21]

Jonny was cleared of any blame and in May 1938 left Moscow for Brazil, on a mission to obtain Ewert's release. He travelled first to Copenhagen, where he had arranged to meet Foley, then to the UK, where he spent several days at an English country house, providing Vivian with a detailed update on the latest information from inside the Comintern. Jonny described the complete shake-up within the organisation in reaction to the Nazis' successes and the Communists' failures in Germany, and the fiascos in China and Brazil. The failure in Germany dominated the debate, taking the heat away from Jonny and the problems in China and Brazil. The Comintern leadership had made the mistake in 1932 of ordering the German Communist Party to co-operate with the Nazis. There was a thorough clear-out of every member of the Comintern leadership, with the single exception of Manuilsky. The disgraced Comintern leaders were arrested and accused of supporting Leon Trotsky, who had himself been sacked and exiled in the late 1920s to remove the main threat to Stalin's power. Supporting Trotsky was now a capital offence in Stalin's Russia. All but two of the German Communist Party leadership were sacked, and even the two that remained, Wilhelm Pieck and Walter Ulbricht, were now effectively Stalin's puppets, with the party completely controlled from Moscow. The entire leaderships of the communist parties in Poland, Bulgaria, Hungary, Latvia and Finland were also arrested, but no-one from the British or French communist parties was touched.

Jonny told Vivian that Stalin had ordered all Russian officers fighting in the Spanish Civil War to return home in a *de facto* acceptance that Franco would win and that Soviet operations in Latin America were being funded via the US and Canada. Jonny then returned to Brazil, continuing in his role as a British agent-in-place inside Soviet military intelligence and the underground sections of the Comintern until 1940. The material he produced led MI5 to describe him as a 'very valuable agent' while Vivian would later tell new recruits to MI6 that the case of Jonny de Graaf provided 'an example of the outstanding success of penetration of Russian secret organisations'. To this day, and despite the subsequent defections of a number of senior Soviet intelligence officers during the Cold War, he is regarded as one of the best agents ever to be recruited by SIS.[22]

TWENTY

Preparing for another war –
'Scratching the surface'

GERMANY and Japan had been high up on the intelligence priorities of both the War Office and the Admiralty at the end of the First World War, but the latter was a 'very difficult' target for a Western intelligence service to work on and required large sums of money for no immediate product. Cumming had opened a bureau in Japan in 1917, appointing Captain Godfrey Scott-Pearse as his representative there. Sir William Conyngham-Greene, the British ambassador, praised Scott-Pearse's 'great service' and urged that a senior MI1c officer be appointed, a rare gesture of support for secret service operations from a British envoy, but when he left in 1919 more normal ambassadorial views took hold, with the new envoy, Sir Charles Eliot, trying to block the appointment of a new SIS bureau chief. There was also a conflict between the presence in Tokyo of a consular officer, Colin Davidson, who ran a successful network of agents, and someone from C's organisation. There was a good deal of truth to Eliot's complaint that it would have been more sensible to use the money spent appointing C's new man, Colonel David Drummond Gunn, on providing Davidson with competent staff, but taking the most sensible option would have meant bringing Davidson onto the SIS staff, which is unlikely to have been what Eliot had in mind. Gunn was appointed passport control officer in Yokohama, based at the British consulate-general in the Japanese port. By 1923, the Yokohama passport control office had gone and Cumming was spending £1,080 a year on a Tokyo bureau, £480 of it on agents, using a consular officer plus two locally employed staff. A major earthquake in 1923 forced the SIS officers to withdraw and an agent run from China maintained a relatively unproductive network until 1928 when the Foreign Office pulled the plug for financial reasons, leaving Japan largely covered by the SIS representative in Hong Kong, Charles Drage. [1]

By contrast, Germany was watched very carefully throughout the inter-war period from a number of SIS bureaux, including a consistently well-staffed Berlin bureau; several Germany-based sub-bureaux, in Frankfurt, Hamburg and Munich, and, in the immediate aftermath of the First World War, two officers at the British Army of the Rhine headquarters in Cologne. Germany was also watched from the bureaux in Paris, Brussels, Warsaw, Berne, Vienna, Copenhagen, and Rotterdam, from where Richard Tinsley continued to operate until 1923. From the very start, extremist groups were a key target and the emergence, in 1923, of a young Adolf Hitler as a leading figure among the right-wing war veterans was noted with interest by SIS, which began issuing reports on the future German dictator under the serial number CX10746. [2]

Hitler had taken control of a small right-wing group, the Nationalsozialistische Deutsche Arbeiterpartei (National Socialist German Workers Party). Both the title and the policies of the Nazi Party, as it swiftly became known, were aimed at appealing across the social divide. Despite the party's right-wing make-up, socialists were wooed with calls for the nationalisation of large companies and the abolition of unearned income, but the essential focus of the party's 25-point programme was the abrogation of the humiliating post-war treaties and the creation of a greater German 'nation', including ethnic German areas of neighbouring countries. 'None but those of German blood, whatever their creed, may be members of the Nation,' it read. 'No Jew, therefore, may be a member of the Nation.' The two main groups attracted to the party were the middle classes, small businessmen and shopkeepers who saw the Jews as stealing their trade, and the young ex-soldiers who had drifted into the Freikorps after returning from the front to poverty and now found a new home in the Nazi Party's brown-shirted paramilitary wing – the Sturmabteilung or SA.

'This consisted largely of rootless ex-servicemen who, if not of the middle-class, nevertheless clung, with a pertinacity that sprang from their qualifications, to the belief in their superiority to the working class,' one British observer noted. 'These were frustrated men, forever regretting the loss of the figure they had cut in the Army, the discipline that had relieved them of personal responsibility, and the security of regimentation.' The financial crisis had dramatically increased the number of Nazi Party members, and Hitler was now an all-powerful leader of his party; the title of *Führer* was used within the Nazi Party from this time onward. Hitler decided the time was ripe to stage his own coup. He would march on Berlin, mustering support along the way, much as Benito Mussolini had come to power in Italy the previous year. The Nazi leader persuaded General Erich Ludendorff, joint commander of Germany's forces on the Western Front during the First World War, to head the march.

The British were warned in advance of these plans by an agent who had infiltrated the Nazi Party and was run by Ernan Forbes Dennis in Vienna. 'On 3 November, a trustworthy German informant ascertained the following personally, and in confidence, from Hitler and Ludendorff,' the SIS political section under Major Malcolm Woollcombe, reported on 6 November 1923. 'On the night of 5 November, a courier was to leave Munich for Holland with a communication from Ludendorff to the Crown Prince, begging the latter not to return from Holland until Hitler had succeeded in establishing a military dictatorship in Berlin. Ludendorff pointed out that otherwise, the reactionary forces would be split up between Hitler and the Crown Prince, and the success of the movement would thus be prejudiced. The informant was at the same time told that Hitler was averse to taking action pending the Crown Prince's reply, but that circumstances might force an immediate march on Berlin.' The agent, codenamed MV44 (MV being the identifier for Vienna-run agents), said that General Paul Emil von Lettow-Vorbeck, who symbolically had commanded German troops in Africa, where they were never beaten, was waiting to join the march in the north and Hitler believed he had support in Saxony.

The SIS report was circulated on 6 November. Two days later, on the night of 8 November 1923, Hitler and 600 members of the SA hijacked a political meeting in the Bürgerbräukeller, where the *Führer* announced that 'the national revolution has broken out'. The next morning, accompanied by Ludendorff and several thousand Nazis, he marched on Munich, but the police were waiting for them, blocking their path in the narrow Residenzstrasse. Shooting broke out, leaving sixteen Nazis and three police officers dead. Hitler fled, but Ludendorff marched on defiantly before being arrested. Hitler was captured and put on trial for high treason. Despite his failure, the SIS agent reported that Hitler's audacious move had gained him support among the estimated 185,000 war veterans who were members of the Deutsche Ehrenlegion (German Legion of Honour). 'The Ehrenlegion has placed itself unreservedly at the disposition of General Ludendorff and, although an unpolitical organisation, appears to be tending in Hitler's direction,' agent MV44 reported.

Given a nationwide platform, Hitler turned the subsequent court case into a denunciation of the government for having failed the German people, attracting a good deal of favourable publicity for both himself and his party. His five-year prison sentence was extremely light given the charge against him, and he ended up spending only seven months in jail, a period which he used to outline his political doctrines, and in particular his hatred of the Jews, in *Mein Kampf* (My Struggle), a book written with the assistance of his political aide and fellow prisoner, the former First World War fighter pilot Rudolf Hess.[3]

The Nazi Party was by no means alone in its eagerness to escape the humiliation of the Versailles Treaty, with its restrictions on military forces and activity, and on the manufacture of conventional and chemical weapons. Co-operation with the Soviet Union had begun more than a month before the Versailles Treaty was signed, with an agreement between Germany and Russia on military assistance under which the Germans would send 'several thousand military instructors' to Russia while the latter would 'render Germany military support'. The reports came from multiple 'reliable' sources in Petrograd, Copenhagen,

Gothenburg and Germany itself. A formal agreement signed in Genoa in May 1922, as a secret clause to the so-called Rapello Agreement, therefore came as no surprise in Whitehall. Within days, SIS was reporting that the Germans, who were banned under Versailles from having their own air force, were secretly sending military aviation instructors to Russia. By 1926, SIS was warning that any information passed to the Germans was likely to find its way immediately to the Russians and, by 1929, it was reporting on formal exchange arrangements which had been in place for a number of years, under which German staff officers lectured their Soviet counterparts on military tactics and in return the Soviet Union allowed the Germans to get round the Versailles ban on a German air force by training military pilots in Russia.[4]

It was already clear that the dismissal by many in Whitehall of Germany as a realistic military threat was simply wishful thinking, given Britain's own rapid disarmament in the wake of the First World War. Perhaps the most astonishing example of this naïvety, in the face of SIS reporting to the contrary, came in the response by Austen Chamberlain, the Foreign Secretary, in April 1929, to a copy of the German plans for mobilisation in the event of war, which an SIS agent had managed to photograph in Berlin. The mobilisation plans were signed by Otto Gessler, who was German Minister for War in December 1927 when they were compiled.

There was no question in the minds of either Hugh Sinclair or the War Office analysts who had pored over them that these plans were genuine. 'A preliminary study of this document, which with its tables and appendices consists of seventy pages, has been made, and all indications point to its being genuine,' the War Office said. The mobilisation plans stated that universal military conscription would be introduced on the outbreak of war. 'At the same time, the armed forces of the Reich will be expanded to such a size as is commensurate with the size of the population and the extent of the frontiers of the Reich,' they said. What staggered even those officials aware of the extent of the secret military co-operation with the Soviet Union was the speed with which the German armed forces would be able to mobilise, given that under the

Versailles Treaty, the German Army was limited to just ten divisions. The War Office report said:

> The expansion is very great – from seven infantry and three cavalry divisions to sixty-three infantry, one cavalry and one composite division. The rate of mobilisation is extraordinarily rapid – the first twenty-one divisions having to be ready in thirty-six hours. Arrangements are made for the formation within four weeks of a total of 192 infantry regiments (576 battalions). This would appear to indicate no great shortage of rifles or light machine-guns. The total requirements in rifles would be about 500,000 as opposed to the authorised number of about 110,000. The scheme allows for the formation of armoured car, tank, anti-aircraft and flying units all of which are forbidden by the Treaty. The scheme arranges for the expansion of the Regular Army while it is still handicapped by the limiting restrictions of the Treaty of Versailles. This document definitely confirms the fact that the peace-time army is being trained, not as a weapon in itself, but as a cadre.

Both Chamberlain and his permanent under-secretary, Sir Ronald Lindsay, accepted that the document was genuine. 'An SS [secret service] agent has got hold of and photographed a German War Office document giving the whole German scheme of mobilisation,' Lindsay told the Foreign Secretary. 'C feels absolutely sure of its authenticity. Certainly, it embodies arresting features.' But his acceptance that it was genuine did not mean that he accepted its significance.

> Prima facie, it seems to me that so long as Germany has millions of men, nothing can stop her elaborating schemes by which they are formed into battalion, brigades and corps. The crux is equipment, rifles, machine-guns, guns, tanks etc., etc., and though I don't understand this WO [War Office] summary as well as I should like to, it seems to me to fail to show that there is in existence anything like the equipment which would be wanted for even a small part of these service battalions. Hitherto, the WO has held that Germany is practically without warlike

equipment. I never heard it seriously maintained that any large caches existed. When there is serious evidence to the contrary, then there will be ground for very serious alarm.

Thus a man who by his own admission did not understand military matters, even so relatively simple as laid out in the War Office report, who appeared to think that 400,000 rifles would be difficult to hide even in a country the size of Germany, and who had clearly also ignored the reports of German military co-operation with Russia, dismissed the potential German threat. Chamberlain's response was equally dismissive of the German ability to obtain the necessary weapons. 'Probably, they have more than are allowed,' he said. 'It would be rash to assume that they have all they require for the scheme.' He and Lindsay agreed to suppress the report. They should keep it 'absolutely secret and communicate its existence to no-one.'[5]

While the Service was certainly watching German military resurgence, even before Hitler came to power, it was giving far less attention to Italy, which was originally watched from Switzerland. SIS did have a good source in Rome in 1919 on the rise of 'the notorious agitator Mussolini' with increasing support from right-wing disgruntled military veterans, but the general view in Whitehall was that Italy, even after Mussolini came to power in 1922, was an ally rather than a potential enemy. The main focus remained on the Soviet Union and Germany; everything else was liable to be cut.[6]

An economic section, Section VI, was set up sometime around 1927 and swiftly became the focus of attention for Desmond Morton, who was rightly convinced that economic intelligence on potential enemies was vital to collect; apart from assisting Britain to maintain a dominant position in the world trade markets, it would clearly provide important target information for the RAF in any future war. Given that Morton still retained his other responsibilities as head of Production, Franklin Clively was allocated to Section VI to assist him. The creation of the economic section reflected a feeling within Whitehall that the Soviet Union and Germany were greater economic threats to Britain than they were military threats, although the threat of Soviet subversion remained the greatest concern to the Service's customers. Morton attempted initially to work on both his economic and production responsibilities, but by 1931, economic intelligence had become his sole focus and he created a new organisation, the Industrial Intelligence Centre (IIC), which would subsequently be removed from SIS and taken over by the Board of Trade, with Morton as its head. A small under-staffed Section VI, made up solely of Major Humphrey Plowden and working effectively as a sub-section of Section IV (the War Office section), continued but, with Hitler's takeover in Germany and the rise of Japanese and Italian military power, SIS struggled to allocate resources to economic intelligence.[7]

During the 1930s, the lack of intelligence on Japan and Italy, largely the result of serious under-funding, became very clear, the first trigger event being the Japanese occupation of Manchuria and Britain's lack of intelligence on what was going on inside Japan as it sought to negotiate a settlement between the Chinese and Japanese. SIS had not ignored the threat from Japan, far from it. Sinclair had made serious representations as far back as 1926 that if, as the armed forces had already said, intelligence 'in this very difficult country' was an important priority, then 'it would be necessary to guarantee large sums, and the establishment of a good Secret Service would probably take some years'. His proposals were turned down as too expensive. By 1928, the War Office, which would later complain furiously about the lack of secret intelligence from inside Japan, was actively blocking the dispatch of an SIS officer to Tokyo on the grounds that the goodwill created by successive military attachés was 'a far more valuable potential source of information than anything which could possibly be obtained by SIS'. By the end of 1932, with Japan fully in control of Manchuria, the situation had changed again, with the Service ordered to set up an intelligence network in Tokyo, albeit without any extra funding. 'In consequence, money had to be found by diverting sums being spent, with valuable results, on other countries,' Sinclair said. 'The amount so found is wholly insufficient, and only suffices to maintain a skeleton organisation.'[8]

One of the key areas to suffer as a result of the financial cuts was

Switzerland, with the Service withdrawing all representation during the early 1930s, seriously limiting coverage of Italy. The Italian invasion of Abyssinia in October 1935, led to demands for more material on Mussolini, much to Sinclair's frustration. 'This necessity for spreading the butter thin has proved particularly unfortunate in the present Italian crisis,' he said. 'As for years Italy has been regarded as a friend and ally, intensive SS work was not pursued against that country, the main effort being directed towards Germany. When the crisis occurred, not only had funds to be diverted from other work, for work against Italy, but large sums had to be expended on obtaining intelligence of a nature which SIS is not normally expected to supply in peace time.'[9]

Unfortunately, Sir George Warner, the British ambassador in Berne, vetoed any SIS officers being based in his embassy, even to monitor Italy, and the Foreign Office declined to overrule his judgement. 'Right up to the outbreak of [the Second World] war, cases occurred in which a head of mission who was hostile to secret intelligence withheld his position and other arrangements had to be made,' said Robert Cecil, a Foreign Office official who worked inside SIS during the Second World War. 'Hostility arose partly because some heads of mission objected to transmission of intelligence to London from an unknown source and partly because of fear that the activities of the Passport Control Officer might land the mission in trouble.'[10]

The Abyssinia crisis also resulted in a brief reprise for Cumming's 'very noted international spy' Enrique Lorenzo Bernstein, this time as Colonel Pedro Lopez, a freelance arms dealer allegedly working for the Abyssinians, in reality employed by the Italians to provide evidence that Abyssinian forces were buying illegal 'dum-dum' bullets from British armaments companies. Having conned a British manufacturer into selling him a single box of the illegal rounds and providing him with a letter guaranteeing the bullets were supplied by a British company, Bernstein passed both to the Italians, leading to Italian newspaper articles attacking the British for their illegal sale to the Abyssinians. British Foreign Secretary Anthony Eden was forced to deny the charges in the House of Commons, describing 'the individual styling himself Colonel

Pedro Lopez' as 'a notorious purveyor of false information and forged documents'. Tracked down by the *News Chronicle* a few days later, Bernstein adopted the standard defence of the would-be spy exposed as a fraud, insisting that his real role was still too secret for the truth to come out. 'What I did in connection with dum–dum bullets was done purely from patriotic motives, not for personal gain and greed,' he insisted. 'The authorities know everything. Time will reveal that I am the most patriotic man in the country.'[11]

Intelligence on Italy and Japan might be in short supply, but Germany remained well covered, from France, the Netherlands, Denmark, Austria, Belgium and Poland, and with a number of German officials unhappy at where Hitler was taking the country, Frank Foley was also the recipient of material from dissidents within the Nazi regime. By the mid-1930s, the Service had filed more than thirty different personal reports on Hitler in the CX10746 series, recording various details about his background, his beliefs, his lack of understanding of foreign affairs, the difficulty of predicting his behaviour, which often defied reason, and the nervous condition that led him to fly into rages.[12]

One of the Service's best agents in Germany, certainly on naval matters, remained Karl Krüger, agent H16, still handled from the Netherlands. From 1922 onwards, Krüger had been reporting on a covert German submarine construction programme that used a company set up in Holland, Ingenieurskantoor voor Scheepbouw (IvS), to circumvent the Versailles ban on Germany having any submarines or developing new ones. The company produced a number of prototypes, building them in Spain and Finland, as part of the development of a new German U-boat. By November 1934, now designated agent 33016, Krüger was reporting that the Germans had begun a domestic U-boat construction programme in breach of the Versailles Treaty but, just as Chamberlain and Lindsay had ignored the report on military mobilisation plans, the Admiralty dismissed Krüger's reports on submarine construction on the grounds of 'improbability'. There was a palpable feeling of shock in the Admiralty when the first German U-boat was commissioned seven months later. Within months, Krüger had produced the German

U-boat mobilisation plans, under which thousands of workers were being trained to mount round-the-clock mass production of U-boats at six German naval shipyards. The programme would use prefabricated parts produced in factories across Germany. Four thousand workers were already being trained to take part, with the target put at a total of 13,000, able to produce seven new boats a month. Morton's IIC reported Krüger as saying that 'the construction plan depends – apart from the utilisation of a number of factories to manufacture sections – on the intensive training by shipyards of squads of selected workmen to carry out assembly'. The construction had been 'largely reduced to a drill'. This intelligence presaged the Kriegsmarine's use of U-boats on a large scale to disrupt Allied shipping, in particular the 500-ton Type-VII boat, which was one of three designs initially developed by IvS and would be the most commonly used German U-boat during the Second World War.[13]

In Berlin itself, Foley was driven, by the sheer availability of valuable intelligence from German officials disenchanted with the Third Reich, to ignore the 'third country rule'. One of those he recruited in 1935 was a Luftwaffe colonel working in the German Air Ministry, who volunteered his services in return for cash. Given his access to high-grade intelligence from the office of Hermann Göring, the minister in charge of the Luftwaffe, and the panic in London over a claim by Hitler that the Luftwaffe had reached parity with the RAF, the Service agreed to pay him for his information. Budgets had been urgently increased in the wake of Hitler's decision to build up his armed forces, so there was hard cash available for good intelligence. But just as the Admiralty refused to believe Krüger on the German submarine construction, the Air Ministry rejected the intelligence from Foley's Luftwaffe colonel, largely because it contradicted their own more conservative estimates. Lord Londonderry, the British Secretary of State for Air, dismissed the SIS reporting on aircraft numbers – a typical example of the difficulties the Service faced in putting across information where the source could not be disclosed. 'He [Londonderry] doubted whether the opinion of the Secret Service in a matter of this kind, which had some technical aspects, was as good as that of the department concerned,' the cabinet minutes record. 'The Air Ministry interpretation and deduction was more likely to be the correct one.' The Air Ministry was wrong. Over the next three years, Foley met the Luftwaffe officer every two weeks, regularly receiving photocopies of top secret documents with details of both the structure of the rapidly expanding air force and its strategy. But when Nevile Henderson, the British ambassador in Berlin, found out about the source, Foley was ordered to drop him. 'I had an agent who was a very friendly colonel in the Luftwaffe HQ,' Foley later told a colleague. 'He passed me reports twice a month – all top level stuff. But at the end of 1938, I was instructed by the Foreign Office to drop this chap. Just imagine, the best source we had in Germany and in a strategic position.' The Air Ministry was subsequently the loudest in its complaints of insufficient intelligence from SIS.[14]

The continued lack of funding, the difficulties tracking the rise of what would become the Axis powers, the complaints from within Whitehall over a lack of coverage of areas for which money was simply not provided and, perhaps most of all, the sure and certain knowledge that war with Hitler's Germany was unavoidable, resulted in October 1935 in a typically robust memorandum from Hugh Sinclair addressed to Warren Fisher, the head of the civil service, Robert Vansittart, permanent under-secretary at the Foreign Office, and the chiefs of staff, in which he took advantage of the concern in Whitehall over the Abyssinia crisis and argued that the Service had been 'constantly hampered by lack of funds' with the effect even greater in the previous few years. Referring specifically to the warnings on Germany that Chamberlain and Lindsay had agreed to suppress, Sinclair said:

Other nations have turned Great Britain's gesture in unilateral disarmament to account by seizing the opportunity to rearm secretly. During this period, official sources of information have proved even worse than useless, because replies deliberately calculated to deceive, have been returned to official queries. The most glaring case in point has been that of Germany. Until the German authorities themselves made the facts public, practically the only sources of information on her rearmament were those available to the Secret Service, and it is a melancholy fact that the march of events has proved their information correct.

What has been done by the Secret Service has been accomplished only by the most intensive efforts on the part of all those concerned, and a great deal more could, and would, have been accomplished had the Service been in possession of adequate funds. These funds are supposed to cover the whole of the world, except Great Britain, India and the Colonies. When this amount, which only equals that spent every year on the maintenance (net the cost) of one of HM Destroyers in Home Waters, is contrasted with sums openly acknowledged by foreign nations in their budgets, as spent on Secret Service, in addition to the considerable sums known to be spent for the same purpose under suitable camouflage, it is indeed remarkable that such results have been achieved at all.

At present, owing to lack of funds, it is not possible to maintain any service in such countries as Switzerland, Spain, Yugoslavia, Albania and Arabia, and, in consequence, a great deal of information about other and neighbouring countries, which could be obtained in these countries, escapes us. It must be borne in mind that even when adequate funds are available, it takes at least two–three years, under the most favourable circumstances, to establish a satisfactory Secret Service in any country. Living, as it does, a hand to mouth existence, with vast areas to cover, it is, as things are, only possible for SIS to scratch the surface. To obtain really inside information means spending big money.

Even this scratching the surface can only be guaranteed up to the development of a period of tension or crisis. A Secret Service which will continue to function during periods of tension, and after War has broken out, can only be ensured by maintaining a network of resident agents in all countries, who will be able to remain there under any circumstances, and whose communications are arranged for by cast-iron methods. Hitherto, in consequence of the hopeless inadequacy of the Funds supplied, it has not been possible to do this, except in a few limited instances, and in exceptional circumstances.

Whatever may be the outcome of the present crisis, it is plainly apparent that, in the future, Germany, Japan and Italy will have to be regarded as potential enemies from without, as well as Soviet Russia from within. This situation cannot possibly be covered by the existing SIS organisation, depending, as it does, upon a limited number of Passport Control Officers and representatives anchored to their posts in the capital, and possessing neither the means nor the mobility for covering the many industrial and strategic posts from which essential information can alone be obtained. A complete plan, details of which are available, if required, has been worked out for the establishment of a network of permanent resident agents at the vital points in the three countries in question. To put this plan into execution will necessitate a large increase in Secret Service Funds. It is considered that the sum of £1,000,000 per annum should in future be provided for the Service, and it must be clearly understood that, failing such provision, no guarantees can be given that the SIS will be able to meet the demands of the Armed Forces Departments in times of crisis, for information on the scale of that which the Italian crisis has shown is necessary and in demand.[15]

The result was an increase in the secret service budget from £180,000 to £350,000. Not quite the million-pound budget that Sinclair had sought, but at least an improvement. The Service was forced to concentrate on Italy and Germany, with Claude Dansey, now Rome bureau chief, being called back to London to set up what was to become known as the Z Organisation. The story was put around that Dansey had been thrown out of the Service after a financial scandal. He set up an export agency, Geoffrey Duveen and Company, at Bush House in Aldwych in central London, using it as a base from which to recruit a number of journalists and businessmen, some with previous connections to SIS. They included William Stephenson, the Canadian businessman whose company, Pressed Steel, made everything from biscuit tins to car bodies; many of the Vienna-, Rome- and Berlin-based British newspaper correspondents; and Sir Alexander Korda, the film producer, who allowed Dansey to use his company, London Films, as cover for a number of his agents.[16]

Norman Dewhurst, who had left SIS in 1922, was one of those recruited by Dansey, who sent him to Italy to contact a potential agent and then find out about the construction of a new Italian battleship at Genoa. 'Luck plays a part in many ways and a few days after my arrival, I just happened to see some anti-aircraft gun emplacements being completed,' Dewhurst said. 'No fewer than eight guns were involved. It was pure chance, I was taking a stroll on the promenade at Genoa, and there was work going on before me. I just casually sat down on the seawall and watched the bathers with one eye and noted the calibre of the guns with the other. I passed that way the day after, only a blank wall between the houses was to be seen. Had I not seen it with my own eyes, I would never have thought that eight guns nestled there.'

On his return to London, he was trained up for a period undercover in Nazi Germany, with Dansey apparently having organised a training course in breaking and entry by a former Scotland Yard detective. 'Every morning for the next few weeks, I quietly made my way to a special office where I received a course of training in lock-picking; inks; codes; wireless telegraphy; and the photographing of documents,' Dewhurst said. 'This was followed by a period of intense study of the organisation of the German Army, with special reference to its different sections and to badges and other distinguishing markings. I was scheduled to go into Nazi Germany for eighteen months. I studied hard. I not only wanted to be a good spy, but also to dodge the Gestapo.' Dewhurst's cover in Bavaria was as a writer, setting himself up in a house with a German widow whom he met at a hiking club. He reported on military activities, including the construction of military airfields and even information from an SS corporal on what was happening inside the Dachau concentration camp. Dewhurst filed his reports by courier, or directly to Dansey at meetings in Zurich and Paris. In mid-1938, he was sent back to Latvia, where Leslie Nicholson was now bureau chief, running a network of agents he codenamed Alex.[17]

'My best agent was known as "Alex", although Alex was not a single person and I never knew the majority of the persons of whom Alex consisted,' Nicholson wrote. 'One of Alex's mainstays, however – I had better call him Alex No. 1 – was a German. He had worked at one stage in the vast Krupp organisation, but he had been sacked for political reasons. I never knew the ins and outs of it, but he became a first-class British agent. I first made his acquaintance through a member of the local British community, who told me that he was very anti-German, which seemed to me a bit unlikely. In fact, he was not at all anti-German, but he was a confirmed opponent of Hitler's expansionist plans. I subsequently met him on several occasions at the Englishman's flat, but it was not until I felt I really knew him that I put the question to him of working as an undercover agent for me. Alex was a man of many parts, he eventually brought in several of his business friends, mostly Latvians, who travelled to Germany on legitimate grounds and also had commercial reasons for visiting satellite countries. Alex No. 1 had a very sharp brain and, under instruction, he developed a remarkable flair for intelligence work.'

Nicholson found that while the agents produced very good intelligence on what was going on inside Germany, including the weekly output of the German shipyards, Head Office often appeared uninterested in the really good reports, and obsessively keen on material of no major importance. 'I was sometimes surprised at the seemingly inconsistent way in which London evaluated reports,' Nicholson said. 'Often a report compiled from accurate information slowly and painfully acquired, of which we felt rather proud, would receive scant recognition – probably, we guessed, because they had already obtained the information elsewhere. Other reports, which we ourselves had rated lower, might be more generously rewarded. If indeed London had a yardstick, its scale of values was difficult to comprehend.'[18]

While Nicholson was the official face of British intelligence in Latvia, Dewhurst operated for the Z Organisation under 'natural cover' as the co-owner of a ships' chandlery, his real role kept from Nicholson, whose agents were soon reporting that Dewhurst was a Nazi sympathiser. 'This really proved how well I was in,' Dewhurst later claimed. Unfortunately for him, the German agents were not so easily fooled as Nicholson's men and at least some of the agents Dewhurst sent into Germany to collect information on tank manufacture were in fact double-agents working for the Abwehr, German military intelligence, and feeding him false information. Dewhurst was not alone; SIS officers and agents operating into Germany from Austria, Denmark, Belgium and the Netherlands were also being fed 'intelligence' by sources who were in fact run by the Abwehr, although Lieutenant-Colonel Edward Calthrop, the Brussels bureau chief, was aware of the Abwehr activity and avoided being deceived. Calthrop was running two successful networks and four individual agents inside Germany, using the captain of a Rhine tugboat as a courier. One of those who did fall victim to the German penetration of British intelligence operations was Captain Werner Aue, British consul in Hanover, who had his recognition withdrawn after being caught in an Abwehr sting.[19]

The non-SIS role of the passport control offices involved issuing visas to anyone wanting to come to the UK or anywhere in the British Empire, including Palestine, which at the time was administered by Britain under mandate from the League of Nations. As war loomed, British passport control offices across central Europe were swamped by requests from Jews for visas to go to Palestine. A few officials undoubtedly took advantage of the situation, the most serious being in the passport control office in The Hague, where Hugh Dalton, the bureau chief, started diverting money paid for Jews trying to get to Palestine in order to fund an expensive love affair. When the shortfall became apparent, in the summer of 1936, Dalton committed suicide.[20] Notwithstanding the Dalton scandal, many passport control officers did what they could to help. One man went much further than any of his colleagues. Frank Foley, the bureau chief in Berlin, is estimated to have saved 'tens of thousands' of Jews from the Holocaust. Most wanted to go to Palestine, but the very strict quotas imposed by the British meant that few were eligible. Foley realised the danger they were in and tore up the rulebook, giving out visas that should never have been issued, hiding Jews in his home, helping them to obtain false papers and passports and even going into the concentration camps to obtain their release.

'He was a quite outstanding character,' one former SIS officer said. 'Schindler pales into insignificance besides his work on getting Jews out of Germany and he was also an outstanding officer. There would be lots of people waiting for Foley to hand out the visas so the Gestapo would come round and try and frighten them away. Foley would come out and say: "You gentlemen have come to apply for a visa, I suppose. Could you join the queue?" And when they said: "No we haven't," he'd reply: "Well, could you kindly get out because this room's a bit crowded." A very, very able man, who I don't think ever got the recognition he should have done, outstanding.'

During the 1961 trial of Adolf Eichmann, the SS official dealing with 'the Jewish question', Benno Cohen, former chairman of the German Zionist Organisation, described the reign of terror under which Germany's Jews lived in the run-up to the Second World War and how few people reached out to help them.

> There was one man who stood out above all others like a beacon. Captain Foley, passport officer in the British consulate in the Tiergarten in Berlin, a man who in my opinion was one of the greatest among the nations of the world. He brought his influence to bear to help us. It was possible to bring a great number of people to Israel through the help of this most wonderful man. He rescued thousands of Jews from the jaws of death.

Günter Powitzer had been arrested at the beginning of 1937 for 'race defilement', after getting his non-Jewish girlfriend pregnant. Powitzer was jailed for 18 months, during which time the couple's son Walter was born. Powitzer's brother, who had successfully emigrated to Palestine, set about trying to get him out. Eventually, he was put in touch with Foley, but by now Powitzer was close to the end of his prison sentence. The day of release was the most dangerous time for so-called Jewish 'criminals', who were likely to be moved immediately to a concentration camp. Powitzer was taken first to police headquarters in the Alexanderplatz and then to the Sachsenhausen camp, north of Berlin. One of the camp guards would stand resting an axe on his shoulder as he called out the names of the condemned before they were led away. He was known to the prisoners as 'the man with the violin'. Powitzer knew his name must soon appear on his list, but continued working in the camp's brick factory, hoping for a miracle. One day, he was tipped off not to go to work, to plead illness. When he said he was not well, he was sent to the camp kitchen where a guard forced him to run around with a sack of potatoes on his back. Returning late at night to the hut, bruised and tired, he found it empty. When he asked where everyone was, he was told simply: 'They tried out a new machine-gun today.'

A few days later, Powitzer heard he had a visitor. An SS guard told him to have a shower and took him to the clinic where they treated his whip wounds. The guard then threw a grey greatcoat over him to cover up all his wounds. He led Powitzer into the camp office where a small owlish looking man with glasses was sat behind the desk. It was Frank Foley. 'My name is Foley,' he said in English. 'I am from the British Consulate in Berlin.' Powitzer asked if he could have an interpreter and when the guard went out to fetch one, he turned to Foley and told him that he understood English. Foley smiled and told him he would be released the next day and there were papers ready for him to go to Palestine. 'What about my child?' Powitzer asked. Foley replied: 'Don't worry, he is also registered on the papers. We have taken care of everything.' The next day, someone was waiting at the camp gates to pick Powitzer up and take him to collect his young son. Shortly afterwards, they were on their way to Palestine.

This is not to be taken lightly either in human or espionage terms. Given that he was now ignoring the 'third country rule' and, like most SIS officers during this era, had no diplomatic immunity, Foley operated at considerable risk to himself, his operations and – since he was hiding 'four or five a night' in his home – his family. Increasing the numbers of refugees coming into Britain was also opposed by Hugh Sinclair. But such was Foley's willingness to help that he even put Jewish activists in touch with his agents on the German borders, most of them clergymen opposed to Hitler, who could spirit people out of Germany.[21]

Foley's work on behalf of the Jews brought him a number of useful agents, in particular Paul Rosbaud, a young Austrian scientist who was scientific adviser to Springer Verlag, one of Germany's largest publishing houses. Rosbaud's wife was Jewish and Foley helped him get her to England, cementing an already productive relationship. Shortly before Christmas 1938, two German scientists, Otto Hahn and Fritz Strassman, working at the Kaiser Wilhelm Institute of Chemistry in the Berlin suburb of Dahlem, carried out a momentous experiment. By bombarding uranium atoms with slow-speed neutrons, they had created new elements of much lower atomic weight. They were aware that their experiment was important but unsure of its full significance. They turned to the Jewish physicist Lise Meitner, who was their adviser on the series of experiments and was now living in Sweden. She discussed the experiment with her nephew Otto Frisch, himself a prominent physicist, and they realised that Hahn and Strassman had split the atom, paving the way for the creation of an atomic bomb. One of the few people Hahn told was Rosbaud, a close friend, who passed the information to Foley. Shortly afterwards, the Nazis ordered German nuclear physicists to start work on an atomic bomb. A strict ban was imposed on any public discussion of the experiments, but Rosbaud, with his relationship to Hahn, remained inside the loop and throughout the war was able to keep SIS informed of the lack of progress made by the German atomic weapons programme.[22]

The expansion of the Passport Control Offices in central Europe to collect intelligence on Germany and cope with the flood of Jews attempting to obtain visas brought a number of young women into the Service, many of them working on both the visa applications and intelligence operations. Marjorie 'Peggy' Weller was twenty-five when she was sent to Sofia in January 1936 completely unaware that she had joined the Secret Intelligence Service. 'I went out on the Orient Express, very grand. I went into the Passport Control Office and they said: "There's a lot to do and there's a [purloined diplomatic] bag. I said "What's a bag?" They pushed something at me and I said: "Oh, really. Nobody told me it was this." I thought it was very funny, but they had a lot of trouble with people who wouldn't do the work. I had two years in Sofia. I used to joke that I had a pile of passports on one side and a pile of secret ink letters on the other. Our staff consisted of the passport control officer, who was a retired army officer, me, and a Russian called

[Wodin] Grenovich, who was the so-called messenger. He had been given a British passport. He had never set foot in England in his life. His English was reasonable and he always said to me: "If you ever see me walking out in the park, or wherever, don't recognise me. You've never seen me before." The retired army officer [Major Charles Mackinnon Gray] picked up a Hungarian cabaret artiste and, before we knew where we were, he and the cabaret artiste had vanished. They sent a man out from London to replace him, Wing-Commander "Teddy" Smith-Ross, RAF, with a very nice German wife.'

Even as the Service was building up new networks that would help produce intelligence throughout the war, so it was losing other agents. One of the worst blows came with the loss of Karl Krüger. In April 1938, he was arrested while trying to collect intelligence on a secret airfield. He managed to talk his way out of it but was now under suspicion and when he next crossed the border, he was subject, unusually, to a thorough search. All meetings were suspended for at least two months and at the first meeting thereafter, he was shadowed throughout by one of the Hague bureau's leading agents, Folkert van Koutrijk. Unfortunately, van Koutrijk had been bought by the Germans. Eventually Krüger was arrested for a second and final time. Shortly after the outbreak of the Second World War, the Germans announced that he had been executed by axe after being found guilty of 'working against Germany in favour of foreign powers'. This was not the Abwehr's only penetration of SIS operations in Europe. Dick Ellis, who worked for Wilfred Dunderdale in Paris, was also providing intelligence to the Germans. In an astonishingly risky move, SIS also tried to reactivate the First World War network La Dame Blanche, even though the Germans were fully aware of the names of all of its members because they had all been awarded medals and decorations which had been published in the *London Gazette*. [23]

The problems facing SIS as they collected intelligence on Hitler's intentions were not helped by the Gestapo's decision to arrest Captain Thomas Kendrick, the SIS passport control officer in Vienna, in August 1938. 'They shut him up for two days,' said his deputy, Kenneth Benton. 'I don't think they tortured him but they gave him a bad time. They

showed him just how much they knew and it was really terrifying.'
This led SIS to recall Foley and some of his staff from Berlin and Harold
Gibson from Prague where he was bureau chief, disrupting the collection
of intelligence. In an attempt to supplement the intelligence on German
and Italian preparations for war, Sinclair set up a London-based agent-
recruiting system quite separate from the Z Organisation. It was known
as 'the 22000 system', since the UK's country designator was 22, and its
role was to recruit Britons who had a legitimate reason for going into
Germany and Italy. These agents were largely businessmen, academics
or journalists operating under natural cover.[24]

With war now inevitable, SIS produced a controversial assessment
of Britain's options in the face of the rising threat from Nazi Germany.
Written by Malcolm Woollcombe in September 1938 and entitled:
'What Should We Do?', this was a far more complex document than it
is sometimes portrayed as being. It argued the case for appeasement, in
the short term, on the grounds that the disarmament measures during the
1920s and early 1930s left Britain needing to rebuild its defences before
taking on Hitler. The paper began with a very accurate prediction of
German intentions. It then made a number of suggestions that would
delay the need for confrontation. Examined in isolation, some of these
were morally reprehensible, including as they did a suggested agreement
to allow Germany to annex the Sudetenland, with its much quoted
proposal to 'forestall the inevitable and make the Czechs realise that
they stand alone if they refuse a solution'. This was not the only dubious
measure proposed; the other related to the moves by the League of
Nations to create a Jewish state in Palestine and the need to keep the
Arab world from siding with Germany against Britain. Woollcombe
suggested the League's decision should be pre-empted by the creation
of 'a mere token state for the Jews, with rigid safeguards against Jewish
expansion. Better still, Jewish cantonisation in an Arab state.'

As regards Germany's other territorial ambitions, 'international steps
of some sort should be taken, without undue delay, to see what really
legitimate grievances Germany has and what surgical operations are
necessary to rectify them,' Woollcombe said. 'It may be argued that

this would be giving in to Germany, strengthening Hitler's position and encouraging him to go to extremes. Better, however, that realities be faced, and that wrongs, if they do exist, be righted, than leave it to Hitler to do the righting in his own way and time.' Criticism of such measures has to be tempered by the position in which Britain now found itself, with no potential ally that would be capable of, or interested in, standing against Hitler's bid for domination of Europe. 'We cannot really trust any foreign country,' Woollcombe said. Britain had to tie itself closer to France and encourage it to rearm. 'But it seems doubtful whether there is any other European country with whom we could be really, and with confidence, allied, or be on terms even approximating those with France. As regards other countries, their positions, interests and/or temperaments stand in their way.'

At the same time, Britain should reach out to Japan and Italy to try to split them off from Germany. While all of these measures might prevent or forestall war in the short term, in the longer term, 'it seems to go without saying that, whatever else we should or might do, above all we should unremittingly build up our armaments and defensive measures and maintain them at the highest possible level, never relaxing. Platitudinous though it may be, our only chance of preserving peace is to be ready for war on any scale, without relying too much on outside support.' Woollcombe added one postscript on a target that had by now slipped down the list of intelligence priorities, Stalin's Soviet Union: 'We can never bank on this country,' Woollcombe said. 'But to keep on the right side of this devil, we must sup with him to some extent, adapting the length of our spoon to circumstances at any given moment.'[25]

Despite arguing that Britain should play for time, Hugh Sinclair was already preparing for war, expanding SIS and buying a war station at Bletchley Park, now more famous for the codebreakers who worked there during the Second World War. He set up three new sections, again in preparation for war. Section VII set up a network of stay-behind intelligence agents across the country that would form the basis for an intelligence network should the Germans invade the UK. It recruited people who would have a key role in society even after an invasion, including 'doctors, dentists, chemists, bakers and small shopkeepers'. Section VIII, under Richard Gambier-Parry, recruited from Philco, where he was general sales manager, would produce up-to-date wireless transceivers and set up radio networks to ensure reports from both officers and agents abroad arrived in time to have any effect.

Sinclair is alleged to have told Gambier-Parry: 'I get a great deal of valuable information. They drive it round Europe in a *carrozza* before it reaches me. Your job here will be to do something about it.' SIS had a small radio station based at Barnes in south-west London, with transmitters at Woldingham in Surrey. The Barnes office also worked on producing communications systems for use by bureaux around the world and for agents in the field, the latter including a radio receiver hidden in a bar of soap. Gambier-Parry set up radio communications links between the SIS bureaux across Europe, often meeting resistance from ambassadors who believed the use of wireless transmitters breached the Geneva Conventions.

Leslie Nicholson recalled Gambier-Parry's deputy, Lieutenant-Colonel Ted Maltby, visiting the Riga bureau where he and the lead Alex had installed a radio transmitter and receiver that was formerly on a ship, buying it piece by piece to get around local laws that prevented the purchase of a radio transmitter without a licence.

> Alex took the pieces to his flat and there he reassembled the set. Although I had warned him of the danger of having such a compromising object in his apartment, he would not trust anyone else with it. Then came a memorable day when we switched the machine on. There was a gentle background hum as the valves warmed up and then we were thrilled to receive London, loud and clear.

Unfortunately they could receive but they could not transmit. Eventually Alex sorted the problem out, only to find an even more worrying one. Every time the radio transmitted messages, the drain on the electric power in Alex's block of flats was such that everybody's lights flickered on and off. The radio was moved to the seaside *dacha* of another of Nicholson's agents.

'In the spring of 1939, a telegram arrived from Warsaw announcing the arrival of a senior colleague on tour from London, whom I had not met and whose name [Maltby] was unfamiliar to me,' Nicholson said. 'I was asked to meet his train the following day and the telegram ended: "Will be wearing Old Etonian tie." How typically English, I thought. I felt sorely tempted to cable back: "Regret unfamiliar with OE colours", but I thought better of it. The Warsaw train was packed and the Old Etonian finally emerged, surrounded by a crowd of chattering peasants, duly wearing his black and light blue tie. He was a tall man and so unmistakably English that even without his distinctive haberdashery, I should have had no difficulty in singling him out from the other passengers. He was apparently going round checking up on communications; my masters were leaving nothing to chance.'[26]

The second new section set up, based on an idea originally put forward by Stewart Menzies, was for a sabotage unit, Section IX, more commonly known as D Section, quite literally D for destruction. Lieutenant-Colonel Lawrence Grand of the Royal Engineers, a tall dapper man who habitually wore a carnation in his jacket lapel, was selected for the job and asked by Sinclair to prepare a report on what might be done. Grand recalled:

A war was coming with Germany and he wanted someone to look after sabotage; was I interested? I said that I was due to go abroad. I could undertake to do a report on what could be done and how to do it. He said that would be all right; had I any questions to ask? My first question was 'Is anything banned?' He replied: 'Nothing at all.' I left very bemused and challenged since I realised the task was considerable. On 1 April 1938, I reported and was taken up to C. He seemed as strange and intelligent and dominating as ever. He asked me if I had thought about the job. I said I had but I didn't know enough yet to be intelligent about it. He then said one thing that proved very true. He said: 'Don't have any illusions. Everything you do is going to be disliked by a lot of people in Whitehall – some in this building. The more you succeed, the more they will dislike you and what you are trying to do.

There are a lot of jealous people about so don't tell anyone more than you have to.' I was given an office on the ground floor with a bare table and chair and found next door another new boy, Gambier-Parry, who turned out to be a wireless expert. We were both very vague as to what we had to do, in fact, we soon realised that we had come to fill a complete vacuum. There were no real secret communications and there was no organisation for anything except the collection of intelligence. We were starting from scratch with a vengeance.

During the Munich crisis of September 1938, Section D set up a sabotage network in the Škoda armaments factories in Czechoslovakia. It sent officers into the Balkans with the intention of sabotaging German access to oil, although not on the scale that Cumming's men had managed in 1916; an agent was recruited within the Romanian oil industry, but the only significant sabotage carried out before the war was caused by army officers sent into Romania in civilian clothes who disrupted rail supplies to Germany by putting sand in the axle boxes of trains. Grand sent A. F. 'Freddie' Rickman to Sweden to gather intelligence on iron ore supplies to Germany, under cover of writing a book, which duly appeared. The section set up links with a number of left-wing organisations and unions to provoke strikes in key German industries, claiming that a strike at the Krupp factory a few weeks before the war was a result of these activities. One of those recruited by Grand, in December 1938, was Guy Burgess, the first of the Cambridge spies to infiltrate the Service and the man who brought in Kim Philby.[27]

In early 1939, SIS began reporting that Hitler was planning to invade Czechoslovakia, reports that were reinforced by an MI5 source, Wolfgang zu Putlitz, a German diplomat based in the London embassy, and separate German contacts of Robert Vansittart, now the government's chief diplomatic adviser. SIS also reported a similar threat to the Netherlands, intelligence that was passed on to Britain's allies. This enraged George Mounsey, an assistant under-secretary at the Foreign Office, who complained that it ran counter to the government's policy of appeasement, risking provoking a crisis rather than preventing it. 'This seems to me a very serious matter,' Mounsey said. 'Are we going to remain so attached to reliance on secret reports, which tie our hands in all directions, that we are going to continue acting on them, in disregard of the clear warnings we now have of the effect which such action may have?'

By the time Gladwyn Jebb, private secretary to Alexander Cadogan, the Foreign Office permanent under-secretary, responded, Hitler's troops had marched into Czechoslovakia. 'I am afraid I have taken a long time to comment on your notes on secret service reports,' Jebb began. 'A good deal has happened since they were written. The policy of appeasement, for instance, seems to have receded rather into the background for the time being, and I must say that I personally doubt whether this unfortunate fact can be attributed to the provocation of Herr Hitler by the broadcasting of unjustified reports! I think that from what you say, you have the impression that the reports of the SIS, which are circulated in the office, are obtained by "hired assassins", who are sent out from this country to spy out the land. This is not at all how the system works in practice so far as the SIS are concerned. Their reports are based on conversations recorded by agents in the countries concerned and collated, first of all abroad, and later in the organisation here. No agent's report is ever put forward unless he has been tested over a long period and the reliability or otherwise of his reports proved beyond doubt.'

Jebb accepted that too many reports were coming from conflicting sources, but a new system had been introduced to ensure all such reports were vetted by Sinclair or one of his officers. Sinclair was 'a man of really remarkable intelligence and discretion', he said. 'He has been doing the job for over fifteen years, reads all Foreign Office telegrams and despatches and is in constant contact both with the Heads of the Departments here and with myself.' All of these colleagues had told Jebb 'what value they attach to his reports. All of them would regard a suggestion that they should be suppressed with frank dismay, I really do not myself think that your criticisms of the kind of report which he produces are justified at all.'

Jebb's boss also felt the need to defend the Service as it came under attack from within Whitehall and the three armed services. Responding to Mounsey's criticism, Cadogan said: 'I cannot ignore that they did warn us of the September crisis, and they did not give any colour to the ridiculous optimism that persisted up to the rape of Czechoslovakia, of which our official reports did not give us much warning.' In a separate minute, Cadogan added:

> Our agents are of course bound to report rumours or items of information which come into their possession. They exercise a certain amount of discrimination themselves, but naturally do not take the responsibility of too much selection and it is our job to weigh up the information which we receive and try to draw more or less reasonable conclusions from it. In that, we may fail, and if so it is our fault, but I do not think it is fair to blame the SIS.

One important piece of intelligence that SIS did not pass on to the Foreign Office, or any other government department, was that the Germans were negotiating a secret non-aggression agreement with the Russians – the so-called Molotov-Ribbentrop Pact – that would ensure Russia kept out of the war in return for half of Poland. This was reported in the spring of 1939 by an agent codenamed Baron and run by Harry Carr from Helsinki. But the desk officer in London refused to believe it. When the pact was announced in August 1939, there was a scramble within headquarters to avoid being blamed for having missed such a potentially useful piece of intelligence.[28]

One of the main critics of SIS was the RAF, despite its dismissal of the figures supplied direct from Frank Foley's Luftwaffe staff officer and its own failure to provide the Navy with aerial photography of the German naval dockyards. Frederick Winterbotham, the head of Section II, the Service's air section, set about remedying the lack of photographic intelligence by recruiting Sidney Cotton, an Australian pilot, to provide the aerial pictures of Germany that were required. Cotton carried out a number of missions, some in co-operation with the French, to photograph border areas of Germany and Italian-occupied territory in the Mediterranean and east Africa. The first flight over Germany came in March 1939, when Cotton used a German-made Leica camera to photograph Mannheim. During July and August 1939, he flew an SIS Lockheed 12A deep into German territory, masquerading as a businessman and amateur pilot and photographing a number of locations of interest to British intelligence, including Berlin and the German naval base at Wilhelmshaven. John Weaver, a member of Cotton's unit, described how shortly before the outbreak of war, Cotton flew to Berlin's Tempelhof airport.

> Göring and his lieutenants were there. Seeing the aircraft, they made enquiries as to whom it belonged. On finding out, they approached Cotton for a flight and asked where he would take them. Cotton said: 'I have a dear old aunt who lives in such an area and if you have no objections we could fly over there.' It was agreed and off they set. But what they did not know was that dear old Sidney was pressing the tit the whole time, taking photographs.[29]

In the months before the war, parts of the Z Organisation were merged with the passport control system. This odd decision was taken, ostensibly on security grounds, to allow the Z officers to use the technical facilities – couriers, radio communications and ciphers – of the normal bureaux and to 'avoid the mutually dangerous duplication of agents' work'. It is difficult to see how this was more secure than keeping the identity of the previously undeclared Z officers secret. The error was compounded by a joint operation mounted by Major Richard Stevens, the passport control officer in The Hague, and his Z officer equivalent, Sigismund Payne-Best. As war grew closer, and in the first few months of the war, there were a number of people on both sides trying to mediate a settlement between Germany and Britain, all of which were doomed to failure. There was, however, reason to believe that various German elements could be split off from Hitler, either to form a credible government that could find a way to avoid war, or to provide an internal resistance once war broke out. In search of such elements, the Service was drawn into an elaborate deception plan in which agents of the Sicherheitsdienst (SD), the Nazi

Party's internal intelligence organisation, posed as members of the anti-Hitler opposition offering to set up just such a government. Payne-Best and Stevens were lured to a small hotel near Venlo on the Dutch–German border for a series of negotiations with opposition 'emissaries' aimed at deposing Hitler and removing German troops from Czechoslovakia, Austria and Poland. At a meeting on 9 November 1939, in what became known as 'the Venlo incident', they were kidnapped and taken to Berlin. Not only did the Nazis gain a propaganda victory by alleging that Payne-Best and Stevens were part of a British plot to assassinate Hitler, but the 'Most Secret' Z Organisation was blown and SIS networks across Europe compromised.[30]

In the middle of the negotiations, on 4 November 1939, Sinclair died of cancer and Stewart Menzies, the man he had anointed as his successor, was put in charge, the navy's choice having been vetoed by the Foreign Office.[31] With senior forces officers intensely suspicious of secret intelligence, and the networks across Europe suffering as the Nazis advanced, Menzies was given a difficult task, but more of the networks survived than is generally believed, others were swiftly built up, and alliances with governments in exile, in particular the Poles, the Czechs and the Norwegians, were to produce excellent results, many of them sadly under-rated. The myth of the intelligence war is that SIS, or MI6 as it would soon become, had a poor war, relying on the work of the codebreakers at Bletchley Park for its triumphs. While the breaking of Enigma was one of the critical intelligence contributions to the Allied victory, it was not alone. SIS was to have a much better Second World War than is commonly believed to be the case.

Written instructions for MI1c officers tasking agents operating behind enemy lines during the First World War. These were given to Redmond Cafferata, who was based in Switzerland and was taught agent-handling by Richard Tinsley's staff in Rotterdam. They were almost certainly produced by Tinsley.

INSTRUCTIONS OF AGENTS

It is plainly to our interest that no agent should set out without being completely equipped to succeed. In addition to the material preparation (papers, perfectly plausible motives, and a clear history from the time of the mobilisation) he must be prepared from the technical point of view.

His research work would be advantageously limited if he were told the kind of information which is useless to us, but which (experience has proved) regularly attracts the attention of incompletely instructed agents.

This indication, illustrated by examples, may be given to the agent; at the same time as he is told briefly of his mission, and it may be seen whether he fulfils at first sight the material and moral conditions requisite.

It will often be advantageous, when relations are first opened with an agent, for two people to interview him, one playing a silent role: experience has proved that in this way one often remarks hesitations, reticences, or assurance of a bad quality that a single interlocutor does not always notice.

The agent, thus roughly instructed in what is required of him, can theoretically immediately receive the complete instruction as to the details with which he should be acquainted. But, as he is not always apt to profit from too long an interview, it is better to leave him a few hours for reflexion to enable him to draw up a small programme regarding what he has just heard, he will then better grasp the signification of what will then be explained to him.

He will, therefore, be asked to return the following day when his instruction proper will be commenced, and for the same reason this instruction will be continued for 30 to 45 minutes only per half-day until completed.

The programme of this instruction corresponds to the memorandum attached.

This instruction should be illustrated by numerous examples for which one should not hesitate to show drawings, photographs representing the things spoken of, nor to make rough sketches so as to present the instruction in a tangible form and fix the attention.

Everything which is not indispensable, and everything which is complicated should be avoided.

Particular care should be taken to make the agent pass through a period of observation making him state the means he expects to employ or that he would wish to employ on the spot. His attention should be drawn to the necessity for our being informed of the daily duration of his observation.

He should be advised to always indicate clearly the source through which he has obtained the information that he gives, and to be content to state what he has seen, or what he has been told without drawing his own conclusions.

One should examine with him the precautions he should take when noting his observations, hiding his notes, communicating with his correspondents when this is necessary.

The dispositions that he would take should be criticised from the point of view of the interest attaching to the information and the personal safety of the agent.

The method of transmitting reports and the channel through which the agent is to receive his salary should be arranged.

If several agents are employed in connection with each other the method of working for the group should be studied in such a manner that nothing is left to chance.

Care should be taken to give confidence to the agent by giving him the impression that we are perfectly informed regarding the movements of the enemy, that he is entering a solid organisation and that nothing will go wrong if he acts as he should.

He should be put on his guard against gossip, the cabaret and women, and told how these were the cause of the recent arrests and executions. He should also be put on guard against German agents both on the journey and after his arrival.

No opportunity should be lost of showing the agent the facility of his mission. In particular, by drawing up false certificates of identity for him or giving him false papers, and showing him the security attached to their possession.

On the map or in imagination the agent should be made to follow his route in such a way as to make him go through a general repetition of his mission.

When the agent has understood well all that has been taught him, he should be told, if necessary, the means which should be employed by him for the transmission of information. When he is working quite alone, this process consists of sending letters into Holland, which are posted there by smuggler.

He should then be given a series of written reports corresponding to the observations that he might be able to make, including useful and useless information mixed, with indication of the dates and hours, and be told to make a report of them, first 'en clair' and then in the form to be adopted for correspondence (invisible writing).

The latter should be revealed to him if necessary, after having made him remark the result (which always strikes the agent). His sorting of information should then be criticised.

This should be recommenced until the lesson has been well learnt. Five to six hours should be reckoned, i.e. six to eight séances, to instruct a medium agent.

The following applies to the instruction of ordinary agents. It is naturally insufficient for the instruction of special technical agents.

Do not attempt to teach those with inferior intelligence more things than are necessary, but always enter into the detail of the subject under consideration.

Experience has shown that, for reasons difficult to discover (often dramatic) agents attach much more importance to certain observations which strike them, than to clear and precise facts which they might note. Example: out of ten agents passing through Brussels nine will report the guns in front of the Palais de Justice; agents will pass along a railway and never fail to report the trainloads of wounded or 'dead' without observing the train carefully so that it could be identified. Others go to inconceivable trouble to take the number of fifteen men of the Landsturm who are in a village or to follow the flight of an aeroplane.

Too much attention cannot therefore be given to explaining clearly to agents the kind of information we require and that which only encumbers their notes and memory, detracting their attention from essential points.

Useless information
When no special mission is in question the following may be considered as useless: all information which does not enable us to follow a movement or identify a concentration of troops: local defensive organisations far from the front, emplacement of isolated anti-aircraft guns or searchlights situated on the aviation field itself, complaints of soldiers regarding their food or the length of the war, details as to their billets or cantonment, names of officers other than colonels or generals, position of Kommandanturen, number of men on guard, numbers of motor-cars circulating, indications relative to columns at halting places when these are not abnormal, local events without importance from a military point of view (café regulations, different fines, requisitions of food, news of political men, rigorous measures taken against the population etc.). The following are also useless: histories of events going back more than a month, as also news regarding actions on the front, which is always fantastic.

Observation in general

Agents should have the idea firmly imprinted on their minds that only precise observations are really useful: by the juxtaposition of precise observations, a conclusion is arrived at. It is therefore necessary for each to report what he has seen as completely as possible and without additions.

The observation may be either instantaneous or permanent. The agent may be in a position to pass a complete report, or he may not.

All momentary observation is not without value if the exact duration is known. In any case, permanent observation is always the surest and most economical process especially in regard to railways.

It is easily understood that the facility for transmitting the agent's reports must greatly influence their context thus under the most unfavourable conditions the agent or the courier has to retain these by memory, and one would thus be obliged to give them, for example for a railway report, under the form: 'From the 15th to 18th – usual movement; the 19th – ten trains to X..., empty trains from X...' This case would necessitate a more extended instruction of the agent who would have to distinguish the grouping of trains transporting constituted units, and avoid losing himself in detail: whilst the more favoured observer has only to copy his observations *in extenso*.

Above all the method of reporting a movement noted in the course of a visit with exactitude but omitting to indicate the duration of the observation should be avoided.

Never report a movement which has not been personally seen without giving the source of the information, and indicating whether the person who has given it saw it personally and duration of the observation.

The agent should note the date with the great precision and not under the form 'Saturday' or 'Sunday' but as 'the 29/1' or 'the 30/1'.

Never give rough information, for instance 'Such and such army corps is round X...' but give the elementary indications.

Observation of railways

When fixed agents can frequently send their reports or pass them in security it is advantageous to have them note all the trains. When the volume of their report has to be small, it is necessary for them to know how to eliminate the trains which have no interest. They should be advised then only to note:

1. Military trains.
2. Empty trains considered capable of transporting a constituted unit.

Under the most unfavourable conditions (information transmitted verbally) the agent will only consider movements of constituted units and very large movements of empty trains.

The observations should bear in the case of each train: the hour, the number of wagons containing men, number of horse wagons, number of wagons containing regimental rolling stock. Indication should also be given of the number of travelling kitchens and guns. If possible the unit transported should be identified, also the appearance of the material (whether new or apparently withdrawn from the front).

The direction is indicated by the station to which the train is certainly going.

Trains transporting constituted units should be carefully distinguished from those bearing reinforcements. This distinction is made by observing the rolling stock: the trains with reinforcements carry all kinds and nearly always without the horses to correspond. The trains transporting constituted units have from thirty-five to fifty wagons, including wagons containing men, horses and rolling stock corresponding to the unit.

The observation of trainloads of material, if restricted, should only be concerned with unusual movements of munition trains and the passage of material that one is not accustomed to see.

The observation of the trainloads of wounded is without interest.

The indications relating to empty trains should include the number of the wagons for men and those for horses and the number of flat trucks. For these the hour is equally indispensable (especially when it is a question of material which is being returned).

The identification of the unit transported is rarely arrived at by the helmets (the men generally wear the calotte), very seldom by the shoulder-straps, much better by the inscriptions on the rolling stock. Artillery material in particular is an excellent means of identification.

The indication of a suspension of traffic (commercial) for a stated period is always very interesting, especially in frontier regions, and on the large German lines.

Movements by road

This information is only of interest when it relates to units and not to isolated people: if the agent has to select his observations, he should be recommended to leave on one side movements of companies or battalions of Landsturm. (See further on the method of distinguishing these.)

The direction of the march should always be indicated by the name of the locality nearest to the point from which it could no longer be followed.

The point where the troops were should also be indicated as well as their certain place of origin.

The identifications, when these relate to important columns, may nearly always be arrived at through the clothing accoutrements. It is, however, well to indicate the inscriptions seen on several carriages (these are generally covered by a piece of cardboard, but it is very rare when some of these are not missing, at any rate in the case of artillery this indication is easy).

The agent should state whether the troops are followed by their regimental equipages (or by their 'fighting train'). If he is able to count the travelling kitchens, the strength of the troops can be estimated (two to four kitchens per battalion): if the agent is careful to note also the time taken to pass, reliable information will have been obtained. But in this case he must keep account of the intervals and not report six battalions passing at regular intervals of one hour as having taken six hours to pass.

It is equally important to note the appearance of the troops: that of the men coming from the front is characteristic, small horses nearly always denote troops from the eastern front (or having been there).

In the towns the troops which have disembarked or who are going to entrain are generally recognised by their march by battalions or batteries at regular intervals (generally one hour).

Garrisons and concentrations of troops
Do not pay any attention to the usual Landsturm garrisons but to important concentrations.

To the sources of identification already given should be added the indications afforded by the cantonment notices, the linen lists, the carriages in the park, the address of the letters received by the soldiers (try to take an envelope if an opportunity occurs, but naturally without asking for it as the soldiers are warned), the money they use to pay their expenses (often vouchers from towns or foreign money indicates whence they have come). Note carefully the indications on the notices (posters) of the Staffs (with the exception of the *Kommandanturen*).

Note if lists of officers arrive and recruits. Repeat this for the different villages of a zone where troops are stationed. Ascertain the data of their arrival and whence they come (immediate if nothing better is possible).

Note the signs of an early departure (reviews, loading of vehicles).

Notice whether the troops are drilled together.

When troops bearing various numbers are permanently in the same town it frequently signifies a depot for recruits. This can be confirmed by observing their drills. In this case it is well to try and find out whether there are men of the 1916 class amongst the recruits.

On the departure of the troops try and determine their itinerary as far as possible. If they entrain do not omit to indicate the direction of the trains. See whether they leave with their regimental material.

Agents should devote particular attention to certain organs of the army corps, very little employed near the lines and consequently cantoned fairly far behind, in the zone of their army corps (bridge makers, munition and food columns, bakeries, demount depots). They should periodically report their presence at their usual quarters, and in case of departure report the date and direction. This information, which sometimes enables a conclusion to be arrived at concerning the troops themselves, is always of importance.

It sometimes happens that the arrival of troops in a certain region is announced for a certain date. It is well in this case to verify that the advice has been given in the various villages. Always indicate whether this measure has been commenced to be executed; it often happens that the troops announced do not arrive.

Particularities to be noted
When showing the agent pictures of uniforms his attention should be drawn to the following:

1. In general the divisions are distinguished by their head-dress: Hussars – Chasseurs – Dragoons and Cuirassiers – Uhlans – infantry – artillery and engineers. New helmet, which appears to be common to all – field-grey colour with no cover.
2. The Landsturm men are now nearly all dressed in grey with a helmet, but have numbers in copper on the collar, whilst the others have the numbers on the shoulder-straps. It often happens that the helmet covers do not bear any numbers. As a rule the Landsturm men only have covers when they are being sent to the front.
3. Certain corps have initials instead of numbers on their shoulder-straps. In this case, to shorten their description it is better to observe the colour of the border of the shoulder-straps. For example W with a crown and red border immediately identifies the 124th Infantry.
4. The men of the Guards and certain corps have on their collar and cuff-facings two white stripes with a red line in the middle. Before noting this peculiarity, observe whether all the men of the unit possess it. Do not confuse this with the non-commissioned-officer's stripes, which go all round the collar.
5. The Saxon troops may be identified by the cut of the basque of the tunic (straight piping instead of two arcs of a circle).
6. The blue and white cockade distinguishes the Bavarian troops.
7. The artillery has always a grenade with figure or letter on the shoulder-

straps. This identification is always very good on condition that the material which accompanies the men is indicated. Count the guns.

8. The infantry has always the red band on the calotte (cap). The artillery and Pioneers have a black band: various other colours denote cavalry men.

9. The silhouettes of the guns are characteristic; field gun, light howitzer, heavy howitzer, mortar.

10. The most important abbreviations employed on the notice boards and vehicles are:

    AOK IV: 4th Army
    VII AK: 7th Army Corps
    III RAK: 3rd Reserve Corps
    13 ID: 13th Infantry Division
    5 RID: 5th Reserve Division
    7 KD : 7th Division Cavalry
    IR 87 : 87th Infantry Regiment
    RIR 28: 28th Infantry Reserve Regiment
    RAR 25: 25th Field Artillery Regiment
    RFAR 50: 50th Artillery Reserve Regiment
    Fs AR4: 4th Foot Artillery Regiment
    etc.

    It is best to note the number of the regiment as well as the army corps.

    The initials EKK27 refer to automobile columns. The inscription naturally does not include the number of the army corps, but sometimes a number in Roman figures which denotes the army.

11. The rifles bear, stamped on the end of the butt, the number of the regiment and that of the company in the form 8 R4 (4th company of the 8th Infantry) or the 6th reserve, followed by a number which is without interest (number of the division). In the example SR 4 186, the indication SR 4 is the only one to be remembered.

Aeronautics
The complete number of the Zeppelins is always interesting, as well as the sheds where they are stationed. Example: LZ77 seen on the 15th

January at Cognelée. It is useless to give other details except an idea of their size in the form 'ordinary size' or 'larger than the Zeppelins seen up to the present'.

Aeroplanes should only be reported: if the agent has seen an aviation field (give situation); if their silhouette is abnormal (give number of guns, of planes); if seen at close quarters (number of places, of motors, disposition of seats and of the mitrailleuse [machine-gun] or mitrailleuses).

Various materials

The transports of wire, wood, gravel from the Rhine etc. are only to be reported when they exceed the normal or when the materials are discharged at an unusual place.

The cisterns on wagons do not contain gas, but liquids.

The gas chambers are generally in the form of long steel tubes, or 3 cylinders placed on a wagon, perhaps also in the apparent form of large parallel-piped cases on small wheels.

If the agent is identifying a factory to which such wagons go, he should observe all the materials taken there and those which leave. Note whether the establishment is near a dirigible shed.

Fortifications

Numerous agents have reported, in an airy way, the presence of fortifications, which were in reality only practice trenches.

The latter are recognised on account of their proximity to garrisons, and extend for a very small distance: other works of a similar nature will not be found on their left or right: troops from the garrison practise there in small parties, and the trenches are not guarded.

When the agent has observed an extended line of fortifications, he should note the site and also position according to the cardinal points, and report: if provided with wire entanglements and guarded by sentinels; if battery emplacements exist behind; if these are armed or not; if the trenches are concreted; if communicating trenches exist behind; if there are several successive lines. Indicate from which point to which point the organisation has been seen to extend.

Various indications

Agents operating near the front should report, as soon as possible, the villages from which the Germans evacuate the inhabitants, and the date of the evacuation.

All those who operate in a zone behind the lines should note every change in the connection of the Kommandanturen to an army, as well as the date on which the change of zone takes place.

German agents (or agents in Germany)

The following indications do not include those relative to political, economic or technical questions.

Bear in mind:

The trains crossing or passing the train in which one is sitting. Only give your attention to movements involving a series of trains. Note exactly the date and itinerary followed, even if nothing is encountered, this precise information has its value.

The series of trains passing through the locality in which the agent is, or stopping for entrainments (only trains with constituted units).

Interruptions of traffic remarked or announced.

The addresses of the soldier relatives of the families that are visited. Repeat carefully all conversations on this subject.

The dates and where soldier relatives of the families visited have been killed, etc.

Places not far removed from the front where there are factories engaged on war materials.

The numbers [of units or formations] above 381 – Try and ascertain if these formations are in the place where you are.

New formations – Ascertain whether any are in cantonments in the surroundings. They are recognised by their unusual numbers. Do not confuse then with Landsturm formations, which wear their number in the form of a fraction, the numerator being that of the region.

The classes – Try and ascertain from proclamations, conversations etc. whether the 1918 class has been called up.

The depots – Try and find out in what manner they are filled. Each regiment forms an ersatz battalion (or division).

Notice whether the standard is as important as formerly, whether the units are composed of young men.

The numbers of Zeppelins observed.

Destructions

It is well for agents who show themselves to be resolute, to be instructed in the use of explosives on railways (choice of point, installation of charge). They should be advised to use these only during large movements executed by the enemy by rail, at a time when an important engagement is certain to take place.

Document from the Cafferata family archives, reproduced by kind permission of Richard Cafferata.

APPENDIX 2

These instructions, which were in the possession of Redmond Cafferata in his role as a senior MI1c officer in Switzerland, are believed to have been prepared by the staff of Richard Tinsley, the MI1c representative in Rotterdam, who ran many of the most successful British agents operating inside Germany, including Karl Krüger, agent H16.

INSTRUCTIONS FOR AGENTS GOING TO GERMANY

Every agent proceeding to Germany should be made to realise the importance of the mission he sets out to accomplish. It is absolutely vital to have, behind the enemy's lines, agents who are willing and capable of furnishing particulars of the movements of troops, concentrations, defences, new measures of offense and the hundred-and-one details which are impossible to obtain by 'contact' information at the Front.

By means of listening posts, examination of prisoners, patrols, aerial observation etc. at the front, our HQ is fully acquainted with the actual enemy forces opposing it on each sector. But it is impossible by these methods to establish what troops are being transported behind the lines, and in what direction, and therefore, without the aid of reliable information received through our agents in the enemy country, it is impossible for our HQ to determine with any degree of accuracy, and in sufficient time, where a concentration of enemy troops is taking place, where the enemy is weakening his line by the withdrawal of effective etc., etc. The value of such information is very great, for it is only when in possession of all particulars regarding the disposition of enemy troops, both at the front and in reserve, that our HQ can decide on the possibilities of future operations.

At times when the enemy is carrying out some exceptionally large concentration at a certain part of our front, information received from our agents on such a subject is of incalculable importance and has often been a means of carrying out a successful operation or saving a serious defeat and the lives of many of our soldiers.

The chief qualifications necessary to make a successful agent – intelligence of a high order, absolute discretion, patience, perseverance and constant attention to duty – are too well known to need but passing mention. Stress should be laid, however, on care in the receiving and expenditure of money. More agents come under the suspicion of the authorities through reckless expenditure of money (especially where no real source of income is apparent) than by any other means.

As will be seen in subsequent lessons the work of our agents can be divided broadly into two classes, the first of which is by far the more important:

1. Movement of troops and their identification.
2. Information dealing with:
    a) Aviation
    b) Depots and new formations
    c) Munitions and factories
    d) New inventions
    e) Economic, industrial and political information.

Special lessons have been drawn up on each subject.

For information on the movement of troops the agent should make a special study of the chapters on the 'Organisation of the German forces' – 'How to identify troops'; 'How troops are moved'.

Special stress should he laid on the fact that an agent in his report should only give us the details of his observations – what he has actually seen himself – we do not want him to draw his own conclusions from what he sees for the obvious reason that it is only possible to draw accurate conclusions from certain facts by having a full knowledge of all other information from every source on that particular subject.

The importance of train-watching is gone into fully in the lesson on 'How troops are moved'. It is impossible to be correctly informed of the changes in the disposition of the enemy forces without having an organised system of train watchers who are installed *à poste fixe* at regular intervals along all the principal railway lines.

In addition to receiving reports on the movements of large masses of troops on the railways it is also necessary wherever possible to obtain particulars of the identity of the troops moving. Such information will give us value to the information on the movements of the troops.

The following example will explain the importance of identifying the troop movements. As already pointed out, our HQ by means of contact information keeps itself acquainted with the various regiments and divisions which form the German front lines. We will assume that one of our agents is able to identify a certain regiment believed by our GHQ to be at the front, en route at say 60 or 70 kilometres from the front. As will be shewn later it is seldom that an isolated regiment is removed so far from the front, without the entire division, of which it forms a part, leaving the line.

Our agent's information in this case would therefore be of the utmost value to our HQ advising them as it does that the enemy has withdrawn probably an entire division from the front or reserve lines. Our HQ will then ascertain by means of raiding parties, if the gap caused by the withdrawal of the notified regiment has been filled by extending the remaining units or if a new formation has been introduced. In the former case an attack on the weakened line might bear excellent results. If our agent has been unable to identify the regiment the value of his information would have been largely discounted, as the sector of the front which had thereby been weakened would have been unknown.

It is often extremely difficult or impossible for train watchers to obtain identification of the troops being moved. It then becomes necessary to appoint a mobile agent, who has the entry to the nearest stopping station or refreshment halt. There he is able to mix with the troops or at any rate to get sufficiently near to identify one or two of the units. This agent may or may not act in conjunction with the train watcher, on that sector of the line, but in any case the reports from these two agents will be confirmatory one of the other.

The various methods of transmitting reports from enemy to neutral territory is gone in fully in the subsequent lesson. The speed with which this is done is second in importance only to the accuracy and amount of detail of the information transmitted.

The question of agents' cover should be carefully discussed and the utmost care should be given to make this as sound as possible. Especially at the beginning of an agent's visit to G[ermany] he should devote a considerable amount of time every day to the building up of his business connections. Especially in the case of a neutral, certain suspicion is attached to every arrival in a German town, and it is essential that for some time at least an agent should occupy himself entirely with his cover business, by calls, correspondence, note books etc.

This would apply to a man who is going to G under the cover as representative or traveller of a neutral House. The agent who takes up a fixed post in a German firm which will tie him to definite office hours can obviously be of little or no use to us, whilst so employed, but this may be a means for him to get into G and after some time he could find an excuse to leave his employment and launch out for himself.

Students in art, music, medicine etc. find good cover for train-watching, as also do professionals such as doctors dentists, architects, and those whose profession or business enable them to dispose of their time as they will and to establish themselves as they wish in localities of their own choice.

Document from the Cafferata Family Archives, reproduced by kind permission of Richard Cafferata.

BIBLIOGRAPHY

Agar, Augustus, *Baltic Episode*, Naval Institute Press, Annapolis (MD), 1963

Andrew, Christopher, *The Defence of the Realm: The Authorized History of MI5*, Allen Lane, London, 2009

Andrew, Christopher, *Secret Service: The Making of the British Intelligence Community*, Heinemann, London, 1985

Andrew, Christopher and Dilks, David (eds), *The Missing Dimension: Governments and Intelligence Communities in the Twentieth Century*, Macmillan, London, 1984

Bainton, Roy, *Honoured by Strangers*, Airlife, Shrewsbury, 2002

Baron, Nick, *The King of Karelia*, Francis Boutle, London, 2007

Batey, Mavis, *Dilly: The Man Who Broke Enigmas*, Dialogue, London, 2009

Bazhanov, Boris, *Avec Staline dans le Kremlin*, Les Éditions de France, Paris, 1930

Bazhanov, Boris and Doyle, David W., *Bazhanov and the Damnation of Stalin*, Ohio University Press, Athens, 1990

Bennett, Gill, *'A Most Extraordinary and Mysterious Business': The Zinoviev Letter of 1924*, FCO, London, 1999

Bennett, Gill, *Churchill's Man of Mystery: Desmond Morton and the World of Intelligence*, Routledge, Abingdon, 2007

Best, Antony, *British Intelligence and the Japanese Challenge in Asia 1914–1941*, Palgrave Macmillan, Basingstoke, 2002

Bottome, Phyllis, *The Goal*, Faber & Faber, London, 1962

Brook-Shepherd, Gordon, *Iron Maze: The Western Secret Services and the Bolsheviks*, Macmillan, London, 1998

Brook-Shepherd, Gordon, *The Storm Petrels: The Flight of the First Soviet Defectors*, Ballantine, New York, 1977

Brown, Anthony Cave, *The Secret Servant: The Life of Sir Stewart Menzies*, Michael Joseph, London, 1988

Bywater, Hector C. and Ferraby, H. C., *Strange Intelligence: Memoirs of Naval Service*, Constable, London, 1931

Campbell, John, *Jutland: An Analysis of the Fighting*, Conway, London, 1987

Carr, E. H., *The Twilight of Comintern 1930–1935*, Macmillan, London, 1982

Chambers, Roland, *The Last Englishman: The Double Life of Arthur Ransome*, Faber & Faber, London, 2009

Childers, Erskine, *The Riddle of the Sands: A Record of Secret Service*, Penguin, London, 1995

Christmas, Captain Walter, *The Life of King George of Greece*, Eveleigh Nash, London, 1914

Christmas, Walter, *Svend Spejder* (Svend the Scout), Miloske Boghandels Forlag, Copenhagen, 1911

Clayton, Anthony, *Forearmed: A History of the Intelligence Corps*, Brassey's, London, 1993

Cook, Andrew, *Ace of Spies: The True Story of Sidney Reilly*, History Press, Stroud, 2004

Cook, Andrew, *M: MI5's First Spymaster*, Tempus, Stroud, 2004

Cook, Andrew, *To Kill Rasputin: The Life and Death of Grigori Rasputin*, History Press, Stroud, 2006

Cullen, Richard, *Rasputin: The Role of Britain's Secret Services in His Torture and Murder*, Dialogue, London, 2010

Davies, Philip H. J., *The British Secret Services*, ABC-Clio, Oxford, 1996

Davies, Philip H. J., *MI6 and the Machinery of Spying*, Frank Cass, London, 2004

Dear, I. C. B. and Foot, M. R. D. (eds), *Oxford Companion to World War II*, Oxford University Press, Oxford, 2002

Dewhurst, Norman, *Norman Dewhurst MC*, H. J. Edmonds, Brussels, 1968

Dukes, Paul, *Red Dusk and the Morrow: Adventures and Investigations in Soviet Russia*, Doubleday Page, New York, 1922

Eatwell, Roger, *Fascism: A History*, Vintage, London, 1996

Everitt, Nicholas, *British Secret Service during the Great War*, Hutchinson, London, 1920

Ferguson, Harry, *Operation Kronstadt*, Arrow, London, 2010

Fisher, John, *Gentleman Spies: Intelligence Agents in the British Empire and Beyond*, Sutton, Stroud, 2002

Foot, M. R. D. and Langley, J. M., *MI9*, Bodley Head, London, 1979

Fowler, W. B., *British–American Relations 1917–1918: The Role of Sir William Wiseman*, Princeton University Press, Princeton, 1969

Gaunt, Guy, *The Yield of the Year: A Story of Adventure Afloat and Ashore*, London, Hutchinson, 1940

Golikov, D. L., *Krushenie antisovetskogo podpol'ya v SSSR* (Collapse of the Anti-Soviet Underground in the USSR), vol. 1, Politizdat, Moscow, 1986

Hill, Capt. G. A., *Go Spy the Land: Being the Adventures of IK8 of the British Secret Service*, Cassell, London, 1932

Hoare, Sir Samuel, *The Fourth Seal*, Heinemann, London, 1930

Honan, William H., *Bywater: The Man Who Invented the Pacific War*, Futura, London, 1991

House, Edward Mandell and Seymour, Charles, *The Intimate Papers of Colonel House*, Kessinger, Whitefish (MT), 2005

Jeffery, Keith, *The Secret History of MI6 1909–1949*, Penguin, New York, 2010

Judd, Alan, *The Quest for C: Mansfield Cumming and the Founding of the Secret Service*, HarperCollins, London, 1999

Kennan, George F., *Russia Leaves the War*, Princeton University Press, Princeton, 1956

Kramish, Arnold, *The Griffin*, Macmillan, London, 1986

Krasilnikov, R. S., *KGB protiv MI-6: okhotniki za shpionami* (KGB against MI6: Hunters, Spies), Tsentrpolograf, Moscow, 2000

Landau, Henry, *All's Fair: The Story of the British Secret Service Behind Enemy Lines*, G. P. Putnam's Sons, New York, 1934

Landau, Henry, *Secrets of the White Lady*, G. P. Putnam's Sons, New York, 1935

Landau, Henry, *Spreading the Spy Net: The Story of a British Spy Director*, Jarrolds, London, 1938

Lawson, J. C., *Tales of Aegean Intrigue*, Chatto & Windus, London, 1920

Le Queux, William, *The Invasion of 1910*, Hurst & Blackett, London, 1906

Le Queux, William, *Spies of the Kaiser: Plotting the Downfall of England*, Hurst & Blackett, London, 1909

Lockhart, Robert Bruce, *Memoirs of a British Agent*, Putnam, London, 1932

McKay, C. G., *From Information to Intrigue: Studies in Secret Service Based on the Swedish Experience 1939–1945*, Frank Cass, London, 1993

Mackenzie, Compton, *Aegean Memories*, Chatto & Windus, London, 1940

Mackenzie, Compton, *First Athenian Memories*, Cassell, London, 1931

Mackenzie, Compton, *Gallipoli Memories*, Cassell, London, 1929

Mackenzie, Compton, *Greek Memories*, Cassell, London, 1932

Massie, Robert K., *Castles of Steel: Britain, Germany, and the Winning of the Great War at Sea*, Jonathan Cape, London, 2003

Maugham, W. Somerset, *Ashenden*, Mandarin, London, [1928] 1991

Maugham, W. Somerset, *The Summing Up*, Heinemann, London, 1938

Morgan, Janet, *The Secrets of Rue St Roch*, Allen Lane, London, 2004

Neave, Airey, *Saturday at MI9*, Coronet, London, 1971

O'Brien-ffrench, Conrad, *Delicate Mission: Autobiography of a Secret Agent*, Skilton & Shaw, London, 1979

Occleshaw, Michael, *Armour against Fate: British Military Intelligence in the First World War*, Columbus, London, 1989

Occleshaw, Michael, *Dances in Deep Shadows: Britain's Clandestine War in Russia 1917–1920*, Constable, London, 2006

Pares, Bernard, *A Wandering Student: The Story of a Purpose*, Syracuse University Press, Syracuse (NY), 1948

Pidgeon, Geoffrey, *The Secret Wireless War: The Story of MI6*

Communications 1939–1945, UPSO, London, 2007

Popplewell, Richard J., *Intelligence and Imperial Defence: British Intelligence and the Defence of the Indian Empire 1904–1924*, Frank Cass, London, 1995

Powers, Thomas, *Heisenberg's War: The Secret History of the German Bomb*, Jonathan Cape, London, 1993

Ransome, Arthur, *Racundra's First Cruise*, Jonathan Cape, London, 1927

Ransome, Arthur, *Russia in 1919*, BiblioLife, Charleston (SC), [1919] 2009

Reilly, Sidney and Reilly, Pepita, *Britain's Master Spy: The Adventures of Sidney Reilly*, Harper, New York, 1933

Rintelen, Captain Franz von, *The Dark Invader: Wartime Reminiscences of a German Naval Intelligence Officer*, Penguin, London, 1933

Rose, R. S. and Scott, Gordon D., *Johnny: A Spy's Life*, Pennsylvania State University Press, University Park, 2010

Samson, Charles Rumney, *Fights and Flights*, Battery Press, Nashville, 1990

Saparov, A., *Bitaya karta: khronika odnogo zagorova, v sborniki chekisti* (Chronicle of a Conspiracy: The Cheka Collection), Lenizdat, Leningrad, 1982

Sheffy, Yigal, *British Military Intelligence in the Palestinian Campaign 1914–1918*, Frank Cass, London, 1998

Smith, Michael, *Foley: The Spy Who Saved 10,000 Jews*, Hodder & Stoughton, London, 1999

Smith, Michael, *New Cloak, Old Dagger: How Britain's Spies Came In from the Cold*, Victor Gollancz, London, 1996

Smith, Michael, *The Spying Game: The Secret History of British Espionage*, Politico's, London, 2003

Smith, Michael and Erskine, Ralph (eds), *Action This Day: Bletchley Park from the Breaking of the Enigma Cipher to the Birth of the Modern Computer*, Bantam, London, 2001

Soutar, Andrew, *With Ironside in Russia*, Hutchinson, London, 1940

Spence, Richard B., *Trust No One: The Secret World of Sidney Reilly*, Feral House, Los Angeles, 2002

Stagg, Frank Noel, *West Norway and Its Fjords: A History of Bergen and its Provinces*, Allen & Unwin, London, 1954

Sumner, Ian, *'Despise It Not': A Hull Man Spies on the Kaiser's Germany*, Highgate, Beverley, 2002

Teague-Jones, Reginald, *The Spy Who Disappeared: Diary of a Secret Mission to Russian Central Asia in 1918*, Victor Gollancz, London, 1991

Tennant, Peter, *Touchlines of War*, University of Hull Press, Hull, 1992

Thwaites, Norman, *Velvet and Vinegar*, Grayson, London, 1932

Tomaselli, Phil, *Tracing Your Secret Service Ancestors*, Pen & Sword, Barnsley, 2009

Tunney, Thomas J. and Hollister, Paul Merrick, *Throttled: The Detection of the German and Anarchist Bomb Plotters*, Small, Maynard, Boston, 1919

Verrier, Anthony, *Agents of Empire: Anglo-Zionist Intelligence Operations 1915–1919*, Brassey's, London, 1995

Volkov, S. V., *Ofitsery flota i morskogo vedomstva: opyt martirologa* (The Officers of the Fleet and the Navy Department: The Experience of Martyrdom), Russkii Put', Moscow, 2004

Waack, William, *Die vergessene Revolution*, Aufbau, Berlin. 1994

Walker, Mark, *German National Socialism and the Quest for Nuclear Power 1939–1949,* Cambridge University Press, Cambridge, 1990

Watson, Fernando, *Olga*, Peter Halban, London, 1990

Watson, Jeffrey, *Sidney Cotton: The Last Plane Out of Berlin*, Hodder Headline Australia, Sydney, 2002

Weldon, Captain L. B., *Hard Lying: Eastern Mediterranean 1914–1919*, Herbert Jenkins, London, 1925

West, Nigel, *At Her Majesty's Secret Service: The Chiefs of Britain's Intelligence Agency MI6*, London, Greenhill, 2006

West, Nigel, *Historical Dictionary of British Intelligence*, Scarecrow, Lanham (MD), 2005

West, Nigel, *MI6: British Secret Intelligence Service Operations 1909–45*, Weidenfeld & Nicolson, London, 1983

West, Nigel and Tsarev, Oleg, *The Crown Jewels: The British Secrets at the Heart of the KGB Archives*, HarperCollins, London, 1998

West, Nigel and Tsarev, Oleg, *Triplex, Secrets from the Cambridge Spies*, Yale University Press, New Haven, 2009

Whitwell, John, *British Agent*, Frank Cass, London, 1996

Willoughby, Charles A., *Sorge: Soviet Master Spy*, William Kimber, London, 1952

Woolley, Leonard, *As I Seem to Remember*, George Allen & Unwin, London, 1962

NOTES

CHAPTER 1: 'CAPITAL SPORT'

1. William le Queux, *The Invasion of 1910*, Hurst and Blackett, London, 1906; William le Queux, *Spies of the Kaiser: Plotting the Downfall of England*, Hurst and Blackett, London, 1909.

2. Christopher Andrew, *Secret Service: The Making of the British Intelligence Community*, Heinemann, London, 1985, p. 43; Michael Smith, *The Spying Game: The Secret History of British Espionage*, Politico's, London, 2003, p. 65.

3. The UK National Archives, Public Record Office (hereafter TNA PRO), HD3/131, agent reports on suspicious German in Suffolk, 18 November 1905 and 21 November 1905; Chalmers to Sir Thomas Sanderson, 30 November 1905.

4. TNA PRO HD3/111, Everett to Sanderson, 8 February 1901; Court to Sanderson, December 1901.

5. TNA PRO HD3/128, Alan Johnstone to Thomas Sanderson, 10 October 1905 and 17 October 1905.

6. TNA PRO KV1/2, Ewart to CGS dated 12 January 1909; KV1/4 Edmonds, Intelligence Methods, undated.

7. TNA PRO KV1/8, memoir of William Melville, 31 December 1917; HD3/130, Henry to Davies, 21 January 1905; Sanderson to Davies, 26 January 1905.

8. TNA PRO HD 3/138, Intelligence Division of the War Office SS accounts for August 1909; list of 'Permanent Agents'; HD 3/139, SS accounts for June and July 1909; FO 1093/29, list of salaries for 'Secret Service Bureau' and 'Secret Service Agents' for 1909–10; HD 3/138, Intelligence Division of the War Office List of 'Permanent Agents'.

9. TNA PRO KV6/47, letter from Long to Melville, 5 March 1909, letter from Edmonds to Melville, 10 March 1909, letters from Long to Melville, 11 March 1909 and 23 March 1909 (I am grateful to Dr Nicholas Hiley for sight of his annotated note on the origins of the TR designation).

10. TNA PRO CAB16/8, report and proceedings, Sub-Committee of the Committee of Imperial Defence, Appointed to Consider the Question of Foreign Espionage in the United Kingdom.

11. TNA PRO KV1/3, Memorandum re Formation of Secret Service Bureau, 26 August 1909; ADM196/39; WO106/6292, conclusions of the sub-committee requested to consider how a secret service bureau could be established in Great Britain, 28 April 1909; Judd, *The Quest for C*, pp. 1, 20; Nigel West, *At Her Majesty's Secret Service: The Chiefs of Britain's Intelligence Agency MI6*, London, Greenhill, 2006, pp. 21–2.

12. The letter from Bethell to Cumming can be seen on the SIS website at http://www.sis.gov. uk/output/Page557.html; Judd, *The Quest for C*, pp. 1, 83–4.

13. TNA PRO KV1/3, Memorandum re Formation of Secret Service Bureau, 26 August 1909; FO1093/29, SS Expenditure, Revised Estimate of Salaries during 1910–1911; FO1093/27 Suggestions by the General Staff Regarding a Secret Service Bureau; Judd, *The Quest for C*, pp. 95–8, 105.

14. Christopher Andrew, *The Defence of the Realm: The Authorized History of MI5*, Allen Lane, London, 2009, p. 26; Keith Jeffrey, *The Secret History of MI6 1909–1949*, Penguin, New York, 2010, pp. 9–10

15. TNA PRO FO1093/29, Secret Service Expenditure, Estimate for 1910–1911, dated 31 January 1910; Notes on Estimates for 1913/1914; Judd, *The Quest for C*, pp. 92–120.

16. TNA PRO FO1093/29, various accounts listing Cumming's agents for the period 1909–11; Judd, *The Quest for C*, pp. 124, 325; Walter Christmas, *King George of Greece*, tr. A. G. Chater, Eveleigh Nash, London, 1914, p. 23.

17. 'Work of the Secret Service: how Germany's preparations became known to the Admiralty', *Daily Telegraph*, 24 September 1930; Judd, *The Quest for C*, p. 134.

18. TNA PRO FO1093/29, various accounts listing Cumming's agents for the period 1909–12; see in particular Service Expenditure, Estimate for 1910–1911, dated 31 January 1910, and Supplementary Estimate of SS Expenditure for Quarter Ending 31 March 1911, dated 19 January 1911; WO374/65422, High Court Petition Launched by Captain Bertrand Stewart, March 1914; Hector C. Bywater and H. C. Ferraby, *Strange Intelligence: Memoirs of Naval Service*, London, Constable, 1931, pp. 175–6; Judd, *The Quest for C*, pp. 157, 160–61, 167, 175; Nicholas P. Hiley, 'The Failure of British Espionage against Germany, 1907–1914', *Historical Journal*, 26 (1983), pp. 872, 889.

19. Judd, *The Quest for C*, pp. 136–9; *Burke's Landed Gentry 1936*, Burke's Peerage and Gentry, London, 1936. I am grateful to Roger Fairholm for his assistance in tracking down the details of the Fairholme family.

20. Churchill College Cambridge Archives MCKN3131 I am grateful to Phil Tomaselli for providing me with a copy of this document; Phil Tomaselli, *Tracing Your Secret Service Ancestors*, Pen and Sword, Barnsley, 2009.

21. Judd, *The Quest for C*, pp. 215–16, 230–36, 270; Compton Mackenzie, *Greek Memories*, Cassell, London, 1932, pp. 411–12.

CHAPTER 2: PREPARING FOR WAR

1. Erskine Childers, *The Riddle of the Sands: A Record of Secret Service*, Penguin, London, [1903] 1995.

2. Alan Judd, *The Quest for C: Mansfield Cumming and the Founding of the Secret Service*, London, HarperCollins, 1999, pp. 177, 188–9; 'Alleged espionage in Germany', *The Times*, 21 September 1910.

3. 'The examination', *The Times*, 22 December 1910; 'British officers on trial at Leipzig', *The Times*, 22 December 1910; 'The German High Sea Fleet', *The Times*, 30 August 1910; Judd, *The Quest for C*, pp. 136–9.

4 'The alleged espionage in Germany', *The Times*, 26 August 1910; 'Alleged espionage in

Germany', *The Times*, 21 September 1910; 'The alleged espionage in Germany', *The Times*, 26 September 1910; 'The alleged espionage in Germany', *The Times*, 16 November 1910; 'British government's demand to be represented at hearing of espionage case not definitely granted', *New York Times*, 18 November 1910; 'British officers on trial at Leipzig', *The Times*, 22 December 1910; 'The examination', *The Times*, 22 December 1910; 'The Leipzig trial British officers found guilty', *The Times*, 23 December 1910; Hector C. Bywater and H. C. Ferraby, *Strange Intelligence: Memoirs of Naval Service*, London, Constable, 1931, pp. 165–73; Judd, *The Quest for C*, pp. 179–81, 188–97.

5.   TNA PRO CAB63/192, The Origins and Development of SIS, Appendix A, Minute Issued by Brigadier-General Macdonogh on 31 October 1910.

6.   Imperial War Museum (IWM) WK9 Kirke diaries, vol. I, 3 December 1915; 'The espionage trial at Leipzig: heavy sentences', *The Times*, 14 December 1911; 'Germany punishes five English spies', *New York Times*, 14 December 1911; Bywater and Ferraby, *Strange Intelligence*, p. 91; German prison record C27/27 for Max William Emil Heinrich Schultz 293, kindly provided by Ian Sumner.

7.   'The espionage trial at Leipzig: heavy sentences'; Judd, *The Quest for C*, pp. 219–21; 'Mr C. Grahame-White', *The Times*, 20 August 1959; 'Mr Grahame-White on the future of flying', *The Times*, 24 December 1910; German prison record C27/27 for Max Schultz.

8.   Max Schultz memoir, courtesy of Ian Sumner. PO Box 500 became so closely associated with the MI5 that even today either 'Box 500' or simply 'the Box' is used by some within the forces and other government departments to refer to it.

9.   TNA PRO KV 1/7, 'Special War List: Wanted or to be Watched if in Great Britain', Folio 7; KV 1/10, Kell's office diary for 7 December 1910, Folio 47; National Maritime Museum, London, Oliver papers, OLV/12, H. F. Oliver, 'Recollections of Rear Admiral R. D. Oliver CBE DSC', vol. II, pp. 99–100; 'Reported arrest of spies at Hamburg', *The Times*, 20 March 1911; 'Espionage trial at Leipzig', *The Times*, 7 December 1911; 'The alleged espionage in Germany', *The Times*, 24 March 1911; 'Espionage Trial at Leipzig: Heavy Sentences'; 'Germany punishes five English spies'; 'Espionage in Germany', *The Times*, 2 February 1912; TNA PRO FO1093/25, Minutes of the Proceedings of a Meeting held at the Foreign Office on 23 May 1911; FO1093/29, various War Office estimates of SS expenditure; German prison record C27/27 for Max Schultz. I am grateful to Dr Nick Hiley for sharing his research on the interesting life of Henry Lawrence Bernstein.

10.   'Work of the secret service: How Germany's preparations became known to the Admiralty', *Daily Telegraph*, 24 September 1930.

11.   Ibid; Bywater and Ferraby, *Strange Intelligence*, p. 91; TNA PRO FO1093/25, Minutes of the Proceedings of a meeting Held at the Foreign Office on 23 May 1911.

12.   The paperback edition of Judd's *The Quest for C* (pp. 475–8) gives details of a meeting between Cumming and a potential officer or agent based in Germany in June 1910. The agent is described in Cumming's diary as HC, the initials of Bywater's Christian names, and all details given of him match those of Bywater. But he does not replace Byzewski on the accounts released to the National Archives until February 1912. This follows a meeting of officials overseeing the secret service bureau in May 1911, at which Bethell successfully cut Byzewski's salary in half because he had 'not provided any information of value'. If

he did not improve within six months he was to be sacked. When the committee next met on 23 November 1911, it was agreed that "'B" should be discharged at a convenient opportunity'. The timing of the recruitment is confirmed by Bywater's timing of his first major mission – a visit to Borkum – as being after 'the Brandon–Trench affair' and presumably also Stewart's arrest in August 1911. (See TNA PRO FO1093/25, Minutes of the Proceedings of a Meeting Held at the Foreign Office on 23 May 1911 and Minutes of the Proceedings of a Meeting Held at the Foreign Office on 23 November 1911. See also Bywater and Ferraby, *Strange Intelligence*, p. 151); TNA PRO FO1093/29, Estimates of SS Expenditure for 1 April 1911 to 31 March 1912 and for February and March 1912; Bywater and Ferraby, *Strange Intelligence*, pp. 5–6; William H. Honan, *Bywater: The Man Who Invented the Pacific War,* Futura, London, 1991, pp. 30–44.

13. TNA PRO FO1093/29, Estimates of SS Expenditure for February and March 1912, February and March 1913, and for 1 April 1913 to 31 March 1914; WO339/13678, Personal File of Major T. S. Laycock; Bywater and Ferraby, *Strange Intelligence*, pp. 5–6; Army Lists 1909–1914; Phil Tomaselli, *Tracing Your Secret Service Ancestors*, Pen & Sword, Barnsley, 2009.

14. 'Intelligence from Germany: narrative of a correspondent's successes and failures', *Daily Telegraph*, 26 September 1930; 'The espionage charges in Germany', *The Times*, 2 July 1912; 'Espionage trial in Germany', *The Times*, 31 January 1913; 'The sentence for espionage in Germany', *The Times*, 1 February 1913; German prison record C27/27 for Max. Schultz.

15. TNA PRO FO1093/29, Minutes of Meeting held at the Foreign Office on 8 November 1912 (The minutes give the Mr Archer concerned as 'Late US Board of Agriculture' but this appears to be a mistransliteration by the typist of the longhand notes, which presumably read 'Late AS Board of Agriculture' with AS standing for 'assistant secretary'. The minutes also note that Archer's son had recently retired from the Royal Navy in the rank of lieutenant. Hugh Archer is the only RN officer named Archer who retired as a lieutenant in the period in question); Navy Lists 1896–1912; 'Mr Walter E. Archer CB', *The Times*, 28 September 1917; 'Captain H. E. M. Archer RN', *The Times*, 6 January 1931; Marriages, *The Times*, 11 November 1905; 'Political notes', *The Times*, 3 May 1912; Marriages, *The Times*, 14 March 1910; Judd, *The Quest for C*, pp. 265–6.

16. TNA PRO WO374/65422, High Court Petition Launched by Captain Bertrand Stewart, March 1914; Secret Memorandum Assessing Accuracy of Stewart Petition, dated 25 May 1914; certificate of death dated 27 August 1918 (I am grateful to Phil Tomaselli for drawing my attention to this document); 'Heavy sentence on Mr Stewart', *The Times*, 5 February 1912; Judd, *The Quest for C*, p. 223; TNA PRO FO 1093/29, SS Expenditure, Revised Estimate of Salaries During 1910–1911; '"Espionage" in Germany', *The Times*, 9 August 1911; 'The Alleged espionage at Bremen', *The Times*, August 1911; 'Statement by the Belgian informer', *The Times*, 14 February 1912; 'Espionage trial at Leipzig', *The Times*, 1 February 1912; 'The trial of Mr Stewart', *The Times*, 3 February 1912; 'Poet jailed as a spy', *New York Times*, 4 February 1912; Letter from Reginald Arkwright, *The Times*, 5 February 1912.

17. TNA PRO FO1093/29, Estimate of SS Expenditure for February and March 1912, February 1913; War Office SS Accounts, Estimate of SS Expenditure for February and March 1913, Estimates of SS Expenditure from 1 April 1913 to 31 March 1914; 'The

Edinburgh necklace affair', *The Times*, 9 March 1911; 'The Edinburgh pearl necklace case', *The Times*, 4 May 1911; 'The pearl necklace case', *The Times*, 5 June 1911; 'The Edinburgh necklace affair', *The Times*, 2 June 1911; 'An officer's chivalry: imprisonment to screen his wife', *The Times*, 25 June 1914; Judd, *The Quest for C*, pp. 244–6.

18. TNA PRO FO1093/29, Minutes of Meetings Held at The Foreign Office in November 1910, May 1911, May 1912, November 1912, and May 1913; FO371/2163, DMO to Under-Secretary of State for Foreign Affairs, dated 7 August 1914; death notices, *The Times*, 6 May 1907; Hugh Barty-King, *Maples: A Household Name for 150 Years*, Quiller Press, London, 1992, pp. 87–102; Nicholas P. Hiley, 'The Failure of British Espionage against Germany 1907–1914', *Historical Journal* 26 (1983), p. 881.

19. TNA PRO FO371/2163, DMO to Under-Secretary of State for Foreign Affairs, dated 7 August 1914 (I am grateful to Phil Tomaselli for drawing my attention to this document); 'Demetrius Boulger', *The Times*, 17 December 1928; Judd, *The Quest for C*, pp. 244–6.

20. TNA PRO FO1093/25. Minutes of Meeting held at the Foreign Office on 23 May 1911; FO1093/29, Macdonogh to Onslow, 31 January 1913; ADM340/136, R. B. Tinsley naval service record; 'A British subject excluded from Holland', *The Times*, 2 March 1911; 'The case of Mr Tinsley', *The Times*, 15 May 1911. Interestingly the British minister in The Hague who persuaded the Dutch government to have the expulsion order rescinded was Alan Johnstone, who had previously represented the Foreign Office view in the discussions on 'Secret Service Arrangements in the Event of War with Germany', insisting that, whoever acted as the 'collector', it was 'undesirable that members of His Majesty's embassies and legations should be in any way connected with espionage'. It is unclear if he had any role in putting forward Tinsley's name as a potential 'collector' and 'forwarder' but the case was so well publicised in the UK that it is unlikely to have escaped Cumming's notice.

21. Bywater and Ferraby, *Strange Intelligence*, pp. 137–8.

22. Judd, *The Quest for C*, pp. 265–6.

CHAPTER 3: TURF WARS WITH THE MILITARY

1. TNA PRO FO371/2159, Secret Note from Nicolson to Sir Edward Grey, Foreign Secretary, dated 31 July 1914; Alan Judd, *The Quest for C: Mansfield Cumming and the Founding of the Secret Service*, London, HarperCollins, 1999, p. 268; Hector C. Bywater and H. C. Ferraby, *Strange Intelligence: Memoirs of Naval Service*, London, Constable, 1931, p 40. Bywater was certainly back in the UK when war was declared: William H. Honan, *Bywater: The Man Who Invented the Pacific War*, Futura, London, 1991, p. 45.

2. TNA PRO CAB63/192, The Origins and Development of SIS, p. 2; Judd, *The Quest for C*, p. 268; Anthony Clayton, *Forearmed: A History of the Intelligence Corps*, Brassey's, London, 1993, p. 20.

3. TNA PRO ADM340/136, Service Record of Captain R. B. Tinsley RNR; 'The Volturno inquiry', *The Times*, 29 November 1913; Christopher Andrew, *Secret Service: The Making of the British Intelligence Community*, Heinemann, London, 1985, p. 156; Captain Henry Landau, *Spreading the Spy Net: The Story of a British Spy Director*, Jarrolds, London, 1938, p. 31.

4. Captain Henry Landau, *All's Fair: The Story of the British Secret Service behind the German Lines*, G. P. Putnam's Sons, New York, 1934, pp. 44–7.

5. Frans Kluiters, *R. B. Tinsley: A Biographical Note*, January 2004 available at http://www.nisa-intelligence.nl/PDF-bestanden/Tinsley.pdf; TNA PRO WO106/6189, Lieutenant M. R. K. Burge, History of the British Secret Service in Holland, August 1914–February 1917, p. 1; WO106/1510, Report on Violation of Dutch Territory dated 2 June 1916.

6. 'A prisoner's career of adventure', *The Times*, 7 August 1914; National Maritime Museum, Oliver papers, OLV/12, H. F. Oliver, 'Recollections for Rear-Admiral R. D. Oliver, CBE, DSC', vol. II, pp. 99–100; Judd, *The Quest for C*, p. 279.

7. TNA PRO WO319/7419, Personal file of Lieutenant Alastair Smith-Cumming, Extract from the Meaux Register of Death Certificates for 1914; Compton Mackenzie, *Greek Memories*, Cassell, London, 1932, pp. 90–91.

8. IWM WK9 Kirke diaries, vol. I, entries for period from 22 October 1914 to 7 November 1914, and for 20 February 1915; TNA PRO T1/11937, letter from War Office Assistant Secretary B. B. Cubitt to Treasury Secretary, 26 November 1914; WO32/10776. Historical Sketch of the Directorate of Military Intelligence During the Great War, 1914–1919, p. 5; WO339/13678, personal file of Thomas Spencer Laycock; Judd, *The Quest for C*, pp. 275–9. Laycock's position as the head of MO6c was to set the precedent for its later evolution into MI1c and eventually MI6, giving the deliberately misleading impression that the officers in charge were part of the War Office rather than, as was the case, the secret service itself.

9. IWM WK9 Kirke diaries, vol. I, 6 November 1914; TNA PRO WO106/6192, lists of British agents awarded honours; Captain Henry Landau, *Secrets of the White Lady*, G. P. Putnam's Sons, New York, 1935, pp. 13–14.

10. IWM WK9 Kirke diaries, vol. I, entry for 19–20 November 1914; TNA PRO WO95/1483, War Diaries 2 Battalion Seaforth Highlanders, November 1914, pp. 10–12; WO106/6189, Lieutenant M. R. K. Burge, 'History of the Secret Service in Holland August 1914–February 1917', p. 2; Medal Roll Index Card for Captain K. Forbes-Robertson; Judd, *The Quest for C*, p. 285.

11. TNA PRO WO32/10776, Historical Sketch of the Directorate of Military Intelligence During the Great War, p. 5; WO106/6189, Lieutenant M. R. K. Burge, 'History of the Secret Service in Holland August 1914–February 1917', pp. 4–5; Medal Roll Index Card for Major Lawrie Oppenheim.

12. Landau, *All's Fair*, pp. 53–54.

13. Judd, *The Quest for C*, pp. 286–8, 297–8, 328; TNA PRO ADM337/119/165; 'A great Oxford oarsman', *The Times*, 3 November 1948; Compton Mackenzie, *First Athenian Memories*, Cassell, London, 1931, p. 316; IWM WK9 Kirke diaries, vol. I, 24 March 1915. Initial CX usage information provided to the author in confidence, see also Michael Smith, *The Spying Game: The Secret History of British Espionage*, Politico's, London, 2003 and Phil Tomaselli, *Tracing Your Secret Service Ancestors*, Pen & Sword, Barnsley, 2009. For Foreign Office previous usage see TNA PRO FO421/91, Further Correspondence – Part CX, December 1887.

14. TNA PRO WO106/45, 'History of I(b) GHQ 1917–1918, Part 1: The Secret Service', p. 10; Landau, *Secrets of the White Lady*, pp. 16–21; 'Belgians executed for alleged espionage', *The Times*, 17 June 1915; 'Death sentence on spies at Dunkirk', *The Times*, 21 June 1915; 'German barbarity in Belgium', *The Times*, 21 December 1916.

15. Landau, *Secrets of the White Lady*, pp. 291–2.

16. IWM WK9 Kirke diaries, vol. II, entries for March through to May 1915; TNA PRO WO106/6189, Lieutenant M. R. K. Burge, 'History of the Secret Service in Holland August 1914–February 1917', pp. 6–11; Judd, *The Quest for C*, pp. 301, 310; Michael Occleshaw, *Armour against Fate: British Military Intelligence in the First World War*, Columbus, London, 1989, p. 150

17. Judd, *The Quest for C*, pp. 312–18, 328–9; TNA PRO ADM337/121/122, RNR record of Lieutenant Alfred George Jolley; death notices, *The Times*, 28 February 1942; Medal Roll of Captain L. Maurice Cockerell Int. Corps OBE; 'Mining news', *The Times*, 18 September 1936; 'Dinner, Digger's Club', *The Times*, 13 November 1937.

18. IWM WK9 Kirke diaries, vol. II, entries for July to September 1915; TNA PRO WO106/6189, Lieutenant M. R. K. Burge, 'History of the Secret Service in Holland August 1914–February 1917', pp. 11–14; Judd, *The Quest for C*, pp. 314–15, 323.

19. TNA PRO WO106/6189, Lieutenant M. R. K. Burge, 'History of the Secret Service in Holland August 1914–February 1917', pp. 6, 9, 10; IWM WK9 Kirke diaries, vol. II, entries for 25 February 1915 to 3 March 1915, and vol. III, for 30 November 1915; Landau, *All's Fair*, p. 134.

20. M. R. D. Foot and J. M. Langley, *MI9: The British Secret Service That Fostered Escape and Evasion 1939–1945, and Its American Counterpart*, Bodley Head, London, 1979, p. 42; Airey Neave, *Saturday at MI9: A History of Underground Escape Lines in North-West Europe in 1940–5 by a Leading Organiser at MI9*, Coronet, London, 1971, p. 69; Tomaselli, *Tracing Your Secret Service Ancestors*; TNA PRO WO208/3242, Colonel Norman Crockatt, Historical Record of MI9; CUST49/448, Arrangements for Bringing Body of Nurse Edith Cavell into England; HO45/10794/302577, Nurse Edith Cavell: Removal of Remains from Belgium to UK; KV2/822, Edith Cavell; KV2/844, Gaston Georges Quien; MT25/32, Re-interment of Remains of the Late Miss Edith Cavell in England; FO383/15, Belgium: Prisoners, Including: Miss Edith Cavell, English Nurse in Brussels, Arrested and Executed by the Germans for Assisting Allied Soldiers to Escape from Germany.

21. Judd, *The Quest for C*, pp. 328–9; IWM WK9 Kirke diaries, vol. III, entries for 29 November to 3 December 1915; TNA PRO WO106/6189, Lieutenant M. R. K. Burge, 'History of the Secret Service in Holland August 1914–February 1917', pp. 10, 22–23.

22. Judd, *The Quest for C*, p. 331; Landau, *All's Fair*, p, 48; IWM WK9 Kirke diaries, vol. III, 29 November 1915; TNA PRO WO106/6189, Lieutenant M. R. K. Burge, 'History of the Secret Service in Holland August 1914–February 1917', pp. 22–3; for the type of information collected inside Germany by Tinsley's press monitoring unit see for example WO106/313, Effect of Military Operations on Political Situation In Germany, written by Macdonogh and dated 13 October 1917; KV1/43, MI5 Historical Reports: 'G' Branch Report, vol. V, 1916, folios 156–7; KV4/113 Principal German Intelligence Agents Captured in the UK by MI5 1909–1919, May 1919; University of Leeds, Liddle collection, DF148, Radcliffe, Sir E. T.; Andrew Cook, *M: MI5's First Spymaster*, Tempus, Stroud, 2004; Christopher Andrew, *The Defence of the Realm: The Authorized History of MI5*, Allen Lane, London, 2009, pp. 72–5.

23. TNA PRO WO32/10776, Historical Sketch of the Directorate of Military Intelligence During the Great War, 1914–1919, p. 6; Landau, *Secrets of the White Lady*, p. 48; Captain Henry Landau, *All's Fair: The Story of the British Secret Service behind the German Lines*, pp. 44–7.

CHAPTER 4: LA DAME BLANCHE

1. 'Lieutenant-Colonel F. H. Browning', *The Times*, 15 October 1929; Sir Samuel Hoare, *The Fourth Seal: The End of a Russian Chapter*, Heinemann, London, 1930, p. 33; Alan Judd, *The Quest for C: Mansfield Cumming and the Founding of the Secret Service*, London, HarperCollins, 1999, pp. 326–9. The title Special Intelligence Service remained in place for some years before being changed to Secret Intelligence Service in 1919.

2. TNA PRO WO106/6189, Lieutenant M. R. K. Burge, 'History of the Secret Service in Holland August 1914–February 1917', pp. 23–4; WO158/897, Macdonogh to Charteris, 25 July 1916; Captain Henry Landau, *Secrets of the White Lady*, G. P. Putnam's Sons, New York, 1935, p. 16.

3. Landau, *Secrets of the White Lady*, pp. 18–22; 'German fears in Belgium, frontier precautions', *The Times*, 18 March 1915; 'Belgians executed for alleged espionage', *The Times*, 17 June 1915.

4. TNA PRO WO158/897, Charteris to Macdonogh, 15 January 1917, p. 2; Report on 'Secret Service (War Office, Admiralty, Air Ministry, Foreign Office)', January 1919; Cafferata family archive, Instructions of Agents, undated.

5. Conrad O'Brien-ffrench, *Delicate Mission: Autobiography of a Secret Agent*, Skilton & Shaw, London, 1979, p. 45.

6. TNA PRO FO 383/413, translation note verbale from German Foreign Office to Dutch government for British government, undated but January 1918; note verbale from German Foreign Office, 18 January 1918; note verbale undated; note verbale from German Foreign Office, 30 April 1918; Agnew to Vansittart, 10 June 1918.

7. TNA PRO WO158/897, Charteris to Macdonogh, 15 January 1917, p. 2; IWM WK9 Kirke diaries, vol. II, 11 October 1915, and vol. III, 17 and 25 April 1916; Judd, *The Quest for C*, p. 319.

8. Captain Henry Landau, *All's Fair: The Story of the British Secret Service behind the German Lines*, G. P. Putnam's Sons, New York, 1934, p. 53.

9. IWM WK9 Kirke diaries, vol. III, entries for 30 April 1916 to 30 May 1916; Christopher Andrew, *Secret Service: The Making of the British Intelligence Community*, Heinemann, London, 1985, p. 153; TNA PRO WO158/897, Charteris to Macdonogh, 28 July 1916.

10. TNA PRO WO339/12456, minute sheet signed by Cumming requesting that Landau be 'attached to this department for special duty', dated 19 June 1916; Landau, *All's Fair*, pp. 42–3.

11. TNA PRO WO339/12456; Landau, *All's Fair*, pp. 50–51, 142; 'German activity at Zeebrugge, G E steamer captured', *The Times*, 26 June 1916; 'Captain Fryatt's action', *The Times*, 29 July 1916; 'Captain Fryatt's murder', *The Times*, 1 August 1916.

12. Landau, *All's Fair*, pp. 295–7.

13. Judd, *The Quest for C*, pp. 347, 350; IWM WK9 Kirke diaries, vol. I, 23 January 1915; TNA PRO ADM337/121/409, personal file of Lt Thomas Ralph Merton RNVR; 'Merton, Sir Thomas Ralph', *Oxford Dictionary of National Biography*, Oxford University Press, Oxford, 2004 (Merton's *DNB* entry says he was mentioned in dispatches for his work with MI1c but his RNVR record makes clear this was not the case); 'Dr H. Granville-Barker', *The Times*, 2 September 1946; 'Granville Barker back to stage play', *New York Times*, 3 January 1917.

14. TNA PRO WO106/6189, Lieutenant M. R. K. Burge, 'History of the Secret Service in Holland August 1914–February 1917, Part II', p. 2; 'Dutch mail steamer seized', *The Times*,

11 November 1916; 'Batavier VI taken to Zeebrugge', *The Times*, 14 November 1916; 'Dutch ships taken to Zeebrugge, British steamer seized', *The Times*, 25 September 1916; 'German barbarity in Belgium', *The Times*, 21 December 1916; Landau, *All's Fair*, p. 128.

15. TNA PRO WO106/6189, Lieutenant M. R. K. Burge, 'History of the Secret Service in Holland August 1914–February 1917, Part II', pp. 2–22.

16. 'German barbarity in Belgium, *The Times*, 21 December 1916'; Judd, *The Quest for C*, p. 351; TNA PRO WO106/6189, Lieutenant M. R. K. Burge, 'History of the Secret Service in Holland August 1914–February 1917, Part II', pp. 2–22; WO158/897, Macdonogh to Charteris, 28 December 1916.

17. TNA PRO WO106/6189, Lieutenant M. R. K. Burge, 'History of the Secret Service in Holland August 1914–February 1917, Part II', pp. 2–22; WO158/897, Charteris to Macdonogh, 27 January 1917; Janet Morgan, *The Secrets of Rue St Roch: Hope and Heroism behind Enemy Lines in the First World War*, Allen Lane, London, 2004, pp. 18–19.

18. TNA PRO WO106/45, 'History of I(b) GHQ 1917–1918, Part I: The Secret Service'.

19. Landau, *Secrets of the White Lady*, pp. 24–57.

20. Landau, *Secrets of the White Lady*, pp. 59–89; University of Leeds, Brotherton Library, Liddle Collection, GS1786, papers of Major S. H. C. Woolrych, Notes on Various Means of Transmission etc., written by Major Cecil Aylmer Cameron.

21. Cafferata family archive, MI1c Instructions for Military Agents.

22. Landau, *All's Fair*, pp. 96–7, 128; 'The Munich libel trial', *The Times*, 27 October 1925.

23. Landau, *All's Fair*, pp. 93–101.

24. Judd, *The Quest for C*, pp. 383–5, 408; Compton Mackenzie, *Aegean Memories*, Chatto & Windus, London, 1940, p. 404; TNA PRO WO32/21380, Report on 'Secret Service (War Office, Admiralty, Air Ministry, Foreign Office)', January 1919. The actual numbering of the sections detailed here differs in some respects from that generally found in the existing literature, which is largely based on the system in place following subsequent minor reorganisations during the early 1920s. The first switched political intelligence and Foreign Office liaison from Section V to Section I, the second, in 1925, saw Section V assigned to counter-espionage and liaison with MI5. A chart giving the numbering of the circulating sections from the 1917 Dansey reorganisation until at least 1921 can be found in TNA PRO KV4/182; Keith Jeffrey, *The Secret History of MI6 1909–1949*, Penguin, New York, 2010, p.60.

25. Landau, *Secrets of the White Lady*, pp. 75, 116–17; TNA PRO WO106/45, 'History of I(b) GHQ 1917–1918, Part I: The Secret Service'; Morgan, *The Secrets of Rue St Roch*; Judd, *The Quest for C*, p. 361.

CHAPTER 5: AIR OPERATIONS – CUMMING'S JESUIT PRIEST

1. I am grateful for Phil Tomaselli's efforts to uncover O'Caffrey's story, which is told in his book *Tracing Your Secret Service Ancestors*, Pen & Sword, Barnsley, 2009; TNA PRO HO 144/3470, Memorial by P. M. C. O'Caffrey with Regard to Application for British Citizenship, dated 9 February 1924; Charles Rumney Samson, *Fights and Flights*, Battery Press, Nashville, [1930] 1990, pp. 13, 16–18, 47; TNA PRO AIR 1/305/15/226/157, letter from O'Caffrey to Captain Murray Sueter, Director Air Department, Royal Navy, dated 15 February 1915.

2.   TNA PRO HO 144/3470, Memorial by P. M. C. O'Caffrey with Regard to Application
     for British Citizenship, dated 9 February 1924; IWM WK9 Kirke diaries, vol. I, 5
     November 1914, 29 November 1915 and 3 December 1915.

3.   TNA PRO HO 144/3470, Memorial by P. M. C. O'Caffrey with Regard to Application
     for British Citizenship, dated 9 February 1924; AIR 1/305/15/226/157, letter from Sueter to
     Rear-Admiral Hall, DID, undated; 'The War in the Air: Bombers: Germany, Zeppelins', First
     World War.com website, http://www.firstworldwar.com/airwar/bombers_zeppelins.htm,
     accessed 12 June 2010; 'The War in the Air: Bombers: Britain', First World War.com website,
     http://www.firstworldwar.com/airwar/bombers_britain.htm, accessed 12 June 2010.

4.   TNA PRO AIR 1/305/15/226/157, letter from O'Caffrey, probably to Sueter, 17
     November 1914; 'Bombs on Zeppelin sheds', The Times, 22 December 1914; 'Successful air
     raids', The Times, 4 January 1915; 'Bombs on Zeppelin sheds', The Times, 28 September 1916.

5.   TNA PRO AIR 1/305/15/226/157, letter from O'Caffrey, probably to Sueter, 17
     November 1914; NASF 110, 'Bomb Targets, Bruges', dated 25 May 1915.

6.   Samson, Fights and Flights, pp. 157–8; TNA PRO HO 144/3470, Memorial by P. M. C.
     O'Caffrey with Regard to Application for British Citizenship, dated 9 February 1924; CAB
     16/8, Report of Proceedings, Sub-Committee of the Committee of Imperial Defence, 'The
     Question of Foreign Espionage in the United Kingdom', p. 4; AIR 1/305/15/226/157,
     letters from O'Caffrey to Sueter dated 10 and 15 February 1915; letter from CO RNAS
     Dunkirk to Director Air Department dated 19 February 1915; O'Caffrey to Lambe dated
     23 February 1915; Director Air Department to O'Caffrey and to DID dated 10 June 1915;
     NASF120, dated 10 June 1915, p. 6; NASF121, Aircraft, Sheds, Evere, dated 12 June 1915;
     'The Zeppelin raiders', The Times, 2 June 1915; 'German version of the Zeppelin raid', The
     Times, 4 June 1915; Alan Judd, The Quest for C: Mansfield Cumming and the Founding of the
     Secret Service, London, HarperCollins, 1999, p. 315.

7.   TNA PRO HO 144/3470, Memorial by P. M. C. O'Caffrey with Regard to Application
     for British Citizenship, dated 9 February 1924; AIR 1/305/15/226/157, extensive
     reporting on Belgian airfields and targets signed by O'Caffrey dating from the second half
     of 1915; NASF 166, Zeebrugge submarine sheds, dated 4 September 1915; NASF176, Gas
     factories from Aircraft Lommel, dated 26 September 1915; NASF188, Aircraft Evere, dated
     15 October 1915; 'Effects of Zeebrugge bombardment', The Times, 3 September 1915;
     'Zeebrugge bombardment', The Times, 10 September 1915; 'News in brief', The Times, 15
     June 1915; 'Honour for airmen', The Times, 23 June 1915; Judd, The Quest for C, p. 350;
     IWM WK9 Kirke diaries, vol. III, 29 November 1915.

8.   IWM WK9 Kirke diaries, vol. III, 6 September 1915; Nicholas Everitt, British Secret Service
     During the Great War, Hutchinson, London, 1920, pp. 53–4, 71–3.

9.   TNA PRO ADM 137/4679 MI1c/10197, Copenhagen, 6 December 1917, from D17,
     folio 16; ADM 137/4305, Airships etc. 1917, MC686 Copenhagen, 27 October 1917, folio
     247; ADM 137/4125. Extract from Weekly Summary of Aeronautical Information No. 13,
     3 November 1918; WO 158/960, Ritson to BGI (France), 2 February 1918; TNA PRO
     ADM 137/4125, Bases (L/A) Germany, Staaken, 'C' June 1919; Bases (L/A) Germany,
     Berlin – Tegel, 'C' June 1919; Bases (L/A) Germany, Airship Base, Ahlhorn, southern
     Oldenburg.

CHAPTER 6: HUNTING THE HUN FROM SWITZERLAND – 'DENY EVERYTHING!'

1. Alan Judd, *The Quest for C: Mansfield Cumming and the Founding of the Secret Service*, London, HarperCollins, 1999, pp. 288, 393; Richard J. Popplewell, *Intelligence and Imperial Defence: British Intelligence and the Defence of the Indian Empire 1904–1924*, Frank Cass, London, 1995, pp. 138–41, 216–18; Nigel West, 'Wallinger, Sir John Arnold (1869–1931)', *Oxford Dictionary of National Biography*, Oxford University Press, Oxford, 2004.

2. IWM WK9 Kirke diaries, Vols I & II, entries for 9 November 1914–22 June 1915; TNA PRO WO 339/27657, Personal File of Edward Béla Josepff Harran, Intelligence Corps; 'Colonel George Pollitt', *The Times*, 12 March 1964; medal roll cards of Lt-Col George P. Pollitt and Maj. E. B. J. Harran; information kindly supplied by Judith Wilde of Brunner Mond.

3. Judd, *The Quest for C*, pp. 288, 310, 324, 331, 393; IWM WK9 Kirke diaries, vol. I, entries for 23 January 1915 & 30 November 1915; 'A journey across the great Sahara', *The Times*, 20 July 1906; TNA PRO HO 144/690/104282, Naturalisation of Hanns Vischer.

4. TNA PRO WO 339/22200, Protection Certificate for Capt. Lewis Campbell Int Corps, dated 1 April 1919; Judd, *The Quest for C*, p. 331; IWM WK9 Kirke diaries, vol. II, entry for 30 November 1915.

5. Judd, *The Quest for C*, pp. 323–4; 'German agents in Switzerland, intrigues against the Allies', *The Times*, 4 September 1915. Despite being naturalised as a British citizen, under Swiss law Vischer remained a Swiss citizen, see TNA PRO HO 144/1572/275113, Note on Status of Swiss Citizens Naturalised as British Citizens, 8 August 1919.

6. W. Somerset Maugham, *Ashenden*, Mandarin, London, [1928] 1991, pp. 24–5, 109–10; IWM WK9 Kirke diaries, vol. II, 3 December 1915.

7. Cafferata family archive, list of Lausanne district agents compiled by Redmond Cafferata, undated but post-January 1917; list of Zurich district agents compiled by Redmond Cafferata, undated but post-February 1917; letter from Robert Sahli to Redmond Cafferata, 26 October 1918; IWM WK9, Kirke diaries, vol. III, 29 November 1915 & 17 April 1916; Judd, *The Quest for C*, p. 393; TNA PRO FO 371/4139, letter from W. G. Middleton Edwards to C. J. Phillips, Foreign Office, 18 November 1918; WO 157/717, Political Intelligence War Diary entry for 19 July 1917.

8. TNA PRO WO 158/897, Charteris to Macdonogh, 12 July 1916; Macdonogh to Charteris, 17 July 1916; Macdonogh to Charteris, 25 July 1916; Charteris to Macdonogh, 13 August 1916; IWM WK9 Kirke diaries, vol. IV, 23 & 24 July 1916.

9. *London Gazette*, 8 August, 1916, p. 7787; Cafferata family archive, list of Lausanne district agents compiled by Redmond Cafferata, undated but post-January 1917; list of Zurich district agents compiled by Redmond Cafferata, undated but post-February 1917; Cafferata Memo 139 to Captain Ernest Anson, 1 April 1917; Cafferata memo re vice-consul system, 4 June 1917; Cafferata passport issued by British Consulate, Berne, dated 1 September 1916; TNA PRO HO 144/1260/236187, Memorial of Robert Sahli; use of 'the Nunnery' from Nigel West, *Historical Dictionary of British Intelligence*, Scarecrow Press, Lanham, MD, 2005, p. 293.

10. Cafferata family archive, list of Zurich district agents compiled by Redmond Cafferata, undated but post-February 1917.

11. Cafferata family archive, Cafferata memo re vice-consul system, 19 April 1917.

12. Judd, *The Quest for C*, p. 394; Hoover Institution Archives, George Davis Herron papers, Doc XI/XI, Whittall to Herron, 17 September 1917; Doc VI/VII, Middelton Edwards to Herron, 14 November 1918; TNA PRO FO 371/4139, letter from W. G. Middleton Edwards to C. J. Phillips, Foreign Office, 18 November 1918; Compton Mackenzie, *First Athenian Memories*, Cassell, London, 1931.

13. TNA PRO FO 371/2885, Samson letter from Paris to MI1c, 21 August 1917; Samson (R) personal letter to Cumming (Captain Spencer), also 21 August 1917, folio 168090; Macdonogh memorandum, 23 August 1917, folio 167852; Heard memo M48 and M49, 15 & 16 August 1917; WO 157/736, unnamed officer report to R on Bulgarian discussions, 4 November 1915.

14. Cafferata family archive: Agent CX, 'Le Contre-espionage en Suisse', undated.

15. Judd, *The Quest for C*, pp. 396–7.

16. Cafferata family archive, memo L/130 from Cafferata to Dansey, 25 November 1917.

17. Cafferata family archive: 'Mission anglaise, Pontarlier, rapport Grob', 12 March 1918; TNA PRO HO 144/1572/275113, Grob, British Subject Accused of Espionage, CID Investigation, 12 April 1915; Memorial of Franz Bruno Grob No 275113, 12 February 1915, FO minute, 17 May 1919; FO 371/3758, British Subject Accused of Espionage.

18. Janet Morgan, *The Secrets of Rue St Roch: Hope and Heroism behind Enemy Lines in the First World War*, Allen Lane, London, 2004, p. 98 (this excellent book is based on papers left by Bruce and is by far the best account of the operation); TNA PRO WO 106/45, 'History of I (b) GHQ 1917–1918, Part I: The Secret Service', pp. 19–21.

19. Hoover Institution Archives, Herron papers, Doc. XI/X, Whittall to Herron, 4 September 1918; Doc. II/XLIV, Intelligence Report from G29, 3 September 1918; R. S. Rose and Gordon D. Scott, *Johnny: A Spy's Life*, Pennsylvania State University Press, University Park, 2010, p. 172.

20. Hoover Institution Archives, Herron papers, Doc. XI/XI, Whittall to Herron, 17 September 1917; Doc. VI/VIIa, Herron to Wilson, dated 1 March 1918; Doc. I/XVI, Herron to Wilson, dated 14 May 1918; Doc. XI/VII, Herron to Dolbeare, 16 June 1918; Doc. XIII/I MacHugh to Herron, 1 November 1918; 'Bogus peace offer made to American', *New York Times*, 10 May 1918; 'Disavow peace offer', New York Times, 12 May 1918; 'Quidde denies proposals', *New York Times*, 16 May 1918; 'Finds modern war folly', New York Times, 16 July 1918.

21. TNA PRO WO 374/44294, Protection Certificate for Colonel R. J. MacHugh, 15 September 1919; minute sheet entry 28, dated 14 November 1918; Hoover Institution Archives, Herron papers, Doc XIII/I, MacHugh to Herron, 1 November 1918; 'Colonel R. J. MacHugh', *The Times*, 7 July 1925; House of Lords Record Office, Lloyd George papers, LG/F/49/1/1, MacHugh, British Passport Office, to Lloyd George, 21 January 1919.

22. University of Leeds, Brotherton Library, Liddle Collection, RUH20, papers of Wallace Ellison, Ellison to Mr Gordon, 25 January 1965.

CHAPTER 7: NAVIES AND NEMESIS

1. TNA PRO ADM223/637, various reports from agent TR/16 (German Travelling Agent 1 appears for example in a report from Rotterdam dated 16 September 1915); Alan Judd, *The*

Quest for C: Mansfield Cumming and the Founding of the Secret Service, London, HarperCollins, 1999, p. 340; information supplied to the author in confidence.

2. TNA PRO ADM337/120/119, service record of Charles Louis Power; the bulk of TR16's reports appear in TNA PRO ADM223/637. The two on submarine construction cited here are Folio 1, Naval Intelligence Rotterdam, 10 April 1915, and Folio 2, Submarines Rotterdam, 28 April 1915. The special reports on a possible invasion appear at Folio 71, Naval Intelligence Rotterdam, 5 January 1916 and Folio 6, Naval Intelligence Rotterdam, 10 January 1916; Captain Henry Landau, *Spreading the Spy Net: The Story of a British Spy Director*, Jarrolds, London, 1938, p. 31; Captain Henry Landau, *All's Fair: The Story of the British Secret Service behind the German Lines*, G. P. Putnam's Sons, New York, 1934, pp. 143–9. I am grateful to Oliver Lörscher for details of actual German submarine construction during this period.

3. TNA PRO ADM223/637, the explosion on board the Seydlitz is in Folio 9, 9 February 1916; The FLBs are reported on in Serials 14 and 15, dated 16 March 1916 and 12 April 1916, in Folio 37, Report H1/571/d, 19 April 1917 and Folio 38, Report H1/575/c, 18 May 1917.

4. 'German estimate of forces', *The Times*, 6 June 1916; 'Fate of the *Derfflinger*', *The Times*, 6 June 1916; 'Britannia still rules the waves', *The Times*, 6 June 1916; 'Germany and the *Lützow*', *The Times*, 10 June 1916; TNA PRO ADM223/637 CX183, 19 June 1916, report from D15 passed on by N1 (British naval attaché in Copenhagen); D15's report is compared here to data in what is recognised as one of the best accounts of damage to the German ships: John Campbell, *Jutland: An Analysis of the Fighting*, Conway Maritime Press, London, 1987.

5. TNA PRO ADM223/637, Folio 58 R9/458, report from R16, 27 June 1916; Folio 59 R1/459, report from R16, 28 June 1916; Comparisons are again based on German data in Campbell, *Jutland*; see also Robert K. Massie, *Castles of Steel: Britain, Germany, and the Winning of the Great War at Sea*, Jonathan Cape, London, 2003.

6. TNA PRO ADM 137/4679, MI1c Section XVI, Note Regarding the Reception of Wireless Messages from the North Hinder Lightship, 11 January 1917; Wireless Signals from North Hinder Lightship, ID Air Section, 18 December 1916; letter from G[ascon] Duquesne, MI1c, Section XVI, re North Hinder Lightship wireless operator, 11 January 1917.

7. TNA PRO ADM223/637, labour difficulties at Folio 17, 14 April 1916 and Folio 23, 19 July 1916; Kiel walks at Folio 22, 29 June 1916.

8. TNA PRO ADM223/637, Folio 37, 19 April 1916, includes the claim that the Germans have 357 submarines, and official scepticism over the figure. Folio 39, 25 September 1917, notes Krüger's return to the British fold after four months.

9. TNA PRO ADM223/637. The references to the Kaiser Wilhelm supergun, which inspired the Iraqi supergun designed by Gerald Bull in the 1990s, appear at Folio 45, CX029069, 31 March 1918; Folio 46, CXN66, 19 April 1918 and Folio 49, CX038561, 27 June 1918.

10. TNA PRO ADM223/637, black market in food from Folio 45, CX029069, 31 March 1918.

11. TNA PRO ADM223/637, effects of air raids from Folio 48, CXN167, 8 June 1918 and Folio 52, CX048543, 4 September 1918.

12. TNA PRO ADM223/637, troops mutiny and unrest from Folio 54, CX056069, 19 October 1918 and Folio 55, CX058029, 15 November 1918.

13. Judd, *The Quest for C*, pp. 270, 408; TNA PRO ADM137/4697, Folios 184–6, assessment of reports by T Rotterdam on German ships operating off coast of Flanders 18 April 1918 to 20 May 1918; KV 1/43, MI5 Historical Reports: 'G' Branch Report, vol. V, 1916, Folios 156–7; Nicholas Hiley, 'Landau, Henry (1892–1968)', *Oxford Dictionary of National Biography*, Oxford University Press, Oxford, 2004.

14. TNA PRO ADM196/49/144, Personal Royal Navy file of Commander Frank Noel Stagg; ADM223/637 CX183, 19 June 1916, Report from D15 passed on by N1; Rigsarkivet (Danish National Archives),Copenhagen, 10 D 27h Klager & Henv. fra tysk Gskab under Stormagtskrigen 1914–18, Auszug aus einem der Kaiserlichen Regierung zur Verfügung gestellten Privatbrief; 'En britiske Norgesvenn', *Aftenposten*, 21 January 1972; email correspondence with Holme's grandson Henrik Sinding-Larsen, 14 February 2009; IWM WK9 Kirke diaries, vol. III, 17 April 1916; Judd, *The Quest for C*, pp. 314, 317, 318 & 350; 'Cmdr F. N. Stagg, British friend of Scandinavia', *The Times*, 12 November 1956; 'Cmdr F. N. Stagg', *The Times*, 23 November 1956.

15. Stagg to Liddell, 26 October 1915; newspaper cutting: 'Worthless declarations, neutral countries and enemy trading; contraband Scandinavia, handling of contraband questions in Denmark', 22 November 1915; letter to Findlay from Eyre Crowe, 29 November 1915; Folio 177143, R. Cecil to Hopwood, 14 November 1915; Stagg to Pollock, 29 November 1915; Pollock to Cecil, 6 December 1915; FO to Lowther, 7 December 1915; Sir H. Lowther, telegram to FO, 10 December 1915; Admiralty Flint to Hall, 25 December 1915; Judd, *The Quest for C*, p. 331; Svendborg Historie Gå til f, Walter Christmas, by Thomas Mathiasen http://www.svendborghistorie.dk/post.asp?m=16&id=86 (accessed 10 February 2009); Keith Jeffrey, *The Secret History of MI6 1909–1949*, Penguin, New York, 2010, p. 87

16. 'Court of Criminal Appeal, trading with the enemy, Rex v Goodsir', *The Times*, 2 November 1915; TNA PRO FO372/958, Treasury Dennis to FO for Eyre Crowe, 30 March 1916; Folio 70, affidavit of Frank Noel Stagg, 30 March 1916.

17. TNA PRO FO 372/944, Dansey to Wellesley, 25 May 1916; Frank Noel Stagg, *West Norway and Its Fjords: A History of Bergen and Its Provinces*, Allen & Unwin, London, 1954 (see flyleaf); Rigsarkivet, Copenhagen, 10 D 27h Klager & Henv. fra tysk Gskab under Stormagtskrigen 1914–18, Auszug aus einem der Kaiserlichen Regierung zur Verfügung gestellten Privatbrief; Peter Tennant, *Touchlines of War*, University of Hull Press, Hull, 1992, p. 3.

18. 'Baron had deadly pencils, bombs and bacilli found in von Rosen's baggage in Norway', *New York Times*, 27 May 1917; 'Sugar infected with anthrax', *The Times*, 3 September 1917; 'Norway unearths bomb conspiracy', *New York Times*, 25 June 1917; 'Deadly relic of the Great War', *Nature*, 25 June 1998; 'Sugar cubes are relic of biological warfare scheme in World War I', Associated Press, 26 June 1998; 'Norway's 1918 lump of sugar yields clues on anthrax in war', *New York Times*, 25 June 1998; 'Above all, do no harm', *Natural History*, 1 October 1998; 'Sugar lumps reveal deadly relic of wartime spy's sabotage plot', *Independent*, 25 June 1998; 'Anthrax in sugar cube proves wartime plot', *The Times*, 25 June 1998; Judd, *The Quest for C*, p. 322.

19. TNA PRO ADM137/4687, Folio 183, 'C' Reports; ADM196/49/144, personal Royal Navy file of Commander Frank Noel Stagg; FO 372/944, Dansey to Wellesley, 25 May 1916; ADM 196/63, personal file of Major Kenneth Lawrance; IWM WK9 Kirke diaries, vol. III, entries for 11 March, 8 June & 1 July 1916; Judd, *The Quest for C*, pp. 351–2.

CHAPTER 8: ENGLISHMEN IN NEW YORK

1. 'Ambassador strike organizer', *The Times*, 7 September 1915; 'The Archibald Papers', *The Times*, 22 September 1915; 'Ambassador Dumba's plan', *New York Times*, 6 September 1915; 'Austria agrees to recall Dumba', *New York Times*, 28 September 1915; 'Arrested on liner in passport fraud', *New York Times*, 1 October 1915; 'Discloses charges against von Papen', *New York Times*, 17 August 1916; 'German plots in the US', *The Times*, 22 September 1917; All details of arrivals and departures from New York used in this chapter are taken from the immigration records held online at www.ancestry.co.uk and www.ellisisland.org.

2. Alan Judd, *The Quest for C: Mansfield Cumming and the Founding of the Secret Service*, London, HarperCollins, 1999; 'Sir Guy Standing: stage and film', *The Times*, 26 February 1937; 'Sir Guy Standing drops dead at 63', *New York Times*, 25 February 1937; W. B. Fowler, *British–American Relations 1917–1918: The Role of Sir William Wiseman*, Princeton University Press, Princeton, 1969, pp. 16–18; Rhodri Jeffreys-Jones, 'Wiseman, Sir William George Eden, Tenth Baronet (1885–1962)', *Oxford Dictionary of National Biography*, Oxford University Press, Oxford, 2004; 'Sir William Wiseman dies at 77', *New York Times*, 18 June 1962; 'Sir William Wiseman', *The Times*, 18 June 1962.

3. Richard B. Spence, 'Englishmen in New York: The SIS American Station 1915–21', *Intelligence and National Security* 19, 2004, pp. 515–17; Norman Thwaites, *Velvet and Vinegar*, Grayson, London, 1932, pp. 119–20; TNA PRO WO339/19912, personal file of Lt-Col N. G. Thwaites, Thwaites to Secretary War Office, 18 December 1914; Thwaites to War Office, 19 November 1934; 'N. G. Thwaites, 83, Aide to Pulitzer', *New York Times*, 27 January 1956; IWM WK9 Kirke diaries, vol. III, 2 February 1916; Guy Gaunt, *The Yield of the Year: A Story of Adventure Afloat and Ashore*, London, Hutchinson, 1940, p. 190.

4. Spence, 'Englishmen in New York', p. 515; 'Admits that boy-ed joined in ship plot', *New York Times*, 20 November 1915; 'Uncover German plot to embroil US with Mexico', *New York Times*, 8 December 1915; Captain Franz von Rintelen, *The Dark Invader: Wartime Reminiscences of a German Naval Intelligence Officer*, Penguin, London, 1933, p. 121.

5. Thwaites, *Velvet and Vinegar*, pp. 131–6; 'Bomb plot men deserted in jail may name chiefs', *New York Times*, 15 April 1916; 'Scheele got money from Rintelen too', *New York Times*, 16 April 1916; 'Nine are indicted in ship bomb plots', *New York Times*, 29 April 1916; 'Seize Scheele in Cuba and send him here', *New York Times*, 14 March 1917; 'Found Irish plot in von Igel papers', *New York Times*, 8 July 1917; 'Secret service in New York', *The Times*, 4 July 1919.

6. 'Secret service in the war, Sir R. Nathan's work', *The Times*, 28 June 1921; TNA PRO KV1/52, list of officers working in G Division as at August 1915; FO371/3065, minute, 14 March 1917; Richard J. Popplewell. *Intelligence and Imperial Defence*, Frank Cass, London, 1995, pp. 219–20.

7. Thwaites, *Velvet and Vinegar*, pp. 152–5; 'Blames her temperament', *New York Times*, 8 December 1918.

8. Thwaites, *Velvet and Vinegar*, pp. 164–8; 'Eight taken here as German spies', *New York Times*, 7 April 1917; 'Secret service in New York', *The Times*, 4 July 1919.

9. TNA PRO ADM223/758, Tom Rotterdam to Admiralty, 29 December 1917 and 1, 2 & 4

January 1918; Popplewell, *Intelligence and Imperial Defence*; 'Commerce raiders, German ships that never left New York Harbour', *Daily Telegraph*, 29 September 1930.

10. Judd, *The Quest for C*, pp. 347, 350; Spence, 'Englishmen in New York', pp. 516–17, 520; 'English army officer reports theft of money, gold bars, and valuable papers', *New York Times*, 7 December 1917; 'Granville Barker back to stage play', *New York Times*, 3 January 1917.

11. Edward Mandell House and Charles Seymour, *The Intimate Papers of Colonel House*, Kessinger, Whitefish, MT, [1926] 2005, pp. 399–400; Fowler, *British–American Relations 1917–1918*, pp. 11–15, 24.

12. 'Must exert all our power', *New York Times*, 3 April 1917; 'Expect action by Wilson today', *New York Times*, 19 March 1917; 'Germans using caution', *New York Times*, 4 February 1917; 'Great mass meeting here', *New York Times*, 6 March 1917; George F. Kennan, *Russia Leaves the War*, Princeton University Press, Princeton, 1956, p. 14; Mavis Batey, *Dilly: The Man Who Broke Enigmas*, Dialogue, London, 2009, pp. 23–7.

13. TNA PRO FO371/3065, CX610, 16 March 1917, Wiseman on US authorities; Wiseman telegram to London marked 'Following from Napier', 11 March 1917; 'German and Hindu held here in plot for India uprising', *New York Times*, 7 March 1917; 'German arrested for making bombs', *New York Times*, 6 March 1917; Thwaites, *Velvet and Vinegar*, pp. 144–9; Thomas J. Tunney and Paul Merrick Hollister, *Throttled: The Detection of the German and Anarchist Bomb Plotters*, Small, Maynard, Boston, 1919, p. 76.

14. Tunney and Hollister, *Throttled*, pp. 98–9.

15. 'Thirty-nine men indicted as German plotters', *New York Times*, July 1917; 'San Francisco consuls sentenced to prison', *New York Times*, 1 May 1918; 'Two Hindus slain in federal court', *New York Times*, 24 April 1918; 'Murder at a trial', *The Times*, 25 April 1918; 'Indian prisoners shot in court', *The Times*, 24 April 1918.

16. TNA PRO KV2/502 CX625, Wiseman to C, 22 March 1917; CX637, Wiseman to C, 28 March 1917; CX677, 10 April 1917; CX015649, 19 January 1918; Dansey to Anson, 21 January 1918; 'Socialists Conservative', *New York Times*, 5 March 1917; Tunney and Hollister, *Throttled*, p. 263; Christopher Andrew, *The Defence of the Realm; The Authorized History of MI5*, Allen Lane, London, 2009, p. 884.

17. Spence, 'Englishmen in New York', pp. 516, 526–7; 'Vernon Castle dies in airplane fall', *New York Times*, 16 February 1918; 'L. R. Grossmith, 66, an actor 47 years', *New York Times*, 24 February 1944.

18. Spence, 'Englishmen in New York', p. 527; Judd, *The Quest for C*, pp. 383–5; 'Written on the screen', *New York Times*, 12 January 1919.

19. TNA PRO FO371/2146, Attitude of the Armenians, Francis Blyth Kirby to the Secretary, the Foreign Office, 6 November 1914; KV 21/827, extracts from Air Ministry and War Office files, 22 June 1931; Richard B. Spence, *Trust No One: The Secret World of Sidney Reilly*, Feral House, Los Angeles, 2002, citing SIS archives CXM212 dated 29 March 1918; Gordon Brook-Shepherd, *Iron Maze: The Western Secret Services and the Bolsheviks*, Macmillan, London, 1998, pp. 13–20; Michael Smith, *New Cloak, Old Dagger: How Britain's Spies Came In from the Cold*, Victor Gollancz, London, 1996, pp. 87–88.

20. Thwaites, *Velvet and Vinegar*, pp. 181–5.

21. TNA PRO KV21/827, letter from T. H. Owens Thurston dated 19 January 1918; Spence, *Trust No One*, citing CX021744, dated 3 March 1918.

22. TNA PRO KV21/827, MI5 observation reports, 7–9 March 1918; telegram sent by Reilly to Litvinov, 22 March 1918; Thomson to Kell, 6 April 1918; Rowe (MI5) to Kendall (MI1c), 27 April 1918; Judd, *The Quest for C*, p. 429; Sidney and Pepita Reilly, *Britain's Master Spy: The Adventures of Sidney Reilly*, Harper, New York, 1933, p. 6.

23. Thwaites, *Velvet and Vinegar*, p. 183.

24. TNA PRO HO45/19966, minutes of the Aliens and Nationality Committee, 3 October 1919; Passport Control Committee report, 15 September 1919; FO366/791, Staff of Passport Control Office, New York, 1920; WO339/27657, demobilisation papers of Edward Béla Josepff Harran, 8 November 1919; Spence, 'Englishmen in New York', pp. 527–33; Spence, *Trust No One*, p. 290; 'Col Thwaites wed to Mrs Greenough', *New York Times*, 10 December 1919; 'Rush on to Europe', *New York Times*, 11 February 1920; Keith Jeffrey, *The Secret History of MI6 1909–1949*, Penguin, New York, 2010, p. 250

CHAPTER 9: MIDDLE EAST ADVENTURES – 'BRIGANDS AND TERRORISTS'

1. TNA PRO FO 371/2146, Samson to FO, 20 October 1914; FO286/638, Instructions of Aegean Intelligence Service and Instructions to Intelligence Officer Mitylene, 9 June 1917; Compton Mackenzie, *Gallipoli Memories*, Cassell, London, 1929, pp. 249–59; Compton Mackenzie, *First Athenian Memories*, Cassell, London, 1931, pp. 10–15, 72–5, 209; Compton Mackenzie, *Greek Memories*, Cassell, London, 1932, p. 2; Alan Judd, *The Quest for C: Mansfield Cumming and the Founding of the Secret Service*, London, HarperCollins, 1999, p. 305; Godfrey diaries, 4 June 1915; medal roll card for Lt-Col George Monreal, 3rd Wilts Regt.

2. TNA PRO FO 141/801, intelligence reports to Capt. Clayton, Cairo from October 1914 to February 1915 and intelligence reports from Samson from 1 March 1915 to 5 May 1915; WO 157/739, series of reports from HBM Minister Athens, and MAs in Petrograd and Paris to GOC from June 1915 to February 1916; WO 157/739, Athens to Cairo 7 October 1915, 10 October 1915 and 11 October 1915.

3. Judd, *The Quest for C*, pp. 296, 304–5; TNA PRO ADM 337/119/243 RNVR, service records for George G. Eady and Edwin Whittall; FO1093/47 to FO1093/57 contain details of Zaharoff's negotiations; WO157/717, Political Intelligence war diary for the months of July, August and September 1917; 'Mr F. E. Whittall', *The Times*, 6 March 1953.

4. TNA PRO ADM 337/119/243, RNVR record for George G. Eady; FO371/3065, Nathan to Lyons, re two Indians suspected of going to US, 31 January 1916; FO 372/944, Dansey to Wellesley, 25 May 1916; WO 32/21380, note by Admiralty; Judd, *The Quest for C*, pp. 312–18, 328; Mackenzie, *Greek Memories*, pp. 2, 117, 373; medal card for Lt-Col Edmund Vivian Gabriel; 'Sir Vivian Gabriel', *The Times*, 16 February 1950; Mackenzie, *Greek Memories*, p. 397.

5. Mackenzie, *First Athenian Memories*, pp. 11–14, 25, 72–8, 107, 209, 257; Mackenzie, *Greek Memories*, p. 5.

6. Mackenzie, *First Athenian Memories*, p. 111.

7. Ibid., p. 204.

8. Ibid., p. 124; Mackenzie, *Greek Memories*, pp. 29–33; TNA PRO FO 655/939, Henry Cauchi's passport.

9. Mackenzie, *First Athenian Memories*, pp. 198–9; 'A loss to scholarship', *The Times*, 24
    February 1920.

10. Mackenzie, *First Athenian Memories*, p. 241; Mackenzie, *Greek Memories*, pp. 525–6; 'Mr H.
    E. C. Whittall', *The Times*, 19 August 1959; Capt. G. A. Hill, *Go Spy the Land: Being the
    Adventures of IK8 of the British Secret Service*, Cassell, London, 1932, pp. 59–65.

11. 'Sir John Myres', *The Times*, 8 March 1954; Mackenzie, *First Athenian Memories*, pp. 171–3,
    249–50; Compton Mackenzie, *Aegean Memories*, Chatto & Windus, London, 1940, p. 136;
    Mackenzie, *Greek Memories*, p. 234; Norman Dewhurst, *Norman Dewhurst MC*, H. J.
    Edmonds, Brussels, 1968, p. 61.

12. J. C. Lawson, *Tales of Aegean Intrigue*, Chatto & Windus, London, 1920, pp. 29–36.

13. Mackenzie, *Gallipoli Memories*, pp. 86–7; Judd, *The Quest for C*, p. 316; TNA PRO
    WO157/736, various MI1c reports issued by R between August and December 1915.

14. TNA PRO FO 882/2, H. McMahon to Sir Arthur Nicolson, 2 February 1916; KV
    1/17, Proposals for the Organisation of a Special Intelligence Bureau for the Eastern
    Mediterranean Area; Mackenzie, *First Athenian Memories*, pp. 44–9, 389; IWM WK9
    Kirke diaries, vol. III, 2 February 1916; 'Mr Everard Feilding', *The Times*, 10 February
    1936; Yigal Sheffy, 'British Intelligence and the Middle East 1900–1918: How Much
    Do We Know?', in *Intelligence and National Security* 17, 2002; Judd, *The Quest for C*,
    p. 350.

15. Mackenzie, *First Athenian Memories*, pp. 254–55; Yigal Sheffy, *British Military Intelligence in the
    Palestinian Campaign 1914–1918*, Frank Cass, London, 1998, p. 86; Bell letters to mother,
    30 November 1915 and 20 September 1916 (Bell letters from the University of Newcastle's
    Gertrude Bell Project http://www.gerty.ncl.ac.uk/); TNA PRO WO 106/1510,
    Memorandum of the Intelligence Service in Mesopotamia, May 1916.

16. 'Miss Gertrude Bell', *The Times*, 15 July 1926; Bell letter to father, 18 May 1917.

17. Sheffy, *British Military Intelligence in the Palestinian Campaign 1914–1918*, pp. 82–3, 146–7;
    Captain L. B. Weldon, *Hard Lying: Eastern Mediterranean 1914–1919*, Herbert Jenkins,
    London, 1925, pp. 110–11.

18. Leonard Woolley, *As I Seem to Remember*, George Allen & Unwin, London, 1962, pp. 97–
    104, 110–13; Weldon, *Hard Lying*, pp. 153, 160–73, 176, 199–200; TNA PRO WO
    157/717, Political Intelligence War Diary for the month of August 1917, entry for 3 August
    1917; Anthony Verrier, *Agents of Empire: Anglo-Zionist Intelligence Operations 1915–1919*,
    Brasseys, London, 1995, pp. 224–75; Keith Jeffrey, *The Secret History of MI6 1909–1949*,
    Penguin, New York, 2010, p. 132

CHAPTER 10: MIDDLE EAST ADVENTURES 2 – 'THE BRITISH SECRET SERVICE GANG'

1. Compton Mackenzie, *First Athenian Memories*, Cassell, London, 1931, pp. 341–4; Compton
    Mackenzie, *Greek Memories*, Cassell, London, 1932, p. 141.

2. Mackenzie, *First Athenian Memories*, pp. 356, 358–61.

3. Ibid., p. 356; 'Bombs on Salonika', *The Times*, 1 January 2009; 'Suspected of espionage',
    The Times, 1 January 2009; 'Enemy archives examined, widespread espionage', *The Times*,
    3 January 1916; 'Lieutenant Pirie-Gordon', *The Times*, 30 June 1915; Norman Dewhurst,

Norman Dewhurst MC, H. J. Edmonds, Brussels, 1968, pp. 44–50; Mackenzie, *Greek Memories*, pp. 127–8.

4. TNA PRO FO372/936, Elliot to Nicolson, 18 June 1916, Memorandum on Proposals for Control of Passenger Traffic from and to Greece.

5. TNA PRO FO372/936, Elliot to Hardinge, 4 July 1916; MSC memo, 5 July 1916; WO 106/6191, Organisation of British Intelligence in Spain since August 1914; WO 158/897, Charteris to Macdonogh, 15 January 1917; Macdonogh to Charteris, 19 January 1917; ADM 337/119/200, personal RNVR file for Lt Windham Baring; WO 339/26150, personal army file for Capt A. E. Forbes Dennis; WO 374/44860, personal file of Lt M. B. Maclachlan, Browning to MI1c & MI6, 18 May 1916; Phyllis Bottome, *The Goal*, Faber & Faber, London, 1962, p. 38; Mackenzie, *Greek Memories*, pp. 221–34, 549–78; Alan Judd, *The Quest for C: Mansfield Cumming and the Founding of the Secret Service*, London, HarperCollins, 1999, pp. 345, 348–50; medal roll card for Philip James Griffiths Pipon; Keith Jeffrey, *The Secret History of MI6 1909–1949*, Penguin, New York, 2010, p. 93

6. Mackenzie, *Greek Memories*, p. 103; Judd, *The Quest for C*, pp. 402–3.

7. Mackenzie, *Greek Memories*, pp. 262–83, 324–40; 'Greece and the war', *The Times*, 4 September 1916; 'Arrest of enemy agents', *The Times*, 5 September 1916 ;'Purging Greece of enemy agents', *The Times*, 6 September 1916; 'Allied black list at Athens', *The Times*, 7 September 1916.

8. Mackenzie, *Greek Memories*, pp. 392–6, 407–8; Judd, *The Quest for C*, p. 402; Nigel West, *Historical Dictionary of British Intelligence*, Scarecrow Press, Lanham, MD, 2005, pp. 292–3; TNA PRO WO 339/84337 personal file of Capt Edward Knoblock; HO 144/1454/312791, naturalisation file of Edward Gustavus Knoblauch.

9. Mackenzie, *Greek Memories*, p. 408.

10 Supplement to *London Gazette*, 17 January, 1917, p. 678; TNA PRO WO 106/6191, The Controls in Athens; 'Reign of terror at Athens', *The Times*, 6 December 1916; 'The full story of the outbreak', *The Times*, 9 December 1916; Mackenzie, *Greek Memories*, pp. 464–547; Compton Mackenzie, *Aegean Memories*, Chatto & Windus, London, 1940, pp. 1–255; Dewhurst, *Norman Dewhurst MC*, p. 56.

11. Mackenzie, *Aegean Memories*, p. 286; Cafferata family archive, Cafferata to Dansey, 25 November 1917, Cafferata to Dansey, 12 August 1918; Captain L. B. Weldon, *Hard Lying, Eastern Mediterranean, 1914–1919*, Herbert Jenkins, London, 1925, pp. 198, 223.

12. Mackenzie, *Aegean Memories*, pp. 355–407; Dewhurst, *Norman Dewhurst MC*, pp. 59–61; TNA PRO FO 286/637, Mackenzie to Tucker, 21 June 1917; Crackenthorpe to Hardinge, 24 June 1917; Crackenthorpe to Hastings, for Z, 29 June 1917; Beaumont to Crackenthorpe, 5 July 1917; Z (Director Aegean Intelligence Service Aegis, Syra) to Crackenthorpe, CXC14, 2 July 1917; Crackenthorpe to Thursby, 10 July 1917; Crackanthorpe to Hardinge, 8 August 1917; Crackanthorpe to Thursby, 13 August 1917; Hardinge to Crackanthorpe, 13 August 1917; FO286/638, Thursby to Crackanthorpe, 19 August 1917; Beaumont to Thursby, 20 August 1917; Crackanthorpe to Thursby, 20 August 1917; Balfour to Crackanthorpe, 12 September 1917; Granville to Hardinge, 30 August 1917; RAE to Hall, 30 August 1917; CXC 39, 5 September 1917; Beaumont to Granville, 13 October 1917; Granville to Fremantle,

16 October 1917; Fremantle to Granville, 31 October 1917; West, *Historical Dictionary of British Intelligence*, p. 293.

13. Dewhurst, *Norman Dewhurst MC*, p. 69; Cafferata to Dansey, 12 August 1918; Yigal Sheffy,' British Intelligence and the Middle East, 1900–1918: How Much Do We Know?', in *Intelligence and National Security* 17 (2002); Cafferata family archive, Myres to Cafferata, 21 April 1918; TNA PRO ADM 137/4697, CX 027625, Report by Eastern Mediterranean Special Intelligence Bureau, Jerusalem, 19 March 1918; F0 286/638 Athens/D6159 6 August 1918; WO 374/32170 Personal file of Captain J. T. Hayward; 'Professor A. W. Gomme, Greek scholar', *The Times*, 20 January 1959.

14. Cafferata family archive, Draft Form of Instructions to Agent, Patras, 18 March 1918.

15. TNA PRO FO 286/638, minutes of proceedings of a conference held at the British legation, Athens, 6 August 1918 on 'the Functions and General Position of the Organisation of which Commander Myres RNVR is the Head'; Macdonogh to Fairholme, 3 August 1918; Talbot to Hall, 2 August 1918; Hall to Talbot, 3 August 1918; Opinions of Commander Talbot RNVR, 9 August 1918; Cafferata family archive, Cafferata to Dansey, 12 August 1918.

16. Cafferata family archive, H547, Rivoli to Cafferata, 7 August 1918; A15631, Sykes to Myres, 31 July 1918; list of Lausanne district agents compiled by Redmond Cafferata; CX/ MD/047995, 12 September 1918.

17. TNA PRO FO 286/637, Dansey to C, 1 November 1918; FO 371/3449 CX 089004, Dansey, Sofia, to C, 23 November 1918; Dewhurst, *Norman Dewhurst MC*, pp. 67–9; medal card for 2nd Lt Henry Albert Bowe.

18. Weldon, *Hard Lying,* pp. 222–3 ; Dewhurst, *Norman Dewhurst MC*, p. 68; TNA PRO WO 158/961, French to BGI France, GHQ Egypt, Mesopotamia, Salonika, Italy, Aden, East Africa, North Russian Expeditionary Force, 1 December 1918.

CHAPTER 11: MURDER AND MAYHEM IN RUSSIA

1. Alan Judd, *The Quest for C: Mansfield Cumming and the Founding of the Secret Service*, London, HarperCollins, 1999, pp. 277–80; Short memoir written by Stephen Alley and held in the Alley papers (henceforward Alley memoir). I am grateful to Andrew Cook for providing me with a copy.

2. Alley Memoir, p. 1; TNA PRO WO 106/6190, Burge History.

3. TNA PRO FO 371/2175, Buchanan to London, 17 October 1914, folio 318.

4. Alley memoir, pp. 3-4.

5. TNA PRO WO 106/6190, Lt M. R. K. Burge, History of the British Intelligence Organisation in Russia from 1914 to February 1917; FO 371/2446, Buchanan to Foreign Office, 20 December 1914; Buchanan to Foreign Office, 3 January 1915, folio 415; Buchanan and Knox insisted that the Russian military did not like Campbell and Ferguson, an impression that is countered by the records in the Russian military archives and by a final Russian report on their work; WO 374/24004, telegram from Russian General Staff to Russian ambassador to the UK, 17 April 1915; Alley memoir, p. 4.

6. Alley memoir, pp. 10–11.

7. Ibid.; 'Colonel C. J. M. Thornhill', *The Times*, 13 August 1952, 16 August 1952, 23

430   NOTES TO PAGES 193–202

August 1952; Judd, *The Quest for C*, pp. 309, 347; Andrew Soutar, *With Ironside in Russia*, Hutchinson, London, 1940, p. 135; TNA PRO WO 106/6190, Burge history.

8.   Cambridge University Library, Templewood papers, Part II, file 1, item 38, Cumming to Hoare, 12 May 1916; Sir Samuel Hoare, *The Fourth Seal: The End of a Russian Chapter*, Heinemann, London, 1930, pp. 28–30.

9.   TNA PRO FO 1093/61, Secret service budgets for 1916/17; Templewood papers, Part II, file 1.

10.   Liddell Hart Centre for Military Archives, King's College London, Steveni memoir, 1/1–2; 4/2–4; The claim that a warning from the Petrograd bureau played a role in the battle is backed up by Cumming's diaries, see Judd, *The Quest for C*, p. 300; TNA PRO WO 106/1146 contains a number of Russian daily War Office summaries sent to London by the MI1c officers.

11.   Hoare, *Fourth Seal*, p. 186; TNA PRO WO 106/6190, Burge history.

12.   Scale details from the Scale papers. The author is grateful to Scale's grandson Edward Harding-Newman for providing access to the papers. Scale's memories of the Astoria come from his monograph on his arrival in Russia and subsequent operations in Romania entitled 'A Glimpse of Petrograd and a Journey', pp. 3–4.

13.   Ibid.; TNA PRO WO 106/6190, Burge history; FO 371/3350, Capt. George A. Hill, Report of Work Done in Russia to End of 1917, p. 5; FO 371/3319, Vladivostok to London, 29 December 1917; KV1/21; KV1/30; ADM 337/122/113, RNVR service record of Leonard F. Binns; ADM 337/123/276, RNVR service record of Harry Anderson; ADM 337/123/350, RNVR service records of Frank Ball and Harry Gruner; Alley memoir; Gill Bennett, *Churchill's Man of Mystery: Desmond Morton and the World of Intelligence*, Routledge, Abingdon, 2007, p. 49; Phil Tomaselli, *Tracing Your Secret Service Ancestors*, Pen & Sword, Barnsley, 2009, p. 118; Judd, *The Quest for C*, p. 347; Urmston, a lance-corporal in the Liverpool Regiment, was like Tinsley brought up in the Bootle docks, and had been plucked from the ranks, and commissioned into the RNVR because of his Russian background.

14.   Scale papers, A Glimpse of Petrograd and a Journey, pp. 9–10; 'Rasputin's secret burial', *The Times*, 24 March 1917.

15.   The involvement of Rayner, Scale and Alley in the plot to murder Rasputin was first revealed by the BBC *Timewatch* programme on 1 October 2004 and recorded in Andrew Cook, *To Kill Rasputin: The Life and Death of Grigori Rasputin*. But the full extent of the brutality of the murder, and in particular the torture involved, were uncovered by Richard Cullen, the former Scotland Yard detective who advised *Timewatch* and has since investigated the murder in far more extensive detail. The account of his investigation is published as *Rasputin: The Role of Britain's Secret Service in His Torture and Murder*, Dialogue, London, 2010.

16.   Cambridge University Library (CUL), Templewood papers, Part II, file 1, no. 48, Private to C; 1 January 1917, no. 49, Letter to B [Browning], 1 January 1917.

17.   'Scotland Yard from within', *The Times*, 1 December 1921; Scale role in Romanian operation a result of the need for him to be out of Russia from Edward Harding-Newman, Scale's grandson.

18.   CUL, Templewood papers, Cumming to Hoare, 28 April 1916; Judd, *The Quest for C*, pp. 343, 350, 390–91.

19. TNA PRO FO 371/2869, report on the destruction of Romanian oilfields, by Lt-Col J. Norton-Griffiths, 22 January 1917; WO 339/13678, handwritten Army record for Thomas Spencer Laycock MC; WO 339/28053, Army record of Sir J. Norton Griffiths KCB DSO MP (Norton Griffiths was a Royal Engineer Lt-Col who had raised a special tunnelling company for work undermining the German trenches on the Western Front and was therefore an expert in demolition and the use of explosives); WO 374/32170, personal Army record of Captain J. T. Hayward MC; Scale papers, Scale, 'A Glimpse of Petrograd and a Journey', pp. 41–2; 'Lt-Col E. G. Boxshall', *The Times*, 7 February 1984; 'Company meetings, Roumanian Consolidated Oilfields', *The Times*, 28 February 1918; 'Oilfields useless to Germans', *The Times*, 11 December 1916; IWM WK9 Kirke diaries, vol. III, entries for 9 February 1916 and 17 April 1916; medal roll cards for Lt-Col Sir John Norton-Griffiths KCB DSO MP and Capt. Philip Huntingdon Simpson MC; 'Sir John Norton-Griffiths', *The Times*, 29 September 1930; Cook, *To Kill Rasputin*, p. 216.

20. Scale papers, Scale to Ismay, 19 September 1940; Hoare, *Fourth Seal*, pp. 156–7; Alley papers, Alley to Scale, 17 January 1917.

CHAPTER 12: 'THE ACE OF SPIES'

1. TNA PRO 371/3005, Hoare to Balfour, 18 February 1917.

2. Scale papers, memo 'For British Officers in Case of Panic or Anarchy in Petrograd'; TNA PRO FO 175/6, letters from K1 to London, dated 13, 18 and 19 July 1918; information provided by Phil Tomaselli.

3. Bernard A. Pares, *Wandering Student: The Story of a Purpose*, Syracuse University Press, Syracuse, NY, 1948, pp. 191, 212–15; 'Order of the British Empire, awards for war service', *The Times*, 9 January 1919.

4. TNA PRO WO 106/1146, Scale report sent from Blair to DMI, 18 June 1917; Thornhill report from HQ Romanian Front, serial no. 307; Macdonogh to Knox, 18 July 1917; Scale report from Jassy sent by Knox to Macdonogh, 20 July 1917.

5. TNA PRO KV 2/585 CX, report from MCO Berne, dated 21 April 1917; CX report from SW5, Berne, dated 13 April 1917; KV 2/498, Russo–German Pacifist Movement in Switzerland, report from G284, 14 September 1917; Russo–German Pacifist Organisation, report from G26, 24 October 1917; Scale papers, Nabokov to Scale, 11 October 1916 and Report of a Meeting of the Anglo-Russian Commission, 29 August 1917; Hoover Institution Archives, George Davis Herron papers, Doc. XI/VIII, 20 July 1917; Alan Judd, *The Quest for C: Mansfield Cumming and the Founding of the Secret Service*, London, HarperCollins, 1999, p. 427.

6. W. Somerset Maugham, *The Summing Up*, Heinemann, London, 1938, pp. 203–5; 'Fear she met fate of Edith Cavell', *New York Times*, 19 July 1916; 'Says enemy spies betrayed sister', *New York Times*, 30 July 1918; 'Government joins 'Red' investigation', *New York Times*, 25 July 1918; Yale University Library, William Wiseman papers, Folder 112, Wiseman memo to London dated 21 October 1917; Maugham to Wiseman, 19 September 1917 and 21 September 1917; WW to WSM, 22 September 1917; CX159, Wiseman to London, 24 September 1917; W. Somerset Maugham, *Ashenden*, Mandarin, London, [1928] 1991, pp. 290, 314–315; Keith Jeffrey, *The Secret History of MI6 1909–1949*, Penguin, New York, 2010, p. 118

7. TNA PRO WO 32/5669, Lindley to WO, report no. 87, 10 January 1918; CX020636-7 P/C/145, P2 to C, 23 February 1918; CX 021635/11395/M, Petrograd to London, 1 March 1918; CX205, Petrograd to C, 8 March 1918; Lockhart Moscow to FO no. 30, 20 March 1918; CX027184 M/13054, Moscow to London, 9 April 1918; CX028699 M/14126, Moscow to London, 20 April 1918; BRITSUP Petrograd to RUSPLYCOM Charles, received 25 April 1918; Lockhart to WO, no. 110, 19 April 1918; Nick Baron, *The King of Karelia: Col. P. J. Woods and the British Intervention in North Russia 1918–1922 – a history and memoir*, Francis Boutle, London, 2007, p. 163; Andrew Soutar, *With Ironside in Russia*, Hutchinson, London, 1940, p. 136; 'The Birth of the ILO: The Personal Memories of Edward Phelan, pp. 165–6, available at www.ilo.org/public/english/century/ information_resources/download/phelans.pdf, accessed 15 June 2010.

8. Scale papers, CX023829, letter to Major J. D. Scale dated 12 March 1918; Judd, *The Quest for C*, p. 429; TNA PRO FO371/3319, French to Campbell, 10 October 1918, folio 450.

9. Andrew Cook, *Ace of Spies: The True Story of Sidney Reilly*, History Press, Stroud, 2004, p. 156.

10. Sidney and Pepita Reilly, *Britain's Master Spy: The Adventures of Sidney Reilly*, Harper, New York, 1933, pp. 8–9; Cook, *Ace of Spies*, p. 157.

11. Cook, *Ace of Spies*, pp. 157–8.

12. Reilly, *Britain's Master Spy*, pp. 12–13.

13. TNA PRO CX031272, issued 15 May 1918, folio 126833.

14. Robert Bruce Lockhart, *Memoirs of a British Agent*, Putnam, London, 1932, pp. 276–7.

15. Reilly, *Britain's Master Spy*, pp. 14–15.

16. TNA PRO WO 32/5669 CX 013592/M/143893, issued 4 June 1916; CX034216, Thornhill to DMI, 1 June 1918; CX034907/M/14635, from Moscow 29 May 1918; CX035402/P/C/350, 29 May 1918; CX035176/M/14636, from Moscow 3 June 1918.

17. Capt. G. A. Hill, *Go Spy the Land: Being the Adventures of IK8 of the British Secret Service*, Cassell, London, 1932, pp. 87–8, 188–93.

18. TNA PRO WO 32/5669, Lockhart to WO, no. 110, 19 April 1918; CX038103, Petrograd 16 June 1918 is an example of an intercepted German telegram; FO 371/3350, Capt. George A. Hill, Report of Work Done in Russia to End of 1917, pp. 7–11; Scale papers, memo 'For British Officers in Case of Panic or Anarchy in Petrograd'; supplement to *London Gazette*, 12 February 1919, p. 2238; letter from Cumming to Sale, 21 May 1918, kindly supplied by Phil Tomaselli.

CHAPTER 13: 'DECEPTION, DIRT AND MEAN BEHAVIOUR'

1. Capt. G. A. Hill, *Go Spy the Land: Being the Adventures of IK8 of the British Secret Service*, Cassell, London, 1932, p. 20.

2. Phil Tomaselli, *Tracing Your Secret Service Ancestors*, Pen & Sword, Barnsley, 2009, p. 116; TNA PRO WO 33/962, DMI to Poole, 28 May 1918; Poole to DMI, 29 May 1918; Steveni, Tokyo to DMI, 5 June 1918; Steveni, Harbin to DMI, various reports dated 18 June–9 September 1918; Knox to WO, 7 October 1918; Blair to WO, 26 October 1918; Knox to WO, 12 December 1918; Knox to WO, 15 December 1918; FO 371/4009, CV for 2nd Lt L. Collas; ADM 223/758, SNO Murmansk for Admiralty, telegram no. 470, 29 May 1918; medal roll cards for McLaren, Small, Calder, and McGrath; *London Gazette*, 25

November 1918, p. 13876; Calder role in Murmansk from RGVA (Russian State Military Archive) Moscow, Fond 4031, Opis 1, file 8, p. 2; Alley position from RGVA, Fond 40311, Opis 1, file 5, p. 2; see also Judd, *The Quest for C*, pp. 430–31.

3.   Andrew Soutar, *With Ironside in Russia*, Hutchinson, London, 1940, pp. 135–6.

4.   TNA PRO FO 371/3350, Capt. George A. Hill, Report of Work Done in Russia to End of 1917, pp. 12–13; ADM 137/1714, Wilson letter, 18 April 1918, folio 91.

5.   TNA PRO FO 371/3350, Capt. George A. Hill, Report of Work Done in Russia to End of 1917, pp. 12–13.

6.   Ibid.; Hill, *Go Spy the Land*, pp. 215–19.

7.   TNA PRO FO 395/185, CX044633, report by ST, 13 July 1918; H. Stuart Jones, Section V to Sir William Tyrrell, 16 August 1918.

8.   TNA PRO FO 371/3350, Hill, Report of Work Done in Russia, pp. 14–15.

9.   Robert Bruce Lockhart, *Memoirs of a British Agent*, Putnam, London, 1932, pp. 314–16; Roy Bainton, *Honoured by Strangers*, Airlife, Shrewsbury, 2002, pp. 238–42.

10. Reilly, *Britain's Master Spy*, p. 27.

11. Hill, *Go Spy the Land*, p. 238; Reilly, *Britain's Master Spy*, p. 26; TNA PRO FO 371/3350, Hill, Report of Work Done in Russia, p. 19.

12. John W. Long, 'Plot and Counter-Plot in Revolutionary Russia', *Intelligence and National Security* 10, 1995, pp. 131–3.

13. Richard B. Spence, *Trust No One: The Secret World of Sidney Reilly*, Feral House, Los Angeles, 2002, pp. 225–32; Reilly, *Britain's Master Spy*, pp. 30–32.

14. Gordon Brook-Shepherd, *Iron Maze: The Western Secret Services and the Bolsheviks*, Macmillan, London, 1998, p. 107.

15. Andrew Cook, *Ace of Spies: The True Story of Sidney Reilly*, History Press, Stroud, 2004, pp. 168–70.

16. Information provided to the author in confidence by former SIS officer who subsequently worked in the SIS archives.

17. TNA PRO ADM 137/4183, CX 048699, Petrograd to C, 9 September 1918; HO405/4803, MI5 naturalisation application ref. B26874/3/Nat Div; Boyce to Under-Secretary of State at Home Office, 10 October 1945; Metropolitan Police Special Branch report on Nikolai Bunakov, 16 October 1945; 'British released from Russia', *The Times*, 18 Oct 1918.

18. TNA PRO BT 62/1/13, BECORS to F. G. A. Butler, Board of Trade, 8 August 1918; FO 371/3334, DMI to Steveni, Harbin, 31 July 1918; FO, Sir G. Clerk to DMI, 8 August 1918; Steveni to DMI, 1 July 1918; FO 371/3888, folio 152; FO 371/3975, Merrett to Foreign Secretary, 4 May 1920; Bulmer to FO, 29 June 1920; W. H. Murray-Campbell to FO, 15 July 1920; 'The Russian terror', *The Times*, 24 October 1918.

19. TNA PRO BT61/60/9, particulars of service of Franklyn Frederick Clively; WO 95/4960, Major G. M. Goldsmith, Acting British Military Agent, Army of Caucasus Front to Director of Military Intelligence, 1 July 1919; CAB 23/41, minutes of war cabinet meeting, 24 June 1918, p. 4; Gökay Bülent, 'The Battle for Baku (May–September 1918): A Peculiar Episode in the History of the Caucasus', *Turkish Yearbook* 25, 1995, p. 35; Judd, *The Quest for C*, p. 447; Teague-Jones, Reginald, *The Spy Who Disappeared: Diary of a Secret Mission to Russian Central Asia in 1918*, Victor Gollancz, London, 1991, pp. 9–13, 119–22.

20. Hill, *Go Spy the Land*, pp. 263–6; Brook-Shepherd, *Iron Maze*, pp. 151–62; Hill and Reilly MCs from supplement to *London Gazette*, 12 February 1919, p. 2238; Hill DSO, supplement to *London Gazette*, 27 June 1919, p. 8060.

21. RAF service record for Sidney George Reilly; Spence, *Trust No One*, citing SIS memo Morton to Maw, 31 Jan 1922; Gill Bennett, *Churchill's Man of Mystery: Desmond Morton and the World of Intelligence*, Routledge, Abingdon, 2007, pp. 48–51; information provided to the author in confidence.

CHAPTER 14: RED DUSK

1. TNA PRO KV 2/498, Dukes, Reports on Political Suspects, undated but file cover indicates sent sometime in early August 1918; Campbell to Kell, 20 August 1918.

2. Paul Dukes, *Red Dusk and the Morrow: Adventures and Investigations in Soviet Russia*, Doubleday Page, New York, 1922.

3. Ibid., pp. 11, 76–82, 107–116 (Merrett is referred to by Dukes as Marsh); John Fisher, *Gentleman Spies, Intelligence Agents in the British Empire and Beyond*, Sutton, Stroud, p. 170.

4. TNA PRO T 161/30, ref. 197690/38, letter from Paul Dukes to Under-Secretary of State at Foreign Office.

5. TNA PRO ADM 223/637 CX062092, Stockholm, 20 December 1918; CX062597, Stockholm, 24 December 1918; translation of report sent from Petrograd by ST25 to ID, 9 January 1919; CX063671, from N63, Christiania, 10 January 1919; CX064290, following from ST25, 7 January 1919; CX064775, from ST25, Stockholm, 23 January 1919; CX065263, Stockholm, 25 January 1919; CX065264, Stockholm, 25 January 1919; CX066471, Stockholm, 13 February 1919; CX066477, Stockholm, 18 February 1919; 'Reval under British protection', *The Times*, 21 December 1918; 'Exchange of prisoners with Bolsheviks', *The Times*, 23 May 1919.

6. *Krasnaya kniga VChK* (Red Book of the Cheka), vol. II, Politizdat, Moscow, 1990, pp. 43–5, 48, 57–8, 320, 339–40, 346–7, 366–7, 380–81; D. L. Golikov, *Krushenie antisovetskogo podpol'ya v SSSR* (Collapse of the anti-Soviet Underground in the USSR), vol. I, Politizdat, Moscow, 1986, pp. 294–5; R. S. Krasilnikov, *KGB protiv Mi-6: ohotniki za shpionami* (KGB against MI6: Hunters, Spies), Tsentrpolograf, Moscow, 2000, p. 72; A. Saparov, *Bitaya karta: khronika odnogo zagorova, v sborniki chekisti* (Chronicle of a Conspiracy. The Cheka Collection), Lenizdat, Leningrad, 1982; 'Mr Harry Charnock', *The Times*, 8 June 1963; Harry Ferguson, *Operation Kronstadt*, Arrow, London, 2010, pp. 76–7; TNA PRO FO 511/5 HB, Quarton to British Embassy Helsingfors, 31 October 1920; KV 2/503 CX2419, Report on Visit to Petrograd by ST65, 30 September 1920.

7. TNA PRO FO511/2, Report on the Passage of the British Embassy at Petrograd through the Finnish Fronts, 21 March 1918; FO 371/3208, report by Arthur Cotter and E. W. Michelson, 3 May 1918; Supplement to the *London Gazette*, 1 January 1919, p. 80; Conrad O'Brien-ffrench, *Delicate Mission: Autobiography of a Secret Agent*, Skilton & Shaw, London, 1979, pp. 53–6.

8. Ferguson, *Operation Kronstadt*, pp. 146–50, 181–5.

9. Augustus Agar, *Baltic Episode*, Naval Institute Press, Annapolis, MD, 1963, pp. 27–32; John

R. Bullen, 'Agar, Augustus Willington Shelton (1890–1968)', *Oxford Dictionary of National Biography*, Oxford University Press, Oxford, 2004.

10. Agar, *Baltic Episode*, pp. 31–2, 37.

11. Ibid., pp. 66–78; TNA PRO ADM1/8563/208 CX 073696 and CX 073697, reports by Lt Sindall on attempts 'to put Sokolov ashore behind Bolshevik lines', Stockholm to London, 28 June 1919; 'Mr Harry Charnock', *The Times*, 8 January 1963. I am grateful to Yury Totrov for the information on the respective football careers of Sokolov and Hall.

12. TNA PRO ADM137/1679, folios 247–8, Agar Report on Sinking of the Oleg, 24 June 1919; folio 255, Draft Citation for Agar VC; *London Gazette*, 22 August 1919, page 10631; Agar, *Baltic Episode*, p. 87.

13. TNA PRO ADM 137/1679, Cmdr Claude C. Dobson, General Narrative of Operation RK, folios 387–91; ADM 137/1686, Agent's Report, 30 September 1919; Agar, *Baltic Episode*, p. 167.

14. TNA PRO ADM 137/1679, Minute Sheet no. 1, folio 576, *London Gazette*, 11 November 1919, pp. 13743–4.

15. 'The Kronstadt raid', *The Times*, 5 September 1919.

16. TNA PRO ADM 137/1679, Agar report of activities at Terijoki from 19 June 1919 to 14 August 1919, dated 14 August 1919; Cumming letter dated 18 September 1919, folio 595; S. V. Volkov, *Ofitsery flota i morskogo vedomstva: opyt martirologa* (The Officers of the Fleet and the Navy Department: The Experience of Martyrdom), Russkii Put', Moscow, 2004; Agar, *Baltic Episode*, p. 207.

17. TNA PRO ADM 137/1686, agent's report, Helsingfors, 29 September 1919 (This informally styled and highly insecure type of report, which in this case includes Hoyer's name typed in the top left-hand corner, only occurred during a brief period at Terijoki); copy of order to Baltic Fleet in Petrograd, 15 September 1919; report on Kronstadt and Krasnaya Gorka, Helsingfors, 16 October 1919; ADM 137/1735, CX6551, 25 October 1920; FO 371/12593, Memorandum by Mr A. J. Cave, Leningrad Spy-Case, 8 September 1927, folio 131; Riksarkivet Sweden, report from Consul Olof Hedman to Torvald Höjer, UD [Swedish Ministry for Foreign Affairs], Reval, 14 June 1921, 'Concerning the Danish Citizen, Albert Hoyer, who is under surveillance', Utrikesdepartementets Arkiv, 1920 Års Dossiersystem, vol. 1458, HP 32 D (III); 'Says British hoped to take Leningrad', *New York Times*, 7 September 1927; 'Soviet executions antagonize England', *New York Times*, 15 September 1927.

18. 'British arrested at Petrograd', *The Times*, 1 December 1919; *Vladimir Il'ich Lenin, biograficheskaya khronika*, Politizdat, Moskva, 1976, pp. 284, 292; *V. I. Lenin i VChK: sbornik dokumentov (1917–1922)*, Politizdat, Moskva, 1975, pp. 217–18; *Leninskii sbornik*, vol. XXXV, Politizdat. Moskva, 1975, p, 68; RGASPI (former Party Archive), Fond 4, op. 2, delo 2802, pp. 1–4, 10–13; GARF (National Archive), F. 130, op. 3, d. 132, pp. 422–427; *Krasnaya kniga VChK* (Red Book of the Cheka), vol. II, pp. 43–5, 48, 57–8, 320, 339–40, 346–7, 366–7, 380–1; Golikov, *Krushenie antisovetskogo podpol'ya v SSSR*, vol. I, pp. 294–5; Krasilnikov, *KGB protiv Mi-6*, p. 72; Saparov, *Bitaya karta*; Volkov, *Ofitsery flota i morskogo vedomstva*; TNA PRO FO 511/5 HB, Quarton to British Embassy Helsingfors, 31 October 1920; FO 371/8212, Report by ST28 in Petrograd on Soviet Removal of Valuables from

Petropavlovsk Cathedral, 9 July 1922; HO 405/4803, Special Branch Report on Nikolai Bunakoff, 16 October 1945.

19.   TNA PRO FO 371/4375, Conflicting Reports on Conditions in Soviet Russia, 16 October 1919; Dukes, *Red Dusk*, pp. 219–20.

20.   'The Russian decision', *The Times*, 20 September 1919; Michael Hughes, 'Dukes, Sir Paul (1889–1967)', *Oxford Dictionary of National Biography*, Oxford University Press, Oxford, 2004.

21.   TNA PRO KV2/1904, MI5 to Morton MI1c, 10 August 1921; Liddell memo, folio 107a, 6 August 1921; FO 395/185, undated minute from Walpole to Eassle[?], 'Hanged as Red agent', *New York Times*, 1 August 1919; 'Confesses crimes of murder band', *New York Times*, 6 October 1919; 'Lynching a Bolshevist', *The Times*, 5 August 1919; 'Tsarists' confession', *The Times*, 16 August 1919; 'Sordid Cossack crime', *The Times*, 18 August 1919; 'Stockholm murders', *The Times*, 29 August 1919; 'Find maze of dark intrigue', *Marion Daily Star*, 27 August 1919; 'Bolshevik Murder League, with pretty girl as decoy, uncovered at Stockholm', *Syracuse Herald*, 31 August 1919; 'Bolshevik Murder League uncovered in Sweden, beauty lures lovers to death', *Indiana Evening Gazette*, 18 September 1919; 'Slew Soviet agents', *Washington Post*, 19 October 1919; Scale papers: Foreign Office Appointment of Major J. D. Scale DSO as Assistant Military Attaché Helsingfors, Registry no. W144921/30, 19 November 1919.

22.   TNA PRO FO 1093/61, Secret service accounts for 1918/19 and 1919/20; CAB24/88, Baltic letter no. 27/531, 8 September 1919; 'Reported arrest of British journalist', *The Times*, 11 September 1919; 'Mr Goode in Russia', *The Times*, 7 October 1919; 'Mr Goode challenged', *The Times*, 10 February 1920; 'The challenge to Mr Goode', *The Times*, 13 February 1920.

CHAPTER 15: 'A VERY USEFUL LADY'

1.   Roland Chambers, *The Last Englishman: The Double Life of Arthur Ransome*, Faber & Faber, London, 2009, pp. 114–16, 122, 183; Tomaselli, Phil, '"A Thoroughly Mischievous Person" – Arthur Ransome, The Foreign Office and the Secret Intelligence Service', original unpublished version; Scale papers, Nabokov to Scale, 11 October 1916; Arthur Ransome, *Russia in 1919*, BiblioLife, Charleston, SC [1919] 2009, p. 10.

2.   TNA PRO KV 2/1903, Lockhart to FO, 21 June 1918.

3.   Chambers, *The Last Englishman*, p. 181; Hill, Capt. G. A. Hill, *Go Spy the Land: Being the Adventures of IK8 of the British Secret Service*, Cassell, London, 1932, p. 191.

4.   TNA PRO KV 2/1903, Memorandum from S8 re Arthur Ransome (S76), 17 March 1919.

5.   Tomaselli, '"A Thoroughly Mischievous Person"'; TNA PRO KV 2/1903, minute on file cover MI5(e), IP no. 294084.

6.   Robert Bruce Lockhart, *Memoirs of a British Agent*, Putnam, London, 1932, pp. 266–7.

7.   Hill, *Go Spy the Land*, pp. 191–3.

8.   TNA PRO KV 2/1903, Scale to London, CX 050167, 12 December 1918.

9.   TNA PRO KV 2/1903, MI1c to MI5, Ransome, Arthur, B/02573, 29 October 1918; 'British released from Russia', *The Times*, 18 October 1918.

10.   TNA PRO KV 2/1904, Thwaites to Maurice, 2 December 1918.

11.   TNA PRO KV 2/1904, Ransome Telegram, Stockholm to *Daily News*, 30 November

1918; FO 371/3954, Scale to London, CX062390, S76 report, Litvinov on Possible
Ultimatum, 9 December 1918.

12. TNA PRO KV 2/1904, Maurice to Thwaites, 10 December 1918.

13. TNA PRO KV 2/1903, MI1c to MI5(e), Ransome, Arthur, 9 December 1918; MI5 to
MCOs Aberdeen and Newcastle, 18 December 1918.

14. TNA PRO KV 2/1903, Clive, Stockholm to FO, 1 February 1919; MI5 IP extract no.
R459, 8 March 1919; FO 371/3988 Minute 116610/W/38; FO 371/3959, CX066368,
Stockholm, 15 February 1919; CX067247, 11 March 1919; 'Bolshevist policy, Mr
Ransome's telegrams', *Westminster Gazette*, 15 January 1919.

15. TNA PRO KV 2/1903, Memorandum from S8 re Arthur Ransome (S76), London, 17
March 1919; An example of the continued suspicion of Ransome can be found in the same
file, MI5 memo entitled Arthur Ransome, 27 March 1919.

16. TNA PRO KV 2/1904, Oldfield (Aliens Inspector, Newcastle) to Home Office, 27 March
1919; KV 2/1903, Folio 121a, Extract from report received from confidential source, 14
March 1927; MI5(e) to Kell, Ransome, Arthur Mitchell, N3414; FO 371/3988, Thomson
to Cavendish-Bentinck, 25 March 1919.

17. TNA PRO FO 371/4002A, Report on the State of Russia by Mr Arthur Ransome.

18. 'Litvinov reaches Copenhagen', *The Times*, 25 November 1919; 'Litvinoff's meeting with
Mr O'Grady', *The Times*, 26 November 1919; 'Litvinoff conference resumed', *The Times*,
28 November 1919; 'Mr O'Grady's instructions', *The Times*, 18 November 1919; Litvinoff
Conference, 24 December 1919; 'British in Russia to be released', *The Times*, 14 February
1920; 'Sir James O'Grady: some reminiscences, L. M. Gall', *The Times*, 13 December 1934;
London Gazette, 30 December 1919, p. 16097.

19. TNA PRO KV 2/1903, Lockhart to Gregory, 2 May 1919; Gregory to Thwaites, 17 May
1919; Gregory to Thomson, 16 April 1919; 'Mr J. D. Gregory', *The Times*, 30 January 1951.

20. TNA PRO KV 2/1903, Troup to Kell, 14 August 1919; Thwaites to Troup, 16 August
1919; MI5 IP, extract no 9068, 22 October 1919; FO 371/4005, FO to Secretary Army
Council, 5 July 1920; Revelations From the Russian Archives, Library of Congress,
Washington, 1997, Document 265, NKVD account of diamonds smuggled abroad to
support foreign Communist parties, 1919; Chambers, *The Last Englishman*, pp. 286–97, 329;
Tomaselli, '"A Thoroughly Mischievous Person"'; Arthur Ransome, *Racundra's First Cruise*,
Jonathan Cape, London, 1927, pp. 90–92.

CHAPTER 16: POST-WAR OPERATIONS – 'FANTASY AND INTRIGUE'

1.   TNA PRO KV 4/182, 14 November 1918, Thwaites, DMI, to Hall, DNI; WO 32/21380;
Scheme for the Reorganisation and Coordination of Secret Service, Hall to Thwaites,
28 December 1918; CAB 127/356, Report of Secret Service Committee, undated but
sometime in January 1919; Christopher Andrew, *The Defence of the Realm; The Authorized
History of MI5*, Allen Lane, London, 2009, p. 116.

2.   TNA PRO KV 4/182, record of meeting held at the Admiralty on 7 April 1919 to
consider the question of secret service expenditure; FO 1093/61, accounts for foreign secret
service account 1919/20; Espionage accounts 1919/20; FO 366/802 Sykes (1, Adam St)
to Robinson, 4 August 1922; ADM 223/851 'The Origins and Development of the SIS';

Alan Judd, *The Quest for C: Mansfield Cumming and the Founding of the Secret Service*, London, HarperCollins, 1999, pp. 445–6.

3.   TNA PRO FO 366/791, Maintenance of the Passport Control System, folio 149, 14 July 1920; FO 366/791, Passport Control Organisation, folios 122–48; minutes of war cabinet meeting, 18 August 1919; FO 371/3117, minute at folio 377, 15 January 1919; FO 371/3951, Cumming to Hay, 21 May 1919; FO 371/10480, The Visa System, folios 252–9.

4.   Phyllis Bottome, *The Goal*, Faber & Faber, London, 1962, pp. 64–5; Keith Jeffrey, *The Secret History of MI6 1909–1949*, Penguin, New York, 2010, p. 154

5.   TNA PRO CAB 63/192, 'The Origins and Development of the SIS', p. 4; FO 366/794, Johnson, Treasury to Montgomery, FO, 20 January 1921, folios 250–51; Foreign Office minute, folio 258; FO 372/1866, Aliens and Nationality Committee memorandum no. 143, minutes of meeting held 10 June 1921; Minute T5945/G, folio 266.

6.   TNA PRO FO 1093/61, Accounts for Foreign Secret Service Account 1919/20; Espionage Accounts 1919/20; CAB 127/356, Committee to Enquire into Expenditure on Secret Service, minutes, 27 May 1921; GS note on secret service expenditure, 1 June 1921; Conclusions of Conference of Ministers [re Secret Service], 20 February 1922; Cabinet Report of Sir Warren Fisher's Committee on Secret Service, 20 February 1922; Secret Service Committee, minutes, 24 March 1922; CAB 128/358, Secret Service 1922/23; KV 4/151, Menzies to Thwaites, plus charts, 19 January 1922.

7.   TNA PRO KV4/182, chart headed Intelligence, Secret Service Vote; FO 371/9347 CX2639, Economic Report on Russia issued by Section Ic, 28 December 1922; Gill Bennett, *Churchill's Man of Mystery: Desmond Morton and the World of Intelligence*, Routledge, Abingdon, 2007, p. 40; Judd, *The Quest for C*, inside jacket cover for chart of the SIS organisation in 1923; Nigel West and Oleg Tsarev, *Triplex; Secrets from the Cambridge Spies*, Yale, New Haven, 2009, p. 20; Anthony Cave Brown, *The Secret Servant, The life of Sir Stewart Menzies*, Michael Joseph, London, 1988, p. 211; Philip H. J. Davies, *MI6 and the Machinery of Spying*, Frank Cass, London, 2004, pp. 75–6.

8.   Judd, *The Quest for C*, p. 436 and inside jacket cover for chart of the SIS organisation in 1923; for coverage of Middle-East from Egypt, see TNA PRO FO 371/6239 Report on sons of Faisal from agents E50 and E51 in Cairo, SIS Section V, 17 May 1921, Folios 186–199 FO 371/8999 CX12051, Situation in Transjordania, 17 December 1923

9.   TNA PRO CAB 127/356, Committee to enquire into expenditure on Secret Service, minutes for meetings on 27 May 1921 and 24 March 1922; GS note on secret service expenditure, 1 June 1921.

10.   TNA PRO WO 188/760 CX9767, Gas Questionnaire for Russia, 19 March 1924; Bennett, *Churchill's Man of Mystery*, pp. 44–45.

11.   TNA PRO FO 371/8215, slip attached to 'A1' Northern Summary no. 725, 19 June 1922, Russia, A German Aviation Mission in Moscow.

12.   Judd, *The Quest for C*, p. 460; TNA PRO FO 371/3776 CX062038, Stockholm to London, 23 December 1918; WO to Tyrrell, 28 December 1918; KV 2/1903, MI5g4a to MI1, 15 April 1919; 'Prostration of Germany', *The Times*, 27 December 1918.

13.   TNA PRO FO 608/128, note from German peace delegation, Versailles, 26 August 1919; report by Captain Laperche, chief of liaison group with the German delegation; ADM

340/136, R. B. Tinsley naval service record; Judd, *The Quest for C*, p. 443; The pressure from financial cuts to axe the Rotterdam bureau is recorded in Bennett, *Churchill's Man of Mystery*, p. 66.

14. TNA PRO FO 366/794, Passport Control Staff for Germany; WO106/45, History of I (b) GHQ 1917–1918, Part I: The Secret Service; Captain Henry Landau, *Spreading the Spy Net: The Story of a British Spy Director*, Jarrolds, London, 1938, p. 233; Landau, Captain Henry Landau, *All's Fair: The Story of the British Secret Service behind the German Lines*, G. P. Putnam's Sons, New York, 1934.

15. Bennett, *Churchill's Man of Mystery*, pp. 49–52; TNA PRO FO 371/3317, minute on Dansey interview with Lord Hardinge, folio 377; FO 371/3951, Cumming to Hay, List of Anti-Bolshevik Officers Abroad, 21 May 1919.

16. TNA PRO 366/791, Passport Control Organisation, Baltic Republics; FO 366/794, Passport Control Rates of Pay for Individual Bureaux; Tomaselli, Phil Tomaselli, *Tracing Your Secret Service Ancestors*, Pen & Sword, Barnsley, 2009, pp. 11–21; Norman Dewhurst, *Norman Dewhurst MC*, H. J. Edmonds, Brussels, 1968, pp. 73–88, 95; Keith Jeffrey, *The Secret History of MI6 1909–1949*, Penguin, New York, 2010, pp 184, 188–190; Information from KGB archives supplied by Yuri Totrov.

17. TNA PRO FO 371/3968 Estonian Relations with the Allies and Russia, 9 June 1919, folio 197 (by L. Webster, Lieutenant RNVR); FO371/5377 Lady Muriel Paget to Curzon, 7 October 1920, folio 122; Webster to Lady Muriel Paget, 24 August 1920, folio 126; Phil Tomaselli, 'C's Moscow Station: The Anglo-Russian Trade Mission as Cover for SIS in the Early 1920s', *Intelligence and National Security* 17, 2002, pp. 173–176; email correspondence with the Charnock family, April 2010.

18. C. G. McKay, 'Our Man in Reval', *Intelligence and National Security* 9, 1994, p. 88; 'Soviet breaks faith, flagrant breach of treaty, Lord Curzon's demand', *The Times*, 21 September 1921; 'Plots against India, indicting the Soviet, text of British note', *The Times*, 21 September 1921; 'Red propaganda in the east', *The Times*, 27 September 1921; TNA PRO KV 2/501, Miller to Major Bell, 15 April 1921; memo no. 141, headed Moscow and Ireland; memo no. 153, headed Bolshevik Support of the Sinn Fein Rebellion; SZ2132, Denniston memo, 16 April 1921.

CHAPTER 17: THE ZINOVIEV LETTER

1. Christopher Andrew, *The Defence of the Realm; The Authorized History of MI5*, Allen Lane, London, 2009, p. 140; TNA PRO ADM 223/851, Secret Service – Naval Representation; HS 7/5, undated grand memoir headed '1938'.

2. Gill Bennett, *Churchill's Man of Mystery: Desmond Morton and the World of Intelligence*, Routledge, Abingdon, 2007, p. 69.

3. TNA PRO FO 1093/67, Sinclair to Crowe, 3 November 1923; FO 1093/66, Sinclair to Crowe, 25 February 1925; Sinclair to Bland, 18 March 1925; Sinclair to Bland, 31 March 1925; FO 1093/68, minutes of meeting of Prime Minister's Secret Service Committee, 2 March 1925; KV4/182, Reorganisation of Naval, Military and Air Force Secret Service, undated but prior to 1 April 1924.

4. TNA PRO FO 1093/69, report of the Secret Service Committee, 1 December 1925.

5. TNA PRO WO 188/760 CX 9767, Russia: The Position of Gas Warfare as, from SIS Information up to 19 March 1924, It Is Believed to Be, 19 March 1924.

6. TNA PRO WO 188/760 CX9767, 7 May 1924; CX9767, Soviet Russia, Revoyensoviet Interest in British Chemical Warfare, 8 September 1924; WO 188/758 CX 7353, 19 August 1924.

7. TNA PRO WO 188/764, Bacteriological Bombs, CX9767 1 December 1924; Soviet Russia, Bacteriological bombs, L3973, 4 November 1924.

8. TNA PRO WO 188/760, Soviet Russia, Bacteriological bombs, L3973, 4 November 1924; CX9767, Russia, Bacteriological Bombs, 28 September 1926.

9. TNA PRO WO 188/761, Soviet Russian Gas Activities, 22 January 1925; Soviet Russian Gas Activities, 23 January 1925, A Confidential Agent Reports, Yperite (Mustard Gas), Formula; Russian Gas, 23 February 1925.

10. '"Spy" trial in Russia', The Times, 14 September 1927; Leeds University Library, Special Collections, Interview with Henry Lambton Carr, MS 1001/4; TNA PRO FO 372/2500, Declaration by Henry Lambton Carr, 30 July 1928; HO 144/11056, various correspondence related to Carr's citizenship; FO 371/4381, Boyce (Vc) to Koppell, 4 July 1919.

11. Bennett, Churchill's Man of Mystery, pp. 80–81; Gill Bennett, '"A Most Extraordinary and Mysterious Business": The Zinoviev Letter of 1924', Historians, LRD 14, February 1999, p. 86; C. G. McKay, 'Our Man in Reval', Intelligence and National Security 9, 1994, pp. 88–111; Sharing intelligence with the Poles from TNA PRO KV 2/2767 CX 434, Bolshevik Propaganda, Reval, 4 October 1920.

12. TNA PRO CAB 23/45 Cabinet 23 (23), 2 May 1923, folio 228, item 1; Cabinet 27 (23), 15 May 1923, folio 283, item 1.

13. India Office Library and Records (IOLR), L/P&J/12/119 SIS A1 report, Russia, 'Anglo-Russian Relations', 24 May 1923, Northern Summary No 1165; SIS Section I to Gregory, 5 June 1923, folio 61; Northern Summary no 1179, 14 June 1923, Russia, graded A2.

14. IOLR L/P&J/12/119, Northern Summary no. 1174, 8 June 1923, Russia, Graded A1, 'Session of the Soviet Peoples Commissaries on 6 May: Discussion of Anglo-Russian Relations in Anticipation of the British Note'; Northern Summary, no. 1178, 9 June 1923, A1 Russia, folio 69–77, 'A Meeting of the Political Bureau of the Russian Communist Party; The System of Government in Russia; Anglo Russian Relations etc.'.

15. TNA PRO FO 371/9337 contains a series of A1 reports from inside the Soviet Union in the early months of 1923 sent by agents including BP16, BP27 and BP42 in Moscow and run from the Baltic republics; FR3 and FR6 in Moscow and FR14 in Latvia, all run from Paris; and BN5 in Berlin.

16. TNA PRO ADM 137/1735, Woodward to C-in-C Mediterranean, 2 August 1920, folio 118; ADM 137/1753, Report of Proceedings, 20 April 1920, folio 208; Report by Sub-Lieutenant Dunderdale, 20 April 1920; Dunderdale report on the Utka affair, 20 May 1920, folio 417; London Gazette, 7 September 1920, p. 9051; John Bruce Lockhart, 'Dunderdale, Wilfred Albert (1899–1990)', Oxford Dictionary of National Biography, Oxford University Press, Oxford, 2004; Nigel West and Oleg Tsarev, Triplex: Secrets from the Cambridge Spies, Yale University Press, New Haven, 2009, p. 319; Keith Jeffrey, The Secret History of MI6 1909–1949, Penguin, New York, 2010, pp 167, 180.

17. Bennett, Churchill's Man of Mystery, pp. 53–4.

18. Bennett, "'A Most Extraordinary and Mysterious Business'", pp. 34–7; TNA PRO 30/69/234, History of the Zinoviev Incident, 11 November 1924; MacDonald to Rakovsky, 24 October 1924; Zinoviev letter, 15 September 1924.

19. Nigel West and Oleg Tsarev, *The Crown Jewels: The British Secrets at the Heart of the KGB Archives*, HarperCollins, London, 1998, pp. 40–43; TNA PRO FO 366/985, Status of Mr Nicholson, Passport Control Officer in Riga, 24 July 1926; John Whitwell, *British Agent*, Frank Cass, London, 1996, p. 65.

20. Bennett, "'A Most Extraordinary and Mysterious Business'", pp. 77–9, 85–6; Andrew, *Defence of the Realm*, p. 151.

21. Bennett, *Churchill's Man of Mystery*, pp. 82–4; TNA PRO KV 2/501 records that the SIS claim to know 'the identity of every individual who handled it' was issued in CX1174 dated 9 January 1924.

CHAPTER 18: MOSCOW RULES – 'A VERY RISKY GAME'

1. 'A petitioner committed for contempt of court', *The Times*, 1 April 1924; 'A woman's committal to prison, Sykes v Sykes', *The Times*, 2 May 1924; 'A woman's release from prison, Sykes v Sykes', *The Times*, 7 May 1924.

2. Sidney and Pepita Reilly, *Britain's Master Spy: The Adventures of Sidney Reilly*, Harper, New York, 1933, pp. 172–203; Andrew Cook, *Ace of Spies: The True Story of Sidney Reilly*, History Press, Stroud, 2004, pp. 230–39, 258–9; Michael Smith, *The Spying Game: The Secret History of British Espionage*, Politico's, London, 2003, p. 156; Keith Jeffrey, *The Secret History of MI6 1909–1949*, Penguin, New York, 2010, p. 184

3. Phil Tomaselli, *Tracing Your Secret Service Ancestors*, Pen & Sword, Barnsley, 2009, pp. 122–4; 'Espionage charges in France', *The Times*, 8 December 1925; 'Three British subjects arrested in France', *The Times*, 9 December 1925; 'The French espionage case', *The Times*, 19 May 1926; 'British subjects sentenced in France', *The Times*, 20 May 1926; 'French espionage case', *The Times*, 2 June 1926; Ban on spying in France from TNA PRO ADM 223/851, 'The Secret Intelligence Service (SIS)'.

4. Gill Bennett, *Churchill's Man of Mystery: Desmond Morton and the World of Intelligence*, Routledge, Abingdon, 2007, p. 91; TNA PRO FO 366/838, Notification of Hiring, folio 133.

5. Christopher Andrew, *The Defence of the Realm; The Authorized History of MI5*, Allen Lane, London, 2009, pp. 122, 128; TNA PRO KV 2/818 CX6239/Prod, MI5 (Mr Farina), Agent Report on ARCOS, 9 October 1920.

6. Bennett, *Churchill's Man of Mystery*, pp. 96–8, 122–4; TNA PRO FO 371/12593, Comrade Rosenholz's Speech at the Anglo-Russian Committee, Moscow *Pravda*, 2 July 1927, folio 91.

7. TNA PRO FO 1093/71, minutes of meetings of the Secret Service Committee, 24 June 1927.

8. TNA PRO FO 1093/71, minutes of meetings of the Secret Service Committee, 24 June 1927; FO 1093/72, minutes of meetings of the Secret Service Committee, 30 June 1927; Mission Collecting Intelligence from KV5/72, Russian Oil Products, undated MI5 memo from December 1930, folio 356.

9. Bennett, *Churchill's Man of Mystery*, pp. 102, 342–3.

10. Ibid., p. 103.

11. 'In Soviet house, nest of secret agents', *The Times*, 25 May 1927; 'Commons and Soviet', *The Times*, 27 May 1927; 'ARCOS White Paper', *The Times*, 27 May 1927; Michael Smith, 'GC&CS and the First Cold War', in Michael Smith and Ralph Erskine (eds), *Action This Day: Bletchley Park from the Breaking of the Enigma Cipher to the Birth of the Modern Computer*, Bantam, London, 2001, p. 27.

12. TNA PRO FO 1093/73 C/2523, Sinclair to Tyrrell, 28 June 1927.

13. 'The OGPU's 20 victims', *The Times*, 11 June 1927; 'Executions spread terror in Russia', *New York Times*, 11 June 1927; 'Bolshevist charges', *The Times*, 13 June 1927; 'Soviet death sentence on naval officer', *The Times*, 17 June 1927.

14. TNA PRO FO 371/12593, *Nasha Gazeta*, Liquidation of the English Spy Organization in Petersburg, 14 July 1927; Montgomery Grove to Tudor Vaughan, 12 July 1927, folio 84; Montgomery Grove to Tudor Vaughan, 14 July 1927, folio 86; 'More arrests by the OGPU, alleged "British agents"', *The Times*, 11 July 1927; 'Cheka's arrest of 26 "British Agents", trial by military court', *The Times*, 31 August 1927; 'Says British hoped to take Leningrad', *New York Times*, 7 September 1927; 'Spy trial in Russia, death sentence on nine people', *The Times*, 14 September 1927; 'Trial by court-martial', *Daily Express*, 19 October 1927; 'Master British spy fabrications', *Daily Express*, 21 October 1927; 'Spying for England', *Daily Telegraph*, 20 October 1927; 'Soviet executions antagonize England', *New York Times*, 15 September 1927; 'Britain and Russia, charge of espionage', *The Argus* (Melbourne), 15 September 1927; 'Moscow lies exposed', *Daily Mail*, 2 November 1927. A good example of an agent weaving truth and fiction to deceive and bewilder interrogators can be read in Nigel West and Oleg Tsarev, *Triplex: Secrets from the Cambridge Spies*, Yale University Press, New Haven, 2009, pp. 251–73. It contains the confession of another SIS Russian agent, Aleksandr Nelidov, who weaves a fantasy, salted with names of real SIS officers, to deceive his Soviet interrogators. Given the timing, Hoyer's original arrest might well have been the result of information provided by Dukes's journalistic contact Kürz-Gedroitz, who was released some time in 1925 or 1926.

15. 'Red police charge British espionage, Soviet chiefs say agents invaded War Office', *New York Times*, 19 October 1927; 'Declares spy scare mere propaganda, British attaché, accused by Soviet, tells of Moscow espionage on mission', *New York Times*, 23 October 1927; 'Trial in Moscow of "British spies"', *The Times*, 24 October 1927; 'Death for 5 "spies" is asked in Russia', *New York Times*, 24 October 1927; 'Moscow spy trial', *The Times*, 25 October 1927; 'Two to prison for selling secrets', *New York Times*, 25 October 1927; 'Three wealthy Russians are sentenced to death for giving British information', *Portsmouth Daily Times* (AP report), 26 October 1927.

16. Boris Bazhanov, *Avec Staline dans le Kremlin*, Les Éditions de France, Paris, 1930, pp. 2–3. Bazhanov's subsequent memoirs avoided such claims, possibly under orders from SIS.

17. Boris Bazhanov and David W. Doyle, *Bazhanov and the Damnation of Stalin*, Ohio University Press, Athens, 1990, pp. 1–6; TNA PRO FO 371/4024, Hill reports in folios 74–90 and 192–216; for Gibson acting as secretary, see High Commission to FO, 2 July 1919, folio 214; FO 371/4021, folios 414–37; for Gibson's importance to mission, see telegram to FO, no. 2, 12 May 1919, folio 436.

18. Bazhanov and Doyle, *Bazhanov and the Damnation of Stalin*, pp. 8–12.

19. Ibid., pp. 16–20, 24–5, 33; Bazhanov, *Avec Staline dans le Kremlin*, pp. 2–3.

20. Bazhanov and Doyle, *Bazhanov and the Damnation of Stalin*, p. 34.

21. Ibid., pp. 135–6, 151, 169–74.

22. Ibid, pp. 185–8; Liddell Hart Centre for Military Archives, King's College London, GB 0099 KCLMA, unpublished memoirs of Colonel Leo Steveni, chap. 16, p. 7, chap. 18, p. 3.

23. TNA PRO KV3/11, A Short Statement about the OGPU – SSSR, B. Bajanov, Simla, 17 May 1928; Bazhanov and Doyle, *Bazhanov and the Damnation of Stalin*, pp. 195–6, 200.

24. Ibid, pp. 199, 203–4; Gordon Brook-Shepherd, *The Storm Petrels: The Flight of the First Soviet Defectors,* Ballantine, New York, 1977, pp. 59–61. On price of agent's reports, see Conrad O'Brien-ffrench, *Delicate Mission: Autobiography of a Secret Agent,* Skilton & Shaw, London, 1979, p. 118.

25. RGVA (Russian State Military Archive) Moscow, Captured Polish Intelligence Files: Fond 453, op. 1, file 54, p. 55; Fond 308, op. 2, file 39, p. 16; Vivian quote information provided to the author in confidence.

CHAPTER 19: THE JONNY CASE – 'A VERY VALUABLE AGENT'

1. John Whitwell, *British Agent*, Frank Cass, London, 1996; Philip H. J. Davies, *MI6 and the Machinery of Spying*, Frank Cass, London, 2004, p. 84.

2 TNA PRO AIR 23/433, Ellington, AOC Iraq to Air Min, 9 June 1927; Carmichael DDO to Dent, Air Int Baghdad, 4 August 1927; Dent to Carmichael, 24 August 1927; Carmichael to Dent Air Staff Intelligence, Iraq, 7 October 1927; Dent, Air Staff Intelligence, Iraq to Carmichael 4 November 1927; Newall DOI (Air) to Ellington AOC Iraq Command, 1 February 1928; Ellington, AOC Iraq Command to Air Ministry, Ref I/438, 23 March 1928; KV5/72, Russian Oil Products, undated MI5 memo from December 1930, folio 356; coverage of Hejaz from FO 371/6239, report on sons of Faisal from agents E50 and E51 in Cairo, SIS Section V, 17 May 1921, folios 186–99; KV5/72, Guy Liddell memo on meeting with Colonel Medlicott of Anglo-Iranian Oil, 26/3/32, folio 322; KV3/326, Agabekov debriefing, paragraph 4, folio 23a, Anglo-Persian Oil Company mail from local branches to its head office being intercepted and read by the Russians; Keith Jeffrey, *The Secret History of MI6 1909–1949*, Penguin, New York, 2010, pp 207–208

3. TNA PRO HW 3/81 HC, Kenworthy, A Brief History of Events Relating to the Growth of the Y Service.

4. Gill Bennett, *Churchill's Man of Mystery: Desmond Morton and the World of Intelligence*, Routledge, Abingdon, 2007, pp. 71–2, 78; intelligence officer's recollections of Max Knight from interview with the late Hugh Astor, 23 January 1998.

5. Bennett, *Churchill's Man of Mystery*, pp. 128–9, 132–4; TNA PRO FO 1093/74, Prime Minister's Secret Service Committee note on discussions in April and June 1931 re 'difficulties which had arisen in the inter-relation between C's organisation and Scotland Yard'.

6. TNA PRO HS 8/986, List of Digraphs for 'Lands and Towns'; HS 8/1014, List of Country Digraphs; KV 2/1106 CX 1713, Russia, Serge S. Maslov, 17 June 1933; Serge Semenovich Maslov, 3 July 1933; KV 2/819 CX 1743, information received from Gutchkov and Baikalov, 18 November 1932, folio 185a; Nigel West and Oleg Tsarev, *The Crown Jewels: The British Secrets at the Heart of the KGB Archives*, HarperCollins, London, 1998, p. 303;

Nigel West and Oleg Tsarev, *Triplex: Secrets from the Cambridge Spies*, Yale University Press, New Haven, 2009, pp. 336–7; Keith Jeffrey, *The Secret History of MI6 1909–1949*, Penguin, New York, 2010, pp 204, 271–2

7. TNA PRO FO 366/884, list of passport control offices in 1930; Sykes to Robinson, DS2197, November 1930.

8. West and Tsarev, *Triplex*, p. 336.

9. TNA PRO FO 371/17269, LO to Secretary of State, 15 April 1933, folios 50–53; Moscow PCO from KV 2/572 1932, SIS to Major W. A. Phillips, MI5, 621626/2, 27 June 1932, folio 11a (by 1936, there was no passport control officer in Moscow, and an attempt to place one there was opposed by the ambassador, Viscount Chilston – Christopher Andrew, *Secret Service; The Making of the British Intelligence Community*, Heinemann, London, 1985, p. 407); 'The evidence, Russian prisoner's "Confession"', *The Times*, 13 April 1933; 'The Moscow charges, first day of "trial", the Soviet case, two prisoners questioned', *The Times*, 13 April 1933; 'Briton confesses at Moscow trial, five deny guilt', *New York Times*, 13 April 1933; 'Marked change in "trial", the prosecution confused, Mr Thornton's stand', *The Times*, 15 April 1933; 'Mystery document in Moscow trial', *Brisbane Courier*, 15 April 1933; 'Moscow sabotage trial, "Whole case a frame-up"', *The Argus* (Melbourne), 17 April 1933; 'Evidence for prosecution', *Sydney Morning Herald*, 17 April 1933; 'The objective proofs, Mr Macdonald's confession', *The Times*, 18 April 1933; 'Speeches for defence, 'discredited' witnesses', *The Times*, 19 April 1933; 'The Moscow prisoners', *The Times*, 20 April 1933; 'The returned engineers, a message from the King, Foreign Office visits', *The Times*, 25 April 1933; 'The Moscow trial, a new survey I – Mr Monkhouse's own story', *The Times*, 22 May 1933; 'The Moscow trial II – Mr Cushny and the OGPU, a personal narrative', *The Times*, 23 May 1933; 'The Moscow trial III – light on the confessions OGPU pressure', *The Times*, 24 May 1933; 'The Moscow trial IV – procedure of the OGPU, incidents in courts', *The Times*, 25 May 1933; 'Release from Russia, prisoners on way home, trade ban raised', *The Times*, 3 July 1933.

10. West and Tsarev, *Triplex*, p. 123.

11. West and Tsarev, *Triplex*, pp. 250–51; SIS file passed to the Russians by John Cairncross and now in the KGB Archives File 72240, vol. 6, p. 93; 'Lived life of intrigue, espionage', *Ottawa Citizen*, 12 January 1954; information provided to the author in confidence; R. S. Rose and Gordon D. Scott, *Johnny: A Spy's Life*, Pennsylvania State University Press, University Park, 2010, pp. 3, 41–9, 68, 101.

12. KGB Archives File 72240, vol. 6, p. 93; Rose and Scott, *Johnny*, pp. 140–63. The Rose and Scott book relies heavily for its narrative on de Graaf's memories, taped in the mid-1970s when he was, by the authors' own account, 'in his early eighties and either slowly becoming senile, forgetting names, or purposefully misrepresenting them to conceal or glorify some unknown fact'. Some of the potentially unreliable elements of de Graaf's memories have therefore been ignored in this account. Rose and Scott have Jonny's UK cover, remembered by de Graaf, as being the same occupation as that cited by Valentine Vivian in the file passed to the KGB – Hamburg wine merchant – but a different name, with the Dinkelmeyer name used for the Romania mission. Given the British interest in the visits to the UK, and Valentine Vivian's fastidious attention to detail, compared to de Graaf's situation at the time of the interviews and his need to remember events that had

occurred forty years earlier, I have judged that the documentary evidence at the time is more likely to be accurate.

13. Details of recruitment by Foley from 'Lived Life of Intrigue, Espionage', *Ottawa Citizen*, 12 January 1954; *Ottawa Journal*, 12 January 1954; KGB archives, file 72240, vol. 6, p. 93; information provided to the author in confidence; Rose and Scott, *Johnny*, pp. 170–73; Foley expert on Soviet operations from TNA PRO KV 3/12 CX report on Soviet Espionage Activities, 17 October 1928; Keith Jeffrey, *The Secret History of MI6 1909–1949*, Penguin, New York, 2010, pp 267–8

14. US National Archives and Records Administration (NARA) RG263, box 7, document 96, pp. 14, 21; TNA PRO FO 369/2189, 3 March 1931, Mounsey to Steptoe; Kelsey minute, 25 April 1931; KV 3/145, Shelley to W. A. Phillips, 20 June and 11 July 1927; Summary of Information Obtained from Raid on Soviet Premises in Peking, 26 August 1927, folio 31a; Notes on Interview with Eugene Pik, folio 33b; Interview with Special Department 'OO', folio 33e; FO 1093/92 CX1434, Communist Activities in China, Federated Malay States, etc. (The Noulens Case), 7 March 1932; Antony Best, *British Intelligence and the Japanese Challenge in Asia 1914–1941*, Palgrave, London, 2002, pp. 50–53, 66, 77–8,114–15; 'Peking police raid', *The Times*, 7 April 1927; 'Soviet plots in China, compromising documents', *The Times*, 18 April 1927; '"Reds" in China', *The Times*, 23 April 1927; Keith Jeffrey, *The Secret History of MI6 1909–1949*, Penguin, New York, 2010, pp 256–9, 266. Foley involvement in Noulens arrest from John Curry, *The Security Service 1908–1945*, The Official History, PRO, Kew, 1999 and information provided to the author in confidence.

15. TNA PRO FO 1093/92 CX1434, Communist Activities in China, Federated Malay States, etc. (The Noulens Case), 7 March 1932.

16. Information provided to the author in confidence; IOLR L/P&J/12/45; William Waack, *Die Vergessene Revolution*, Aufbau, Berlin, 1994, passim; Charles A. Willoughby, *Sorge: Soviet Master Spy*, William Kimber, London, 1952; *All about Shanghai: A Standard Guidebook*, University Press, Shanghai, 1934; Frederick S. Litten, 'The Noulens Affair', *China Quarterly* 138, June 1994; E. H. Carr, *The Twilight of Comintern 1930–1935*, Macmillan, London, 1982; Keith Jeffrey, *The Secret History of MI6 1909–1949*, Penguin, New York, 2010, p. 268

17. Information provided to the author in confidence; Rose and Scott, *Johnny*, pp. 180–93.

18. Michael Smith, *Foley: The Spy Who Saved 10,0000 Jews*, Hodder & Stoughton, London, 1999, p. 57.

19. 'Lived life of intrigue, espionage', *Ottawa Citizen*, 12 January 1954 and from the SIS report on his mission passed to the Russians by John Cairncross which is now in KGB Archives File 72240, vol. 6; Waack, *Vergessene Revolution*, passim.

20. KGB Archives File 72240, vol. 6; information provided to the author in confidence; Waack, *Vergessene Revolution*, passim; Rose and Scott, *Johnny*, pp. 199–211; Fernando Watson, *Olga*, Peter Halban, London, 1990, passim; Keith Jeffrey, *The Secret History of MI6 1909–1949*, Penguin, New York, 2010, pp 269–70

21. 'Lived life of intrigue, espionage', *Ottawa Citizen*, 12 January 1954; Waack, *Vergessene Revolution*, passim; Rose and Scott, *Johnny*, pp. 221–43.

22. TNA PRO KV 3/129, Vivian to Liddell, CX95542, 2 June 1938, folio 86a; five-page report entitled 'The Comintern', folio 86a; IOLR L/P&J/12/144, letter from EMH to Silver, 11 June 1938; KGB Archives file 72240, vol. 6; information provided to the author in confidence.

CHAPTER 20: PREPARING FOR ANOTHER WAR – 'SCRATCHING THE SURFACE'

1. Max Everest-Phillips, 'Colin Davidson's British Indian Intelligence Operations in Japan 1915–1923 and the Demise of the Anglo-Japanese Alliance', *Intelligence and National Security* 24, 2009, pp. 694–5; TNA PRO FO 366/791, List of Passport Control Officers, p. 3; ADM 223/851, memorandum on secret service funds, 9 October 1935; Alan Judd, *The Quest for C: Mansfield Cumming and the Founding of the Secret Service*, London, HarperCollins, 1999, inside back cover; Keith Jeffrey, *The Secret History of MI6 1909–1949*, Penguin, New York, 2010, pp 262–6

2. TNA PRO FO 366/791, Passport Office Capitulation, folio 111; ADM 340/136, R. B. Tinsley naval service record; WO 208/4475 CX 10746, SIS Section I to Cadogan, 6 November 1923; CX 10746, Germany and Austria, the Deutsche Eherenlegion, 9 November 1923. The CX 10746 series was to be used throughout the pre-WWII period for reports on Hitler.

3. TNA PRO WO 208/4475 CX 10746, SIS Section I to Cadogan, 6 November 1923; CX 10746, Germany and Austria, the Deutsche Eherenlegion, 9 November 1923; Roger Eatwell, *Fascism: A History*, Vintage, London, 1996, pp. 89–95.

4. TNA PRO FO 371/4020 CX 071166B, Political – Russia, Russian-Japanese-German Alliance, Stockholm, 17 May 1919, folio 183; CX070779, Political – Russia, German Negotiations with Lenin, 11 May 1919; CX071089, CXP478, 15 May 1919, folio 186; CXM314, Agent Reports, Gothenburg, 15 May 1919, folio 187; FO 371/8187, Northern Summary No. 641, Germany and Russia at Genoa, 21 April 1922; FO 371/8215, Northern Summary No. 725, Russia, A German Aviation Mission in Moscow, 19 June 1922, folio 101; KV 3/11 CX 1570, Menzies to MI5, 21 October 1926, folio 45A; MI1c to MI5, statement from employee of Soviet legation in Europe re Russo-German SS co-operation, 31 May 1927; KV 3/12 CX 1745, Russo-German Military Collaboration, 19 February 1929.

5. TNA PRO FO 1093/78, German Scheme for Mobilisation, MI3/9125; Lindsay to Chamberlain, 15 April 1929; Chamberlain to Lindsay, 15 April 1929; Lindsay to Chamberlain, 16 April 1929.

6. TNA PRO FO 371/4381, Section Vc to Sir William Tyrrell, 3 July 1919; Boyce to P. A. Koppell, Political Intelligence Department, 4 July 1919, folio 329; Koppell to Boyce, 4 July 1919, folio 330; CX073324, Rome, 21 July 1919, folio 331; CX073329, Rome, 25 June 1919, folios 332–6; CX073331, 26 June 1919, folio 337; ADM 223/851, Sinclair Memorandum on Secret Service Funds, 9 October 1935, pp. 2–3.

7. Gill Bennett, *Churchill's Man of Mystery: Desmond Morton and the World of Intelligence*, Routledge, Abingdon, 2007, pp. 136, 141–51, 158.

8. TNA PRO ADM 223/851, Sinclair memorandum on secret service funds, 9 October 1935, p. 3; WO 106/209, Piggott note, 9 February 1928.

9. TNA PRO ADM 223/851, Sinclair memorandum on secret service funds, 9 October 1935.

10. Robert Cecil, 'The Cambridge Comintern', in Christopher Andrew and David Dilks (eds), *The Missing Dimension: Governments and Intelligence Communities in the Twentieth Century*, Macmillan, London, 1984.

11. Hansard, House of Commons, 18 May 1936, vol. 312, cols 838–46; 'Colonel Lopez interviewed, dum-dum bullets', *Melbourne Argus*, 25 May 1936.

12. TNA PRO WO 208/4475 Extract from CX10746/29, 31 May 1934, folio 37; CX10746/30, Herr Hitler's Nerves, 14 May 1935, folio 38; Herr Hitler in the Great War, 20 January 1936.

13. Judd, *The Quest for C*, p. 338; Joseph A. Maiolo, '"I Believe the Hun Is Cheating": British Admiralty Technical Intelligence and the German Navy 1936–39', *Intelligence and National Security* 11, 1996, pp. 32–58; TNA PRO ADM 116/2945, British Legation Helsingfors to Simon, 21 June 1933; CAB 104/29, Industrial Intelligence Centre, ICF/118, 8 April 1936; Nigel West, *MI6: British Secret Intelligence Service Operations 1909–45*, Weidenfeld & Nicolson, London, 1983, p. 51.

14. Smith, *Foley*, p. 119–20; Bennett, *Churchill's Man of Mystery*, p. 192.

15. TNA PRO ADM 223/851, Sinclair memorandum on secret service funds, 9 October 1935; Troup memo, The Naval Intelligence Organization and the Secret Intelligence Service, 14 October 1935.

16. TNA PRO T 160/787 (Pt 4), Civil Estimates, Class 1, 23, Secret Service 1939; Bennett, *Churchill's Man of Mystery*, pp. 192–3; Nigel West, *Historical Dictionary of British Intelligence*, Scarecrow Press, Lanham, MD, 2005, pp. 597–8.

17. Norman Dewhurst, *Norman Dewhurst MC*, H. J. Edmonds, Brussels, 1968, pp. 95–104; Philip H. J. Davies, *MI6 and the Machinery of Spying*, Frank Cass, London, 2004, p. 85.

18. John Whitwell, *British Agent*, Frank Cass, London, 1996, pp. 61, 69.

19. Dewhurst, *Norman Dewhurst MC*, pp. 105–6; TNA PRO KV 3/116, Abwehr Deception Activities in 1939, Second Report, 4 October 1939, pp. 11–12; Bennett, *Churchill's Man of Mystery*, p. 192; Nigel West, *MI6: British Secret Intelligence Service Operations 1909–45*, Weidenfeld & Nicolson, London, 1983, p. 54; 'British consul in Hanover', *Daily Telegraph*, 9 November 1935.

20. TNA PRO CAB 733/322/8, account of fraud by Hugh Dalton, 1 October 1936, folio 10. Much is sometimes made of allegations that a similar fraud was perpetrated by SIS employees in Warsaw, but a Polish police investigation found that, although there was a fraud taking place, it did not involve any embassy employees. See FO 366/966, Kennard to Eden, 1 March 1937, folio 91.

21. Smith, *Foley*, passim.

22. Ibid., pp. 120–22; Arnold Kramish, *The Griffin*, Macmillan, London, 1986; Thomas Powers, *Heisenberg's War: The Secret History of the German Bomb*, Jonathan Cape, London, 1993; Mark Walker, *German National Socialism and the Quest for Nuclear Power 1939–1949*, Cambridge University Press, Cambridge, 1990; 'Focus on 50th anniversary of splitting the atom', Associated Press, 15 December 1988.

23. Judd, *Quest*, pp, 338–40; 'Telegrams in brief', *The Times*, 10 October 1939; West, *Historical Dictionary of British Intelligence*, p. 171; Keith Jeffrey, *The Secret History of MI6 1909–1949*, Penguin, New York, 2010, pp 275, 292

24. Interview with Kenneth Benton, 3 December 1996; Keith Jeffrey, *The Secret History of MI6 1909–1949*, Penguin, New York, 2010, p. 316

25. TNA PRO FO 371/21659, 'What Should We Do?' [Views of SIS, 18 September 1938], folios 62–7.

26. A. O. Blishen, 'Parry, Sir Richard Gambier- (1894–1965)', *Oxford Dictionary of National Biography*, Oxford University Press, Oxford, 2004; Geoffrey Pidgeon, *The Secret Wireless War: The Story of MI6 Communications 1939–1945*, UPSO, London, pp. 14–23; Whitwell, *British Agent*, pp. 84–6.

27. TNA PRO HS7/5, undated Grand memoir headed '1938'; SOE History, Experimental Station 6; Great Britain's Only Successful Experiment in Total Warfare; Appendix III, Sabotage Results; C. G. McKay, *From Information to Intrigue: Studies in Secret Service Based on the Swedish Experience 1939–1945*, Frank Cass, London, 1993, pp. 46–7; Bennett, *Churchill's Man of Mystery*, pp. 194–6.

28. TNA PRO FO 1093/86, Mounsey to Jebb, 3 March 1939 and 6 March 1939; Jebb to Mounsey, 31 March 1939; Cadogan letter, 31 March 1939; FO 800/270, Cadogan memo. Examples of the reporting from Putlitz, and the analysis of its accuracy by SIS, can be found in FO 1093/88; Keith Jeffrey, *The Secret History of MI6 1909–1949*, Penguin, New York, 2010, p. 312

29. TNA PRO ADM 223/475, Adm. Sir John Godfrey on Sidney Cotton; John Weaver at seminar on 'Photographic Reconnaissance during World War II', RAF Museum, Hendon, 10 June 1991; Jeffrey Watson, *Sidney Cotton: The Last Plane Out of Berlin*, Hodder Headline Australia, Sydney, 2002, pp. 88–145.

30. TNA PRO GFM 33, Report to Reichs Minister of the Interior, 413/215837-57, 29 March 1940; Michael Smith, *The Spying Game: The Secret History of British Espionage*, Politico's, London, 2003, pp. 166–7.

31. 'Sir Hugh Sinclair', *The Times*, 6 November 1939; TNA PRO ADM 223/851, Secret Service, Naval Representation, undated but post-WWII.

INDEX